Business Process Management

To our families

Yvonne, Brittany, Connor, Cassie and Kurt

and

Sandra, Angelique and Mystique

*Without the support and inspiration of our families this would not have been possible;
we know it has been tough at times, your understanding will never be forgotten. Thank you.
We will now endeavor to make up the time we have lost with you.*

John and Johan

Business Process Management

Practical Guidelines to Successful Implementations

Second Edition

John Jeston and Johan Nelis

AMSTERDAM • BOSTON • HEIDELBERG • LONDON • NEW YORK • OXFORD
PARIS • SAN DIEGO • SAN FRANCISCO • SINGAPORE • SYDNEY • TOKYO
BUTTERWORTH-HEINEMANN IS AN IMPRINT OF ELSEVIER

Butterworth-Heinemann is an imprint of Elsevier
Linacre House, Jordan Hill, Oxford OX2 8DP, UK
30 Corporate Drive, Suite 400, Burlington, MA 01803, USA

First edition 2006
Second edition 2008

British Library Cataloguing in Publication Data
A catalogue record for this book is available from the British Library

Library of Congress Cataloging-in-Publication Data
A catalog record for this book is availabe from the Library of Congress

ISBN: 978-0-75-068656-3

For information on all Butterworth–Heinemann publications
visit our website at books.elsevier.com

Printed and bound in Hungary

08 09 10 11 12   10 9 8 7 6 5 4 3 2 1

Contents

118086

Contributors

John Jeston has been working in the business and IT industries for over thirty years, covering project management, business process management, business process reengineering, systems development, outsourcing, consulting and general management. In addition to his consulting roles, he has held the positions of financial controller, divisional manager, director of a software company, HR director and CIO.

John now specializes in business process management strategy, coaching, advice and implementations, and runs an independent BPM consultancy practice, *Management By Process Pty Ltd* (www.managementbyprocess.com). John and his team build internal BPM skills and capabilities within organizations; complete Board and CEO process reviews; provide clients with a 'road map' for the creation of a sustainable, successful and repeatable business process improvement programs and organizational culture. He presents at conferences, holds workshops and is an author and course director of a BPM distance learning program in Australia. He also writes a regular column for BP Trends. John can be contacted at johnjeston@managementbyprocess.com.

Johan Nelis has international experience as a hands-on Business Process Management Consultant. He has established and managed a BPM practice of thirty consultants in the Netherlands, and is also co-founder and Vice Chairman of the Dutch BPM Forum. Johan has worked for the United Nations as an Advisor. He is well known for his drive to transfer knowledge and experiences, and has shown that he is capable of motivating and stimulating people. He has initiated many BPM training courses and lectured at a postgraduate course.

Johan has carried out assignments in a wide variety of sectors, with the main emphasis on finance and telecom. He specializes in aligning processes with strategy, business objectives and IT. He has also performed many process audits, and is able to pinpoint fundamental problems, formulate quick wins, and provide innovative and sustainable solutions. Furthermore, he is good at initiating and overseeing implementations of BPM and ensuring that the people are able to perform their activities better and independently. Johan is a lead consultant at a specialist BPM consultancy, where he provides strategic advice on business process services and supervises a team of BPM consultants. He has presented at seminars and hosted workshops at several BPM conferences in Europe and Australia. Johan is an author and course director of BPM distance learning programs in The Netherlands and Australia and writes a regular column for BP Trends. Johan can be contacted at johannelis@managementbyprocess.com.,

Antje Breer has a powerful combination of experience, creativity, international experience, reputation and intelligence and brings these to bear on her consultative approach. She demonstrates a passion for achieving results and building internal capability for businesses around their most critical business process issues. She has in excess of 10 years experience across many industries and has worked with both international consulting organisations, such as IBM Global Services in Germany, and specialized business process management (BPM) firms.

Antje's diverse portfolio of experience has included undertaking process improvement projects, the introduction and implementation of BPM methodologies, development and implementation of Process Management frameworks, conducting methodology workshops and training users in the ARIS toolset, along with the undertaking of pre-sales activities.

Frits Bussemaker has been working in the IT industry for twenty years. He has held various senior commercial positions with companies including Logica, Cambridge Technology Partners and Tibco. He is now a Management Consultant with Ordina. In 2003, he was the founder and chairman of the BPM-Forum Netherlands (www.bpm-forum.org), a neutral expert platform for Business Process Management. He is also the founded and former Chairman of the Dutch chapter of the Association for Strategic Alliance Professionals (www.strategic-alliances.org) and boardmember of the Business Rules Platform (www.brplatform.org). He is a regular speaker on BPM and a columnist in *Business Process Management Magazine* and bptrends.com. He has an MSc from the University of Delft.

Tonia de Bruin is a PhD candidate at Queensland University of Technology, Brisbane, Australia, where she is researching business process management maturity. Following her acceptance as a CPA in 2001, Tonia obtained an MIT from QUT in 2004. Tonia has an extensive background in the financial services sector, where she has worked for more than fifteen years as both a manager and a consultant. Experience managing process improvement projects has seen Tonia develop a strong interest in the relationship between business processes and IT.

Brad Power is the Principal, Palladium Group and Executive Director, Process Management Research Center at Babson College. With over twenty years of management consulting and research experience across a variety of industries around the world, he addresses the important business opportunities and problems of clients by combining human, technological and business perspectives. From 1981 to 1997, Brad worked for CSC Index, the business reengineering firm. In addition to leading many process-innovation consulting projects, he led CSC Index's research service in business reengineering for three years, working with over thirty senior executives leading major reengineering initiatives, and the founders of business reengineering. Brad has an MBA from UCLA and a BS from Stanford University.

Michael Rosemann is a Professor for Information Systems and Co-Leader of the Business Process Management Group at Queensland University of Technology, Brisbane, Australia. He received his MBA (1992) and his PhD (1995)

from the University of Muenster, Germany. His main areas of interest are business process management, business process modeling, enterprise systems and ontologies. In his current research projects he is exploring, among others thing, the critical success factors of process modeling, issues related to process modeling in the large, and the actual application of process modeling. Michael has intensive consulting experience, and has provided process management-related advice to organizations from various industries including telecommunications, banking, insurance, utility and logistics. Besides more than forty journal publications, seventy conference publications and thirty-five book chapters, he has published two books on logistics management and process modeling, and is editor of three books, *Reference Modelling, Business Process Management* and *Business Systems Analysis with Ontologies*. He is a member of the Editorial Board of six journals, including the *Business Process Management Journal.*

Foreword

This book shouldn't be unusual, but it is. It should have been written a long time ago, but it wasn't. All books on business process management should be similar to it, but they aren't. Books that purport to tell people in organizations how to do something should be this clear, but they seldom are. Process management should have already been demystified, but it hasn't been.

What's exceptional about the book is its extraordinary common sense. It suggests seemingly prosaic ideas, such as that multiple different levels of process change are necessary under different circumstances, and that technology alone isn't sufficient to bring about process change. These ideas seem obvious, but they are not often encountered in the world of business process management, or BPM. In fact, in order for you fully to appreciate the virtues of this book, you need to know something about what's wrong with BPM.

A brief history of business process management

The idea that work can be viewed as a process, and then improved, is hardly new. It dates at least to Frederick Taylor at the turn of the last century, and probably before. Taylor and his colleagues developed modern industrial engineering and process improvement, though the techniques were restricted to manual labor and production processes. The Taylorist approaches were widely practiced in the early 1900s, but were largely forgotten by mid-century.

The next great addition to process management was created by the combination of Taylorist process improvement and statistical process control, by Shewart, Deming, Juran and others. Their version of process management involved measuring and limiting process variation, continuous rather than episodic improvement, and the empowerment of workers to improve their own processes. It turned out that Japanese firms had both the business need – recovering from war and building global markets – and the discipline to put continuous improvement programs in place. Other firms in other societies have adopted continuous improvement and 'total quality management' based on statistical principles, but it requires more discipline than most can muster.

Toyota, in particular, took these approaches and turned them into a distinctive advance in process management. The Toyota Production System (TPS) combined statistical process control with continuous learning by decentralized work teams, a 'pull' approach to manufacturing that minimized waste and inventory, and treating every small improvement in processes as an experiment to be designed, measured and learned from. But few firms have been able to successfully implement the TPS, and even Toyota has had more success with the approach in Japan than at its foreign plants. A somewhat less stringent approach to the TPS is present in the 'lean' techniques that many American firms have recently adopted.

The next major variation on BPM took place in the 1990s, when many Western firms were facing an economic recession and strong competition from global competitors, particularly Japanese firms. Business process reengineering added, to the generic set of process management ideas, several new approaches:

- the radical (rather than incremental) redesign and improvement of work
- attacking broad, cross-functional business processes
- 'stretch' goals of order-of-magnitude improvement
- use of information technology as an enabler of new ways of working.

Reengineering was also the first process management movement to focus primarily on non-production, white-collar processes such as order management and customer service. It did not emphasize statistical process control or continuous improvement. Many firms in the United States and Europe undertook reengineering projects, but most proved to be overly ambitious and difficult to implement. Reengineering first degenerated into a more respectable word for headcount reductions, and then largely disappeared (though there are some signs of its return).

The most recent process management enthusiasm has revolved around 'Six Sigma', an approach created at Motorola in the 1980s and popularized by General Electric in the 1990s. In some ways Six Sigma represents a return to statistical process control; the term 'Six Sigma' means one output defect in six standard deviations of a probability distribution for a particular process output. Six Sigma also typically involves a return to focusing on relatively small work processes, and presumes incremental rather than radical improvement. Most frequently, however, Six Sigma improvement techniques have been employed on an episodic basis, rather than continuously, and while employees are somewhat empowered to improve their own work, they are generally assisted by experts called 'Black Belts'. Some firms are beginning to combine Six Sigma with more radical reengineering-like approaches to processes, or with the 'lean' techniques derived from the Toyota Production System. It is simply too early to tell whether Six Sigma will continue to prosper; I see some signs of its weakening, but it is certainly still popular in many US firms.

The approach to BPM described in this book is a welcome amalgam of all of these previous approaches. It doesn't focus heavily on statistical process control or bottom-up experimentation, but addresses the basics of process improvement and change. It doesn't view IT as being the core of process change, but doesn't ignore it as did TQM and Six Sigma. It considers all of the major vehicles by which organizations understand, measure and change how they work.

Lessons from history

What can we learn from this history, and how does it relate to the book you have in your hands? First, it's clear that process management has been somewhat faddish in the past. It has been a bit immature, coming and going in various forms as a management fad. This does not mean that there is no value to the concept – indeed I am a strong believer in it – but rather that managers and firms may have latched onto the more fashionable, short-term elements of the approach instead of the more timeless ones. Some managers have even made comments to me such as the following: 'We're doing Six Sigma – we're not really into process management'. This inability to see the forest for the individual tree is problematic if (or, more likely, when) the appeal of an individual process management offering begins to fade.

Perhaps the excitement of a 'new' approach (or at least a new combination of previous ideas with a new name) is necessary to get people excited, but the problem is that they become less excited after a time with each new variant of process change. Basic business process management – the essence of each of these faddish enthusiasms – may not be sexy, but it is clearly necessary. Perhaps it should be adopted whether it is sexy or not, and then maybe it will persist over the long term at a moderate level of popularity. This book is admirably free of faddish elements, and provides a good guide to the basic principles of process management. The authors refer to the 'demystification' of process management, and they are correct that the field has been clouded by faddishness and mystification for far too long.

It's also apparent that process management, as it has changed over time, is an increasingly synthetic discipline. This book, I am happy to note, also takes a synthetic, broad approach to process management. Each new process management approach has built on previous foundations, and added one or more new elements. Ideally, an organization would be able to draw upon all of the elements or tools available to meet the process management needs of any individual project. However, to wrap all of the possible process management tools into one consolidated approach would be a bit unwieldy. They can't all fit into one normal-sized book. Therefore it seems likely that, in the future, firms will assemble the tools they need to address a particular project using a customized or configured methodology. Such a configuration process would require either very experienced process management consultants who could assemble the proper tools or perhaps even software that could help a less-experienced user configure a methodology.

Despite these methodological issues, process management all boils down to human change. This is true of all variations on process management. As Jeston and Nelis point out, people are the key to implementing new process designs. If they don't want to work in new ways, it is often very difficult to force them to do so. Hence any successful process management effort requires a strong emphasis on culture, leadership and change management. Several chapters of the book are devoted to these issues.

Process management doesn't replace everything else in organizations, and it's not a panacea. There have been other authors and publications that have strongly suggested that all an organization needs to do to be successful is process improvement. This book does not make that mistake; it simply argues that process management must become one of the abiding approaches to managing organizations. It must augment and align with strategy, human resource management, financial management, information management and the other traditional management disciplines. This and other perspectives within the book may appear to be only common sense. They are indeed sensible, but they are not sufficiently common.

Thomas H. Davenport

Preface

This book began in 2003, when I was engaged in the early stages of a BPM project within a large financial organization. Over three decades of consulting and line management positions within both small and large organizations, I have been developing my intuitive project management and business skills. I was then struggling with how to help develop the skills of the consultants in our BPM consultancy practice faster than just 'on the job training'.

I searched the Internet and book shelves for a comprehensive text on 'how to successfully implement a BPM project'. I did not just want a big picture view but a detailed step-by-step guide that we could give to our consultants and clients, and one that would force me to be less intuitive (although I still think this is the most powerful insight one can have) and more formal in approaching BPM projects. So I started to document my thoughts over the next twelve months.

In mid-2004, we received the resume of Johan from the Netherlands. Johan was looking to migrate to Australia from the Netherlands, where he headed up the BPM practice of Sogeti (part of Cap Gemini). Johan had also been working on the development of a framework for BPM projects. Johan joined me in the TouchPoint BPM consultancy practice and soon thereafter we began the journey of completing this book.

John Jeston

I have always found it amazing that in a time of information, the skills and expertise of a BPM consultant are still predominantly based on experience, and grey hair is still an indicator of this. BPM is still more an art than a science. There are very few sources of information for people to rely on when delivering a BPM project: there are very few good books which cover all the relevant aspects; internet searches are crowded with advertising of vendors; and few seminar or training courses live up to their promises.

I have always been very passionate about exchanging expertise and experience – right from my first job at the United Nations Industrial Development Organization which was not just about achieving results but also knowledge transfer. During my career at Sogeti B.V., The Netherlands, I enjoyed the support and opportunities provided to develop process reference models and guidelines; give BPM training and lectures as well as setting up a BPM expert group and the Dutch BPM Forum. Jeroen Versteeg and Klaas Brongers have been very supportive in this regard.

Writing a book which combines both a holistic view and the necessary details has been a long cherished dream. When I joined TouchPoint, Australia, and John Jeston told me about his plans for this book and showed me the outline of the Framework, I knew that this dream would be fulfilled.

Johan Nelis

Introduction

In almost every industry, globalisation is leading to overcapacity, which is leading to commoditisation and/or price deflation. Success, therefore, will go to the fittest – not necessarily the biggest. Innovation in process – how things get done in an enterprise – will be as important as innovation in the products a company sells.

(Louis V. Gerstner Jr, 2002: 270)

Be careful of management buzzwords and techniques and the latest fads – EVA, TQM, Balanced Score Card, Benchmarking, BPR, Six Sigma and now BPM – they all promise a lot and are often seen as a panacea. Managers can hide behind them and say, 'Well, I applied it like I was told to and it still didn't work'.

These 'latest techniques' look simple to apply, but in real life they are complex. Managers still need to look critically at their organization and apply change as 'their' organization needs it – custom-made.

At a time of exceptional change within both organizations and society,

there are a number of imperatives for executives and managers as they lead their enterprises beyond present boundaries into the twenty-first century. They are the following:

- developing global capacity
- positioning for growth
- relentless business improvement
- managing from the outside in.

(Stace and Dunphy, 1996)

Peter Drucker (1991; emphasis added) has stated that:

the single greatest challenge facing managers in the developing countries of the world is to *raise the productivity of knowledge and service workers*. It will dominate the management agenda for the next decades, determine the competitive performance of companies, and determine the very fabric of society and the quality of life in industrialised nations.

What is productivity or relentless business improvement?

Most would argue that productivity or relentless business improvement is doing things faster for less cost. This is certainly a measure, and probably the most basic. Quality must also be added into this equation, as must customer service. Another measure of productivity is the rate at which an organization is responsive to market needs, service or product innovation, and its ability to change as the marketplace demands. There is much talk that an automated BPM implementation can provide an organization with this business *agility*.

It is imperative for an organization to identify what type of productivity is essential or critical to meeting its strategic goals. The easy answer is all of the above (time, cost, quality, customer service, market responsiveness and business agility); however, it is difficult for an organization to target all at the same time, without a structured and planned approach.

As we will discuss in Chapter 13, on the Organization strategy phase, Treacy and Wiersma (1997) say that an organization must choose between three strategic options:

1 Customer intimacy – the best total solution for the customer
2 Operational excellence – the best total costs
3 Product leadership – the best product.

They say it is impossible for an organization to be good at all three strategic options. Organizations must make a choice of one of these dimensions, otherwise they will, according to Michael Porter (1980), become 'stuck in the middle' and will eventually either not perform well or disappear.

It is the role of the leaders to select which strategy is the critical one for the organization, and then identify the business processes to be redesigned, or created, to achieve the desired results. There is a growing number of leaders who have identified how critical this is for the achievement of an organization's strategies and objectives.

This book is about providing organizational leadership with an understanding of BPM and its importance to an organization, and how to make it happen within the organization. It is also about providing BPM practitioners with a framework – and set of tools and techniques that will provide a practical guide to implementing BPM projects successfully.

However, in reading the book it must be clearly understood that BPM projects are complex activities. This is not a book to be read from cover to cover as a piece of fiction, like a novel; it is a reference book for organizations completing BPM projects and provides an holistic approach. The various phases and steps in the framework described are complex and highly interrelated, and for the novice BPM project manager will appear overwhelming on first reading. However, once read, studied and used, the complexities and interrelationships will become clearer and start to fall into place.

The book is divided into four parts. Part I asks and answers ten frequently asked questions about business process management (BPM). These questions are aimed at the business executives of an organization, and take a holistic, organization-level approach to BPM. The questions and the answers provided should not be interpreted as having to be answered or addressed by an organization before BPM or a BPM project can be started within an organization. The questions are not answered at a project level, but at a program or organizational level. They are designed to provide an overall view or understanding of BPM and the move towards a process-centric organization.

Part II introduces the framework, and is for the BPM practitioner. It explains the BPM project framework in detail, which comprises two different likely starting points for a BPM project and the selection of four probable project implementation scenarios. These are followed by ten phases and three 'essentials' of BPM projects. Phases 1 and 2 (Organization strategy and Process architecture) are predominantly aimed at BPM mature organizations and need not always be fully addressed before a BPM project can commence. They are at organization and program levels. Phases 3 to 10 are project-based, and show the reader the activities and steps involved in the successful completion of a BPM project.

The depth and usage of each phase of the framework will depend upon how the organization determined that a BPM project was necessary and the BPM implementation (type of project) scenario was selected. Which scenario is selected will be influenced by the BPM and process maturity of the organization and executives involved, and the particular circumstances of the organization or business unit initiating the BPM project.

Part III is once again aimed at the executives of an organization, and provides insights into how to determine the BPM maturity of the organization or business unit and how to embed BPM within an organization to ensure a continuous business process improvement culture.

Lastly, Part IV is back to the practitioners and comprises a series of appendices relating to all of the framework phases, which will provide the business and a project team with practical tools, explanations and assistance in the successful implementation of a BPM project.

The book also includes in excess of fifty case studies to illustrate various points in the book. Two of these cases are lengthy, to show how entire phases of the framework have been used in practice.

Introduction to the second edition

This second edition, within eighteen months of the first publication and after three reprints, highlights the fact that the demand for pragmatic Business Process Management books is growing **and** that there has been considerable progress in the development of the subject matter.

In other words, Business Process Management (BPM) is coming of age:

* No longer is BPM an academic exercise with 'interesting' but unproven theories
* No longer is BPM seen as just relabelling of the disastrous Business Process Reengineering
* No longer is BPM positioned as just an automated silver bullet to solve all problems instantly.

We have been told that our book has been successful because it is a pragmatic, step-by-step set of guidelines that allows the reader to build internal organization capability for process improvement and the completion of repeatable successful BPM projects.

We see the following trends emerging and/or strengthening within the business process management environment:

1. **BPM focuses on Business Performance Management**

    Executive management will give more and more attention to the business processes within their organization and especially the outcomes of these processes, which of course is the processes performance. With the increasing demand to continue to improve, performance organizations have exhausted the low hanging fruit. Blindly cutting staff numbers across the organization is no longer possible without seriously affecting the performance and compliance of the organization, as many organizations have already 'cut to the bone'. Thus, organizations need to manage performance: cost and benefits, as well as increasing market share through agility. Executive managers cannot afford to be surprised by their performance at the end of the reporting period. The desk of an executive will become more a 'control tower' from where the processes will be run and exceptions will be flagged instantly. Fine-tuning will happen through extensive what-if scenario's. A prerequisite for this to occur is that the processes are adequately modeled; describe how staff work; that staff work according to the processes; and targeted performance levels are actually realized.

2. **Everything is seen from a customer perspective**

    Customer-centric end-to-end process thinking will expand to all activities in the organization. Processes will be more and more viewed from the contribution it makes to add value to the customer and the alignment and realization of the strategic objectives. This will break from the predominantly held view that processes should be modeled from inside out. Process improvement will start by obtaining a better understanding of the customer and their demand on the business. A customer-centric view will also ensure that it becomes easier to incorporate business partners as part of an overall customer proposition.

3. **Knowledge worker**

    Gone are the days where only the repetitive and mundane processes are modeled, as these processes become automated, to a large extent. Knowledge-intense processes will be better managed as processes. The main reasons will be that compliance requires controls around these processes and the knowledge-intense processes are the core of the competitiveness of organizations. They will be better monitored with the knowledge being retained within the organization. A more advanced way of modeling, improving and managing processes will evolve. Key elements will be self-reliance, training and competency and peer-reviews.

4. **Processes as the basis for automation**

    The two main frustrations with process modeling will be resolved: first, the fact that business requirements for IT development are specified independently from the modeled processes; and secondly, the modeled processes once entered in a workflow tool can no longer be modified in the process modeling tool.

    The processes and their documentation will form the basis for BPM automation. The advantages of this approach will ensure that the business requirements are process driven and make use of the available documentation. In addition, the best mechanism to check the validity of the information is that people use the information.

    Process modeling has been completed for many years in an isolated set of activities separated from the actual process execution and the automated support. With the increased awareness that processes need to be approached holistically and with the advancement of technology, the automation can be specified, developed and tested from the modeled processes. One of the main challenges to overcome for workflow and business rules engines is to present the process models in a way that is easy to understand and maintain by the process owners/stewards.

5. **End of the Chief Process Officer**

    This seems to be a contradictory trend, just as more Chief Process Officers (CPOs) are being appointed, we are forecasting their

decline. The main reason for suggesting this is that we consider
the CPO role as a transitional role to ensure that an organization becomes more process focused. Once the customer focussed
end-to-end process thinking is engrained in the organization, the
executive responsible for an end-to-end business process will over-
see the continuous improvement process and will most likely report
to a Chief Operating Officer. The reason that we still propagate
the CPO role in this book is that we see it as an essential interme-
diary stepping stone in achieving a more customer-focussed and
process-centric organization.

6. **Even more internal resources**
    Organizations have learned from the 1990s that large-scale re-
    engineering projects with many external consultants does not
    work. Organizations have experimented with various models using
    more internal resources. It has become obvious to the authors
    that the most successful model is for there to be a relatively
    small Centre of Business Process Excellence within the organiza-
    tion and for the various business units to have subject matters
    experts that are keen to improve their processes. We do not envis-
    age whole batteries of BPM 'Black Belts', but a more across the
    board increasing awareness of BPM. Internal capability will be built
    by increasing the internal skills and knowledge to improve and
    manage processes, thus creating a true continuous improvement
    environment.

7. **Governance as part of process management**
    Governance and compliance of business processes has increased
    significantly in the last few years. Many organizations have moved
    from a situation of scattered governance to a large and elaborate
    framework of governance. Many of these structures will be difficult
    to maintain in the long run. We envisage that more and more
    governance will be included in the main stream of business pro-
    cess management. This will reduce the risks that governance and
    compliance are isolated 'ivory tower' activities. There will always
    be the need to have an independent compliance and governance
    department within an organization, however, the daily validation
    of governance and compliance will be completed as part of the
    process management process.

8. **Accreditation**
    We believe that the process management community is approach-
    ing its next level of maturity which will include the accreditation
    of process analysts, process consultants, process managers (pro-
    cess owners/stewards) and BPM project managers. Several attempts
    have been made by various firms to develop accredited training
    courses; however, most of these courses do not provide the sus-
    tainability of the training material intellectual property, while oth-
    ers have theoretical content without an all encompassing project
    methodology model. Some training organizations provide training
    where their BPM expertise and methodology is only existent in
    the presentation material and not within supporting documenta-
    tion. The strength of IT management and project management

methodologies, such as ITIL and Prince2, is that they have an over-all encompassing detailed model with a consistent approach for each module and has been based on extensive expertise.

9. **Process Community**

There is a greater need than ever for a process (BPM) commu-nity. This is both internally within an organization, and externally between organizations. We have seen various attempts at establish-ing process communities, but the most sustainable are those with no commercial interests that are independent, open for everyone and has the right (and enforced) balance between process users, consultants, vendors and academics – the Dutch BPM Forum is a perfect example of this. It is still growing strong after more than three years (www.bpm-forum.org).

10. **Embedding in the organization**

We believe there will be further embedding of process thinking and management within organizations. The best indicator of this occurring within an organization is the number of times that pro-cesses are discussed at the executive level. These discussions could be related to: solving specific business problems (for example, it could relate to customer satisfaction issues); integration with busi-ness partners; and the importance of processes in mergers and acquisitions. In other words, business processes become an impor-tant starting point for the discussion of problems and opportunities within an organization.

Positioning of this book and our next book

This book provides a practical guide to the successful and repeatable imple-mentation of BPM projects. Three reprints in the first edition and the release of this second edition highlight the enormous demand for practical common sense guidance on successful BPM implementation.

Many readers have reacted and welcomed our suggestions regarding BPM projects. However, many of you now face the next challenge: how to achieve a process-focused organization. That is, not just be able to successfully imple-ment BPM projects but move to the next stage of maturity where an organi-zation needs to support process performance management. This is depicted as part of Figure I.1

Strategy is the foundation and starting point for the formulation of an organization's strategic objectives. However, the strategy is only one part of the journey. Without an outstanding competency in strategy execution, then success will not follow. We believe it is essential to distinguish between two types of execution – project execution and process execution.

Project execution is the topic of this book you are reading now. Process execution is the topic of the new book which is titled: *Management by Process: A Roadmap to Sustainable Business Process Management*. In our experi-ence with coaching and assisting organizations with the implementation of BPM, we have found that the following seven dimensions are critical in the

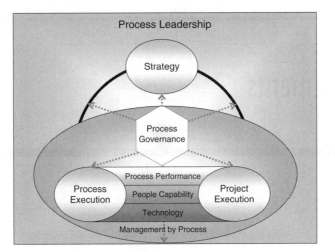

Figure I.1
Management by
Process framework.

achievement of a truly process-focused and high performance management organization:

1. Process leadership
2. Process governance
3. Process performance
4. Strategic alignment
5. People capability
6. Project execution
7. Technology.

In the next book, to be released mid 2008, we examine these dimensions as to their:

- Importance
- Key trends
- Elements that comprise the dimension
- Detailed description of the elements that comprise the ideal or visionary position
- Road map of how to get there from various starting positions.

While much has been written describing the ideal (or visionary) position that an organization must aspire to, there needs to be a recognition that few organizations fully understand what this ideal state is, let alone how to achieve it from its current position or level of process maturity. In our next book, we describe this 'road map' in great detail and how to progress towards the visionary state.

We will also include detailed case studies of successful BPM projects and programs of work.

For more information please visit our website www.managementby process.com

We would be delighted to receive reader's feedback and suggestions. You can provide this by emailing us at: info@managementbyprocess.com

Acknowledgements

It has been a journey for both of us as we have researched and developed the tools and techniques in this book. This is not a text written from academic research alone. The framework, approaches, scenarios, phases, steps, tools and techniques are what we use in our day-to-day BPM consultancy.

However, no book can be written in isolation, and there are many people we would like to thank who have reviewed, contributed to, critically commented and debated with us. These people include Stephen Dawson, Andrew McPherson, Richie Hughes, Brett Walker, Wim Hofland and Michael Oosterhout.

As always, there are special people we would especially like to thank.

Antje Breer, process and business consultant extraordinaire, has donated a significant amount of her personal time in reading and re-reading the draft chapter after chapter, and has spent many hours in robust discussion with us. She has significantly added to the quality of this book, and her contribution cannot be underestimated; it is very much valued and words alone cannot describe our appreciation and respect for Antje and her ability.

Nigel Foote, a senior consultant at Adaptra project management services, has contributed greatly to the chapter on project management; he is an outstanding project manager and thought leader in this area.

Our thanks are due to Professor Michael Rosemann and Tonia de Bruin from Queensland University of Technology and Brad Power from the Babson College at Boston University for their contributions to BPM maturity research and their chapters in this book. We especially thank Michael Rosemann for his encouragement and advice, and Frits Bussemaker for his contribution to Chapter 7, 'How do you sell BPM technology to the organization'.

Finally, we would like to thank our senior editor, Maggie Smith, for her trust, support, never-ending encouragement and good humor throughout this journey.

Training Services

Management by Process Pty Ltd offers complete training and coaching services in Business Process Management. The training courses cover the content of this book and other BPM-related topics. Please refer to www.managementbyprocess.com for more details.

New Distributor and Partner Enquiries

Distributor and partner opportunities are available for qualified BPM experts and expert organizations for the training material and courses. If you are interested please contact info@managementbyprocess.com.

Part I

Frequently asked questions

The important thing is not to stop questioning
(Albert Einstein)

As explained in the Introduction, Part I is aimed at an executive level of questions and takes a holistic view to a process-centric organization. These questions do not all need to be addressed before an organization commences its BPM journey; however, somewhere along that journey they will need to be reviewed.

Part I starts with providing an understanding of why some people find Business Process Management (BPM) a little confusing and why it is different from what has come before – the questions 'How do we demystify BPM?' and 'What is BPM?' are answered in Chapters 1 and 2.

In our experience of implementing BPM projects and programs within organizations, it is important to improve the processes before automating them. This is addressed in Chapter 3.

For an organization and for management, it is important to have an understanding of when you should do BPM and what the main drivers and triggers are. Once management has determined that a BPM project is a good thing for them to do, they need to ask who should be involved. These aspects are covered in Chapters 4 and 5.

There is much literature about aligning BPM with the organization's strategy and the need for a process architecture, and Chapter 6 explains why these points are so important.

It can be difficult for BPM enthusiasts within an organization to successfully sell the concept to management. In Chapter 7, we have asked a successful European alliance manager of a large BPM software organization to tell us how it sells BPM to other organizations.

Finally, we address three important questions in Chapters 8, 9 and 10. respectively:

- What are the critical success factors in a BPM project?
- What are the critical implementation aspects for a BPM solution?
- Why do you need a structured approach to implementing BPM?

All human progress is preceded by new questions

Chapter 1

How can we demystify business process management?

Brief history of business process management

The road to Business Process Management (BPM) has been a difficult one that has gained from the successes and failures of various other attempts at achieving process-based organizational efficiency.

Perhaps it is worthwhile taking a few moments to understand a very brief recent history of management's focus on business processes.

In the 1980s there was a considerable focus on Total Quality Management (TQM). This was followed in the early 1990s by Business Process Reengineering (BPR) as promoted by Hammer and Champy (1990). BPR had a chequered history, with some excellent successes as well as failures.

Following BPR in the mid- and late 1990s, Enterprise Resource Planning (ERP) systems gained organizational focus and became the next big thing. These were supposed to deliver improved ways for organizations to operate, and were sold by many vendors as the 'solution to all your problems'. The ERP systems certainly did not solve an organization's process issues, nor make the processes as efficient and effective as they could have been. Towards the end of the 1990s and in the early 2000s, many Customer Relation Management (CRM) systems were rolled out with extensive focus on the customer view and customer experience. While this provided focus on the front office, it did not improve the back-office processes. More recently, Six Sigma has started to come into its own.

According to Hammer (1993), 'Coming up with the ideas is the easy part, but getting things done is the tough part. The place where these reforms die is ... down in the trenches' and who 'owns' the trenches? You and I and all the other people. Change imposed on the 'trench people' will not succeed without being part of the evolutionary or revolutionary process:

> Forceful leadership can accomplish only so much. The shift from machine-age bureaucracy to flexible, self-managed teams requires that lots of ordinary managers and workers be psychologically prepared.
>
> (Hammer, 1994)

The next big thing (or how mystification begins)

Now, we have BPM, yet another three letter acronym!

So why is BPM considered the 'next big thing', and why do the 'next big things' invariably come and go?

There are usually four steps to the creation of a 'next big thing':

1 The concept promoters (vendors/analysts, etc.) hype it up to the market in their advertising, sales pitches, promotional materials, research and successful case studies.
2 These promoters then tend to disparage all the 'old big things' that have preceded it, and promote the new big thing as simply the best.
3 The next step is to make the 'new big thing' very simple, so that the decision-makers can understand it, the message being that it is not complicated and can be easily implemented.
4 Finally, the promoters (vendors in particular) market their existing products and service offerings with this new label (in this case BPM), even if the offerings do not meet the generally accepted definitions of the label. This leads to there being almost as many definitions of the label as there are vendors.

In this case, the new label is 'BPM' and the same problems are beginning to emerge. If you examine the historical 'next big things', there is a common thread running through them: they are all about business processes and trying to make them better.

Vendors and consultants all latch onto new ideas, which are often extremely good, and hype them up until the idea matures and is able to be used or implemented in a sustainable way.

BPM hype cycle

The BPM hype cycle in Figure 1.1 shows a summarized view of how the process cycle has progressed over the last two decades.

Six Sigma was invented in 1986, and created an awareness of 'processes'. This was followed in July 1990 by Hammer and Champy's (1990) *Harvard Business Review* article 'Don't automate, obliterate', and the BPR movement started. While BPM has been around for some time, *BPM: The Third Wave* (Smith

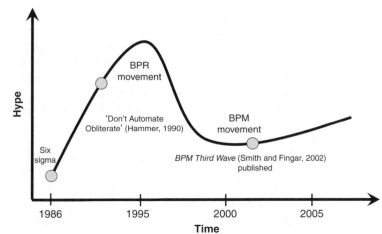

Figure 1.1
BPM hype cycle.

and Fingar, 2002) created significant interest and discussion; it could now be argued that BPM is the most important topic on the management agenda.

What is mystifying about BPM?

BPM is advocated by its proponents as being different from and better than what has been available in the past. The major advantages promoted are outlined in Table 1.1, as are our comments supporting or refuting them.

Table 1.1
Promotion v. reality

BPM major 'mystifying' points versus Reality
1   BPM is better than the past options for process improvement.   BPM has certainly raised the visibility of process improvement for many organizations. BPM has also focused many academics and consultants back onto processes and several organizations have been created solely to focus on process (e.g. BPMI.org/BPM Group). This is definitely a good thing, as the discussion on standards and BPM in general continues to raise its profile and maturity in the marketplace. Learning from past experience, such as BPR, has also been taken into consideration. *The key point is that BPM is only as good as the buy-in you get from the organization and management.*
2   BPM uses new and better technology.   There are far too few fully automated enterprise-wide BPM implementations to validate this claim at this point in time. In our experience, technology should not be the initial focus in a BPM implementation. The initial work should relate to reviewing the current processes with a goal of increased efficiency and effectiveness (the importance of establishing process goals is discussed in more detail in
(Continued)

Table 1.1   *(Continued)*

> Chapters 14, 15 and 17). While these new improved processes *could* (if appropriate) contain suggestions for automation, significant process improvements can be achieved without the use of technology. *People become carried away with the 'bells and whistles' and look at what the technology* could *do for the organization, rather than what it* needs *to do for the organization.*
>
> 3   There is a robust methodology to support BPM.   There are methodologies for parts of BPM, and few fully developed methodologies for the implementation of a complete BPM solution. *Be careful: a methodology or framework can be a millstone as much as a saviour, it is how you use it that matters.*
>
> 4   BPM is simple (and, in fact, often oversimplified).   BPM is anything but simple. There are many components and elements to a BPM implementation, and one of the purposes of this book is to explain this in more detail. *You do not need to solve all the organizations process problems in one go with BPM. Start small, with one project. As the organization matures, BPM can be expanded.*
>
> 5   External people are needed to implement BPM.   This very much depends upon the maturity of the organization and the skill levels and experience within an organization. *Certainly external consultants can assist either in a coaching or in a consulting role if the organizational maturity and/or skill levels are not sufficient. An experienced external BPM project manager can provide significant project focus that, sometimes, internal project managers are unable to bring to a project.*

BPM is not a simple concept nor is it simple to implement – it is extremely complex and difficult.

While the introduction of technology can be a useful contributor for many organizations, BPM does not always need technology to be successful. It is far more important to get your processes right *before* you consider the implementation of technology.

The iceberg syndrome

Icebergs typically only show about 10 percent of their mass above the water. BPM is often like an iceberg; people and organizations only see what is above the water. The interesting observation is that what appears above the surface depends upon the viewer's perception. For example, a vendor sees technology above the surface; a process analyst sees the processes; human resources sees change management; IT sees the technology implementation; business management sees short-term gains (quick wins), cost reductions and simple measures of improvement; and the project manager sees short-term completion of project tasks and the deliverables of the project.

People often see the 'perception' component as the completion of 'pretty pictures' or process models, whereas 'reality' is addressed in the

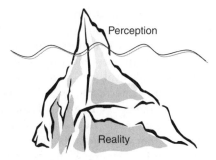

Figure 1.2
Perception, the tip
of the iceberg called
'reality'.

implementation of these processes and the achievement of business benefits. An excellent strategy is of no use unless it is well executed.

Unfortunately, a BPM implementation is a multi-faceted activity, and Figure 1.2 shows that 'reality' is what appears below the water line. Unless all the 'reality' associated with a BPM implementation is addressed, the risk to the project increases. This 'reality' needs not only to be addressed, but also made visible to the organization. A ship could cruise very close to an iceberg on one side and not hit anything, and yet do the same on the other side and sink. *The visibility of issues and activities is an important part of addressing them.*

We will now briefly explore one of these 'realities'

Exploring 'reality'

The most important component in any BPM implementation is the management of organizational change and the associated people (staff) impacts. As mentioned earlier, the implementation and its success are owned by the people in the trenches. People and their engagement in the implementation are critical, and a holistic approach in meeting the people, cultural and 'process factory' aspects of managing an organization is crucial. The key to engaging the people in the trenches is leadership from their line managers. These line managers must be engaged first. The project manager or project team cannot achieve people engagement on their own. (Note: so what is a 'process factory'? Any organization that has a back-office operation that processes a large volume of throughput and has a large number of hand-off points could be referred to as a process factory.)

It is the people who will determine the success (or otherwise) of your BPM project. You can have the most effective and efficient new or redesigned processes in the world, but unless you can convince people to use them efficiently or at all then you have nothing. People need to be included as an integral part of the development journey. They need to be consulted, listened to, trained and communicated with on a regular basis. If they do not understand the processes, the reasons for the new processes and why changes to the existing processes are necessary, how do you expect people to take ownership and responsibility for them?

People need to understand clearly what is expected of them and how they fit into the new structure and processes. Their performance measures need to be developed in consultation and agreement with them.

What is the role of management in the transformation? While it may seem obvious that managers need to *manage* the operation of the organization and process factory, this is in fact *not* what most managers do in their current positions. In our experience, with rare exceptions, today's managers spend most of their time reacting to critical situations and treating the symptoms and not the causes – commonly referred to as 'crisis management'.

This is not to be critical of managers. In general, they are well-meaning and hard-working individuals who generally do a great job with the tools they have to work with. There needs to be a considerable effort in any BPM project to work with the management and determine what information managers require to *manage the business*. You need to ensure that there is a deep and thorough understanding of how the business operates; what reports are required, and how to provide information in a timely manner, to enable managers to move from reactive to proactive management and then to predictive management. It is this journey of management maturity that provides the organization with a long-term continuous and sustainable increase in productivity.

Change management and performance measurement

The people change-management components of projects need to address the organizational culture and modify it towards a new set of management behaviors that will translate into the behaviors of the people they manage.

To support the drive to implement cultural change, management incentives need to be aligned with the management information available, the process goals and organizational strategy. Incentives and targets via performance measurement need to be well known and realistic. They must also allow the best performers to overachieve, and the rewards need to be worthwhile. This does not always translate as money incentives; human resource departments can be very creative in providing other non-monetary options. The challenge is how to measure this change in an effective and acceptable way.

Conclusion

Many people are still confused about what constitutes BPM, which is not surprising when the BPM community itself has not yet agreed on a common definition and approach. BPM is all about the efficient and effective management of business processes – people are at the center of business processes, so make them part of the solution. As Stephen Schwarts, from IBM, stated so well: 'We had improvement programs, but the real difference came when we decided it was no longer a program, it was a business strategy'. We believe this is one of the keys to a successful BPM implementation. Without trivializing the work involved in the implementation, the project is the easy part. It is the institutionalization of process improvement as a fundamental management practice that is the key, and this cannot be effectively achieved without the ability to *manage* your processes proactively and predictively.

Chapter 2

What is business process management?

This is a question that needs to be asked and addressed right at the very beginning to ensure that we have a common understanding. There are as many answers to this question as there are vendors, analysts, researchers, academics, commentators and customers.

We would like to clarify one thing straight away. In our opinion, BPM does *not* equate to a technology tool or initiative for business processes. In our experience, there is significant business process improvement that can be achieved without technology. Can BPM involve technology, and is technology a good thing? Absolutely, in the right circumstances and when it can be justified. Are process modeling and management tools useful for achieving process improvements in non-technology circumstances? If the tools referred to are process-modeling tools, then yes, they can be extremely useful in this process. In fact, it is difficult to complete complex process improvement projects in a time-effective manner without the use of these tools.

One word of caution: There is a danger of organizations believing that once they have purchased a process-modeling tool, it will solve all their problems and the process improvements will just follow. Nothing could be further from the truth. A process-modeling tool is just a piece of software, and without a methodology or framework, skilled resources to use it and a genuine commitment from organizational leadership, it is useless.

Refer to Appendix L for how to select a process-modeling tool.

BPM is just like many other three-letter abbreviations in the recent past, such as CRM and ERP, which have been misused and misinterpreted.

Currently, BPM is being used by:

- some vendors who only focus on the technology solution of process improvement
- other vendors who think of BPM as business process modeling or business performance management
- some consultants who use BPM to continue their message on BPR
- some managers who want to jump on the BPM bandwagon, with no idea where it is going
- some process analysts who use BPM to inflate their process-modeling aspirations.

Table 2.1
Definition of terms used in our definition of BPM

Achievement	Realizing the strategic objectives as outlined in the organization's strategic plan. At a project level, it is about realizing the value or business benefits as outlined in the project business case.
Organization	The organization in this context refers to an enterprise or parts of an enterprise, perhaps a business unit that is discrete in its own right. It is the end-to-end business processes associated with this part of an organization. This end-to-end focus will ensure that a silo approach does not develop.
Objectives	The objectives of a BPM implementation range from the strategic goals of the organization through to the individual process goals. It is about achieving the business outcomes or objectives. BPM is not an objective in itself, but rather a means to achieving an objective. It is not 'a solution looking for a problem'.
Improvement	Improvement is about making the business processes more efficient and effective.
Management	Management refers to the process and people performance measurement and management. It is about organizing all the essential components and subcomponents for your processes. By this we mean arranging the people, their skills, motivation, performance measures, rewards, the processes themselves and the structure and systems necessary to support a process.
Control	BPM is about managing your end-to-end business processes and involves the full cycle of plan–do–check–act (Deming circle, Walton, 1986). An essential component of control is to have the ability to measure correctly. If you cannot measure something, you cannot control and manage it.
Essential	Not every process in an organization contributes towards the achievement of the organization's strategic objectives. Essential processes are the ones that do.
Business	An implementation of BPM must have an impact on the business by delivering benefits. It should focus on the core business processes that are essential to your primary business activity – those processes that contribute towards the achievement of the strategic objectives of the organization.
Processes	What is a process? There are as many definitions of process as there are processes. One we agree with is Roger Burlton's, where he says that 'a true process comprises all the things we do to provide someone who cares with what they expect to receive' (Burlton, 2001: 72). This covers a true end-to-end process, from the original trigger for the process to the ultimate stakeholder satisfaction. Burlton adds that the '. . . final test of a process's completeness is whether the process delivers a clear product or service to an external stakeholder or another internal process'.

Many of the industry commentators and vendors provide definitions that specify technology (automation tools) as an essential component of BPM – in fact, they say that BPM is technology. However, if you take a simple and commonsense view of BPM, it is obviously about the *management of business processes.*

With this simple statement in mind and the organization as the primary focus, we would suggest that BPM is

> The *achievement* of an *organization's objectives* through the *improvement, management* and *control* of *essential business processes.*

It is important to have a common understanding of what we mean by each of the *italicized* words in our definition, so each is defined individually in Table 2.1.

We are happy to see that there is currently a movement towards an agreement that BPM is about the management of business processes. Paul Harmon, of *Business Process Trends,* recently defined BPM 'as a management discipline focused on improving corporate performance by managing a company's business processes' (Harmon, 2005a).

Thus, process management is an integrated part of 'normal' management. It is important for leadership and management to recognize that there is no finish line for the improvement of business processes; it is a program that must be continually maintained.

BPM is

- more than just software
- more than just improving or reengineering your processes – it also deals with the managerial issues
- not just hype – it is an integral part of management
- more than just modeling – it is also about the implementation and execution of these processes, which requires analysis.

Last but not least, as a management discipline, BPM requires an end-to-end organizational view and a great deal of common sense, both of which can often be in short supply.

Chapter 3

Why is it important to improve business processes before automating them?

The first rule of any technology is that automation applied to an efficient operation will magnify the efficiency.
The second is that automation applied to an inefficient operation will magnify the inefficiency.

(Bill Gates, Microsoft Corporation)

Humans are attracted to easy solutions to complex problems. In the business world, we learn to solve problems quickly and move on fast. When we can't get our work done quickly enough, we've discovered we can automate! In the office we've perfected this ability over the past 100 years to the point that we now automate almost everything in order to get more done faster – first letter-writing, then bookkeeping, reporting, inventory, sales and order processing and, more recently, business workflow and document management. Thus, when confronted with productivity, efficiency and business control issues today, our first temptation is to buy an automated solution to our problem.

So, what's the problem?

Businesses today, especially large organizations with complex service products, are realizing that there's only so much their IT systems can achieve in improving their business operations. Even where core systems are effective and efficient (which is not always the case), it is becoming increasingly difficult further to improve the overall operating efficiency and customer service effectiveness to the extent necessary to meet customer and shareholder expectations at a rate faster than our competitors. Even Bill Gates, the ultimate advocate of technology, notes that automation is only effective when applied to efficient operations.

So, having solved the immediate challenges of automating operational business systems and having achieved most of the 'easy' systems benefits, organizations are now turning to some of the more difficult and systemic operational efficiency areas to achieve their required 'step change' business improvement benefits: the operational back-office processes themselves. What is our intuitive solution to these age-old areas of inefficiency? *Automate them!* After all, it worked for systems throughput and productivity, and there are now plenty of vendors keen to provide automated workflow and document imaging solutions – often 'out of the box' – for your industry or environment.

Why isn't this working?

There are often two reasons why this isn't working. The first we refer to as the *black box syndrome*, where executives see their processes as a 'black box'. They don't know the details, but somehow the processes produce outcomes. The executives have a feeling that these processes may not be as efficient or as effective as they could be (quality and rework are not measured), but at least they work, and managers are afraid to change anything because change might disrupt these fragile 'black box' processes – and fixing a problem is tough when you do not understand it. Automating the 'black box' is therefore easier, because it becomes a project and businesses 'do' projects.

The second reason we refer to as the *looking at the edges syndrome*, where the processes and associated people are treated like sacred objects: executives cannot or do not want to discuss the efficiency and effectiveness or ask the tough questions. They keep 'looking at the edges' of the problem and not at the heart – solving symptoms rather than the cause. For these organizations, bringing in a new technology sounds so much easier because there is no talk about people or processes – just technology.

If business process inefficiencies could be easily solved by automating them, why are consultants often called in after an organization has purchased an expensive automated workflow solution that has failed to 'solve' the problem? Why do automated solutions fail to deliver their expected business benefits? In fact, often organizations experience an *increase* in paper work or *increased* rework and *diminished* quality following automation of key business processes and workflows.

Why do automated solutions fail to deliver expected benefits?

The answer lies in Bill Gates' observation. Automating something doesn't fix its underlying problems; it just helps them to occur more quickly, in vastly increased numbers and at greater frequency. The notion that 'we're going to replace what's broken with something much better' is almost never realized in a mature organization, owing to the difficulty of making instant process and cultural change on a broad scale while still running the business. At best a compromise solution is achieved, often following sizable project over-runs in time and cost budgets. At worst, the project fails completely and the *status quo* is maintained. In both cases, the expected benefits are not realized and employee and customer satisfaction levels may decline dramatically.

The obvious question would seem to be, 'Why don't organizations fix their processes *before* they look to automation solutions?'

In most large organizations, the basic back-office processes have remained predominantly unchanged for many years – even decades. In the financial services industry, for example, basic banking, insurance and investment processing procedures have been passed down for generations.

Historically, organizations haven't been able to fix their operational back-office (business processes) easily because they are perceived as being either easy (and all we need to do is automate them to make them faster and take people out of the equation as much as possible) or hard (and too difficult for management to fix because they do not have the expertise, and the temptation is to purchase a solution which will 'solve' the problem – so back to the easy option).

What have we learned from history?

In Chapter 1, we learned that none of the management trends of TQM, BPR, CRM, ERP or Six Sigma has delivered the total solution to the business benefits that an organization requires in their back-office operations areas. So what makes today's management think that BPM automation will be any different?

BPM automation has the potential capability to contribute towards achieving success, if the processes are improved first and all other aspects of a BPM project are addressed. *But are we addressing business process improvement change correctly?*

Organizations have said: 'we have been doing continuous improvement for years, so we are already in a position to automate'. Well, have they? Is continuous improvement the appropriate strategy, and has continuous improvement really dealt with the causes rather than just the symptoms?

Continuous improvement, even if appropriate, is an extremely difficult program to implement 'continuously', year after year. It requires managers to be in control of their business, and unfortunately most managers are *not* in control of their business. They mainly provide what has been referred to as 'band-aid' management, whereby they continually fix issues and problems for their staff and the business. The real issue is how much of their time is actually spent on prevention of problems by addressing fundamental process improvements.

There is a simple measure for this, and it is the answer to the question, 'how many of your critical business processes or process steps rely on spreadsheets?' It is the Spreadsheet Index. Many organizations would fail to function effectively if spreadsheets were taken away. When they are used to manage processes, the business has the potential to lose control as each person creates their own versions or 'control' mechanisms. If used for critical business processes, the information cannot be easily shared and controlled. Adequate systems should make the use of spreadsheets unnecessary.

Another indicator is to take a minute and answer the following questions truthfully:

1   Are your managers introducing new spreadsheets and small satellite database solutions into the processes, or business units, they manage?
2   Are your managers predominately focused on short-term tactical issues, and not process improvement based upon root cause analysis?
3   Is quality measured by periodic sampling?
4   Is your backlog growing, or at least not reducing?
5   Do your managers and you have no accurate measure of the level of rework within your organization and departments?
6   Do you have no idea what this rework costs the organization?
7   Does your organization have no accurate knowledge of the actual cost of executing a transaction or process?
8   Are your staff performance measures mainly focused on measuring throughput?
9   Are your managers primarily focused on cost reduction?
10 Are less than 80+ percent of projects completed to realize the benefits outlined in the business case?
11 Are your processes just focused on internal aspects?

If the answer to any of these questions is 'yes', then you and your managers are not managing the business processes. By addressing these types of questions, the organization will be getting to the root cause of process issues and taking the first steps towards a continuous business process improvement program.

Conclusion

Management, at the operational level, is predominantly about the improvement and control of the processes essential to your business to achieve the objectives of the organization. Setting the direction and goals for business process improvement is a critical step, and one that needs to be addressed by higher management.

While the introduction of technology can be a useful contributor for many organizations, business process improvement does not always need technology to be successful. It is far more important to get your processes right *before* you consider the implementation of technology. *In our consulting engagements, we find that the majority of improvements in the short term can be achieved without automation.*

It is executive management's responsibility to ensure there is a clear link between the process improvement projects undertaken by the business, and the organization's strategy and objectives. If the project cannot make a strong case on how it contributes and adds value to an organization's objectives, the project should not be undertaken.

Chapter 4

When should you do BPM — what are the main drivers and triggers?

These are difficult questions to answer in a generic manner. The real answer is, 'it depends'. It depends upon the circumstances of the organization and the organization's process maturity, and these will vary from organization to organization, and from situation to situation.

We have categorized some of the likely drivers and triggers that may cause an organization to consider BPM as a possible solution, looking at these drivers and triggers from organizational, management, employee, customer, supplier/partner, product or service, process and IT perspectives. We have listed the possible drivers and triggers under each of these categories (Table 4.1). Obviously, there are many occasions where the drivers and triggers overlap with each other.

If one or more of the triggers apply it is important to complete a root-cause analysis, as too often organizations take the easy way out and fight the symptoms rather than taking fundamental and structural steps to tackle the cause.

Drivers and triggers for the organization to consider an automated solution may include the following:

- a high volume of similar and repetitive transactions
- a clear flow of high-volume transactions that need to be passed from one person to another, with each adding some value along the way
- a need for real-time monitoring of transactions (a need to know a transaction status at all times)
- a critical issue with processing time – that is, time is of the essence
- a need to complete many calculations within the transaction
- transactions or 'files' need to be accessible by many parties at the same time.

However, never over-automate processes to the extent that the organization loses sight of the need for people involvement. People are best at managing

Table 4.1
Drivers and triggers that may cause an organization to consider BPM

Category	Drivers and triggers
Organization	• High growth – difficulty coping with high growth or proactively planning for high growth • Mergers and acquisitions – they cause the organization to 'acquire' additional complexity or require rationalization of processes. The need to retire acquired legacy systems could also contribute. BPM projects enable a process layer to be 'placed' across these legacy systems, providing time to consider appropriate conversion strategies • Reorganization – changing roles and responsibilities • Change in strategy – deciding to change direction to operational excellence, product leadership or customer intimacy • Organization objectives or goals are not being met – introduction of process management, linked to organizational strategy, performance measurement and management of people • Compliance or regulation – for example, many organizations have initiated process projects to meet the Sarbanes Oxley requirements; this has then provided the platform to launch process improvement or BPM projects • The need for business agility to enable the organization to respond to opportunities as they arise • The need to provide the business with more control of its own destiny
Management	• Lack of reliable or conflicting management information – process management and performance measurement and management will assist • The need to provide managers with more control over their processes • The need for the introduction of a sustainable performance environment • The need to create a culture of high performance • The need to gain the maximum return on investment from the existing legacy systems • Budget cuts • The need for the ability to obtain more capacity from existing staff for expansion

(Continued)

Table 4.1   (*Continued*)

Category	Drivers and triggers
Employees	• High turnover of employees, perhaps due to the mundane nature of the work or the degree of pressure and expectations upon people without adequate support • Training issues with new employees • Low employee satisfaction • The expectation of a substantial increase in the number of employees • The wish to increase employee empowerment • Employees are having difficulty in keeping up with continuous change and the growing complexity

Customers/ suppliers/ partners	• Low satisfaction with service, which could be due to:
	  • high churn rates of staff
	  • staff unable to answer questions adequately within the required timeframes
	• An unexpected increase in the number of customers, suppliers or partners
	• Long lead times to meet requests
	• An organizational desire to focus upon customer intimacy
	• Customer segmentation or tiered service requirements
	• The introduction and strict enforcement of service levels
	• Major customers, suppliers and/or partners requiring a unique (different) process
	• The need for a true end-to-end perspective to provide visibility or integration

Product and services	• An unacceptably long lead time to market (lack of business agility) • Poor stakeholder service levels • Each product or service has its own processes, with most of the processes being common or similar • New products or services comprise existing product/service elements • Products or services are complex
Processes	• The need for provision of visibility of processes from an end-to-end perspective • Too many hand-offs or gaps in a process, or no clear process at all • Unclear roles and responsibilities from a process perspective

(*Continued*)

Table 4.1   *(Continued)*

Category	Drivers and triggers
	• Quality is poor and the volume of rework is substantial • Processes change too often or not at all • Lack of process standardization • Lack of clear process goals or objectives • Lack of communications and understanding of the end-to-end process by the parties performing parts of the process
Information technology	• The introduction of new systems, for example CRM, ERP, billing systems • The purchase of BPM automation tools (workflow, document management, business intelligence), and the organization does not know how to best utilize them in a synergistic manner • Phasing out of old application systems • Existing application system overlaps and is not well understood • Introduction of a new IT architecture • A view that IT is not delivering to business expectations • A view that IT costs are out of control or too expensive • The introduction of web services

relationships, and their involvement must be engineered into the process in the appropriate way.

As stated at the start of this chapter, when to commence a BPM project is a difficult problem. For any given organization, it will be appropriate to start a BPM project when the right number and combination of the above drivers and triggers occurs. This will be different for every organization, and for every situation within the same organization.

Chapter 5

Who should be involved in BPM?

Many articles have been written about what process management is, and some would argue that consultants are the experts. However, little has been written about who should be involved in BPM within an organization. 'Involved', in this instance, includes such diverse aspects as process reviews, process modeling, process redesign or innovation, metrics analysis, BPM implementation, and ongoing management and improvement. We will spend time reviewing the role of internal and external personnel in BPM within an organization, and the various types of process management.

Processes are not a goal in themselves, as they are simply a means to achieve a business objective. Processes will not achieve a business objective automatically or by chance; they need continuous and effective management. As mentioned previously, process management is the management and organization of processes crucial for your business. Figure 5.1 shows how processes support and contribute towards the fulfillment of strategic, tactical and operational objectives, with the assistance of technology and people. They need to be as efficient and effective as possible. This can be achieved by periodic projects (step improvements), and then sustained by ongoing management and measurement.

Management of business processes

We would suggest that there are two aspects to operational management of business processes:

1 Management of business processes as an integral part of 'management'
2 Management of business process improvement.

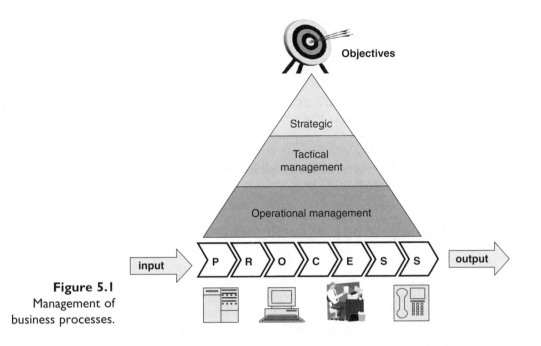

Figure 5.1
Management of
business processes.

Management of business processes as an integral part of 'management'

This type of management is responsible for the realization of the business objectives and organization strategy. This management of business processes should be performed by line management (or business process owners/ stewards), and cannot be delegated to internal or external BPM consultants, as this role forms an integral part of management as usual. For example, senior managers should be responsible for the end-to-end processes, while middle management should be responsible for the individual process(es) that comprise the end-to-end process or parts of the process. It is crucial for line managers that they are the owners of these processes. Typical process ownership–related responsibilities include the following:

- specifying objectives (goals) and measures that relate to the objectives and targets to be achieved – these targets should be broken down into daily or weekly measures to enable continuous monitoring and management
- communicating the objectives, measures and targets to the people executing the processes and, if necessary, providing rewards and incentives
- monitoring and managing progress of the targets, and verifying whether the objectives and measures are still accurate and relevant
- motivating staff to exceed objectives and deal with process disturbances
- encouraging staff to identify bottlenecks and possible process improvements.

These line-managers can be classified according to their main scope of activities:

- Operational managers should be working with clearly defined processes and related objectives. Their main involvement in the processes are to adjust the resourcing of the people aspect of the process(es) (for example, more or less staff) and solve operational problems (for example, errors as a result of the processes).
- Tactical managers will be looking at improvements of the processes.
- Strategic managers will be looking at the business model and the related processes.

Management of business process improvement

This role relates to the identification, development and roll-out of the benefits of BPM. These managers are responsible for supporting the business/organizational managers in improving their processes, and they should not be responsible for the day-to-day management of the business processes. We call these managers BPM managers, and distinguish between the following types:

- The BPM project manager, whose main responsibility is to ensure that the objectives of the BPM project, as outlined in the business case, are being met
- The BPM program manager, whose main responsibility is to facilitate multiple BPM projects so they meet the program's objectives and, by sharing best practices and lessons learned, to do it in the most effective and efficient way
- The manager of the Center of Business Process Excellence, whose main responsibility is to ensure that the business and processes are aligned to ensure that the maximum benefits are obtained from the business processes
- The chief process officer, whose main responsibility is to ensure that the processes and IT are aligned with the strategy, business and organization, and that this initiative is continuously managed from the executive level of the organization.

Close to the business

All the BPM managers must understand that their role is to assist in the achievement of targets established by the line managers/process owners/process stewards, and not building an empire. The people working with or reporting to the BPM managers should ideally be sourced from the business units involved with the project, as these people will provide the opportunity for a 'closeness' to the business and processes that cannot be obtained from non-business people from a central process unit. Large, central units are unable to obtain this 'closeness' to the business. The main reason for this is that designing processes on paper is easy, but to be able to keep on executing them as things change is a challenge and will remain a challenge long after the project is complete.

Remember that the most important criteria for success are *not* to have the best 'looking' process models or solution, or the most sophisticated process modeling and management tools. The most important criteria for success are that the organization actually uses the BPM solution and that the designated results are being achieved or exceeded.

On average, about 80 percent of a business line manager's time should be spent on business-as-usual activities, such as reviewing results, coaching and solving problems, and only about 20 percent on new process development or business initiatives. On the other hand, BPM managers will spend in excess of 80 percent of their time on process improvement activities. (Note: these percentages can of course vary from time to time and situation to situation; this is also dependent on other factors, such as the personality of the managers, workload of the business-as-usual activities and so forth.)

This difference of focus between the two roles is a reason for tension between the line manager and the BPM manager: the line manager focuses on achieving the short-term target, and any change can affect his or her ability to do this, in the short term. The BPM manager focuses on change, better to achieve the long-term objectives. Successful managers are those able to agree a win–win solution.

Use of external BPM experts

By its very nature – namely, managing people and processes – it is recommended, in the long term, that it is always internal personnel who fulfill the management roles discussed above, to ensure continuity and acceptance. In the initial phases of an organization's BPM maturity and its first few projects, it will be appropriate for the organization to appoint external BPM experts and BPM project managers to assist in bringing BPM experience and knowledge transfer to the internal staff.

After the initial projects, and as the organization maturity grows, external support for the managers can take on a different set of responsibilities, such as:

- *Setting up a project, program or Center of Business Process Excellence.* External consultants can leverage their experience from multiple organizations and provide guidance. This can be of particular assistance in ensuring that the scope of the activities is not too ambitious or has ambitions that are too small (although the latter is preferred over the former). The activities should start pragmatically (think BIG, start small). Having no ambition will lead to no fundamental change, while the lack of a pragmatic approach leads to the inability to meet expectations or maintain the initial effort.
- *Monitoring the progress of a project, program or Center of Business Process Excellence.* An external consultant has the ability and independence to ask tough questions. Many people become engrossed in the details of

process models and the structure of the project, program or Center of Business Process Excellence, and can lose sight of the overall objective.

- *Monitoring the performance of the business and identifying areas for improvement.* The external consultant can periodically review the performance of the business unit and staff. These reviews can then be discussed with the line manager for corrective action, if necessary.
- *Conflict resolution and project/program revival.* The external consultant can assist the organization if the original project/program or Center of Business Process Excellence does not deliver the agreed results. The first step is to identify the core problem(s) and determine whether the original objectives can still be met; the necessary steps can then be taken. An external consultant can function as an icebreaker.
- *Support for the manager.* The external consultant can assist the BPM manager if he or she is overburdened with work – which can especially occur with large organizational changes. The external consultant becomes the right-hand man/advisor to the BPM manager. The BPM manager should still be responsible for stakeholder management and decision-making, and the consultant can assist in analyzing and overseeing the various activities under responsibility of the BPM manager.
- *Evaluating (or auditing) project(s) and program(s).* At the end of the project or program it is crucial that the results are evaluated; this will assist with formulating lessons learned for the next initiatives and may also assist in evaluating and identifying outstanding key issues that have not yet been addressed within the project. In these situations, an external consultant can ask unpopular questions.

BPM projects can be extremely complex, and there is a growing trend towards providing internal business project managers and BPM managers with a BPM coach. This role is typically filled by a senior BPM consultant (internal or external), who will coach a BPM manager/project manager on a frequent basis (once or twice a month) about the main challenges and how to deal with them. This can also be appropriate for business line managers who want to introduce process thinking among the employees to achieve sustainable improvements. Most of these coaching engagements commence with a project or workshop, followed by the ongoing coaching sessions.

Chapter 6

Why are organizational strategy and process architecture important in BPM implementation?

The first question that the business should be asked at the commencement of any BPM project is, 'what objectives and goals do you have for your processes?' The reply is often, 'we have not yet formulated those aspects, but could we first start with reviewing and improving our processes?' This is absolutely the wrong way of approaching BPM, and even though organizations often understand this, they want to do it anyway to obtain quick wins and easy results.

Organization strategy

Why is organization strategy important to business processes?

Organization strategy is sometimes not considered in business processes. Here, we list the reasons for this and discuss the conclusions that have emerged from our experience and research.

1   *There is no explicit strategy available.* In most cases an implicit organization or business strategy exists, and it has the potential of causing a conflict with any available explicit information. Another way of approaching this is to look at the organization's objectives and how it proposes to implement or achieve them.

    In order to ensure that business processes are effectively and efficiently contributing to the organization's strategy, it is essential that the objectives, and an outline of the strategy, are explicitly specified. Without agreed upfront process goals, it is impossible to improve the processes while ensuring that they add value and contribute to the organization's strategy and objectives. How does the project team know it is 'heading in the right direction'? The best thing to do in this situation is to delay the process improvements project(s) until the main objectives and strategic choices have been made.

2 *Obtaining the strategic information will take too long.* In this case, the strategic information is not either communicated or scattered throughout the organization.

   It is important to spend adequate time upfront in understanding and obtaining this information rather than starting to look at processes only to find at the end of the project that the assumptions made at the start were incorrect. One method is to use project meetings with major stakeholders to elicit the strategic information and promote the benefits of the project.

3 *People involved are not capable of strategic thinking.* Some believe that operational personnel should not be bothered with, or confused by, the strategic issues, on the basis that such personnel should be focused only on operational issues.

   This is not the case, as it is important for operational personnel and managers to understand the strategic choices and their consequences. If this is not clear, then workshops are a useful method of imparting this information and demonstrating how the strategic issues affect their work and how they can contribute in making a strategy successful. Operational participants start to highlight operational issues that they know are at odds with the strategic direction. Without operational managers and personnel being informed of and committed to the strategic direction, it is very challenging to have a successful and effective business operation.

4 *We have already prepared a list of wishes; we do not need to involve strategy.* Many projects start with a predefined 'wish list' of improvements. Most of these proposals are very operational and actually take the current processes and settings for granted.

   Often the biggest impact and success comes when strategic considerations are included in the analysis. This provides an opportunity to question and challenge some of the stubborn and ignored tacit assumptions and constraints. 'Wish lists' tend to be very operationally and short-term focused, whilst most organizations are faced with fundamental changes which have substantial impact at the strategic level.

What should be included within organization strategy and process architecture in order to have the right context for process review and process improvement?

Sometimes discussions regarding a process review or process improvement can take an unnecessarily long period of time, as people within the same organization don't always have the same mindset when reviewing the processes because the information is tacit (in people's heads). After providing everyone with the same context, most process issues can be resolved in a fraction of the time it would have taken via the traditional method of discussion. Unless there is a clear structure, all the various issues will be mixed up (e.g. objectives, strategy, constraints, principles and guidelines). An explicitly formulated context ensures that every new argument can be placed within the agreed context to determine the impact on the processes.

At a minimum, the issues that should be considered are the objectives of the organization (the Balanced Score Card (BSC) is a good method to specify and measure these objectives), the strategic choice (e.g. customer intimacy, operational excellence or product leadership strategy), the business model (the relationship with the customers, partners, competitors and the community at large) and the main guiding principles of the organization (this includes the values of the organization). In addition, there should also be principles specifically for processes. We refer to all these elements together as 'process architecture'.

Process architecture ensures that all the relevant information, which consists of the foundation and guidelines for the process review and improvement, are made explicit and can be referred to. The impact of any internal and external change can easily be determined.

Process architecture

Why do people fail to use the process architecture? Our research has shown that people quote the following reasons:

1   *We already have process models.* Many people confuse process models with a fully-fledged architecture. We have seen people who proudly show their elaborate process models, which have been published in color on a poster. However, they become very quiet when asked when it was last updated and how it is continually maintained.

   Process architecture is much more than a process model; it also includes the objectives, principles, strategies and guidelines that are the foundation of the models. A process model is just a snapshot of the current thinking, and does not provide sufficient guidance for reviewing existing or creating new processes. In fact, the process the organization goes through to create a commonly agreed process architecture is more important than the eventual documented architecture itself. It is during the process of creation that all the important decisions are made, and the business gains an understanding and appreciation of the importance of the process architecture.

2   *Creating the process architecture is more effort than the benefits to be derived from it are worth.* If management and the business are, in general, negative about the need for process architecture, then this usually indicates that they do not understand the importance of setting rules and guidelines for process models and process structure. They may not have been through the workshops and decision-making process associated with the creation of a process architecture.

A good process architecture will ensure that more time and effort is saved by its use. It will also provide a means of communicating, specifying and agreeing the process objectives and principles in a way that it is clear for everyone. Where process architecture already exists, it will be much easier to identify the impact of the suggested changes against the agreed standard.

3   *We have process architecture, but no one is using it.* Many architects get carried away with the creation of the organization's process architecture, making it more elaborate than it needs to be and forgetting that its success is measured by the level of its use and the benefits it provides to the organization.

A common mistake made by architects is that when the business and management are not involved with the creation of the process architecture, they run the risk of it becoming more complex and elaborate than it needs to be. The first step is the involvement of all the relevant stakeholders, if buy-in, agreement and usage are to occur. The most successful architectures (that is, those actually being used to support decision-making processes) are relatively short and simple.

4   *We have agreed on a common process architecture, but no one sticks to it.* A common process architecture has been agreed, and before the ink has dried there are already all kinds of drivers to deviate from it – new legislation, new products, a customer request and so forth. Initially the process architecture may be successful in suppressing these exceptions, but it will not be able to withstand the pressure from the business and management. The moment the first exception is granted, exceptions will increase at an alarming rate and within no time the process architecture will become irrelevant. The more projects deviate, the more the project risk increases.

It must be recognized that there will need to be deviations from the agreed process architecture sometimes. The process architecture will need to adjust to business requirements and thus it will need to be dynamic, rather than the static architectures of the past. Therefore, rather than suppressing exceptions it is better actively to manage them, ensuring that there is a valid reason for the deviation, that the deviation is limited (thus remaining within a certain bandwidth of the agreed process architecture), and that measures are being taken to bring it eventually into alignment and compliance with the process architecture.

Chapter 7

How do you sell BPM technology to the organization?

Frits Bussemaker

Even though many internal BPM practitioners have identified substantial business benefits from the use of an automated BPM solution, they have often struggled to convince the rest of the organization, especially the decision-makers and holders of the budgets, to gain funding. Frits Bussemaker, Chairman of the Dutch BPM Forum, describes how an automated BPM solution can be positioned to gain acceptance. The main message is: there are multiple stakeholders, and it is crucial to focus on the business benefits rather than technology.

Business processes are all around us, independent of the market, organization, department or function – whether a telecom operator providing an ASDL connection, a bank processing a loan application, an insurance company handling a claim, or a local government organization processing a request for a new passport. It could be argued that any organization is the sum of its business processes. At least, the business process should be considered as a fundamental part of any organization's infrastructure. In all the above examples, the volume of work and the complexity of the business process demand that organizations look for possible IT applications to support and automate their processes. Throughout the years, many companies have invested millions in all sorts of IT solutions. The marketing department has its Enterprise Content Management (ECM) system, used to inform the consumer of the organization's products or services. The sales department has a Customer Relation Management (CRM) system to allow the company to up- and cross-sell, and finally the delivery department has an Enterprise Resource Planning (ERP) system to process the order and send an invoice. The reality with most organizations today is that these departments operate as independent silos (Figure 7.1).

The consumer is often confronted with poor customer service due to broken processes, inefficient processes and manual processes – that is, the customer is often confronted with the silos of the organization. However, the same

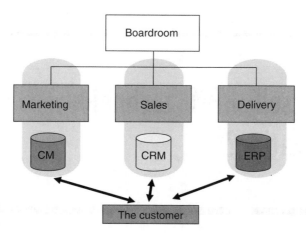

Figure 7.1
Automation of the
functional silos.

consumer is becoming more and more demanding with respect to delivery time – where customers used to expect and accept days or weeks for delivery, over recent years they have moved to ever more real-time expectations. At the same time, the consumer is demanding higher quality of the products or services. Finally, the product or service is becoming more and more personalized (and thus more complex), supported by increased customer services – 'This is what I want, and I want it now'.

How can any organization cope with these increased demands in an environment where, at the same time:

- the number of interfaces with the customers is growing (e.g. phone, fax, email, sms, pda)
- the product, service and price options have increased the complexity of the business
- most organizations have a whole suite of 'build and buy' systems and applications, often each with its own data format
- budgets are being cut.

Organizations must start realizing that all the organization's assets, systems, departments and people are interlinked. There are numerous internal processes that form an internal supply chain, which relate to the end-to-end process of the organization. Basically, one simple interface with the organization would be preferable:

- Marketing – what product or service do you have to offer?
- Sales – please treat me as one single client
- Delivery – please provide the product or service as quickly as possible.

Realizing that an organization could be seen as a sum of its business processes is the key element in selling BPM – that is, BPM automation is not about implementing technology, it is about automating the business processes

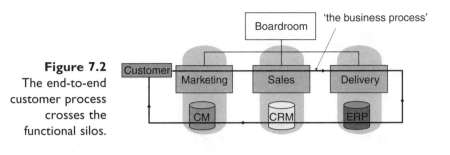

Figure 7.2
The end-to-end
customer process
crosses the
functional silos.

in the right circumstances. Existing applications can be linked to each other by an independent process layer. BPM automation is also about a new way of working, monitoring and managing the organization, which often results in a new organizational structure.

As presented conceptually in Figure 7.2, BPM technology can complement existing (and future) investments in applications. BPM provides a process layer linking the various independent applications needed to execute a single end-to-end business process. BPM technology can then manage the flow of activities along different applications, and the people involved. BPM technology can also reduce execution time. By tracking the business process, an organization can monitor its performance and at the same time audit for compliance. Analyzing this information will also help to improve the business processes further. All this can increasingly be completed in real time; management can make instant changes and validate if the changes are having the desired effect.

As the business process may cover different people working in different departments, the organization must consider allocating issues such as process owners, process managers, and the method of measuring the effectiveness and efficiency of a business process. This also implies that, with most organizations, the business and IT must be aligned. Experience shows that organizations which are successful in exploiting BPM technology start by solving a specific business problem with a clear, short-term return on investment (ROI). Thus, anybody selling BPM, both internal and external to an organization, should consider all parts of the equation:

$$BPM = organization + people + technology.$$

In the end, you are selling a shift in mindset: functional organizations will become process-centric supported through BPM technology.

Can BPM technology realize a more efficient organization at a lower cost? Yes! Just consider the 'old' silo structure, where individual departments spend lots of time and money (effort) but this effort is not necessarily aligned, so that the effort of one department actually contradicts the effort of another department. What BPM can do is assist in aligning the efforts of the individual departments. The sum of the total effort will then increase (Figure 7.3).

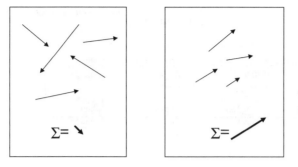

Figure 7.3
Illustration of a
sub-optimal process
versus an
end-to-end
optimized process.

Who is buying BPM technology?

As mentioned previously, both the business and the IT side of an organization are involved in considering BPM technology. As processes are everywhere, this also means that basically the key business manager should be involved. Generic arguments for any business manager include the following:

- BPM technology provides business process transparency
- the business becomes more agile
- productivity is increased at a lower cost
- compliance can be provided
- customer service is improved.

These generic arguments should be presented as specific business benefits where the BPM technology is the means of providing these.

When addressing an IT department, the following issues should be presented:

- with BPM technology, the earlier investment in IT applications will not be wasted
- BPM will link these independent applications together
- the IT department can be more responsive to the changing business requirements
- the new applications can be provided faster, cheaper and more flexibly
- BPM is also a key element in a service-oriented architecture.

Finally, it is important not to forget to involve the senior executives of the organization. As mentioned, BPM and its associated technology will most likely change the way an organization is managed, and even its structure. Senior executive support is therefore essential to enable the shift to a process-centric organization.

Who is selling BPM technology?

In general, we can see the following three parties involved in selling an automated BPM solution:

1   Parties internal to the organization
2   A software vendor
3   A system integrator and/or consultant.

Many organizations have internal sponsors and advocates for an automated BPM solution. There is, however, a shift from enthusiastic individuals to a more structural support, in the form of process owners, Centers of Business Excellence or Senior Executives. In many cases these internal personnel leverage the benefits and lessons learned from earlier implementations.

For a long time, BPM vendors were niche companies in a small market. Pure play BPM software vendors had a background in developing and selling workflow management solutions (e.g. Staffware) or document management solutions (e.g. Filenet). When the first early adopters of BPM technology demonstrated significant business benefits and of course a good ROI, business analysts such as Gartner and Forrester began to notice this. Favorable reports were written on the future and benefits of BPM, and a multi million dollar market was predicted. This has definitely woken up the supplier market. New pure play vendors have emerged, and existing vendors are repositioning themselves from, for example, a CRM or Document Management vendor to a BPM vendor. Others have come into the BPM space through acquisition, for example Tibco software buying Staffware. Finally, the traditional big companies, such as IBM, SAP and Siebel, are offering BPM-type solutions. However, as outlined in this chapter, it is crucial that vendors look at a BPM solution from the specific business perspective and not from a technology point of view.

At the same time, numerous system integrators are investing in BPM knowledge and setting up dedicated BPM practices. Consultancy firms are offering services to design, describe and help implement the business process. It is important to ensure that these organizations are able to provide the best solution and are not limited due to their partnerships or specific package knowledge.

Associations such as the WfMC, BPMI.org have been set up to define BPM standards. BPM communities have been set up, such as the bpm-forum.org and BPtrends.com. Numerous new websites, training courses, postgraduate degrees and dedicated magazines are available.

With all these suppliers, ranging from the pure play BPM software vendor through to consultancy firms to the postgraduate degree, the buyer should be very aware of what the organization's business requirements are when selecting a specific vendor, and should take into account that this explosion of BPM suppliers will sooner or later result in a shake-out of the market.

Case study: BPM automation in a telecommunications organization

A European telecommunications company was faced with an extremely fast-growing demand for broadband services, just as most countries in Europe. The company anticipated the challenge of such high demand, realizing that if it did not update its system for managing customer requests and broadband orders, then business would suffer. The existing system was entirely manual, so every order had to be produced from one system and passed to another by its employees. About eighty processes were divided over twenty systems and ten departments. On average, one order took two days to process. This was proving to be very expensive and a waste of resources, especially since it was a relatively straightforward procedure.

By implementing a BPM infrastructure, the company is now able to process approximately 80 percent of orders automatically, and turns around most orders within two hours, thus reducing the process time by 90 percent. This has also increased quality by reducing errors by 95 percent. A full return on investment was achieved within a year of implementation. On a practical level, the company has learned a lot more about its business and how it operates – 'Now we actually know exactly how our customer order process works'. Using the previous legacy system, it took the company between four and six weeks to make any changes; now, any problems in the processes can be fixed in two weeks.

Chapter 8

What are the critical success factors in a BPM project?

As discussed previously, the *reality* of implementing a BPM solution is far more complex than it first appears to be. A BPM project has the potential to (and usually does) cut across department and, increasingly, organization boundaries, as clients, vendors and partners become more involved. It will involve many varying and complex stakeholder relationships both inside and outside the organization.

While each project will be unique and have its own characteristic success factors, we have identified ten fundamental and critical success factors that apply to all BPM projects:

1   *Leadership*. Much has been written about leadership in a BPM context. It has been suggested that unless you have the undivided and total support of the CEO, you should not attempt any BPM projects. The reality is that few CEOs are yet at the point of turning their organizations into totally process-centric businesses. While there is undeniably a growing awareness of the importance of processes to organizations, there is still a long way to go. As we will discuss later, leadership does not always equate to the CEO; there are many leaders within an organization, some of whom are experimenting with BPM projects. Leadership in this context means having the *attention, support, funding, commitment* and *time* of the leader involved in the BPM project. Obviously, the degree of each of these will vary according to the BPM maturity of the organization and leader. These factors will also have input into the type of BPM project taking place – projects can range from pilots and larger 'experiments' to full-blown divisional or organizational implementations. *Time* is critical to the project, and does not mean that the leader 'turns up' to project steering committee meetings once a month. The time commitment will involve the leader supporting the project amongst

colleagues, stakeholders, customers, suppliers and the people within the organization. The leader is the 'head sales person' for BPM, and will need continually to 'sell' the expected benefits and outcomes and 'walk the talk' of BPM.

2 *BPM experienced business project manager.* In a sense, this role is the next level of leadership. This is the leader of the project team and of all the surrounding personnel, stakeholders and activities. The project manager *must* have significant skills with regard to people change management and stakeholder management. While it may be argued that good project management has always required these skills, it might also be argued that BPM projects require this knowledge to be deeper and better executed than in the past. The other significant aspect to this success factor is the necessity for the project manager to come from the business, and not IT. This is a business project, with business outcomes, and the IT component will either not exist or will be a smaller component of the overall project. Furthermore, a BPM project requires a fundamental and structural change, which is often lacking in a 'traditional' project (this will become evident in Part II).

3 *Linkage to organization strategy.* Projects are created to add value to the execution of the organization strategy and objectives. If this is not the case the project should not exist, unless it has been specifically planned as a tactical short-term solution. Tactical short-term solutions can be extremely dangerous, however. How often have we all seen a tactical solution twenty years later, so ingrained into the fabric of the organization that it is extremely difficult to replace? Managers look at the tactical solution to solve an immediate problem and then their attention is diverted to other issues and they never get the time to refocus upon the original problem, resulting in a string of tactical solutions which become, over time, a significant operational challenge. Organization strategy is the common ground which ensures that all people involved are working towards the same objectives.

4 *Process architecture.* Once the organization has adopted BPM as a strategic direction or has several BPM projects underway or implemented, it is critical that there is a synergistic approach and consistency within the organization to ensure that the maximum benefits are derived. There needs to be a set of agreed guidelines and process directives within the organization, otherwise different parts of the organization will pull in various directions and there will not be a consistent approach. Process architecture is more than just a nice set of models for processes; it describes the founding principles of process (or BPM) within the organization and is the reference for any changes in the way an organization chooses to approach BPM.

5 *A structured approach to BPM implementation.* Without an agreed structured and systematic approach to the implementation of BPM projects that takes into account the organization strategy, how it is to be executed and the significant behavioral aspects of the implementation, a project will be chaotic and have very high risks associated

with it. Too often, BPM projects are executed on the basis of traditional project management or a 'common sense' approach. As the project progresses and the pressure starts to building towards delivery, the 'intuitive' steps lose the systematic and structural approach that is required. The framework described in this book provides this systematic and structured approach.

6   *People change management.* Processes are executed either by people, or by people supported by technology. It is people who will make or break the implementation of a BPM project, and unless they are 'on board' and supporting the project, the chances of failure are high. Human change management can occupy anywhere from 25 to 35 percent of project time, tasks and effort. How often do you hear it said that 'people are our greatest assets'? Yet most organizations spend less than 1 percent of project budgets on the people aspects of the project. This is simply not enough in any project, and with the increased impact upon people of processes, this percentage must increase substantially. The project team needs to spend a great deal of time and effort on human change management. The people aspects of every process change and activity need to be assessed and acted upon in an understanding and sympathetic manner.

7   *People and empowerment.* As indicated in critical factor (6), people are impacted significantly by BPM projects. Their roles may well change quite dramatically with changing tasks and activities. Perhaps they are to be performance managed and measured for the first time. Business team leaders may have to actually 'manage' their processes, work volumes and capacity plan for the first time. These team leaders and staff will need support, not just through traditional training but also via one-on-one coaching and guidance. Team leaders, as their managers, are often forced into the role of 'fire fighter', where they rarely have time to work on the processes and coach their staff. People *are* an organization's greatest asset, so they should not be judged on their performance until the systems (processes) and structure have been changed to support the BPM project. Only then can a person's performance be assessed. Once the processes, people roles, structure and people performance measurements and feedback systems have been redesigned and implemented, personnel should be trusted and empowered to do their job. They should be provided with an environment in which to work that allows for their creativity and flexibility to perform, provided they have been set and understand their role, goals and targets.

8   *Project initiation and completion.* All BPM initiatives within the organization must be aligned with one another and, once they are completed, a post-implementation review must be conducted to ensure that the lessons learned from one project are transferred to subsequent projects. There is much to learn from one project to the next, especially in the selection of where and how to start, how to justify the business case and how to engage the various stakeholders. The business case must not be seen as simply the justification to obtain project funding, but as the main guide for the implementation of

the project. These lessons are invaluable, and must not be lost to the organization.

9   *Sustainable performance.* A project has a defined period of life, whereas processes, if maintained, supported, measured and managed, will continue to exist in a business-as-usual environment far beyond the life of the project. It is a project task to hand over processes in such a way that the business understands how to 'look after' them. The organization must establish a business process structure that maintains the life (efficiency and effectiveness) of its processes.

10 *Realizing value.* Why are projects commenced? To provide and create value that contributes to the organization's strategy. A project is only complete once the reason for its existence has been achieved and it has been handed over to the business in such a way that the business can now sustain the project outcomes. The project manager and project sponsor need to ensure that there is a benefits management structure in place to monitor and realize the value that comes from the project. It is also critical to gather as many 'quick wins' throughout the project as is reasonable and sensible. These quick wins need to be evaluated and implemented, while gathering information on the savings that result from them. This creates funding and further momentum for BPM projects. Always let everyone (all stakeholders) know of the benefits gained from the implementations of quick wins – a great BPM selling tool.

BPM projects are complex business activities that require a defined, structured and organized approach to their implementation, and we will discuss how to address these critical success factors throughout the book.

Chapter 9

What are the critical implementation aspects for a BPM solution?

Implementation is all about balance and cohesion between the organizational (business) and IT aspects. Getting this balance correct will allow the BPM project to be finished in the most effective and efficient way.

A useful metaphor is the Regatta® of Sogeti, The Netherlands, shown in Figure 9.1. The slogan used is 'Speed (effectiveness) and efficiency through balance and cohesion'.

The metaphor goes like this:

- *Speed* (effectiveness) is crucial – the overall aim is to win, and you win by being the first (fastest) across the finish line. In a BPM project/organization, the aim is to focus on realizing benefits from the business processes.
- *Efficiency* relates to ensuring that all the available energy and enthusiasm is used optimally to realize the desired result – that is, to get the best out of the entire team. In a BPM project/organization, the aim is to ensure that everyone is contributing sufficiently to realize the desired results.
- *Balance* is required to ensure that the boat does not lean sideways or tip over, which would not be good for its speed and efficiency. Balance is achieved by carefully matching the strength, weight and experience of all the participants in the boat. In a BPM project/organization, the aim is to ensure that all implementation elements (management, process, people, project management, resources and information) are considered when implementing a solution.
- *Cohesion* is required to ensure that the team rows as one – all rowers have to follow the same rhythm and technique, which gives extraordinary speed. In a BPM project/organization, it is important that all

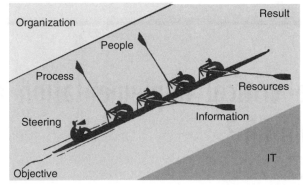

Figure 9.1
Regatta® as a
metaphor for
implementing a BPM
project (reproduced
with kind permission
of Sogeti
Nederland).

the implementation elements are in alignment and are not treated separately.

- *Process* is on the first oar, and this is the person who dictates the speed to other rowers. In a BPM project/organization, the business process should be leading and the technology and people should follow.

- *Management* (project manager, chief process officer, project sponsor) steers the boat in a straight line directly to the finish, ensuring that it does not go off course or get stuck on the shore. If a BPM project/organization places too much emphasis on resources and information (the IT aspects), then the project will be pushed onto, and could get stuck on, the organization bank (aspect) – for example, people who are not committed. Alternatively, if a BPM project/organization places too much emphasis on the people and process (=organization aspects), the project 'boat' could get stuck on the IT bank (aspects) of the project, for example, the resources (hardware and software) which are unable to meet the desired results.

Chapter 10

Why do you need a structured approach to implementing BPM?

The iceberg syndrome discussed in Chapter 1 showed that an organization's *perception* of a BPM program is likely to be only what is above the water line at a project level, but the *reality* is that most of the implementation effort is below the water out of sight. BPM is not about projects; it is about the business opportunity that BPM can provide if a process view permeates every manager and person in the organization. Certainly, a project is often how a BPM effort will commence, but there must be a concerted effort to move a project from the traditional project status to blend into a business-as-usual environment.

The traditional way that most organizations have gone about process improvement projects can be shown with the Deming Cycle (Walton, 1986) of Plan, Do, Check and Act. This evolved over time into the cycle shown in Figure 10.1, which shows the traditional steps a business improvement project would complete, such as:

1. Conduct a review of the areas to be improved, understand the business objectives, collect stakeholder requirements and select the initial processes to be improved
2. Complete the 'As is' mapping in sufficient detail to understand the process and learn how to improve it
3. Agree the timeframe for the delivery of the redesigned processes with the business and complete the 'To be' step to redesign the processes
4. Implement the redesigned processes.

Most organizations have historically stopped at this point, considering that the implementation of the redesigned, more efficient processes constitutes a successful project. In many cases the process redesign project will be repeated within eighteen to twenty-four months, because the business has changed and the processes have thus become inappropriate.

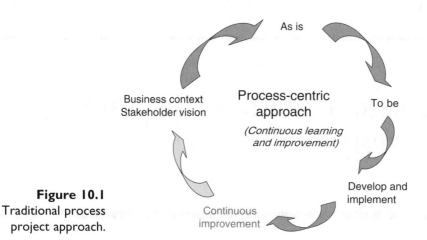

Figure 10.1
Traditional process
project approach.

To overcome this continuous need for new business process improvement projects, organizations establish a continuous process improvement program within the organization to change the processes as the business changes. This completes the feedback loop.

One of the key questions in this approach is, 'have you solved the correct problem?' How can you be certain that the way you have redesigned your processes contributes to the organization's strategic vision or intent?

Stace and Dunphy (1996) say that:

> strategy is the search for directions which energize the life of an organization; structures provide the social organization needed to facilitate the strategy.... Strategy and structure need to be constantly re-examined and realigned to be effective.

The first consideration is therefore to ensure that the organizational strategy and structure support each other. But is that all?

C. K. Prahalad, speaking at a Harvard Change Colloquium ('Breaking the Code of Change') in August 1998, described three agendas that must work simultaneously and continuously together:

1 *The intellectual agenda.* This is what some call strategy; while others have described it as an organization vision or strategic intent. This is referred to as 'Organization goals and measures of organizational success' in Figure 10.2.

2 *The management agenda.* This consists of the structures, technologies and systems of the organization. It includes how management chooses to utilize and move resources within the organization to meet the organization needs. We would explicitly include processes in this agenda, and this is shown as the 'Organization management' column in Figure 10.2.

3 *The behavioural agenda.* This covers the culture, values, ethics, leadership styles, personnel training, skills and key performance indicators (KPIs) of the people within the organization. It is important here to ensure that the reward systems respond appropriately to the behavior you wish to promote. This is shown as the last row ('Performance and measurement') in Figure 10.2.

Performance needs

Performance levels		Goals and measures	Design and implementation	Management
	Organization	Organization goals and measures of organizational success	Organization design and implementation	Organization management
	Process	Process goals and measures of process success	Process design and implementation	Process management
	Performance and measurement	Organizational goals and measures of success	Role design and implementation	People management

Figure 10.2 Performance components. Reprinted from Harmon 2003 with permission from Elsevier.

Prahalad correctly stated that an organization must operate with *all three agendas simultaneously.*

The challenge for the organization's leadership and management is to take these three agendas and determine how to apply them to the business in a practical way. Rummler and Brache (1995) and Harmon (2003) have shown how to achieve these three agendas with their performance levels and performance needs, recreated here as shown in Figure 10.2. It provides an excellent description of an organization's performance levels and performance needs, and how to apply the Prahalad agendas.

Most organizations that wish to improve their business processes start with the middle box, 'Process design and implementation'. They carry out the 'As is' and 'To be' process modeling, implement the new redesigned process, and wonder why the results do not always meet their expectations.

Leo Lewis (1993) stated that 'reengineering is not a bed of roses . . . Some statistics say seven out of ten reengineering initiatives fail'. McKinsey's found that a majority of companies researched achieved less than 5 percent change due to reengineering (*Newsletter for Organizational Psychologists*, 1995).

How can you redesign processes without knowing what you wish to achieve from the project – what the new goal(s) of the process will be? Are you trying to improve processing times from five days to two days, or two hours? If it is two hours, the approach to the redesign will be substantially different than with a two-day goal. Are you endeavoring to increase the quality of your service offering, even though this could mean an increase in the processing time for some transactions? The approach you take to the redesign process will be totally different depending upon your answer to these questions.

Then you must ask, 'how do you know that the process will contribute towards, and add value to, the organization's strategy?' Even if you know the process goals and redesign the processes to meet those goals, will this meet or contribute towards the strategic goals of the organization?

Case study: Importance of understanding organization strategy

We were asked to review the current processes in the operations area of an organization and to recommend how they should go about an improvement program. There were two options put forward. The first was for incremental process improvement, with no additional automation, and the second was for an automated BPM solution. It was interesting that both options met the designated process goals, which the client had documented. So we asked them to describe their organization strategy for the next three years.

The organization's strategic intent was that it:

will place us substantially ahead of our competition, such that it will be difficult for competitors to match the process and systems service levels able to be consistently achieved. This will form the foundation of our competitive advantage in the near and medium term.

The incremental option would have provided incremental improvement. Only three out of the twenty-five processes could be redesigned totally, whereas the remaining processes would have only been incrementally improved.

The automated BPM option would have provided substantial innovation and integration with other critical systems, as well as the ability to provide the organization with continuing business agility.

Message: It became obvious for our client to choose the automated BPM option. Unless the project manager clearly understands the organization's strategy, and ensures that the project satisfies and adds value to this strategy, then the project runs the risk of 'solving the wrong problem'.

Having linked the organization strategy with the supporting process goals and created the redesigned processes, you must ask, 'who will implement these new processes?' The answer is, the people within the organization. Unless the organization structure, role descriptions, skill sets and reward systems support and are in alignment with the organization direction, you will only be covering the first two of Prahalad's agendas.

Once all these areas have been addressed, the organization must ensure that there is an ongoing process to 'manage' and continuously to improve the business processes.

Implementing a BPM project is a multi-faceted and complex process that, if tackled without a structured approach, either will not work or will not meet the expectations of the stakeholders. However, over-applying a methodology or framework will not provide the flexibility required to meet the varying challenges.

What is needed is a practical, comprehensive, structured approach that can be tailored to each organization. We have developed a proven framework that provides this structured and flexible approach for use in the implementation of BPM projects and programs. The framework covers all of the 'reality' of the activities that reside 'below the waterline of the iceberg' in a BPM project, and consists of ten phases and three *essential* components. Each phase is then broken down into logical steps that, if followed and executed correctly, will ensure the success of your project.

These phases, essentials and steps associated with the framework are common sense. However, as Mark Twain is purported to have once said: 'Common sense is most uncommon'. In our experience, even though people know these things, they rarely execute them well, in a logical sequence or, indeed, at all. The framework groups these various aspects of a BPM project into a logical sequence. However, as stated earlier, a framework or methodology can be as much a millstone as a savior, so it is essential that it is used according to the organization's needs.

Conclusion

A rigorous yet flexible framework is essential to facilitate improvements in business processes. Our approach to BPM recognizes that change is ideally driven by people who operate within an organization where the vision and process goals are clear, organization roles and accountabilities are transparent, and systems, process and technologies are supportive of the organization's purpose. This, however, is rarely the case, and the framework provides an approach for how to make them clearer. It also provides a structured approach throughout a BPM project, from project conception and initiation to completion and sustainable business-as-usual.

Part II

The framework

This section of the book comprises an explanation of the BPM implementation framework, its various phases and steps, and how to use it in the successful implementation of BPM projects.

Chapter 11 describes the framework, the ten phases and three components considered to be *essential* to any BPM project.

Chapter 12 explains how the framework can be used, describing two typical ways in which BPM projects are initiated and the resulting four implementation scenarios usually selected by an organization.

Chapters 13–22 then explain each of the ten phases in detail, while Chapter 23 introduces the essentials, which are in turn described in Chapters 24–26.

An important aspect in the use of the framework is that while the phases are shown sequentially and typically follow the order indicated, this is not always the case. There may be occasions when a phase is skipped (e.g., the Understand phase could be skipped if there were no reason to gain an understanding of the existing processes, such as in the case of a green-field start-up organization). Similarly, the phase steps may also be completed in a different sequence. While this is possible, we would strongly recommend that each phase and step is seriously considered, and if the project team determines that it will be skipped, then this should be documented and reported to the project steering committee, justifying the reasons.

It is strongly recommended that the framework section be read in its entirety before an organization commences a BPM project. One of the reasons for this is explained in the previous paragraph. Another reason is that some phases (such as the Realize value phase) do not have their steps completed within their own phase as these must be completed during other phases of the framework. The phases are specified as discrete steps in order to highlight their importance to the project team and organization, ensuring that – in our example of the Realize value phase – the project team focuses on, and brings to fruition, the realization of the benefits shown in the project business case.

It is important to be clear that BPM initiatives will be completed either as a 'project' or as an 'ongoing improvement' activity within the business. The framework described in Part II of this book is applicable to a BPM project. The

Sustainable performance phase described later addresses the handover from project status to a business-as-usual activity. Part III of the book addresses how to embed BPM within an organization to ensure ongoing process management and improvement. However, when an ongoing BPM improvement activity is large enough for the establishment of a 'project', the framework in its entirety will apply again.

Chapter 11

Framework overview

Historically, process literature has suggested that there are three critical aspects to a process improvement project: people, process and systems. While we agree with this in principle, these days 'systems' needs to be interpreted more widely and we have used the term 'technology'. We have also added a fourth critical component: project management. To illustrate this, we have suggested the BPM project success stool (Figure 11.1).

The three components (legs of the stool) are not new; however, the fourth component *is* new, and is the 'seat' upon which 'success' rests. The foundation upon which the stool sits is also critical to success. The legs to the stool are the following:

1 *Process.* There must be an appropriate level of business process innovation or redesign linked to the organization strategy and process goals, and an acceptance of the importance of processes within the organization.
2 *People.* As an organization grows in its maturity of process management, it will understand that people are the key to implementing the proposed new processes. The organization must have the appropriate performance measurement and management structures across key processes. Process management should be proactive and then move towards being predictive, rather than reactive. Amongst other things, this all revolves around the people aspects of a BPM project.
3 *Technology.* This refers to the supporting tools for the processes and people and does not necessarily mean BPM software components or applications (although it could).

The fourth component, which holds these legs together, is the 'seat' of *project management*, for without a well-run project an implementation is destined to failure.

If a leg is missing the stool will fall, and if the seat of project management is missing then all the legs will collapse and the project will fail to meet expectations. BPM projects are complex, and success depends upon all aspects

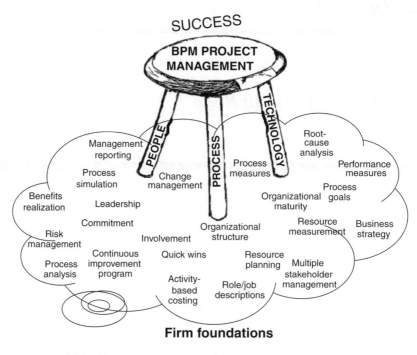

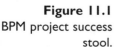

Figure 11.1
BPM project success
stool.

of the project being executed well. These aspects are represented by the 'foundations' upon which the stool rests. If these foundations are soft (or not executed successfully), then the stool will sink and eventually collapse. If the foundations are firm, however, because they are executed well, the stool will be resting upon a solid foundation and the project will be successful.

Organizations routinely attempt to execute significant BPM projects without properly addressing all four of these components and the foundations. Just as with the stool, a weak or missing leg will cause the project to collapse.

Different people (or groups of people) within the organization generally execute these components, and the foundations upon which the project rests. These groups do not always communicate effectively with each other, nor do they coordinate their activities. In fact, it has been suggested that IT, business and customers speak different languages. Project management skills are also often poor within organizations.

Effective execution of all four components and the foundations require different approaches, skills and expertise.

Symptoms which indicate that an organization is struggling with executing these components are that:

- it doesn't know where to start
- it is not making the headway that was anticipated or planned
- it has purchased a technology tool and thinks this is the answer
- redesigned processes are not implemented
- insufficient benefits are being realized
- it is doing process improvement for the wrong reason ('everyone else is doing it, so should we!')

- BPM is making little impact on the organization, perhaps because the scope is too small or too large, or because the organization is endeavoring to be too ambitious.

While there are obviously high levels of commonality between organizations, the emphasis required to apply these BPM implementation components and foundations can be different both across organizations and within an organization. For example, there is much talk about the need to align a BPM project or program of work with the organization's strategy. While this is an extremely desirable objective, it is not the only aspect of an organization that needs alignment. Before an organization can improve business processes, there must be an understanding of factors that influence it. Unless there is full appreciation of the culture and behavior of the people using the processes, you cannot know that the changes will be effective.

This is not just about aligning strategy and processes, but also people and behaviors. Performance management and measures, change management and communication will also impact a BPM project. Effective communication across all organizational levels is critical to BPM project success.

As described in Chapter 10, Figure 11.2 shows the phases and essentials of the framework, and this figure should be kept in mind throughout this chapter.

Organization results are a function of how the critical components are synchronized, and the critical components include the following:

- strategic intent
- strategic vision
- execution
- values/culture/behaviors
- people.

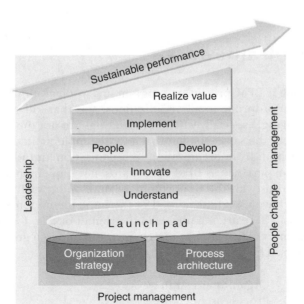

Figure 11.2
BPM project
framework.

Having alignment within the organization of the strategy, vision and process improvement projects will enable the execution of the strategy to be more complete. In an article in the July 2003 *Harvard Business Review*, entitled 'What really works', the authors (Nohria *et al.*, 2003) state that there are four primary practices (strategy, execution, culture and structure) and four secondary practices (talent, leadership, innovation, and mergers and partnerships) that successful organizations execute exceptionally well within themselves. The researchers of the study found that these organizations successfully executed all four primary practices and at least two of the four secondary practices. It is interesting to note that strategy and execution are two of the four primary practices. 'Execution', in this context, is defined by the authors as 'developing and maintaining operational execution'. In their study, they found that successful organizations selected the processes that were the most important in meeting their customers' needs, and they focused on making these as efficient and effective as possible. The organizations were also very clear about the performance measures for these processes.

This alignment must be extended further into the performance measures throughout the organization. The executives, managers, team leaders and personnel must have performance measures that are all consistent with and pulling in the same direction as that of, the organization strategy, if the organization is to be successful.

To implement a successful business process improvement program it must be governed and controlled by a consistent implementation approach, otherwise significant risks will be added to the program. This consistent implementation approach will enable the business to add value to the elements of organizational success only if it is carried through to individual projects, ideally within the BPM program.

Each of these broad levels is now explained in more detail, showing how they relate and how a consistent approach needs to be applied throughout the organization.

The 7FE project framework

Creating a BPM project or program and project implementation framework that is appropriate to all organizations, and that will suit all circumstances, is challenging, especially when organizations are not the same. Even if organizations were the same, the approach to the implementation of BPM varies enormously both from organization to organization and within an organization.

Our experience as BPM consultants and implementation practitioners has provided us with the opportunity of developing such a framework, and one that we have used and refined in the implementation of BPM programs and projects. There are ten phases in the framework, and we will describe them in a little more detail later in this chapter and in much great detail in subsequent chapters. The phases are the following:

1   Organization strategy
2   Process architecture

3   Launch pad
4   Understand
5   Innovate
6   Develop
7   People
8   Implement
9   Realize value
10   Sustainable performance.

Since the publication of the first edition of this book, we have been asked by readers to provide a 'name' for the framework. This has been a difficult tasks (at least we found it to be) because it needs to be relevant and appropriate, and we have decided to call it the **7FE Project Framework**: where the four 'F's' relate to the grouping of our 10 phases and the three 'E's' relates to the three Essentials.

As seen in Figure 11.3 the 4F's relate to Foundations, Findings and Solutions, Fulfillment and Future which group the ten phases.

The explanation of these groupings is as follows:

- **Foundations:** The majority of new BPM projects are initiated from the Launch Pad phase, and the type of project will determine the extent to which the Organization Strategy and Process Architecture phases will be referenced. These three phases form the 'foundations' of any project.
- **Findings and Solutions:** This refers to the findings (or analysis) that must take place of the existing processes and is completed in the Understand phase, with suitable solutions being determined and defined in the Innovate phase.
- **Fulfillment:** Fulfillment is the People and Develop, as well the Implement phases, for the defined solutions.

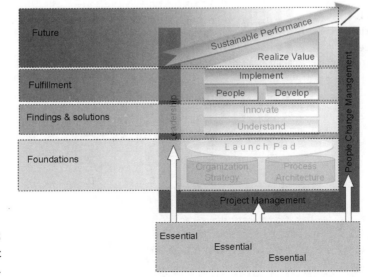

Figure 11.3
7FE Project
Framework.

- **Future:** This relates to setting the project up for the future and this is achieved by the completion of the Realize Value and Sustainable Performance phases. This moves from the project state to a business-as-usual state, thus ensuring that process improvement projects are repeatable and embedded within the organization.
- **Essentials:** The three essentials – *Leadership, BPM Project Management* and *People Change Management* – are simply considered to be necessary or 'essential' throughout the entire project.

Organizational approach to BPM implementations

While business process improvement is considered a high priority by most organizations, their attention to it and approach to BPM or process improvement implementations varies enormously. Therefore, the challenge in ensuring that projects are highly successful is to devise a framework or method of implementation that meets all the likely variations. In the next chapter, we will discuss and suggest two methods for the selection or initiation of BPM projects within an organization.

Figure 11.4 shows phases 1 and 2 of the framework, and subsequent figures will show how these phases fit with the incremental implementation of a BPM program throughout an organization.

Projects typically commence at the Launch pad phase, where a business unit is selected for business improvement, or determines that it is necessary, and the project is scoped, established and commenced (Figure 11.5). From this point, the Understand, Innovate, Develop, People and Implement phases will be utilized to guide the individual project and ensure that all projects are following a consistent framework or approach.

During the final stages of the project (Figure 11.6), the project team should be working with the business to realize the expected value or benefits as

Figure 11.4
Organization strategy and Process architecture phases.

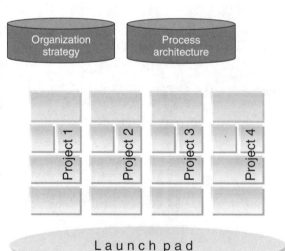

Figure 11.5
Launch pad and program phases.

Figure 11.6
Realize value and
Sustainable
performance phases.

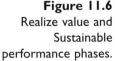

Figure 11.6
Realize value and
Sustainable
performance phases.

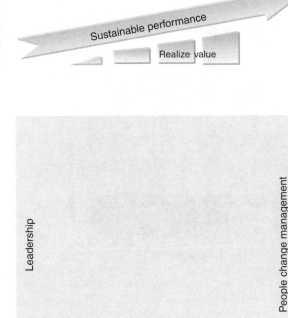

Figure 11.7
The three essentials.

outlined in the business case and to ensure that the transition from a 'project' to normal business operations (business as usual) is as smooth as possible. This will drive the project from a 'project' status to a sustainable performance basis.

Figure 11.7 shows that during the entire project there is a need to be supported by the *essential* components of project management, people change management and committed leadership. Without these essential components, the project risk is significantly escalated.

Once a track record of successful BPM projects has been established within the organization, projects may be commenced on a staggered basis after the previous one has been successfully launched.

Any framework adopted by an organization needs to be flexible and broad enough in its structure to adapt to each unique project, program and organizational approach. Our framework is aimed at providing this necessary breadth and flexibility with a set of phases and steps capable of meeting BPM implementation challenges.

The framework is designed to allow an organization to skip a phase or various steps within a phase if they are not applicable to the particular selected implementation scenario (this is discussed in Chapter 12).

There are ten phases within the framework and three additional components that are referred to as essentials, because they are *essential* to any BPM project (Figure 11.8). While some of the phases may initially be skipped, or partially skipped, in certain implementation scenarios, we believe that all

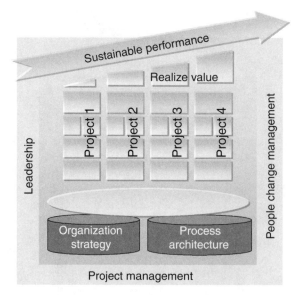

Figure 11.8
The BPM program
framework.

organizations must eventually come back and complete all phases if BPM or a process-centric view is to be seriously adopted as a critical business strategy.

Each of the phases comprises a series of steps that provide a detailed, structured and yet flexible approach to the implementation of a BPM project. The framework steps not only show what tasks are to be completed within each phase; they also provide an understanding of how the phases interrelate.

Framework phases

We will briefly outline each of the phases and essential components here, and then explain them in more detail in the subsequent chapters.

1 *Organization strategy.* This phase includes ensuring that the organization strategy, vision, strategic goals, business and executive drivers are clearly understood by the project team members. Do stakeholders expect short- or long-term gains from this project? Is the value proposition of the organization clear and understood by everyone? It is important to understand that strategy is not a 'plan'; strategy 'is a purposeful process of engaging people inside and outside the organization in scoping out new paths ahead' (Stace and Dunphy, 1996: 63). The strategy must be communicated and sold to all relevant stakeholders (especially the management and staff) until it becomes entrenched in the culture of the organization. Personnel need to take it up with urgency and, ideally, a sense of passion. The strategy needs to be known and understood by the project team, which ensures that the project scope and direction add value to it.

2   *Process architecture.* This phase is where the process architecture is designed. Process architecture is the means by which the organization establishes a set of rules, principles, guidelines and models for the implementation of BPM across the organization. The process architecture provides the basis for the design and realization of BPM process initiatives. It is where the process, IT and business architectures are brought into alignment with the organization strategy.

3   *Launch pad.* This phase has three major outcomes:

  • the selection of where to start the initial (or next) BPM project within the organization
  • agreement of the process goals and/or vision, once the processes have been selected
  • the establishment of the selected project.

Determining where to start is a difficult exercise in its own right, and the framework will provide you with several ways of determining where and how to start. Process goals and vision need to be aligned with the organization strategy and the process architecture to ensure that they are enhancing or adding value to the strategy. Once a business unit and processes have been selected and the process goals are agreed, the project must be established to maximize the likelihood of success. Establishing the project includes deciding the project team structure, the scope, the stakeholder management, creation of the initial business case, and expected business benefits.

4   *Understand.* This phase is about understanding enough of the current business process environment to enable the Innovate phase to take place. It is essential that at least basic process metrics are gathered to allow for the establishment of process baseline costs for future comparative purposes. Other essential steps are root-cause analysis and the identification of possible quick wins. There will be a need to identify, and ideally implement, quick wins along the way, as the business will not (and should not) provide unlimited funding for process improvement projects. The ideal situation is for the project(s) to become self-funding because of the gains made by the implementation of these quick wins.

5   *Innovate.* This is the creative phase of the project, and often the most interesting. It should not only involve the project team and the business, but also relevant stakeholders – both internal and external. Once the various new process options have been identified, there may be a need to run simulations, complete activity-based costing, conduct capacity planning and determine implementation feasibility, to enable the finalization of which options are the best. Additional metrics should be completed to allow a comparison with the baseline metrics established during the Understand phase. Additional possible quick wins are identified and prioritized within the business.

6   *Develop.* This phase consists of building all the components for the implementation of the new processes. It is important to understand

that 'build', in this context, does not necessarily mean an IT build. It could involve the building of all infrastructure (desks, PC movements, buildings, etc.) to support the people change management program and changes in the support of the people who execute the processes. It also involves the testing of software and hardware.

7   *People.* This is a critical phase of the framework and it could put the rest of the project at risk if not handled thoroughly and to a high standard. The purpose of this phase is to ensure that the activities, roles and performance measurement match the organization strategy and process goals. At the end of the day, it is people that will make processes function effectively and efficiently, no matter how much automation is involved. This phase should not be confused with people change management, as this needs attention throughout the project in all the phases.

8   *Implement.* This phase is where the 'rubber hits the road'. It is where all aspects of the project (roll-out of the new processes, roll-out of the new role descriptions, performance management and measures, and training) take place. The implementation plans are crucial, as are roll-back and contingency plans. Many organizations believe that the project has been completed after implementation has been successful. However, in our opinion the next two phases are the most important in a BPM project.

9   *Realize value.* The purpose of this phase is to ensure that the benefit outcomes outlined in the project business case are realized. This phase basically comprises the delivery of the benefits realization management process, and benefits realization reporting. Unless the benefits are realized, the organization should not provide additional funding to continue further process projects. It is the role of the project team, project owner, project sponsor and business to ensure that these benefits are realized. Although this is described as the ninth phase of the framework, it is in fact not a discrete phase in its own right because some of the steps are executed in previous phases. Therefore, we advise the reader to study the appropriate part of this chapter in conjunction with every other phase. The steps have been grouped together in this chapter to provide an end-to-end insight into the role of realizing value in a BPM project and to ensure that the BPM project team takes time after the Implement phase actually to realize the benefits specified in the business case.

10 *Sustainable performance.* It is absolutely essential that the project team works with the business to establish a process structure to ensure that continued process agility and improvements are sustainable. The considerable investment made in process projects must be maintained and enhanced over time. The organization must understand that processes have a lifecycle, and will need continuous improvement after the project's targeted improvements have been realized. If they don't, over time and as the business changes, the organization will simply be running its processes in a sub-optimal fashion. This phase is about the conversion from a 'project' to a 'business operational' activity.

Project essentials

We will now turn our attention to the three BPM project essentials. These are the *essential* components upon which any successful BPM project rests, and they permeate all phases of the project framework.

1   *Project management.* Clients often ask, 'can a normal application or business project manager implement a BPM project?' The answer is a qualified 'Yes, but nowhere nearly as well as an experienced BPM project manager'. The project risks will be significantly higher, and the organization risks missing out on many of the potential benefits that can be achieved from BPM. Can a person without significant project management experience implement a BPM project? This answer is easy – 'no'. Project management is a fundamental skill or requirement for any project, and a BPM project is no different. In fact, the requirement is even higher because of the increased complexity of BPM projects.

2   *People change management.* We will look at the importance of the change process as it specifically relates to the implementation of the personnel aspects of a BPM project. There have been many articles written on why process improvement and BPM project failures occur, and we do not propose to mention all the reasons here. However, there is a growing belief that the personnel aspects of an improvement project have not always been addressed in sufficient detail. As Michael Hammer stated in 1993, 'coming up with the ideas is the easy part, but getting things done is the tough part. The place where these reforms die is... down in the trenches'–and who 'owns' the trenches? The people in the organization.

3   *Leadership.* A point acknowledged by all business process change experts is that any change program *must* have the support of senior leadership/management to be successful. According to Keen (1997: 119), 'These people's commitment to change matters more than the details of the plan for change'. The extent to which executive leaders 'delegate' responsibility is crucial to the effectiveness of the outcomes of BPM projects. We have witnessed extremely successful BPM implementations and some poor ones, and the common thread in both types has always been the commitment, attention and process maturity of the executive leaders. The successful projects had excellent executive commitment, attention and understanding, while the poor ones did not.

If we bring these three BPM project essentials together and show their relationship diagrammatically, it gives us Figure 11.9. This shows that the perception is often that a BPM *project* is seen as being above the visibility line (that is, having a high visibility within the organization) whilst the *business operational* activities are seen as not having as high a visibility and hence as being below the visibility line. Project management relates to projects and people change management primarily relates to the business-as-usual activities, because that

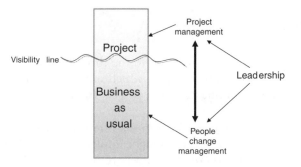

Figure 11.9
Relationship of BPM
project essentials.

is where the business people are. Leadership's role is to ensure that these two essentials are brought together in a harmonious and seamless manner.

It is important to stress that the framework does not need to be followed meticulously; it should be adapted for a specific organization or situation. More details on how to use the framework are provided in Chapter 12.

A process-centric organization

We refer to a process-centric organization later in the book, and it is useful to ensure that we have a common understanding of what this means. The easiest way to describe a process-centric organization is to compare it with an organization that is not process-centric (Table 11.1).

Table 11.1
A process-centric v. a non-process-centric organization

Process-centric organization	Non-process-centric organization
Understands that processes add significant value to the organization; understands that processes are a significant contributor to the fulfillment of an organization's strategy	Does not fully appreciate the contribution that processes make to the organization and the realization of the organizational strategy
Incorporates BPM into the management practices of the organization	Management of processes is not a primary focus
Embraces a BPM strategy	Supports various BPM initiatives
Senior leadership focuses on processes (especially the CEO, because others will follow the leader)	Understands that processes must be important because of the problems they cause (quality, backlogs, etc.)
	(Continued)

Table 11.1   (*Continued*)

Process-centric organization	Non-process-centric organization
Has a clear understanding of their processes	Has a well-defined value chain, list of processes and sub-processes
Understands the impact of processes upon each other	Perhaps has some processes modeled in unsophisticated tools; process models are not linked or related
Organization structure reflects this process understanding, with either a structure designed around process, or a matrix reporting of process and functional responsibilities	Organizational structure is based upon functional departments
Understands that tension can arise between process and functional lines of responsibility and has mechanisms in place to deal with and resolve these tensions – a team understanding and approach	Becomes frustrated with inter-departmental process issues, and could have a blame mentality; perhaps wishes to (or already has) inter-departmental service level agreements
Has appointed senior executives as responsible for processes – perhaps a chief process officer and/or process owners	Functionally based with no cross-departmental responsibilities
Rewards and measures linked to process outcomes	Rewards and measures linked to functional departmental outcomes (silo effect)

A truly process-centric organization would describe itself as follows:

we will live and breathe a customer-centric process design and management organization.

Case study: Leadership is about drive not about position

A senior executive leader within an organization had a strong process-centric view and commitment, and was extremely successful in realizing benefits from processes in one of the major business units of the organization. The CEO of the same organization did not have such a strong process view, and tried to drive process improvement throughout the organization. He could not gain the attention and passion of the other executive leadership. As a consequence, he did not obtain the business benefits he sought within the rest of the organization.

Message: The executive responsible for the implementation of BPM must be passionate and committed to its success, and able to 'sell' this passion and commitment to all others involved.

Chapter 12

Guidelines on how to use the framework

In previous chapters, we have introduced the framework and the importance of a structured approach to BPM projects. This chapter discusses how to use the framework as a result of the way an organization initiates BPM projects, and the project implementation scenario subsequently selected.

Why a 'one approach fits all' philosophy does not work

The difficulty with any structured approach to business projects, whether a BPM project or not, is that organizations often adopt a 'one approach fits all' philosophy.

Many people suggest that a BPM project should start by first obtaining the full and complete support of the CEO, and unquestionably this is the ideal method. In reality, though, most CEOs either do not know about the BPM project or will not be interested because it is considered to be 'just another project'. If they are aware of the project and it is one of the first BPM projects within the organization, they might want proof of the benefits that BPM can bring.

Even if the CEO is interested, it is often the case that the BPM initiative does not get sufficient attention, time and resources from the CEO Business processes are at the heart of an organization and require more than just lip service to monitor, manage and improve them. This lack of attention, time and resources can have a significant negative impact on the execution of the BPM initiative.

In addition, most approaches do not cater for the various stages of experience and embedding of BPM within an organization – from the initial orientation of BPM as an important part of management, through to a business-as-usual activity. Obviously, there will be a fundamentally different approach depending upon the level of organizational experience with BPM.

In the ideal situation, the organization will have established and published its strategic vision, objectives and goals. It will have embraced BPM, aligned the organization strategy with BPM and set about establishing the process archi-tecture – these being the foundations upon which individual BPM projects can be launched. The process architecture will also have been aligned with the organization's strategy and the IT and business architectures. However, most situations are not ideal.

How are BPM projects initiated?

The difficulty with any structured approach to business projects, whether a BPM project or not, is that organizations often adopt a 'one approach fits all' philosophy. This is not reality and is the reason why organizations often state, 'but we are different, we have unique problems and issues.' We would argue that the framework (structured approach) may be tailored to meet the specific requirements of any organization. We have never implemented it within an organization without the need to provide flexibility to meet the specific needs of that organization.

We would suggest that there are three approaches for BPM projects and, in fact, projects in general, and that almost all project initiators can be fitted within one of these approaches.

How a project is initiated is fundamental in the determination of which project approach is to be selected and therefore how the BPM framework will be used. Projects are predominately initiated in one of the three ways:

1. *Strategy-driven project*;
2. *Business issue-driven project*; and
3. *Process-driven project*.

Figure 12.1 shows the three approaches and their interaction with the phases of the Framework, together with some of the possible project triggers of each approach. The three approaches will be individually discussed below.

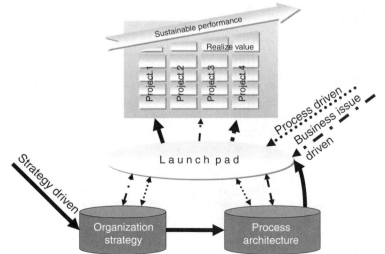

Figure 12.1
Project initiation
approaches.

The strategy-driven approach

The strategy-driven approach assumes that the organization's strategy has been determined and documented, and its implementation has resulted in the initiation of a BPM program/project(s). This is the transition from strategy to an implementation plan, and is 'top-down' management of an organization's processes.

Figure 12.1 shows the impact this will have on the project framework. The sequence is that the organization strategy will have determined that a project(s) is necessary and will know, via the Process Architecture, which processes, applications and data will be impacted, which therefore assists in the determination of the project scope. This will feed into the Launch Pad phase – the place where projects are 'launched.' The Process Architecture will need to be referenced throughout the project. The remaining framework phases will be completed as required.

Figure 12.2 shows how a strategy-driven project would typically be initiated. The steps would be as follows:

- Organization executives create the strategy that results in a number of organizational objectives.
- A number of objectives would be allocated to sub-managers (say, general managers) to be primarily responsible for the strategy's implementation and realization.
- The general managers, their staff and appropriate stakeholders would devise an Action Plan (Terms of Reference) for each objective – this is the commencement of the Strategy Implementation Plan.

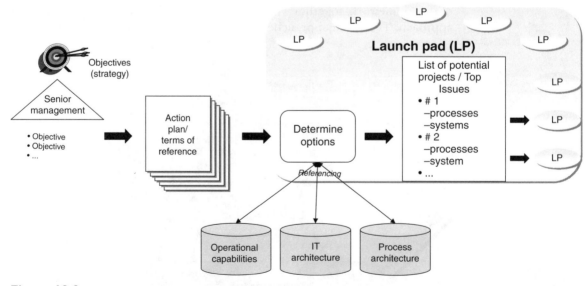

Figure 12.2
Strategy-driven project.

- The Launch Pad phase of the BPM framework would be used to determine and plan the various options available and how these will be turned into projects. This will require the managers to reference the operational capability of the organization to implement the planned projects, the IT architecture and the process architectures of the organization. It will also determine how the projects will be prioritized and then launched (commenced) in an appropriate, structured and controlled manner.

Business issue-driven approach

A business issue-driven initiative will, as the name suggests, be an initiative driven by the operational or business issues of an organization, business unit or department. The triggers for this type of BPM project are likely to originate from a business issue (opportunities, problems or regulatory requirements). Refer to Figure 12.3.

Business issue-driven initiatives will mean that the determination that a project is required occurs at a lower level within an organization than at the strategy level. The likely starting point will be the Launch Pad phase.

A small project team will commence several of the Launch Pad phase steps, after referring to the Process Architecture, to assess and gather sufficient information to know exactly where to start the project and determine its depth. The Process Architecture will provide the information of which

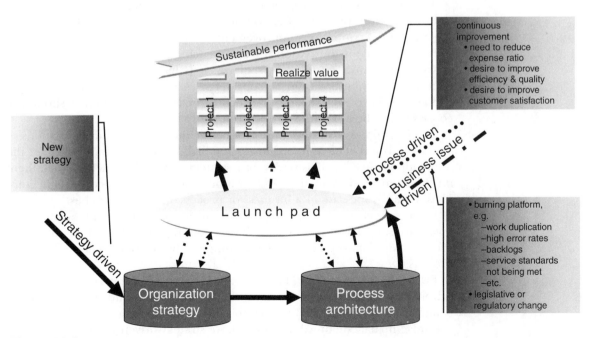

Figure 12.3
Project initiation triggers.

processes, applications and data will be impacted by the required project and the guidelines for the process modeling.

This will mean that the Organization Strategy will only be referenced to ensure that the project is in alignment with the organizational strategy, adding value to it. If the project is not in alignment with the organizational strategy, then it needs to be recognized and accepted as a tactical project, and plans and a timeframe agreed to bring it back into alignment in the future.

Process-driven approach

This refers to a project that is initiated by a process team investigating a part of the business from a process perspective to determine if there are opportunities for business efficiency improvements. The initial investigation will review the high-level processes within the designated business unit/area, establish appropriate high-level metrics, and gain some knowledge of where to start the subsequent detailed process investigation (which steps will be necessary and how they will be executed will be discussed in Chapter 15).

During these steps, the Organization Strategy will only be referenced to ensure that the project will contribute towards the organizational objectives – for example, cost reduction, increased customer service levels. If the project is not in alignment with the organizational objectives (strategy), then it needs to be recognized early and accepted as a tactical project, and then plans and a timeframe agreed to bring it back into alignment in the future (in a similar manner to the business issue-driven approach).

The Process Architecture will need to be referenced and used as required.

Process-driven projects, after completion, must always leave a legacy within the business of continuous improvement.

If compliance is the reason for commencing a BPM project, it should be considered from a strategic perspective. If it has the backing of executive management, then it should be considered as a strategic-driven approach; if it does not have the backing of executive management, then it should be considered to be a business issue-driven approach.

The organization strategy and process architecture are the foundations of any BPM project. The more extensive and bigger the project, the stronger the foundations must be. This is why, in a strategy-driven approach project, there must be more effort in the Organization strategy and Process architecture phases than is the case in a business or process-driven approaches.

In our experience, with rare exceptions, all projects comply with one of these three approaches. Understanding the approach enables the business and project team to have a clear understanding of how to conduct and implement projects.

By far, the majority of BPM projects are initiated as business or process issue-driven approaches. As an organization achieves more and more significant benefits as a result of BPM, the organization's process maturity will grow and executive management will push for more strategy-driven projects.

No matter how the need for a BPM project is determined, the next decision the organization will need to make is what type of BPM project it will be.

Four scenarios in implementing BPM

We distinguish between the following four BPM project scenarios; which one is selected will be determined by many factors, and these are discussed here.

1 *Business as usual.* This will be selected by the most BPM-mature organizations. The organization and business managers will be totally committed to a process-centric organization, and BPM projects are simply business-as-usual activities or projects.
2 *In the drivers seat.* This is the next level of organization BPM maturity, and is where there is a fully informed business manager who is totally committed to the implementation of BPM within the organization or business unit he or she is responsible for.
3 *Pilot project.* This is where there is a fully informed business manager who has yet to be totally convinced of the benefits of BPM and is willing to try it out on a small scale to start with before making a full commitment.
4 *Under the radar.* This occurs in the least BPM-mature organization, and is where there is a partially informed business manager who is not yet committed and is not paying much (or any) attention to BPM within the organization. This scenario could be a project under the guise of process improvement, and BPM may not be mentioned at all. An interesting observation regarding this type of project scenario is that some organizations may complete many 'under the radar' BPM projects and still not obtain the attention of the appropriate business management in order to undertake BPM on a wider scale within the organization.

How to determine which scenario is applicable

The scenario depends upon the involvement and commitment of the business manager. In this context, the business manager is the person who determines the business strategy – for example, the executive general manager or CEO. The more involved and committed this person is, the more impact the project can (and should) have on the organization. This is shown in Figure 12.4, where it is important first to determine the business manager's involvement; only then is it appropriate to review the impact on the organization. Once an organization has fully implemented BPM (is process-centric and BPM mature), all BPM initiatives, whether small or large, will be 'business-as-usual' projects.

Common characteristics of the various BPM scenarios are listed in Table 12.1.

Once the organization has selected the implementation scenario for the BPM project and the project team has a clear understanding of how the BPM project was initiated, it will be able to commence using the framework.

Where appropriate, we have mentioned at each phase in the framework the impact of the scenarios on the steps to be used, and the depth of use that is needed.

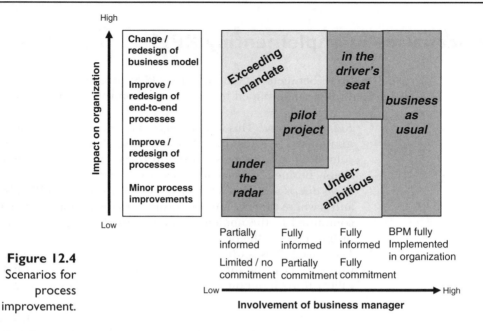

Figure 12.4
Scenarios for
process
improvement.

Table 12.1
Characteristics of different BPM project scenarios

	Under the radar	Pilot	In the driver's seat	Business as usual
Type of BPM initiative	Project	Project or a program	Program or an organizational initiative	Organizational initiative
Experience with BPM	None/ limited	None/ limited; perhaps one or two successful BPM projects	A number of successful BPM projects or programs	BPM embedded within the organization
BPM maturity of the organization	Initial	Initial, repeatable	Repeatable, defined, managed	Managed, optimized
Triggers for BPM initiative	Operational problems	Range of wide operational problems; strategic issues	Strategic issues, e.g. mergers, compliance	From operational problems to strategic issues
People impacted	Limited numbers	Medium numbers	Potentially, everyone in the relevant business unit	Depending on size of project, from small numbers to every one
Organizational level	Department, projects	Business unit	Organization or business unit	Depends on size of project

Skipping of a phase

It is highly recommended that *all* phases of the framework be considered when executing a BPM project; however, there are situations in which not all the steps must be performed for a particular phase. In a green-field situation, organizations may skip the Understand phase. However, it is quite rare that an organization or new business line will start from scratch, from a processes perspective. In many cases, the organization will have already performed the proposed processes on a small scale and simply want to expand the activities on a larger scale. In this situation, it is important to understand the process experience so far (on the smaller scale) in order to be in a better position to formulate appropriate processes for the future (Innovate phase).

If the organization wishes to skip a phase, or one or more steps within a phase, it is crucial that this is thoroughly reviewed and the impact of this action is determined and understood prior to skipping the phase or step(s).

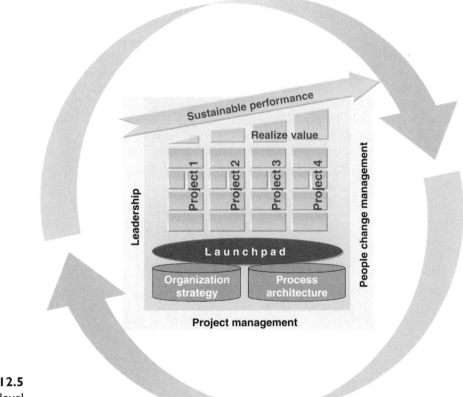

Figure 12.5
Organization-level
iteration.

Iterative approach

At first inspection, it appears that our phased approach looks forward with the completion of one phase before the next phase. However, a closer examination of each phase will reveal that there are links to the phases before and after. There are two different levels of interfaces:

1 *Project level.* These are the interfaces between the various phases of a project. Some phases can be iterative – for example, between the Innovate and Develop phases there could be feedback and feedforward. A BPM solution could be chosen (in the Innovate phase) that, in the Develop phase, provides either additional features or not all the required features, which necessitates going back to the Innovate phase to review the situation and determine how to proceed.

   At the beginning of each phase, we show the main inputs from other phases. At the end of the chapter, we describe the main outputs from the current phase. These provide the main feedforward and feedback interfaces between phases.

2 *Organization level.* BPM itself is also a process and, as we will describe in later chapters, no process is complete without sufficient feedback loops to ensure that the organization learns from their experiences (Figure 12.5). For example, as a result of executing a BPM project, there will be information obtained that may necessitate review of the organization's strategy and process architecture. At a more detailed level, a project post-implementation review will provide lessons learned that can be incorporated into future BPM projects (for example, the business case formulation in the Launch pad phase).

In the next chapter, we will commence the description of each phase of the framework.

Chapter 13

Organization strategy phase

Why?

Organizational alignment is an essential part of getting results within an organization, and there are many elements that need to be brought, or kept, in alignment. There has been a great deal of comment and discussion in BPM literature about the need to align a BPM project or program of work with an organization's strategy, and rightly so. This is the purpose of this chapter.

The goal should be to ensure that BPM projects have a clear link to the organization's strategy and add value to it. Often BPM projects operate within 'pockets' of the organization and appear to have no link to the organization's strategy. However, every organization and every project should spend some time to understand the organization strategy and ensure that the project is adding value towards defined strategic outcomes. The depth and extent of the review depends on the importance of the project to the organization and the management level you are dealing with. If a project cannot clearly demonstrate that it is adding value to an organization and its strategic direction, it should not be undertaken. Many projects are justified because they are of a tactical nature, but many tactical solutions become long-term solutions.

There are many books on strategy, and just as many methods and definitions. We like the approach of Hamel and Prahalad (1994), based on *strategic intent*. They wrote, 'if Strategic Architecture is the brain, then strategic intent is the heart'. The three attributes that an organizational strategic intent will provide are as follows:

1 A sense of direction – a particular point of view about the long-term market or competitive position that an organization hopes to build over the coming decade or so.
2 A sense of discovery – this implies a competitively unique point of view about the future.
3 A sense of destiny – this adds an emotional edge to the strategy, and is a goal that employees perceive as being inherently worthwhile.

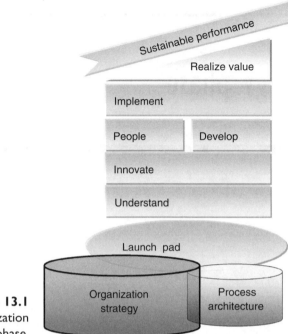

Figure 13.1
Organization
strategy phase.

The purpose of this chapter is not to describe how to develop an organization's strategy, as this topic has been covered in many other publications, but to describe how the organization's strategy, process management and the individual processes relate and interact (Figure 13.1).

Why involve strategy in BPM?

Processes are not an end in themselves, but rather a means to achieving a business objective. The selection of a business objective and the approach to achieving that objective is the strategy of the organization. The management team is responsible for selecting the organization objectives and ensuring that the processes support, or contribute to, the fulfillment of the objectives, as seen in Figure 13.2. Thus processes that are aligned with the strategy and objectives are most effective in achieving these objectives and are more sustainable in the medium to long term.

Case study: Only a view of today

An airline company wanted completely to reorganize its business processes relating to freight. We started this engagement by meeting with all the stakeholders and asking them about their strategic views for the organization. One of the marketing managers objected to this approach, saying that all the requirements for the processes were already specified in the Request for Information (RFI). However, her colleagues were speaking about fundamental business changes – further collaboration with a wide variety of partners, additional products and services, new methods of payments and new business models. After hearing this, the marketing manager realized that she had drafted the RFI on the basis of the current problems within the business processes and focused on the immediate current requirements. If we had proceeded on the basis of the original RFI and redesigned the processes accordingly, without linking them to the organization's strategy, this would have caused the processes to be outdated before they were implemented.

Message: Take time for reflection before getting lost in detail.

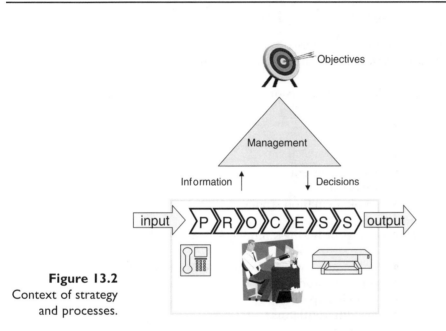

Figure 13.2
Context of strategy and processes.

It is important that while formulating strategy, the current processes, their strengths, weaknesses, possibilities and constraints are taken into account. A significant percentage of failures in deploying an organization strategy, and obtaining the anticipated benefits, are caused by ignoring the impact of the strategy on business processes during the strategy formulation steps. It is easy to develop a strategy in isolation, but to ensure that the strategy actually works throughout the organization is far more challenging.

Case study: Forgetting a detail

A large distributor of goods went through a strategic business re-orientation. Managers decided that they wanted to increase revenue. To achieve this, they needed to significantly improve resource planning and the level of automation within the organization. Their solution was to implement a new ERP system and change all their processes to accommodate the new ERP system.

Instead of obtaining more orders, they experienced a dramatic fall in orders. After analyzing why this had occurred, they realized that they had forgotten one important detail in their strategic analysis: their

(Continued)

Case study: Forgetting a detail (*Continued*)

delivery process was unique, as they were the only organization that provided goods within 24 hours. With the changing of the processes to suit the new system, they were no longer able to meet this deadline.

Message: Validate any process solution with your original business case and your strategy.

Results

The deliverables of the Organization strategy phase have significant input into the next phase, Process architecture, and include the following:

1   A documented version of the organization's:

- vision
- mission
- goals
- strategic intent
- objectives
- implementation strategy.

2   A context or business model, which includes the following:

- customers (type and volume of customers)
- services/products
- suppliers/partners
- key differentiators
- resources.

3   Key differentiators of the organization.

How?

The steps involved in aligning organization strategy and the BPM project are shown in Figure 13.3.

The depth and duration of each of the steps specified varies from project to project and organization to organization. The crucial issue of these steps is that they are at the very least considered before going on to the next step.

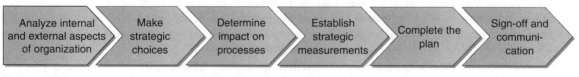

Figure 13.3
Organization strategy steps.

Chapter 12 described how the timing and extent of this phase depends on the approach and scenario chosen:

- in a strategy-driven approach, the Organization strategy phase will be the starting point and requires substantial effort and attention. In an operational initiative approach, the project will only make reference to the Organization strategy phase, ensuring that it is in alignment with the strategy.
- the attention and effort paid to the organization strategy will increase as you move from an 'under the radar' project to a 'pilot' and an 'in the driver's seat' project scenario. In a 'business-as-usual' scenario, this will depend on the scope of the organizational change associated with the project.

Step 1: Analyze internal and external aspects of the organization

During this step, the organization should review the internal and external aspects of the organization. By this we mean understanding the internal strengths, weaknesses, competencies and constraints of the organization and, on the external side, the competitive and environmental impacts upon the organization. The effort and level of detail involved in this exercise depend on the BPM scenario selected. In the case of an 'in the driver's seat' scenario, this step should be completed in more detail than in the case of an 'under the radar' scenario. Useful models to assist in this step are the following:

- SWOT analysis (Porter, 1980)
- core competencies (Hamel and Prahalad, 1994).
- competitive forces (Porter, 1980)
- environmental aspects (Porter, 1980).

Step 2: Make strategic choices

After the analysis step, strategic choices should be made and documented. In the case of an 'in the driver's seat' scenario, it is crucial to ensure that the questions specified below are answered and that the answers are completely up to date. In the case of an 'under the radar' approach, it is usually sufficient to have a clear understanding of most of these elements, without the need completely to rework and align each of the answers with the BPM project.

Key questions

- Vision: what does the organization strive to 'be'?
- Mission: what is the organization in business to 'do'?
- Goals: what does the organization plan to accomplish?
- Strategic intent: how are we going to achieve the goals and objectives?
- Objectives: what results does the organization plan to deliver?
- Implementation strategy: what methods or approaches are used to reach the goals and performance targets?

To answer these questions, we will outline two of the most helpful methods and models that are appropriate for BPM:

1 Treacy and Wiersma (1997) suggest that a company must choose between three strategic options:

   - customer intimacy – the best total solution for the customer
   - operational excellence – the best total costs
   - product leadership – the best product.

   They say that it is impossible for an organization to be a leader in all three strategic options. Organizations must make a choice of one of these dimensions, otherwise they become 'stuck in the middle' (Porter, 1980) and will eventually not survive.

   From a process perspective, this is one of the main choices that will impact each individual business process. From a BPM project perspective, it is crucial to gain a clear understanding of the direction the organization wishes to choose, because the choice will have a significant effect upon the approach to the project.

   Reviewing and (re)designing processes is impossible without this choice, because processes are all about making the right choices to achieve the desired results via the chosen strategy. Without the clear formulation of this strategy it becomes unclear how the processes should contribute to the organizational results, leading to inconsistent choices at the lower management level and, eventually, the inability of the executive management to steer the direction of the processes, organization and people.

2 The strategy maps of Kaplan and Norton (2004) describe how an organization creates value by connecting strategic objectives in explicit cause-and-effect relationships in the four Balanced Score Card (BSC) objectives (financial, customer, business processes, learning and growth).

   The strength of this model is that it involves the same method of formulating the strategy, and eventually measuring its success, through a BSC approach. Processes are crucial in the strategy maps of Kaplan and Norton because they enable the realization of organizational targets and are fundamental in enabling the organization to plan, act, measure and check work. Too often the creation and monitoring of a BSC is completed separately from the processes that must deliver the results. This leads to inefficiency, ambiguity and risk of focusing on the incorrect elements. The strategy maps of Kaplan and Norton ensure that, at the creation of the BSC, the processes are taken into account.

Step 3: Determine impact on processes

In this step, the impact of the organization strategy on the business processes is briefly reviewed. This is applicable to all four scenarios mentioned previously ('business as usual', 'in the driver's seat', 'pilot' and 'under the radar'). The relevant models that have been presented in this chapter will be used to describe the impacts.

The impact on the processes will be influenced not only by the organization strategy, but also by the analysis that should have been completed as part of the analysis of the internal and external aspects of the organization (performed in Step 1) and the determination of the strategy (performed in Step 2). This includes the following:

- strategic choice
- core competencies
- competitive forces
- SWOT analysis.

Strategic choice

Strategic choice should be analyzed from a business process perspective. It is important to obtain upfront consensus on the strategic choices, because only then can agreement be achieved on the processes to support the strategic choice. We have included in Appendix A a useful questionnaire assessment to determine the strategic choices within an organization. Figure 13.4 is the result of a completed assessment. This example clearly shows that the various people have different views on the strategic choices within the organization, and it can be clear that the general manager (operational excellence), the call center manager (customer intimacy) and the marketing manager (product leadership) have very different ideas about the strategy.

Once the strategic choice has been determined and agreed, it is possible to view the impact and consequences of this choice on the processes. In Table 13.1, we have provided some examples of the impact of the strategic choice on the processes.

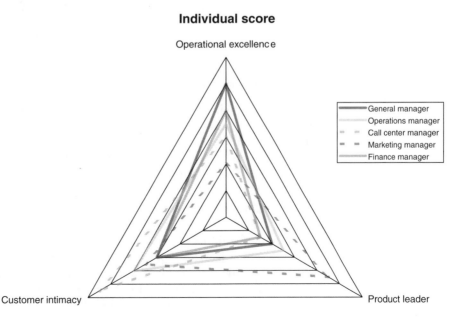

Figure 13.4
Strategic choice questionnaire sample results.

Table 13.1
Impact of strategic choice on business processes

	Operation excellence	Customer intimacy	Product leader
Key processes	• Order fulfillment • Process engineering	• Acquisitions • Delivery • Marketing communication	• Product development • Technical services • Marketing management
Organization and skills	• Centralized decision-making • Supply chain partnering	• Shared trust between sales team and back-office operational staff • Increased partnering skills	• High level of product innovation (patents) and product development • Intelligence at local level
Key process variable	• Low costs • Low lead time	• Flexibility • Staff empowerment	• Flexibility • Product
Management systems	• Key client relationships • Cost improvements • Activity-based costing • Real-time costs	• Customer equity measures (e.g. lifetime value) • Customer satisfaction, share management	• Focus on growth in sales and profitability • Specialized schedule targets

Core competencies

Core competencies (Hamel and Prahalad, 1994) is an inside-outside corporate strategy model that starts the strategy process by thinking about the core strengths of an organization. This is based on the belief that, in the long run, competitiveness derives from an ability to build the following, at lower cost, better or faster than competitors.

1   *New products, services and markets.* Modularity of processes could enable new products or services to be available faster and more cheaply than otherwise. With customers desiring increased personalization of services and products, the ability to build on existing process modules and processes will significantly benefit the competitiveness of the organization. In addition, when an organization has a good product development process that is timely, involves the right people

and integrates product development and operations, it could provide better and faster product and service development.

A variation on this is to adopt a strategy of 'smart adopter'. This implies that the organization does not complete all the ground-breaking research and development itself, with the associated costs and risks. Rather, the organization arranges its processes in such a way that it is able to quickly copy successful products and services from competitors.

2 *Fundamental customer benefit.* All processes should be focused on delivering customer benefit. This doesn't arise by chance, but by systematic and consistent design and execution within an organization's processes. Remember that customer perception is very fragile: it takes a large investment to build it, and it can be lost instantly if one or more of the processes or involved employees don't live up to this expected benefit. The customer benefit must be specified upfront, and every step should specify how it will contribute towards this.

3 *The ability to be competitively unique.* Ideally, all core processes and related supporting processes should include a level of unique competitiveness. To gain a competitive advantage is tough, and ensuring that it is sustainable is even tougher. This requires all processes, including the core and supporting processes, to be focused on maintaining the competitive advantage and taking market trends, competitors and substitutes into account on a continuous basis. Reviewing and maintaining this competitive advantage could involve migrating to another business model or different customers, or including additional products and services.

Case study: Agility as strategy

A telecommunications organization was reviewing its organization strategy and in the process reviewed its value chain. This didn't provide any major differentiators or ideas for the strategy. While reviewing the organization's strengths and weaknesses, managers realized that one of their major strengths was their ability to launch new products and services quickly. As a result of this, they selected agility as a central aspect of their strategy and chose the approach of a smart adopter organization: they would not be at the forefront of innovation in their marketplace, but innovative breakthroughs would be quickly adopted and rolled out.

Message: Selecting the right strategic choice is easier, and likely to be effective, once an organization understands its core strengths. Linking this to processes can provide a source for competitive advantage.

Competitive forces

It is crucial to realize that each of the five aspects of Michael Porter's competitive forces analysis (that is, entry of competitors, threat of substitutes, bargaining power of buyers, bargaining power of suppliers, and rivalry among the existing players) has process components. The bargaining power of suppliers can be reduced if generic processes are in place to deal with suppliers. On the other hand, the bargaining power of buyers can be reduced when the selling organization has been able to 'lock the customer in' with specific customized processes.

These forces are very useful in reviewing the various strategic 'what if?' scenarios and then evaluating the impact on the organization's processes, for example, how will the processes be impacted if more competition or substitutes enter the market, or what will happen with changes in legislation? Without understanding and conducting 'what if?' scenarios, it could be that with a change in circumstances the organization's strategy may have to be changed unexpectedly, or the business processes may require changing at a high cost. On the basis of this, the process management team will need to understand clearly which processes are more likely to change. Understanding this will ensure that the managers of the processes understand the level of resources to apply to ensure flexibility and agility of the processes.

Case study: 'What if?' analysis

A telecommunications organization wanted to introduce a new business unit for a particular market segment. In their initial proposal, managers claimed that they only needed one type of billing process and there was no need for flexibility: time-to-market was essential. Reviewing the requirement the same day, we asked many related 'what if?' questions. It soon became clear to the managers that the organization needed flexibility in its billing processes and to differentiate between residential and business accounts. We were able to prepare these billing processes in a fraction longer than originally planned, but they were able to meet the requirements of the business, not only during launch but long afterwards. The organization was grateful as managers came to realize that this saved them substantial time and money (as they would have had to replace their initial billing system within twelve months) for the small amount of additional time required to conduct 'what if?' reviews.

Message: Think broader than your initial scope by asking many 'what if?' questions.

SWOT analysis

The completion of a business process SWOT analysis may reveal some processes as being significant 'strengths' and others significant 'weaknesses'. This will have major consequences for the business model of the organization. For example, it could allow the processes which are major strengths to become the core processes of the organization and perhaps provide strategic opportunities, such as process 'in-sourcing'. At the same time, if other processes are significant weaknesses, 'outsourcing' could be considered. If the process of the IT helpdesk is a significant weakness, then the organization could decide to outsource these processes and focus all its energy and resources on the processes that are performing well. Whichever choice is selected, the business model will change.

Performance prism

The performance prism (Neely *et al.*, 2002) is a performance measurement and management framework. It considers all the stakeholders in a two-way relationship, on one hand, considering what the stakeholders want and need, and, on the other hand, what the organization itself wants and needs from its stakeholders. It involves the following five facets:

- stakeholder satisfaction
- stakeholder contribution
- strategies
- processes
- capabilities.

Some of the key questions that should be considered are the following:

- What critical processes do we require if we are to execute these strategies?
- What capabilities do we need to operate and enhance these processes?
- What contributions do we require from our stakeholders if we are to maintain and develop these capabilities?

This method helps to bring stakeholders into full context and relate them to the business processes. Leaving them out might result in processes not meeting the requirements of the stakeholders, and eventually requiring changes that were not anticipated and could be expensive and difficult to implement.

Step 4: Establish strategic measurements

In this step, high-level measures should be specified that will provide the organization with the ability:

- to measure and monitor the progress of the strategy execution
- to provide, from middle management downwards, more specific and personal objectives
- to evaluate initiatives and projects by their contribution to these strategic measures.

Balanced Score Card

The BSC (Kaplan and Norton, 1996) provides the ability to quantify the organization's targets in alignment with the strategy and vision. The strategic maps, as outlined previously, can be directly related to the BSC. The four perspectives that are taken into account are the following:

- the financial perspective
- the customer perspective

- the business process perspective
- the learning and growth perspective.

For each of these perspectives, the following items are specified:

- objectives
- measures
- targets
- initiatives.

The BSC is an excellent method to specify organizational objectives at a high level and ensure that the underlying processes and organizational units provide the aggregated output to meet these objectives.

The BSC's four dimensions allow short-term profits and more sustainable actions to be included. As stated earlier, it is crucial that it is related to the business processes and that these business processes provide a real-time view of the status of the progress on the BSC items.

Step 5: Complete the plan

The strategy and main decisions should be documented in a strategic plan. This should contain the overall enterprise objectives, as well as the main strategic choices which have been discussed in the previous steps. Remember that strategy is not just about specifying objectives, it should also provide the organization's guidelines on how to achieve these objectives.

We use the following framework (Figure 13.5), which is the basis for the process architecture that will be developed in the second phase of the framework. The strategic plan should also include an action plan, as well as general principles.

Figure 13.5
Strategic objectives and general principles.

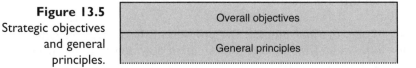

| Overall objectives |
| General principles |

Overall objectives

Overall objectives are those that an organization, or business unit, want to achieve. This information is normally already present within the organization, for example, '10 percent increase of turnover'.

General principles (strategic choices)

General principles are derived from the organization's vision and strategy, and form the strategy level of the organization (process) architecture. They are simple statements that should be able to be understood by everyone in the organization, for example:

- 'the organization follows an Operational Excellence Strategy (this will be taken into consideration while evaluating existing processes and (re)designing new processes)'
- 'the customer has a single point of contact for all his or her questions (all processes will be described as end-to-end processes)'.

Step 6: Sign-off and communication

Last but not least, it is essential to obtain formal sign-off on the results of the previous steps as well as communicating them to all stakeholders. The sign-off is a crucial step, because all the decisions must be completed in a formal way.

The greater the organizational impact of the project (as in the 'in the driver's seat' scenario), the more crucial it is to have true commitment from all key stakeholders rather than just lip service. In the scenarios with limited impact on the organization (e.g. as in 'under the radar'), the sign-off is a formal step of checking that all relevant information has been completed and has been made available.

From the moment sign-off is obtained, there must be a strict change management approach to any additional changes to the organization strategy, just like any scope changes in a project.

Communication of the organization strategy and how it impacts business processes is critical, as it aims to unlock the organization from its current situation.

The Organization strategy phase is the foundation of any BPM program/project: it provides the *raison d'être*, and it guides and motivates the people within the organization and project.

Organization strategy outputs

The Organization strategy phase outputs (Figure 13.6) will provide valuable input into other phases of the framework:

- In creating a process architecture for an organization, the objectives and goals specified in the Organization strategy will need to be understood
- When establishing a project scope and writing the initial business case, the project team must ensure that it is adding value to the objectives and goals of the organization
- The results of this phase should be presented and taken into account during the Innovate phase, as the Innovate phase is where new processes will be developed that need to be inspired by and aligned with the organization strategy.

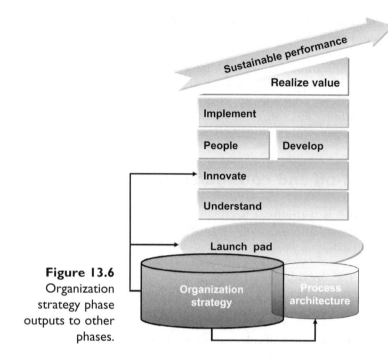

Figure 13.6
Organization
strategy phase
outputs to other
phases.

In fact, all phases of a project will need to reference and clearly understand the outcomes of the Organization strategy phase to ensure that each step in the project is adding value to the organizational objectives.

Organization strategy phase risks

A few of the most common risks involved in the Organization strategy phase are listed in Table 13.2.

Table 13.2
Organization strategy phase risks and mitigation strategies

Risk	Mitigation strategy
1 Reinventing the Organization strategy	Choose clearly at the start of the BPM project the scenario the organzation wishes to follow, and stick to the related depth of the strategy review; do not go any deeper than is required
2 Indefinitely waiting for information on the Organization strategy	If the information is not forthcoming, make assumptions and get them validated; if no answer is supplied, escalate or re-scope the project
3 No commitment from senior management	Start small-scale improvements and achieve quick wins, and obtain commitment incrementally; ask the project sponsor for assistance

Chapter 14

Process architecture phase

Process architecture is the link between the Organization strategy and the Launch pad phases (Figure 14.1). Just like the Organization strategy phase, the Process architecture phase is a prerequisite for any organization wishing to undertake successful process management-related activities, which are

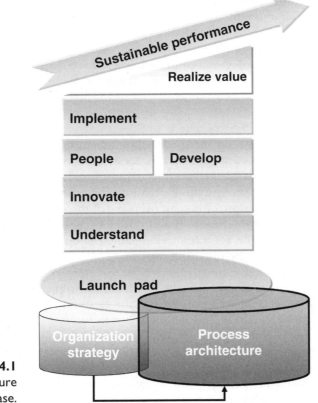

Figure 14.1
Process architecture phase.

sustainable and agile, to continuously meet the objectives of the organization in changing circumstances. The Process architecture phase is the foundation for an organization's process-related projects. We will show in this chapter that good process architecture should be an essential part of a larger organization-driven enterprise architecture.

Why?

Process architecture is an important step in a BPM project and BPM organization. It is too often neglected or just paid lip service. A process architecture ensures that:

- processes to be redesigned, or newly developed, are meeting the organization's objectives and fit within the organization strategy.
- processes are aligned with the way the business is (or should be) performed, and are able to provide the products/services to customers.
- processes are aligned with the IT architecture and applications, as the IT has to support the current and future processes.
- processes are aligned with related processes. Large organizations quite often have several process management initiatives running concurrently, and it is crucial that all these BPM projects are in tune with each other.
- all relevant information and decisions on processes are grouped together. If information is scattered throughout the organization, this can result in duplication, confusion and inconsistencies.
- relevant decisions and high-level processes are presented in an easily understood manner. An effectively aligned architecture is judged solely on how useful it is, and not by how complicated or how nice it looks.

We have often seen that process architecture is built as a result of a long drawn-out analysis and planning process. The resulting detailed models have two main drawbacks: they are too complex and, more importantly, they are always 'too late'. Thus, in these situations the process architecture is recording history rather than providing an overview of the current situation and providing guidance for the future. Both drawbacks cause the process architecture to be more of a hobby for a few well-meaning people, and one that is not being used throughout the organization.

What we describe in this book is an architecture that is comprehensive as well as understandable (that is, it provides insight in a complex situation) and dynamic (that is, it evolves with the business changes). In summary, the architecture should be 'just enough, just in time'.

A process architecture can only work if it is first aligned with the organization strategy and objectives, and secondly aligned with the business, organization and IT architectures.

Lastly, an architecture has to generate (or save) more than it costs to develop and maintain. Too often, dedicated people spend endless time and energy on the architecture, without anyone using it. The only way to develop and maintain a dynamic architecture effectively and efficiently is to make certain that there is an architectural process that ensures that all the triggers, considerations and policies are taken into account when developing, maintaining and using the architecture.

However, there is a fundamental truth regarding architecture, and it is that

> . . . organizational dynamics and culture will always trump architecture. Without a shared sense of purpose and mission, effective governance structure, and executive leadership and commitment, enterprise architecture will only have a minimal impact. Good enterprise architecture is a tool for executive management to improve enterprise efficiency and agility, and to align {with the business}.
>
> (Nelson, 2003)

In this chapter, we focus on process architecture; however, many of the statements regarding this phase are also applicable for an enterprise architecture.

What is process architecture?

There is a saying, 'put ten architects together and you get ten different definitions of architecture!' – so rather than producing yet another definition, we have listed the attributes that comprise good process architecture (inspired by Wagter *et al.*, 2002):

These are as follows:

- there must be a set of rules, principles and models for the processes
- there must be a basis for design and realization of processes of the organization
- processes must be related to organization strategy and objectives
- processes must be aligned with the business architecture, and information and technical architecture, which equates to an organization-driven enterprise architecture
- processes must be easy to understand and apply by all relevant stakeholders
- the process architecture must be dynamic, that is, easily adaptable to the evolving process, business and enterprise changes.

We have studied various process architectures and have found that the model illustrated in Figure 14.2 complies best with all the above-mentioned attributes.

Process guidelines

Process guidelines are the translation of general principles to the process domain. Examples of process guidelines are standards, methods, guidelines, policies and tool selections. Process guidelines provide concrete guidance for

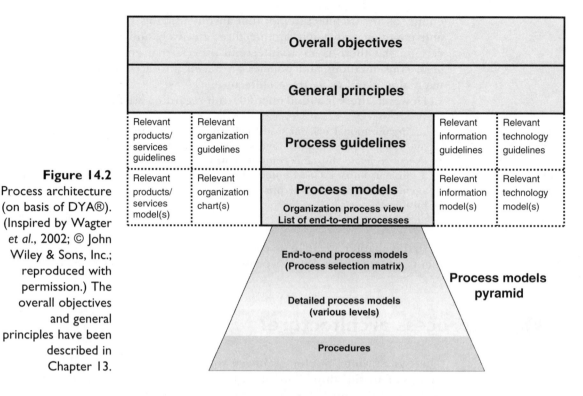

Figure 14.2
Process architecture
(on basis of DYA®).
(Inspired by Wagter
et al., 2002; © John
Wiley & Sons, Inc.;
reproduced with
permission.) The
overall objectives
and general
principles have been
described in
Chapter 13.

process development (and subsequent IT development), and are at a tactical level – for example, the design of the business processes is completed independently of the organization structure.

Process models

Process models are visual representations of high-level processes as well as the high-level links between processes. The pyramid below the architecture shows how the other, more detailed, process models fit into this process architecture. They will be produced in the later phases.

Architectural principles

We use the following architectural principles (Wagter *et al.*, 2002):

- architecture is not a goal in itself, and should support the objectives of the business
- architecture is more than models and documentation; it deals especially with the logic that forms the basis of the models and documentation
- the only way to have an appropriate dynamic architecture that is in line with the strategy and the business is to have an architecture process that deals with all the triggers and subsequent changes

- architecture can be developed incrementally
- non-compliance with the architecture is justifiable in certain circumstances; we call this the 'pressure cooker mechanism', and it will be discussed further in Step 6.

Results

The output from this phase will include the following:

1 A documented and agreed process architecture
2 A project start architecture
3 An organization process view
4 A list of end-to-end processes.

How?

The Process architecture phase, as with the Organization strategy phase, focuses on the organizational aspects of a BPM project. The following information should be taken into account during execution of this phase:

1 *The BPM scenario* (as discussed previously). The criticality and intensity of this phase will be influenced by the BPM scenario chosen by the organization:

- Process management as 'business as usual' – available and relevant information will be assessed (through the use of a project start architecture (PSA), which will be discussed later in this chapter), and any modifications will be raised through the appropriate change management channels. This may result in changes to the process architecture, or a partial and managed exemption might be allowed.
- The 'in the driver's seat' scenario – available information will be assessed and the process architecture will be either amended or developed if this is the first BPM project for the organization.
- The 'pilot' project scenario – available information will be assessed and questions might be asked, for clarification. In addition, the process architecture will be reviewed and required changes may be proposed. The scope of the changes will be limited.
- The 'under the radar' scenario – available information will be assessed and questions might be asked for clarification. The process architecture documentation will not be amended at all, or only in a very limited way.

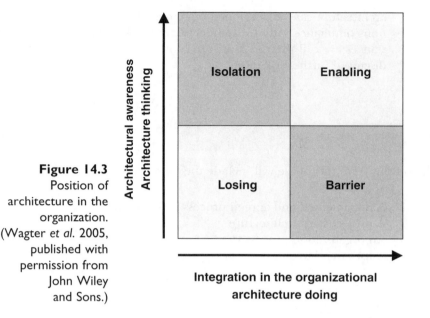

Figure 14.3
Position of
architecture in the
organization.
(Wagter *et al.* 2005,
published with
permission from
John Wiley
and Sons.)

2 *The maturity of the organization in architecture.* The maturity of the organization does not only relate to the level of architecture 'thinking' and implementation, but also to the related architecture 'doing' and the discipline to be able to obey the related discipline (Figure 14.3).

- *Isolation* refers to the situation where architects develop a perfect architecture in an 'ivory tower' and very few people within the organization are aware of it, let alone use it. In this situation, the architects must find more engagement with, and commitment from, the rest of the organization.
- *Barrier* refers to the situation where architects have the required engagement with the rest of the organization but are not very advanced with their architecture. This will mean that the architecture remains predominantly at the operational level, as it is too fragmented and low level to add value at a more strategic level. The organization must include architecture in its strategy.
- *Losing* refers to a situation where the organization has limited awareness of architecture and has partial integration in the organization. This occurs in organizations where everyone is so busy fighting operational fires, there is no time to consider more tactical and strategic options. We recommend starting a step-by-step roll-out of the architecture to address this situation.
- *Enabling* refers to a situation where the organization has adopted architecture as a key enabler. The important challenge is to ensure that architecture remains an enabler and does not become a burden.

3 *The scope and focus of the architecture.* Before embarking on formulating an architecture, it is important to decide on the level of

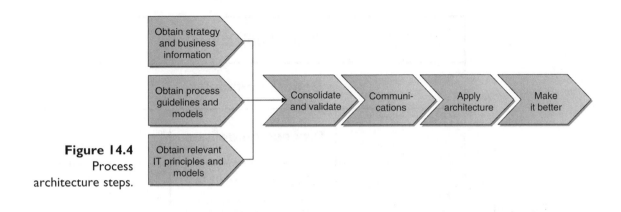

Figure 14.4
Process
architecture steps.

ambition – that is, the scope and focus for the architecture. One of the main choices to be made is whether to start only with a process architecture (normally applicable in the 'under the radar' or 'pilot' scenarios) or whether the entire enterprise architecture will be modeled (normally applicable in the 'in the driver's seat' scenario).

Another important choice is the processes that are in scope for the architecture. A scope that is too small will lead to limited benefits, while a scope that is too ambitious will lead to too much work and reduced benefits.

The steps shown in Figure 14.4 are applicable to the creation of a process architecture, and are described below.

The Process Architecture is usually established in a step-by-step manner rather than in one set of activities. The steps by which it is created are outlined in this chapter and they describe how each of the elements, as outlined in Figure 14.2, are populated.

Step 1: Obtain strategy and business information

Figure 14.5 shows the relevant products/services and organization guidelines and models used to obtain strategy and business information.

The information to be obtained includes the following:

- overall objectives and general principles as specified in the first phase, Organization strategy, completed/updated when appropriate
- relevant business (product and services) guidelines and models
- relevant organization guidelines and models.

We have stated that the process architecture has to serve the business – which is why it's crucial to understand the business fundamentals that will make it easier to provide solutions that fit the business logic. The first phase, Organization strategy, already included some general principles. However, process architecture also has to capture the more implicit assumptions and guidelines, which are more-or-less taken for granted in the strategy. That is why the general principles need to be completed.

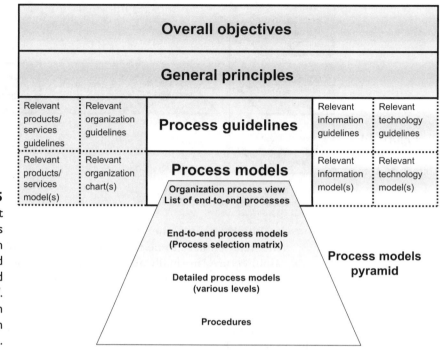

Figure 14.5
Relevant
products/services
and organization
guidelines and
models. Adapted
from Wagter *et al.*
2005, used with
permission of John
Wiley and Sons.

It is important to have explicit agreement on the general principles within the company: these are issues and aspects that form either part of the strategy or a part of deeper embedded implicit assumptions and founding principles within the organization. Because these assumptions and principles are implicit, there is always a danger that they may be ignored or forgotten, or that the relevant people have different views on them. A workshop consisting of the relevant people is the best way to table these assumptions. It is crucial to get a clearly defined and broadly agreed formulation of these assumptions and principles.

It is necessary to capture the relevant information, mostly high level, such as the typology of:

- products and services and the underlying principles and logic
- customers and the underlying principles and logic
- pricing and discounting and the underlying principles and logic
- partners (including suppliers) and distribution and the underlying principles and logic.

Our experience is that obtaining this information can sometimes be a challenge. Although most of the information is there, such as listings of products, customers and partners, the challenge normally lies in obtaining the underlying principles and logic. This is because most of the principles and logic are implicit considerations that the business takes into account, which is another good reason for creating an architecture where the implicit considerations become explicit.

Suggested ways of acquiring this information include the following:

- obtaining listings of products, prices, customers and partners
- obtaining annual financial plans, marketing plans, major account plans and budgets
- discussing with the business managers why they have made their selection for these products, prices, customers and partners, and why others are not included (the *why?* question)
- visualizing the structures (for example, how is a product constructed, does each customer get a unique product, or is the customer solution composed of standard elements?).

Don't try to model all the exceptions – remember, a model is a simplification of the reality and not a complete theory that has to explain everything. Organizations that do not have a clear business architecture often provide solutions that are difficult to put into one comprehensive and understandable architecture. Most business managers and sales managers provide solutions in different ways, which is another good reason to start with a business architecture.

Step 2: Obtain process guidelines and models

In Step 2 (Figure 14.6), the following things have to be specified:

- process guidelines
- process models
- list of end-to-end processes.

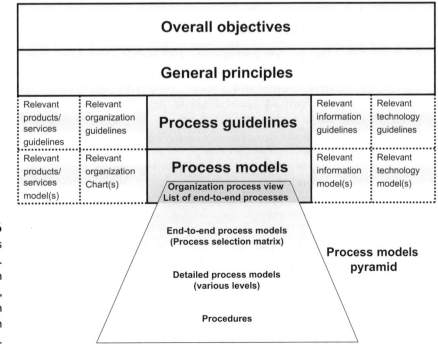

Figure 14.6
Process guidelines and models. Adapted from Wagter *et al.* 2005, used with permission of John Wiley and Sons.

Process guidelines

These are the guidelines that must be formulated for the processes, and include the following:

1 Ownership of the process
2 Scope of the processes – processes are end-to-end or are related to a function or organization entity
3 Selection of a modeling method
4 Selection of a process modeling and management tool
5 Method of governance of the processes
6 Process outsourcing, which is the place where the organization will make a decision whether or not to outsource processes; if it decides to do so, it is important to specify the following:

- type of processes to be outsourced (plus reasons)
- type of processes not to be outsourced (plus reasons)
- minimum criteria that must be met (e.g. security, SLAs)
- considerations to be taken into account (e.g. people involved)

7 Process reference models: the process architecture has to include the choice of relevant reference models. These provide a powerful basis for the processes, as they are based on best practice (e.g. ITIL–Information Technology Infrastructure Library, see www.itil.org.uk) or on industry practice (e.g. eTOM–enhanced Telecom Operations Model, developed by the Telecom Management Forum, see www.tmforum.org) or SCOR–Supply-Chain Operations Reference Model, by the Supply Chain Council, see www.supply-chain.org).

Process models

The process architecture also needs to contain a graphical, high-level representation of the processes. A good way to do this is by the organization process view diagram and a list of end-to-end processes.

Figure 14.7 provides both the organization process view and a more detailed list of end-to-end processes.

Organization process view

The organization process view represents the highest-level view of the organization from a 'process perspective'. Figure 14.7 is an example of an insurance organization. The depiction or grouping of the processes is usually shown in three levels:

1 Strategic processes – this level represents the strategic processes, which must ensure that the underlying processes are meeting, and continue to meet, the specified objectives
2 Core processes – this level represents the core, or main, business activities of the organization
3 Support processes – this level represents the non-core processes, which support the core processes of the organization.

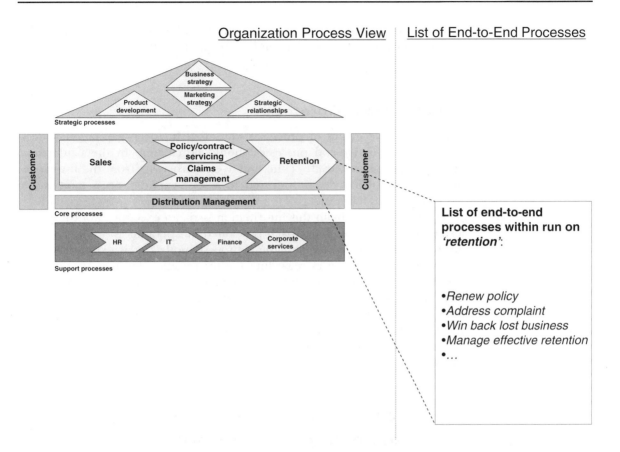

Figure 14.7
Organization process view and list of end-to-end processes. (Reproduced with the permission of MPM Group Pty Ltd, trading as TouchPoint Process Management Services.)

The organization process view diagram has several purposes:

- it should be used to describe the processes of the organization to all staff members and stakeholders
- it could be placed in a prominent position throughout the organization and perhaps on the organization's intranet site (some organizations have used it as their intranet home page)
- it will assist in getting the senior executives and all management and staff to understand the main activities and priorities for the organization from a process perspective, and provides focus for BPM within the organization.

However, this only works when the high-level view has relevant underlying information and is adopted *and* used throughout the organization.

The benefit of the development of an organization process view is that you not only have a high-level model of the organization that can be used to link the lower level processes, but also engage the management in the modeling process. This enables the organization's managers to define the critical process areas upon which they may wish to focus. It will also assist in ensuring that all key executives, stakeholders and participants in the BPM project have a common language and understanding.

List of end-to-end processes

For each of the group of processes identified in the organization process view, a list of end-to-end processes should be created. In the Understand and Innovate phases, each of the end-to-end processes from the list can be described in further detail (referred to as end-to-end process models and detailed process models).

The best way to obtain this information is via an executive workshop, and a suggested agenda and approach is detailed in Appendix E.

During the development of these process models, it is extremely useful to capture various metrics regarding the organization business unit and the processes – for example, capture the number of staff involved in each process or process group, the percentage of business effort involved on a process, the sales value and volume of transactions applicable. This will assist in directing the process team in selecting the processes or areas of the business to start subsequent phases of the framework – such as the Understand and Innovate phases.

Step 3: Obtain relevant information and technology principles and models

During this step, details must be obtained regarding the relevant 'information' aspects (which relate to data and applications) as well as the supporting 'technology' aspects (middleware, platforms and networks) – Figure 14.8. This will include such things as overviews of:

- data models and their underlying principles and logic
- main applications and related interfaces, and their underlying principles and logic
- main middleware and their underlying principles and logic
- main platforms and their underlying principles and logic
- main network(s) and their underlying principles and logic.

Our experience is that one of the main challenges in putting IT information into an enterprise architecture is that, in most organizations, the IT department has an enormous list of tools and applications; the challenge is to focus on the principles and the main choices.

Furthermore, it is important that IT supports the objectives, strategy and business, and this is why it is advisable to have the business and process architecture in place before creating the IT architecture. However, if the architecture development has started with the IT architecture, care has to be taken that IT remains supportive of the business requirements.

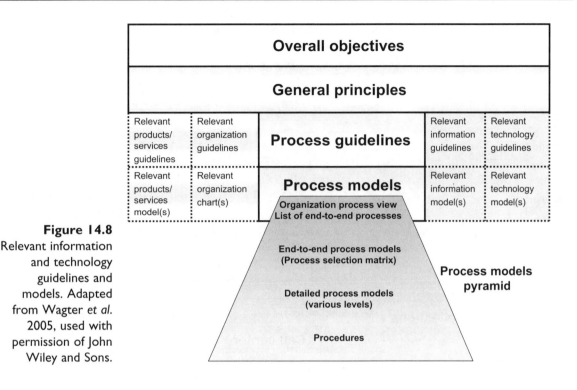

Figure 14.8
Relevant information
and technology
guidelines and
models. Adapted
from Wagter *et al.*
2005, used with
permission of John
Wiley and Sons.

Step 4: Consolidate and validate

In this step, all the information is consolidated and validated for consistency. This often proves to be the most challenging step, as it is where all the conflicting priorities and requirements come together and have to be sorted out. For example, the business may want to have flexibility, while the IT department wants to have standards and uniformity.

One way to consolidate the information collected so far is to relate the various architectural models with one another. For example, the combination of organization charts and processes result in the compilation of the organizational relationship map (Figure 14.9).

The organizational relationship map

The organizational relationship map, as shown in Figure 14.9, shows the high-level relationships and process flows between the various divisions or departments within the organization. It will enable the organization to gain a high-level view of any disconnections in the flow of processes. This provides an especially useful view of how customer end-to-end processes can be scattered throughout an organization structure, which can be a reason for delays and errors. In Figure 14.9, the light grey background box represents the organization, and anything that falls outside this grey box is considered outside the organization.

An example of a process disconnect is also shown in Figure 14.9. In this example, the call center implements and creates the credit guidelines for

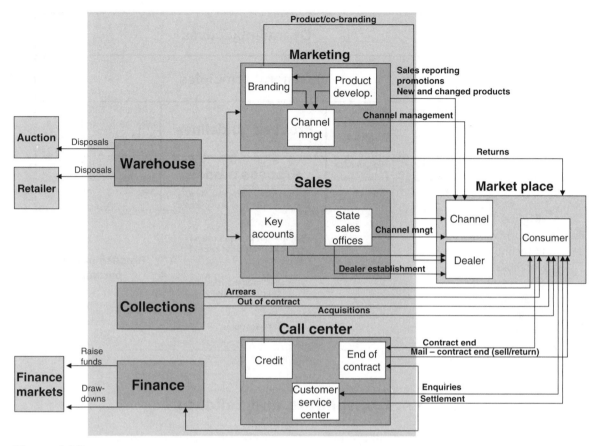

Figure 14.9
Organizational relationship map.

the organization, whereas the collections department collects accounts in arrears. There is no feedback in this figure from the collections department's experience of the effectiveness of the credit guidelines back to the call center, to amend the credit guidelines where necessary. If a bad credit guideline is created, the call center does not receive the feedback.

The best way to make the map is to organize a workshop with all relevant stakeholders, and:

- use the organization objectives and strategy as a starting point
- add all the various requirements and views of the stakeholders
- highlight the relationships and conflicts between these requirements
- discuss the conflicts, and find ways or alternatives of how to deal with these – the challenge here is to think 'outside the box', and dare to make decisions and think about the future instead of being stuck in the present
- prioritize the requirements
- discuss process gaps and remaining conflicts

- prepare action plans to deal with the disconnects and conflicts (including escalation paths)
- present final findings to relevant management, making clear the link to the organization strategy and objectives and specifying how the formulated architecture will help in this regard
- obtain sign-off.

Step 5: Communications

As stated previously, a good architecture is one that is understood, supported and is actually being used as a basis for activities and decision-making within the organization. A useful way to achieve this is by communicating the architecture and its benefits to as many relevant people within the organization as possible. Ways of achieving this include the following:

- displaying posters of the architecture models throughout the organization
- ensuring that all relevant organization charts use the architecture in their scoping and decision-making
- ensuring that projects use the architecture as a starting point.

Step 6: Apply architecture

Any organization wanting to use process architecture needs to develop the discipline required to do so. This means that all relevant projects need to take the architecture into account and specify where they are deviating from the agreed principles.

The ultimate test for any architecture is what the management decides to do in the case of a project wanting to deviate from the agreed process architectural principles. Most textbooks and theories tell us that the architecture must be enforced. In practice, this position cannot be upheld: in reality, in most cases, direct business benefits will prevail over longer-term architectural issues. However, it seems that once people have been granted exemption from the rules of the architecture, they are left completely free to deviate more and more from it. Furthermore, once a person or project has been able to 'break free' from the strict disciplines, others will also do so at an increasing rate. This eventually leads to a situation where it is difficult or impossible to maintain the architecture effectively and efficiently (Figure 14.10).

Figure 14.10
Suppressing exceptions leads inevitably to unmanaged exceptions.

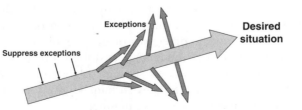

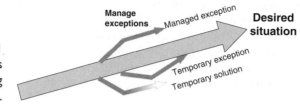

DYA® (DYnamic Architecture; Wagter *et al.*, 2002) has a very pragmatic approach to these situations: it recognizes the fact that there are situations where the immediate business needs should prevail over the architectural issues. However, rather than fighting this, management should focus their energy on containing the impact of this deviation. However, any deviation from the agreed architecture has to meet the following conditions:

- the short- and long-term consequences of the deviation must be specified (e.g. additional maintenance costs)
- the proposal has to contain how the solution will eventually fit back into the agreed architecture – either by phasing the solution out (this is normally done in the case of a one-off project or issue) or eventually moving towards the agreed architecture (as with a new release of the application addressing the required architectural issues)
- the business case to override the architecture has to be approved by the appropriate management level that originally approved the organization's architectural direction.

This approach can be compared with a pressure-cooker mechanism or a safety valve: when the pressure gets too much, it is better to control the lowering of the pressure (Figure 14.11) than to resist it and eventually have an explosion (see Figure 14.10).

Business process architecture committee

A useful way to embed process architecture in the organization is the establishment of a business process architecture committee.

This committee should have the responsibility for maintaining an overview of the entire organization's processes and the process architecture. It should establish and maintain the link between the organization's strategic objectives and the process goals. It should also know the extent to which each process supports a defined strategic goal. (An option is that the project works on the process architecture, and this is added to the process architecture repository.)

When the strategic objectives of the organization change, this committee analyzes the impact of the change and then directs and changes the business processes to fulfill these new strategic objectives. If this impacts the process architecture, then the changes should be given as feedback for its ongoing maintenance and relevance. Remember,

Alignment of organization strategic objectives and the supporting processes doesn't just happen, it must be planned.

The business process architecture committee is an ongoing committee, and is not formed just for a project.

Project start architecture

In order for a project to use the process architecture, the organization should develop a project start architecture (PSA) on the basis of DYA® (Wagter *et al.*, 2002). A PSA ensures that the project has a flying start, as it provides the project team with the relevant parts without overwhelming it with the entire process architecture when it is not necessary. That is, the PSA is a sub-set of the organization's process architecture. The PSA will include models such as an organization chart, product portfolio, process models and application models, as well as the relevant guidelines that relate to these. The advantage of the PSA is that it provides a mechanism of avoiding the weeks and weeks associated with gathering all the required information for a more detailed architecture for the project.

Step 7: Make it better

A process architecture is never finished, it only gets better.

The architecture must always be kept up to date, and a change management mechanism must be established to deal with changes. This is essential, as any change in the architecture may have an impact on the processes that have been designed using previous versions of the architecture. For change management to occur, the ownership of the architecture has to be clearly defined.

This step is where the architecture can be further refined and expanded. In many cases the full architecture for the organization is not defined at the first attempt, and it is often better this way: first, it is important to get people comfortable with the broad architectural issues and concepts and achieve some quick wins. After this, the architecture can be expanded in the following ways:

- in breadth – there may be more issues to include (e.g. IT issues)
- in depth – more details may be included (e.g. more detailed process models)
- in volume – more processes may be included (e.g. complete additional business unit process models).

Last but not least, it is important to ensure that more and more people are using the architecture – for example auditors, IT and business analysts.

The real benefit of process architecture becomes evident over time – when new developments and challenges arise, when the strategy changes, or when a new system is implemented and the process architecture provides guidance for the impact assessment.

Step 7 must ensure that the architecture is evaluated on a regular basis to ensure its usefulness and appropriateness to the organization.

Realize value

The benefits management framework must be defined as part of this phase. For details, refer to Step 1 of Chapter 21, where it is described in the context of realizing value within a project.

Process architecture outputs

The Process architecture phase provides valuable input into other phases of the framework (Figure 14.12), including the following few examples:

- the business process models to be created in the Understand and Innovate phases will utilize the process architecture created or amended here
- the process architecture will provide the guidelines as to how the project should be scoped and established during the Launch pad phase
- it will also provide feedback about the appropriateness to the Organization strategy phase, and the ability of the organization to implement the strategy via its current processes.

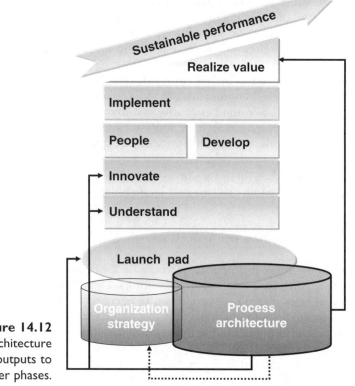

Figure 14.12
Process architecture
phase outputs to
other phases.

Process architecture phase risks

Table 14.1 highlights the commonest risks involved in developing process architecture.

A sample Process architecture phase is provided in Appendix B.

Table 14.1
Process architecture phase risks and mitigation strategies

Risk	Mitigation strategy
1 Architecture has too great an IT focus	Start with the organization objectives and strategy, and involve management and the business
2 Architecture is too detailed	Start with the objectives and strategy, and work down to the generic principles
3 Architecture is not being used	Ensure that the architecture meets the requirements of the management and other stakeholders, and 'sell' the benefits to them
4 Architecture is always too late	Emphasize the importance of a dynamic and compact architecture rather than a meticulous architecture that is difficult to adjust
5 Architecture efforts lead to lots of discussion, but no results	Approach architecture as a project, with a clear deliverable and deadline

Case study: Implement strategy all the way

We evaluated the processes of an organization that wanted to increase market share drastically by having a 'lean and mean' organization (equating to an operational excellence strategy). When reviewing the call center processes, we noticed that the processes were not consistent with this strategy. They were very elaborate and more in line for a customer intimacy strategy. The call center manager wanted to ensure that the customers had a good customer experience, and the 'lean and mean' aspects came secondary to this. Senior managers were surprised how this difference in interpretation could have existed for so many months without being noticed, and they not only changed the Call Centre processes to a more 'lean and mean' practice, but also started with the outline of a business architecture to ensure that the entire organization would take the strategic considerations into account while reviewing and redesigning processes.

Message: Ensure that your strategy is explicit and being used while designing, using and monitoring processes. Process architecture is a good way to achieve this.

Case study: 1+1+1=1

A large organization wanted to work on its processes. The IT department mapped the businesses processes that they needed to support, using process modeling tool 1 and with an IT approach. The business described its processes with process modeling tool 2 and a method related to this tool. The finance department wanted to map the business processes with financial impact for Sarbanes Oxley Compliance with yet another tool. It is obvious that this approach will not obtain any significant, and certainly not lasting, results such as:

- each organizational department will have only a partial view of the organization's processes
- there is no relationship between the various models
- it is questionable whether the process descriptions will be maintained over time
- the cost of maintenance will be high.

Message: A fragmented approach to process modeling and management leads to fragmented usage, resulting in high costs, high frustration and limited value.

Case study: An extreme 80/20 case

A software company producing software packages had difficulties in providing its customers with an overview of their customer service software. The business architect needed more than fifty pages to describe the main processes of its solution, which resulted in nobody having a clear understanding. We were able to provide an overview of 95 percent of the main processes within three simple diagrams and four pages of text (i.e. less than 10 percent of the initial pages). When we spoke to the business architect, he pointed out that some exceptions were not included. However, the business team was delighted that members could easily explain the structure of their product. The exceptions were handled in a different forum.

Message: Whether a process architecture is good or not depends mainly on whether it is actually being used. A short and simple process architecture can thus be much better than a complex, state-of-the-art architecture.

Case study: eTOM

A telecom organization wanted to work closely with another telecom company from a different country. They spent many, many months in talks about how to integrate their respective processes, but all the meetings and efforts were in vain. There seemed to be no progress in coming to a solution; whenever a problem was solved, one or even two additional problems appeared. When we came in, we realized that both organizations had different systems, processes, business and customers, and even a different definition for activities. We used the eTOM model to come to a common understanding and agreement on the processes and related definitions, which clearly allowed the specification of where the interfaces between both organizations should be. This allowed us to complete the work within weeks, providing a robust and acceptable solution.

Message: A common understanding is the basis for results and progress. Reference models and process architecture are vital in this regard.

Case study: Architecture the wrong way around

The IT department of an organization wanted to introduce an enterprise architecture. They started with their own domain: the IT aspects. They produced an 'architecture' with more than seventy pages of technical details. When asked about the next steps, they informed us that they wanted the executive managers to sign-off on this 'architecture' and enforce it. However, they had to acknowledge that the management wouldn't understand the document, let alone be able to enforce it. They realized they needed to develop the architecture the other way around: more pull-based (from the business) than push-based. They went back to the business and started a more demand pull-based oriented architecture, resulting in a comprehensive and generally accepted architecture.

Message: The challenge of process architecture is not in formulating it, but in gaining commitment and having people use it.

Chapter 15

Launch pad phase

It is often very difficult for organizations to determine where to start a BPM project. The organization may know it has operational inefficiencies and issues within a particular business unit; however, how and where to start can be a very difficult decision.

The Launch pad phase (Figure 15.1) is the platform from which BPM projects are scoped, established and launched (Figure 15.2).

In the case of an operational initiative method, sufficient high-level business and process analysis is completed during this phase to enable the organization to determine a logical place to start the initial review of the effort involved in the BPM project along with the possible benefits to be gained. The process architecture can also help for this purpose. In the case of the strategy-driven method, the starting point will predominantly be known (although it may require some refining).

This phase will not only provide a way of starting; it will also complete the steps necessary to establish the project for success. These include the following: project scope; project team selection and structure; stakeholder expectations, establishment and engagement; the establishment of the initial process goals; and the use of the process start architecture to provide a fast start for the project from an architectural perspective. Each subsequent project launched from this launch pad will be able to benefit from synergies and lessons learned from previous BPM projects, rather than starting from scratch and/or reinventing the wheel every time. For an organization to progress, it is crucial that lessons learned are systematically and structurally embedded within the approach.

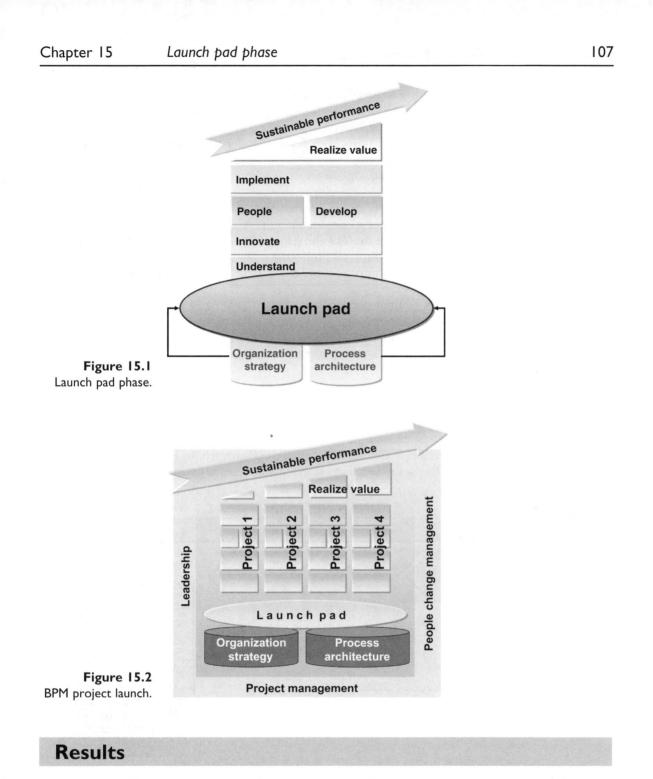

Figure 15.1
Launch pad phase.

Figure 15.2
BPM project launch.

Results

The results that should be expected from the Launch pad phase will include the following:

1   Definition of stakeholders involved or associated with the project
2   Stakeholder engagement and commitment, and documented and agreed expectations

3 Process selection matrix
4 A list of identified business processes and initial metrics
5 A list of agreed process goals
6 Prioritized processes for the Understand phase
7 An initial implementation strategy
8 Project management:

- project charter document
- project scope document
- initial draft of the project plan (the Understand phase plan will be completed in detail)
- determination and documentation of the initial communications strategy
- initial risk analysis

9 Development of the initial business case.

How?

To have a successful outcome from the Launch pad phase, there are several high-level steps that must be followed (Figure 15.3). How the project and the project scenario have been selected will determine the approach.

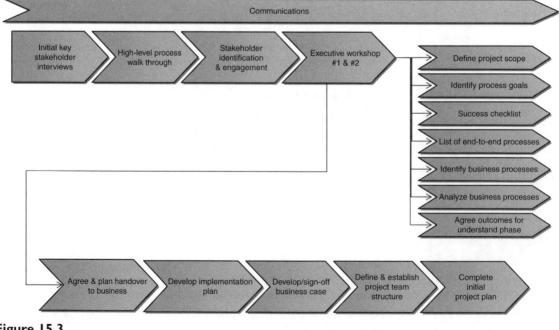

Figure 15.3
Launch pad phase steps.

All steps will still need to be covered; however, the project selection method and scenario will determine the depth of some of the steps. This will be mentioned as each step is described.

Step 1: Communications

Prior to the phase commencing, people within the organization should be informed of the project, its goals, its initial or likely scope, and indicative timeframes. Within some organizations, BPM projects still have a stigma attached to them from the BPR days – the view is that BPR equals down-sizing, and people will be retrenched. This issue needs to be handled at the start with appropriate communication, telling personnel why BPM is different.

Communication must then continue throughout the phase, and the entire project, as the project scope and plans are refined. This communication must include continual updates on:

- how the project will impact on personnel
- how personnel can expect management to conduct themselves
- how people will be treated as a result of the change, how information will be shared and how often, and details of opportunities for people to participate (always be open and honest).

Always anticipate questions and objections and handle them in a proactive way. Perform analysis of the targeted groups and tailor the communications to them, ensuring consistency.

Identify a person to be responsible for communications and human change management, and make that person accountable for this task. The individual should be engaged at this early stage of the project, a communications plan should be drafted and it should start to be executed. (Refer to Chapter 25 for suggestions regarding the contents of the communications plan and how to address change management issues.)

Step 2: Initial key stakeholder interviews

After discussion with the project or business sponsor, a series of interviews with a small number of key internal business stakeholders should be conducted. The purpose of these interviews is to gain an overview of the current business and process environment, and to gather these stakeholders' views of the key areas of process and operational issues. This is not a long drawn-out process, but short and to the point. In the strategy-driven method, the interviews will also cover the communication of how this particular BPM project will contribute towards the successful implementation of the organization strategy.

The outcome of the interviews will be the following:

- building rapport with the stakeholders (part of stakeholder management)
- obtaining a high-level understanding of the issues from a stakeholder perspective
- identification of quick wins, which the stakeholders are passionate about.

This step should not be confused with Step 4, where all project stakeholders are identified for input into the stakeholder management strategies as outlined in Chapter 24.

Step 3: High-level process walkthrough

If the initial members of the project team are not familiar with the processes within the business unit, it can be extremely useful to spend a couple of days speaking to the people who execute the processes *in situ*, and following the processes within the business unit on an end-to-end basis. This provides an excellent overview of how the business is conducted, and provides an opportunity to identify process similarities and differences.

Similarly, a discussion with the IT department is useful to provide a high-level overview of how the business applications and infrastructure (IT architecture) interact with and support the business processes.

These walkthroughs must not replace the activities in the Understand phase, as these provide a more in-depth analysis and understanding.

Step 4: Stakeholder identification and engagement

This is a simple step of brainstorming to discover who the project stake holders are (both from internal and external perspectives). External, in this instance, will include stakeholders outside the business unit and still within the organization who will be impacted by the project, as well as stakeholders external to the organization – such as customers, partners and suppliers.

Once this has been completed, the stakeholders who must contribute to the project are identified and must be kept informed. Important stakeholders (such as customers or suppliers) may need to be not only informed but also involved in and committed to the project. Effort invested in redesigning, developing and implementing new process(es) would be wasted if customers or suppliers refused to use them.

Stakeholder engagement is covered in detail in Chapter 24.

Step 5: Executive workshops

The agenda for these workshops usually comprises two three-hour sessions, and covers the following:

- definition and agreement of the project scope
- identification of the initial process goals
- agreement of the success checklist for the project
- stakeholder identification and categorization
- creation of the initial list of end-to-end process model(s)
- identification of the individual business processes
- an initial analysis of the processes, including high-level metrics
- agreement of the outcomes for the Understand phase.

Each of these is examined in further detail below.

Step 5.1: Define project scope

This is the normal project management scope definition. As described previously, we do not propose to outline a project management methodology within this document. There is, however, one overriding question that needs to be answered: Do we feel confident that, with the initially planned scope, we can deliver the expected results for the stakeholders?

In many situations, the business will already have determined the scope of the project – for example, in the strategy-driven project selection method. At the very least, this 'initial' scope should be revisited within the executive workshop and confirmed as still being appropriate to the business and other stakeholders. If the operational business wishes to change the scope of a strategy-driven method project, it will be necessary to take this back to the project sponsor and executive leadership, as it may have an impact upon the organization strategy. It is important also to make it clear what is *not* included in the project scope.

It is essential that the process(es) within the scope and being 'workshopped' (understood) are completed on a true end-to-end basis. If this means crossing departmental, business unit or even stakeholder boundaries, then this should be done. The Understand workshops must be conducted for the 'process', and not be concerned about organizational boundaries or structure. For example, if a particular department is being examined (represented by the oval in Figure 15.4) and the process proceeds outside this department, it should be

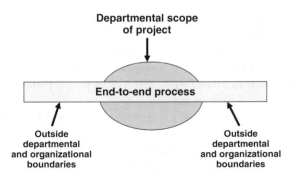

Figure 15.4
End-to-end process.

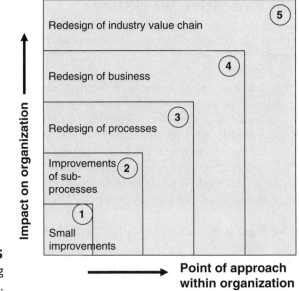

Point of approach
within organization

Figure 15.5
Determining
redesign width.

examined in the other 'adjacent' departments – thus covering the 'upstream' and 'downstream' aspects of the process.

It is, however, necessary to have a common understanding of the 'project width', which will have a significant impact on the project scope.

Project width

This step should also determine the 'width' of the effort in the Innovate phase – that is, agree and document the target, scope and approach of the Innovate phase. Figure 15.5 provides an indication of several possible approaches.

The organization needs to review the purpose of the BPM project. Does the business:

- simply want incremental or small improvements in its business processes?
- wish to redesign the existing processes to make them better (more efficient, effective, improved quality, reduced costs)?
- want to take the opportunity of totally redesigning its business by the use of process innovation?
- wish to evaluate the industry value chain and redesign it?

The impact upon the organization escalates with the 'width' of the option selected, see BPM scenarios in Chapter 12.

Once the 'width' of the project has been determined, the organization will need to look at (if this has not been done already) the driving forces behind the need for process innovation. Is it because the organization:

- *must* change – external or internal forces are demanding process change?
- *wants* to change – there is a realization that unless the processes change, the organization may not survive in its current form; or, there needs to be a substantial increase in the level of customer service; or, there needs to be a significant reduction in the cost model or increase in quality?
- *can* change – the maturity of the organization is such that managers now understand that it can change and, perhaps, for the first time, know how to achieve change successfully on a repeatable scale.

Step 5.2: Identify process goals

It is necessary to develop the process goals at this point so that the project can be planned appropriately. Unless you know the process goals, the organization does not have sufficient information to define and establish the project adequately. In a strategy-driven method project, it would be expected that the high-level goals may already be known and dictated by executive management. In an operational initiative method, the goals will be determined during this workshop.

The process goals will need to be linked to the organization strategy and objectives (as identified in the Organization strategy phase). They must take into account:

- stakeholder needs
- benchmarking against competitors.

There are several inputs in the determination of the process goals, including the following:

- defining the measurement indicators used to evaluate the process performance today and planned to be used in the future
- targeting the degree of performance improvement needed based on potential and risk
- determining the level of improvement expected – targeting an 80 percent improvement is *totally* different to targeting a 10 percent improvement, and the approach will be substantially different. Perhaps the time taken for the process needs to be longer, in order to increase the quality? This needs to be very clearly documented, understood and agreed by all project stakeholders
- identifying process performance measures start with the expected performance measures of the stakeholders and then work backwards to derive the process performance measures
- assessing the performance management and measures – for the individuals executing them (refer to Chapter 18 for more details)

- assessing for measures of: effectiveness, efficiency and adaptability
- keeping the number of performance measures low – certainly no more than five
- looking for an opportunity to establish 'stretch goals'.

Also, look at the change you would like to take place in the behavior of the personnel involved in the process(es) – in managers, team leaders and staff.

All project goals should be made SMART (Specific, Measurable, Achievable, Realistic and Time-related).

Step 5.3: Success checklist

This is an important step in the management of stakeholder expectations and validation of the project scope. From a project and business perspective, it is important to understand what must be achieved for this project to be successful. While the high-level success checklist, for a strategy-driven method, will have been set by the executive, the details will be determined during this step. For an operational initiative method, all the success checklist criteria will be determined here. We apply the 'red wine test' and ask this question:

> It is six weeks after the completion of the project and you are sitting back at home in front of the fireplace having a red wine and reflecting on the project. You decide that it has been outstandingly successful. Why?

The answer to this question will provide the success checklist.

The reasons given during the workshop must cover both project and business deliverables. Projects are not solely delivered by project teams; businesses must be intimately involved and committed. The facilitator of this executive workshop must ensure that the reasons for success are also in alignment with the Organization strategy phase. In Table 15.1, we have provided an example of a few of the likely critical success factors within a BPM project and who is responsible.

Step 5.4: List of end-to-end processes

The end-to-end process model provides an overview of the main processes for the organization. If it has already been created, then review it to confirm its relevance for this business unit. If it does not exist, then create one as per the suggestions in Step 2, Chapter 14.

For an individual project, the completion of an end-to-end process model will provide assistance with the completion of the next step – 'identify individual business processes', which are sub-processes of the end-to-end process model. The best way to obtain this information is via the executive workshop. A suggested agenda and approach is detailed in Appendix D.

Step 5.5: Identify business processes

Prior to commencing a BPM project, there is a need to identify all the relevant individual business processes within the business unit being examined. *It is*

Table 15.1
Critical success factors

Responsibility	Project	Business
1 Deliver the project on time and on budget	✓	✓
2 At the end of the Understand phase, there is a general understanding of the current end-to-end processes by the business and agreed metrics	✓	
3 Key internal and external stakeholders and management understand the root cause of process issues	✓	✓
4 Staff are excited and understand the way forward	✓	
5 Quick wins in the processes are identified and implemented along the way	✓	

important to ensure that the processes identified cover the end-to-end business process.
While there are many methods to achieve this, we have outlined only one
here, the process selection matrix, as it is the one we use on a regular basis
with great success.

The Process Selection Matrix (PSM) is a way of showing, usually on one
page, all the business processes within the business unit. Figure 15.6 provides
an example. Furthermore, the PSM is an ideal way of understanding and
showing the level of process complexity, the number of processes, and the
high-level process metrics within the business.

The vertical axis (main processes) comes from the end-to-end processes
developed as part of Step 5.4. The horizontal axis (scenarios) represents the
dimension that provides more detailed analysis of the processes listed on the
vertical axis. This will vary from situation to situation, it might be represented
by the products of the organization, payment methods, distribution methods,
geographical spread, business units and so forth. The important consideration
is to ensure that the cell at the intersection of the horizontal and the vertical
axes represents an individual business process.

If a process step is unique, the process object should be specified under
that scenario (as in Process 1, Product 1 and Main process A in Figure 15.6).
If there is no process step under a scenario, then no process object should be
specified (for example, Product 1 does not have a process associated with Main
process C). In the case where the process step is the same for several scenarios,
the process object should spread across these scenarios (as in Process 5, where

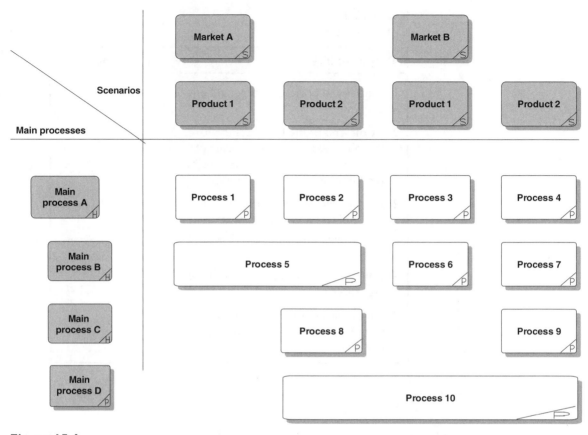

Figure 15.6
Process selection matrix.

Product 1 and Product 2 share the same process related to Main process B). This is normally the case when:

- the scenarios has no impact on the uniqueness of the process step
- processes are carried out by the same business units/roles
- processes are supported by the same IT applications.

Again, the best way to obtain this information is via an executive workshop with appropriate process managers and team leaders in attendance.

The PSM provides an excellent starting point for the project. It can and will be modified during the project, owing to increased insight or changed circumstances.

Step 5.6: Analyze business processes

The selection of which processes to include in the scope of a project sounds easy, and yet it is critical and sometimes difficult to get correct the first time. Most organizations select processes intuitively, based on the problems a process appears to cause the organization or the guesstimated benefits to be derived from the redesign. While this is often a sensible starting point, adding some objective analysis to the selection process is important, if for no other reason than validating the 'gut feelings'of staff and management.

During the completion of the process selection matrix, it is important to gather metrics of appropriate parts of the value chain and processes. Metrics useful for each process/market/product include the following:

- the number of people involved in executing a process
- the number and value of transactions
- the figures on quality (e.g. customer satisfaction, rework, complaints and so forth) which equates to process problem areas
- the metrics on processing time, throughput time and waiting time, which can equate to process bottlenecks.

These will provide guidance for where to commence the more detailed analysis. For example, if Processes 3 and 5 in Figure 15.6 take 70 percent of the process resources, then any improvement in these processes can make a substantial difference to the costs of the business unit. On the other hand, if Process 2 only occupies 4 percent of the resources, then process improvements here might not make a contribution to the cost benefits of the business unit. The metrics collected should be recorded on the PSM, which becomes a powerful 'picture' for management and the project.

If the project has been initiated as a strategy-driven method, while all this information will be useful, the processes to be included in the project scope may already have been determined.

The PSM, however, is not the only procedure involved in process prioritization, especially in an operational initiative method project, as quality and rework are also key inputs.

Another matrix that will add an interesting dimension to the analysis of the business processes is the Keen Process Worth Matrix (Keen, 1997: 26), shown in Table 15.2.

Table 15.2
Process Worth Matrix

	Worth	
	Asset	Liability
Identity Priority Background		
Mandated		

This is a useful way of determining what business processes to invest in; however, it is not always an easy matrix to complete – processes can be difficult to categorize. The definitions Keen uses are the following:

- *Assets* – 'any process that returns more money to the firm than it costs is an asset' (Keen, 1997: 25). However, you must ensure that the determination of cost is correctly calculated – certainly do not use the traditional accounting definition.
- *Liability* – the opposite of an asset.
- *Identity* – defines the organization for itself, its customers and stakeholders. It differentiates the organization from its competitors. For example, McDonald's has a reputation based on fast, consistent service; similarly, AAMI Insurance's reputation is for friendly personalized service. These are the marketing perceptions that these processes *must* deliver. They are processes that define the two organizations' identities. These identity processes are a sub-set of the 'core' processes referred previously to in Figure 14.7.
- *Priority* – these processes strongly support the effectiveness of the identity processes. Customers don't usually see them, but if they fail then the impact is immediate and visible to the stakeholders. In the example of McDonald's above, these processes would include those that are part of the supply chain to deliver the raw materials for the products sold.
- *Background* – these processes support the daily activities of operations within the organization, and include those such as administration, HR and document management. Sometimes they are highly visible and therefore have the attention of management. It is a mistake to invest in these processes ahead of identity and priority processes. Most organizations target these processes for BPM projects, because they can be easy wins. This can be a mistake unless the economic cost/benefit stacks up and even when it does, there should be greater value to the organization by first working on the asset processes.
- *Mandated* – these are processes imposed on the organization by external factors, such as legislation and compliance. The organization does not have any choice but to perform them. Usually these are liability processes, and rarely add direct value to the organization.

Other processes that can exist but don't appear in the matrix are 'folklore' processes. Staff usually describe them as, 'we have always done this'. If you find any, challenge staff to assess their value and necessity, and then either add them to the list of processes or eliminate them.

While the initial process worth matrix may be created during a BPM project, it should not be a one-time exercise. The matrix should be added to the process architecture and refined during future projects and business-as-usual activities. Processes may move from one category to another over time. This is usually caused by the business environment, management decisions, behavior of staff and the organization, and could also be caused by unintentional neglect of a process.

Having gathered the information in the PSM, the process worth matrix, the associated metrics and the process goals, it is all brought together in order to eliminate, select and prioritize the order in which the processes will be addressed within the Understand phase.

When completing this analysis the organization must focus on the creation of *value* – creating benefits from the redesign of a process does not necessarily create value: '*Benefit* is a managerial concept; *Value* is an economic concept' (Keen, 1997: 75).

There are examples of organizations that gained substantial benefits from the redesign of their processes and yet their profit declined. Improvements in processes do not necessarily translate into business benefit. For example, a process may be redesigned to be more efficient, and yet it is of little benefit to the customer or adds no value/profit to the business.

The processes that should be selected for a BPM redesign project are those that will add value to the organization.

Step 5.7: Agree outcomes for Understand phase

Again, this is about stakeholder expectation management. It is much better to inform (and thus set expectations for) the appropriate stakeholders of the deliverables before the phase commences, rather than complete the phase and not deliver to their expectations. If the project team does not set the expectations, the stakeholders will make up their own – and the two rarely coincide.

The deliverables for the Understand phase will include the following:

1   A list of end-to-end process model(s)
2   A list of end-to-end sub-processes
3   Models of the current processes to a level of detail sufficient to enable the Innovate phase to be completed
4   Appropriate metrics, sufficient to establish a baseline for future process comparative measurements
5   A list of major process issues, as determined by the business
6   Identification of innovate priorities
7   Identification of opportunities for quick wins
8   Validation and handover of quick wins for implementation, if appropriate at this stage
9   A report on the phase.

Step 6 Agree and plan the handover to the business

Before doing any further steps it is important to agree and plan the handover to the business. Most projects fail the ultimate test: that the business is able and willing to take over the project as part of business as usual.

This step also serves as a good testing ground to see how the stakeholder management should be completed during this phase. Stakeholder management is always a tough issue, but it is always better to receive feedback early in the project rather than later. This feedback will enable adjustments to be made to the approach.

When creating and agreeing a business handover plan the following issues need to be addressed:

- Project costs
- Required support from subject matter experts during the project, the hand-over and the operational costs
- Risks and issues
- On-going costs and benefits
- Time of handovers
- Implementation fall-back scenarios or contingency plans
- Communication and implementation plan
- Governance and escalation.

We have often seen the following situations:

- **Business does not see the handover as important nor something that needs to be addressed at this stage of the project**. Many business managers are still focused on the short term and want to address today's issues and worry about other issues in the future. However, addressing the business handover plan is necessary at this stage. It would be easy for the project team to give in and delay it to a later stage, but this will only aggravate the situation. Unless the business is fully involved and committed, and understands how it will be handling the project outcomes once the project is completed, then it is a reason to put the project on hold until this can be resolved.
- **Initial hand-over arrangements are modified without adequate change control**. If an initial hand-over plan has been completed and agreed, chances are that these arrangements will be changed in the future, either due to changes in the organization or due to changes in the project or the perception of the project (as the business gains a better understanding of the project and its outcomes). Apply standard project management change control to any changes in the hand-over plans as this may impact the overall success of the project.

Step 7: Develop implementation plan

The importance of implementation cannot be over-emphasized. A common question is, 'what benefit does the project get by spending more time and money on implementation?' The answer is simple, and sometimes the upfront proof is difficult to calculate. A good implementation will ensure that the proposed solution is optimal for the organization and that the organization uses this solution in the best manner and does so in the shortest possible time. If implementation is not completed smoothly, then one or more of the following situations may arise.

- the chosen solution is not optimal for the organization – this can be due to incorrect, incomplete or inconsistent gathering of the requirements; however, it is mostly caused by insufficient participation of the stakeholders and users of the process
- the organization does not use the solution in the best manner because the users are not properly informed, trained and motivated
- the solution cannot be implemented immediately because it needs some modifications, resulting in a longer timeframe for the realization of the benefits – which will not be as great as they should have been.

A traditional implementation is characterized by little upfront effort and investment. By the time the solution is implemented, last minute changes have to be made, resulting in a significant, unforeseen, additional investment and lower sustainable results (Figure 15.7).

If implementation preparation is started during the Launch pad phase of the project, it will initially result in a higher investment; however, once implemented, the solution will be off to a flying start, resulting in quicker and better sustainable results (Figure 15.8) (Regatta® from Sogeti Nederland).

If we compare the two approaches, we can clearly see that despite the early additional investment in implementation thinking, the benefits of this approach are substantial higher than the tradition approach (Figure 15.9) (Regatta® from Sogeti Nederland).

Forrester Research, in the presentation 'Linking IT To Business Performance: It is Implementation that Matters' by George Lawrie, at Amstelveen, The Netherlands, on 21 May 2003 at the launch of the Regatta® book on implementation by Sogeti Nederland, stated that: 'How much you spend on IT

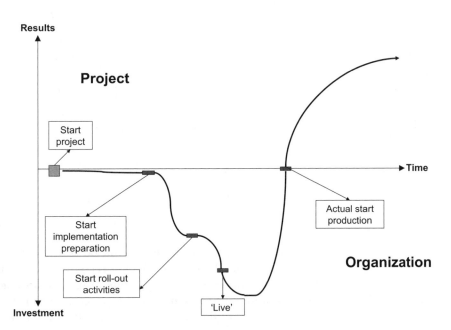

Figure 15.7
Traditional
implementation.
(Regatta® from
Sogeti Nederland,
reproduced with
permission.)

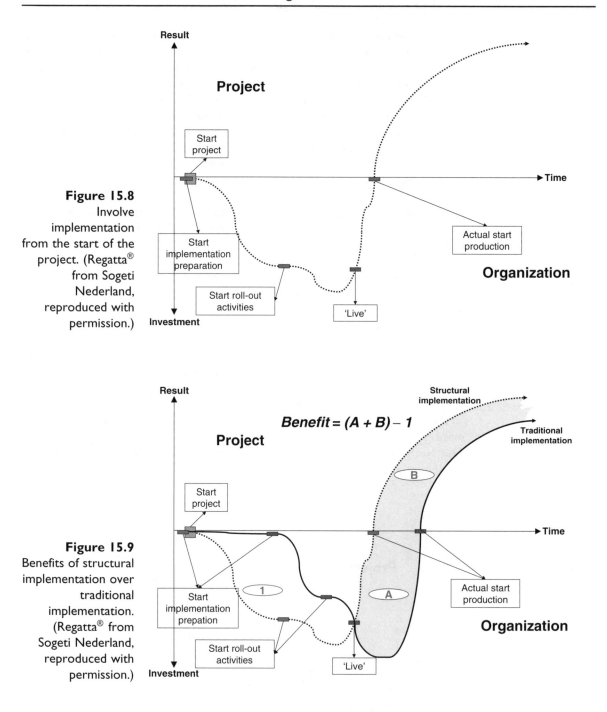

Figure 15.8
Involve implementation from the start of the project. (Regatta® from Sogeti Nederland, reproduced with permission.)

Figure 15.9
Benefits of structural implementation over traditional implementation. (Regatta® from Sogeti Nederland, reproduced with permission.)

$$Benefit = (A + B) - 1$$

doesn't matter, which technologies you buy does matter, how you implement matters the most'. This comes from a recognition that more and more organizations are purchasing and implementing standard packages, which means that the competitive advantage does not come from the tool but more from how this tool is configured and implemented within the organization.

The Implement phase discusses the various options that should be considered during this step. The purpose of this step is to think through the implementation options and select the one appropriate for the project, which will provide guidance for the other phases and steps in the framework as the project progresses.

Step 8: Develop/sign-off business case

The standard organization business case template should be used. Apart from the normal BPM business case content (which is described in detail in Appendix C), the business case should also include the following:

- an Economic Value Add (EVA) analysis
- internal proposal preparation
- documentation of any non-quantifiable operational costs, benefits and EVAs, and examination of the risks of each
- present pros and cons of the various options
- use scenarios and performance evaluation criteria.

The team should *never* defend recommendations; only make them and explain the options in a neutral and objective manner (Burlton, 2001).

Part of the business case development will include the identification of the business person(s) who will be responsible for the process(es) once the project has transitioned from an 'project' to an 'operational' situation. This is to ensure their engagement in the project and project decision-making activities so that they have a level of ownership and responsibility for the project outcomes.

Remember that this is only an initial business case, which may either justify the entire BPM project or provide funding for further investigation to enable the development of a detailed business case for the full project. The business case will need to be updated or completed in the Innovate phase to justify the continuation of the BPM project (refer to Step 14: Identify benefits and update business case, in Chapter 17).

Step 9: Define and establish project team structure

Having decided upon the sequence in which processes will be examined during the Understand phase, the initial project team and business will be in a position to create the BPM project structure and assemble the project team. The structure of a BPM project can be somewhat different to a 'normal' IT or business project. The sample structure shown in Figure 15.10 assumes that an integrated document management system is being implemented simultaneously with the BPM implementation. Roles are discussed in more detail in Appendix C.

This sample project structure is designed for a large-scale BPM implementation program or project, and will need to be modified to suit the particular

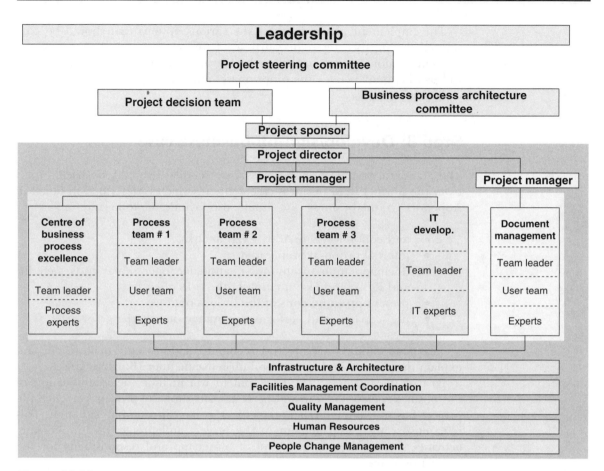

Figure 15.10
Sample project team structure for a large-scale BPM project. (Reproduced with the permission of MPM Group Pty Ltd, trading as TouchPoint Process Management Services.)

organizational and project requirements. Rarely does the team start off this size in the Launch pad phase. However, the future project team structure needs to be determined and planned. The number and make-up of the work-streams shown in Figure 15.10 will depend upon the project and the automa-tion components involved. We have shown one workstream for a document management component; clearly, there could be others for a process engine (workflow) and business rules implementations. This is, however, a structure that has been particularly effective, so modifying it too much may lead to compromising the effectiveness of the project.

Project Steering Committee, project director and project manager

The roles and responsibilities of the Project Steering Committee, project director, project manager and team leaders are close to the normal functions these roles would have in any project. For a detailed list of their roles and responsibilities, refer to Appendix C. We will, however, comment here upon the project manager's role and then the remaining roles.

We highly recommend two key leadership positions within the project structure:

1 The business unit should have its own project manager with overall responsibility for the entire project. This is, after all, a business project, not an IT project. This position is crucial to ensure that the *business* requirements are met and are of primary importance. IT, vendor and all other project components should report to this business project manager. Ideally, this business project manager will be an experienced project manager with BPM expertise. If the project manager does not have BPM expertise (and this means having implemented several BPM projects), then a senior and experienced BPM consultant is required.

2 A senior and experienced BPM consultant is highly recommended, not only to coach the business project manager if BPM expertise is lacking, but also to assist with:

   • objectively managing situations when process or project compromises need to be made during the course of the project as they inevitably will be. Such decisions can have very serious repercussions, and an expert BPM specialist can manage this risk to prevent the BPM project turning into an expensive business process improvement project that yields limited benefits.
   • ensuring that the BPM project remains focused and self-funding, and continues to deliver real business value.
   • identifying additional business opportunities that could be enabled through BPM.
   • ensuring that the required people change management elements are correctly built into the project plan and thereby managed as an essential part of the project.
   • adding value to the stakeholder management and providing the expertise necessary to ensure that stakeholders remain continually engaged and focused towards a successful BPM delivery.

While some of these may sound like the responsibilities of the project director or project manager, we have found that an independent consultant is often able to make judgment calls and express opinions that are politically difficult for an internal person to make.

Project decision team

The project decision team should resolve as many questions as possible to avoid the necessity for them to be referred to the Project Steering Committee.

It should comprise the user leaders of each of the user teams, and be chaired by the chief process officer or the designated process sponsor. The responsibilities for each of these roles are outlined in Appendix C.

The project structure for smaller BPM projects may require some of the roles to be amalgamated; however, leadership is extremely important in any project and particularly important in a BPM project, so never compromise in this area of the project. We will cover leadership in more detail in Chapter 26.

The Steering Committee fulfils the normal role expected from this committee within a project. It usually comprises the project sponsor, project manager, business owner, CIO or senior IT person (where there is a large component of IT within the project), and one or two people who represent the organizational aspects to ensure synergy can be gained across the organization.

Business process architecture committee

This has been discussed in the Process architecture phase.

Process teams

The project team will be broken up into various teams (often referred to as workstreams). Whether the project has one or multiple teams will obviously depend upon its size and complexity. In a large project involving automation, there would be an expectation that the teams would comprise a small team of process experts (probably from the Center of Business Process Excellence), an IT team handling interfacing and other development activities, and a team with document management expertise that will consult to all the team(s) and especially those completing the process analysis and innovation activities. Depending upon the size of the project, each team could comprise the following:

- team leader
- user leader
- user team representatives
- process experts.

Each of these roles is briefly described here, and Appendix C describes them in more detail.

1   *Team leader.* This is the normal project team leader role. The leader will lead the team (workstream) and ensure that appropriate workshops are organized, the project plan is developed (in conjunction with the project manager), the timetable adhered to, budgets met and so on.
2   *User leader.* This individual is a business resource appointed by the business management, and has the authority to make decisions on behalf of the business.
3   *User team representatives.* These are the technical or subject matter experts from the business, and are selected by the user leader.

4   *Process experts.* This group will come from the organization's Center of Business Process Excellence, and will provide the expertise for:

- process design and redesign
- process design tool(s) used in the project
- activity-based costing
- process simulation
- capacity planning
- process interfacing.

If the organization does not have a Center of Business Process Excellence or internal expertise, then these resources may come from an external specialist BPM consultancy.

IT development team

This group predominantly comprise IT experts in systems interfacing. They will provide the expertise and work with each of the other teams to ensure that process interfaces to the various host systems are executed successfully.

Document management team

This group will comprise experts in document management, and business staff who understand how documents flow and are used with the processes in their area of business. This team will work with and provide expertise to all the other process teams in the project, to ensure that documents and images are successfully integrated with each process.

Step 10: Complete initial project plan

The initial project plan must cover the Understand phase in detail, with the Innovate phase steps included but with no timeframes against it at this stage.

In our experience, 'understand' workshops should comprise no more than four three-hour workshops per week, with the time in between scheduled to tidy up the models, review and analyze the findings within the business (including root-cause analysis) and gather and complete metrics analysis. This will be discussed in more detail in Chapter 16.

The number of processes modeled per workshop will depend upon their complexity and size.

Always remember to build contingency into your plan, and remember that the writing of the report at the end of this phase will always take longer than you think, so allow an appropriate amount of time as this should not be rushed. In fact, we always start populating the report as the project progresses. A sample report structure and project plan are provided in Appendix C.

Realize value

Potential benefits must be identified and planned as part of this phase. For details refer to Step 2 of Chapter 21, where it is described in the context of realizing value within a project.

Launch pad phase outputs

The information being developed during the Launch pad phase will have inputs into the various phases shown in Figure 15.11.

The obvious input is into the Understand phase, where the project plan is developed, processes prioritized via the process selection matrix, initial metrics and business case decided, and the project documentation established. Much of this information will also flow over into the Innovate phase, for example process goals.

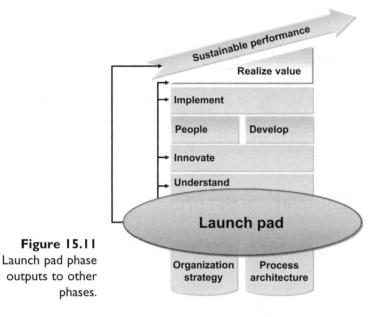

Figure 15.11
Launch pad phase outputs to other phases.

Launch pad phase risks

This phase provides the platform from which projects are launched. Like any project, unless it is established correctly in the first place, it will be difficult to get 'back on track'. There are several risks that must be considered, and mitigation strategies should be implemented to eliminate (or at least reduce) them. These risks include those listed in Table 15.3.

Table 15.3
Launch pad phase risks and mitigation strategies

Risk	Mitigation strategy
1 Project stakeholders are not all identified and/or engaged in the project	This is a critical function for the project manager and the project sponsor, and every attempt must be made to identify all the stakeholders and engage them. Stakeholders will be identified during the project, and Chapter 24 explains how to deal with this situation. Engagement is essential, and unless critical stakeholders are fully engaged, then the project risk is increased and consideration should be given to the continuation of the project
2 The project manager is not experienced in BPM implementations and projects Salience	There are three options available here: (1) replace the project manager with an experienced BPM person; (2) provide coaching and mentoring for the project manager from an experienced BPM project manager; and (3) continue with the inexperienced project manager, recognizing the increased risk to the project
3 The project scope is ill-defined and/or not clear and agreed	The project manager must clarify the scope with the project sponsor, and the project should not proceed until the scope is well defined, agreed and signed off
4 The project is not funded sufficiently or stopping of the project until funding is available	Refer to the Project Sponsor for further funding
5 Handover to the business is not sufficiently planned	Ensure that basic arrangements are made in order to proceed

Case study: Where to start?

A managing director gave directions to the process manager: 'Go and find significant process improvements and identify where I can make large savings within the organization'. The process manager was newly appointed to the task, and did not know where to start. He established several process project teams to process-model various parts of the business in their current state. There was no high-level analysis

(Continued)

Case study: **Where to start?** (*Continued*)

completed to determine the likely areas of savings and focused activity, little or no executive support for the project(s), and no BPM coaching provided to the process manager. The project largely failed to deliver to stakeholders' expectations, and was substantially dismantled a year later.

Message: Without an experienced person leading the project team and a structured approach, the team will find it difficult to know where to start in a disciplined way that will maximize potential effort.

Case study: **The need to follow the framework steps**

An executive workshop of the project steering committee members was conducted and the project scope (as agreed with the project sponsor) was presented. All steering committee members agreed with the scope. Later in the workshop, we asked the 'red wine test' question to elicit the success checklist. During this it became obvious that the steering committee members did not agree with the project scope, as the success checklist described was inconsistent with the proposed scope. We had their minds, they agreed, but not their hearts.

Message: Without completing the success checklist step, the project would have started with a scope that was not what the steering committee wanted. If the project had been completed, it would not have satisfied all stakeholder needs and would have been a waste of time and money.

Case study: **Premature implementation**

We participated in a project where the Managing Director insisted that the project was implemented on a certain date, even though the project manager, IT Director and Operational Director all insisted it was three months too early and implementation at this time would cause significant chaos within the operations area of the business.

The implementation did proceed as instructed, it did cause operational chaos, and we subsequently discovered that the Managing Director did get his substantial bonus for implementing it 'on time'!

Message: Stakeholder analysis and gaining an understanding of stakeholder drivers is essential to a successful project outcome.

Case study: **Need for a business-based project manager with BPM experience**

An organization insisted on appointing a project manager whose responsibility was to bridge the gap between the business and IT. However, the project manager reported to the IT department and had little knowledge of BPM implementation. When the project started to miss scheduled milestones, we were asked to provide a project health check. An outcome of this was coaching and mentoring for the project manager, and one of our senior managers participated in the Project Steering Committee to provide continual comment and advice to the committee and directly to the business project sponsor. Had the organization spent more time in the first place carefully selecting an appropriate business project manager, the project delays and cost overrun could have been avoided.

Message: The selection of an experienced BPM business project manager is one of the most important decisions with regard to a BPM project. Spend the necessary time and money to ensure that the right person is appointed; it will pay for itself throughout the life of the project.

Case study: Working on the right process?

A worth matrix for an organization early in the project showed that two business processes represented 52 percent of the people executing the process. One process (32 percent) was classified as a priority/asset process and the other (20 percent) as a priority/liability process. Of all the process people, 20 percent were involved in the processing of a transaction that had a negative value to the organization! Consideration was given, once further analysis had been completed, to outsource this process.

Message: The completion of the process worth matrix is an extremely useful technique, as it helps management to understand and categorize the organization's processes and thus enable more informed decisions to be made.

Chapter 16

Understand phase

Why?

The purpose of the Understand phase (Figure 16.1) is for the project team members and the business to gain sufficient understanding of the current business processes to enable the Innovate phase to commence. This will include the collection of appropriate metrics to gain further understanding,

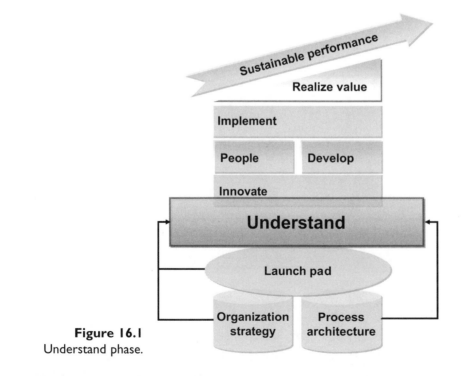

Figure 16.1
Understand phase.

establishing prioritization for innovation/redesign, and baselining the current status. This baseline will enable a comparison with future innovation process scenarios, which will be determined in the next phase (Innovate) when simulation and activity-based costing steps may be completed.

The project team must also understand what the business wishes to achieve from this phase. The process models created may be used for more than input into the Innovate phase, as the business may wish to use the models for documentation and training purposes while the innovation and implementation is taking place.

The Understand phase will also validate the current process reality within the organization and define improvement priorities within the project scope. It will assist in determining changes, if indeed changes to process(es) are necessary at all.

The crucial point here is that the project team and business are seeking to *understand* the current processes – not to document them in excruciating detail. Once a process is clearly understood and documented, stop: this is enough detail. If it has been agreed with the business that the process models may be used for documentation and training purposes, then be sure also to agree the level of detail to be recorded within the process models.

Results

There will be a number of results and outputs that the business can expect from this phase, including the following:

1   Process models of the current processes
2   Appropriate metrics sufficient to establish a baseline for future process improvement measurement, prioritization and selection in the Innovate phase
3   Measurement and documentation of the current or actual performance levels
4   Documentation of what works well (for taking into the Innovate phase) and what could work better
5   Identification of any 'quick wins' that could be implemented within a three- to six-month period
6   A report on the phase.

How?

First, let's spend a few moments to overview the depth and approach for this phase. As stated previously, the Understand modeling should only be completed to the point where all participants (project team and business) have a common understanding of what is going on in the current business process(es) and there is enough information and metrics to commence the Innovate phase. There are several situations to keep in mind during this phase:

- 'understand' what actually goes on, and ensure that what is documented reflects the actual 'as is' situation and not an 'as if' (or 'should be') situation.
- ensure that the process(es) being understood (modeled) are completed on a true 'end-to-end' basis (we will discuss this in more detail in Step 3 of this phase).
- ensure that staff are comfortable within the workshops and do not feel as though they are being evaluated; unless this is the case, participants may tell you what they think you want to hear will not impart their knowledge, or may provide you with incorrect information.
- ensure that timeframes are set regarding the amount of time to be spent on understanding or modeling a particular process, and deliver to this timeframe – in other words, set some milestones and 'time-box' activities. If you don't set milestones, you risk overruns of workshop time and the waste of valuable business subject matter expert time by going into too much detail. Workshops can be fun, and there is a risk of a workshop becoming an end in its own right, which is clearly not the purpose. Alternatively, participants can become bored and start to fail to show up for the workshops.
- use the Pareto principle (80/20 rule) to decide when you are hitting the point of diminishing returns. Always ask, 'do we have sufficient information now and can stop?'

Case study: Having the correct participants in workshops is crucial

We have been in workshops where the business experts came from different regions within the organization and actually 'negotiated' the process in the workshop, in front of us, as we modeled it, until we realized what was happening. We then mutually acknowledged what was happening, and asked them one at a time to explain the process to us, and then requested the others to amend it for their particular region.

Message: Always have people who know the detailed process in the workshop, and if they come from varying offices or regions where the process(es) could be different, then request that the process be modeled for one area at a time until there is confidence that there is a common process(es).

A few of the reasons for and against process modeling in the Understand phase are listed here.

Reasons *for* process modeling in the Understand phase include the following:

1 To gain a common understanding of, and common language for, the problem
2 To show the shortcomings of the current situations
3 To support acceptance for the 'unfreezing' for the project
4 To allow evaluation of the completeness of the innovate process

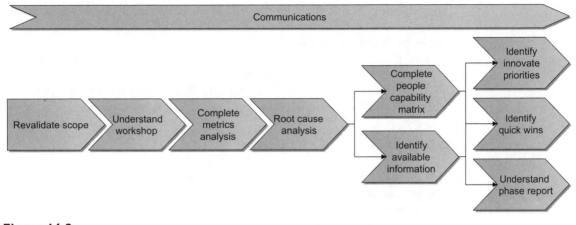

Figure 16.2
Understand phase steps.

5 Models produced may be used as documentation of the process if there is little need to change the process(es)
6 People become used to process thinking and the process modeling
7 To establish a baseline for the relationship of processes with the organization, IT and personnel.

Reasons *against* process modeling in the Understand phase include the following:

1 The current situation as modeled becomes obsolete as soon as the innovate processes are designed and implemented
2 There is always the danger of having a 'narrow focus' process design, thus putting constraints on the thinking for the innovate process
3 It takes time, requires commitment of busy business resources and costs money; in most cases this will be a complicated procedure with a steep learning curve in the first instance
4 There is a danger of doing too much and drowning in the details.

The various steps to be completed within the Understand phase are shown in Figure 16.2.

Step 1: Communications

In this phase, the main communication activities relate to providing information to the stakeholders and people within the organization about the project, its objectives, and how and when people will be involved in the Understand phase. For example, it is during this phase that the project starts to have more visibility within the organization, because personnel are starting to be specifically engaged in project workshops and asked questions regarding their current process activities and associated metrics. This can raise concerns with some regarding their future role within the organization, and whether or not their employment will continue. If these concerns are not addressed early and satisfactorily, it will be difficult to obtain the support of the organization and its people.

The project team needs to create an atmosphere in which people feel at ease in providing the information necessary to the project and the workshops. People should be comfortable in sharing their real issues and problems without fear of any blame.

Step 2: Revalidate scope

It is essential to revalidate the scope of a BPM project on a continual basis, and now is an ideal time – prior to the commencement of the Understand workshops.

It may be useful to go into the various stakeholder organizations (suppliers, customers and distribution channels) and model their processes to understand how they fit in with yours, and how your processes can enhance their business processes. The benefits of this activity include the following:

- helping the organization to gain a clearer understanding of the end-to-end process, thus allowing it to be more effective in the innovation of the process
- providing you with the ability to suggest to the stakeholder(s) that their process(es) should be redesigned as well, and work with them to understand how this could be accomplished and fully integrated with your process(es)
- enabling the organization to minimize duplications and disconnects, and reduce and improve the hand-offs between your organizational processes and those of your stakeholders.

Step 3: Understand workshops

It is important that the project sponsor and business have a clear understanding of why this phase is necessary. We have rarely encountered any resistance to the Understand phase, but we have had executives think that 'it will only take a couple of hours to model all the processes!'

Should you encounter any resistance and need to explain why the Understand phase is necessary, here are a few reasons:

1   To ensure a common understanding of the *facts* about the current process(es), not what management *thinks* happens.
2   To analyze whether improvement is possible, or even necessary. Some processes may need improvement (small changes); others may need to be redesigned using basically the same approach but just doing it more efficiently; others may need innovation using a totally new approach (perhaps from different industries, or taking out steps in the value chain); and yet others will not warrant any change at all.
3   To assist with an understanding of the process interactions and impacts upon other processes within the organization – for example, from one department to another (hand-offs).

4   To understand and document the interfaces to existing legacy systems and applications, which will be essential for the Innovate phase –
especially if process automation is involved.

Various drivers to complete process models, rather than take linear
notes, could include the following: documentation, cost, simulation, improvement, compliance (for example, Sarbanes-Oxley, Basel II), software (selection, evaluation, configuration, development), assistance with the redesign of
enterprise architecture, HR capacity planning, project management, knowledge management, document management and relationship management
(Rosemann, 2005).

Prior to the commencement of the workshops it is important to have a
clear understanding of why you are carrying out process modeling, to ensure
that upon completion the models are relevant for the desired purpose. Don't
strive for perfection; strive to have models that are sufficiently complete and
relevant, and 'fit for purpose'. Always keep in mind Pareto's principle (the
80/20 rule), because 'perfection is the enemy of good'. Perfection at this stage
can be an extremely expensive state to obtain, which can be an issue with the
complete Six Sigma approach.

Questions that should be considered on a continual basis are as follows:

1   Is the process fit for the purpose it is designed to serve?
2   Does the process satisfy the business requirements for which it is
designed?
3   Is the process critical to the business outcomes or objectives?

When organizing the Understand process workshops, there are three steps
necessary to ensure that they run smoothly:

1   Schedule the workshops early, and conveniently for the business
participants (Step 3.1)
2   Ensure that the participants minds are 'framed' appropriately before
the workshop commences, to establish the correct expectations
(Step 3.2)
3   Conduct the workshops in a structured and controlled manner
(Step 3.3).

Step 3.1: Schedule workshops early and conveniently

The Understand workshops can be very time-consuming, and could require
the subject matter experts (SMEs) to be away from the business for quite some
time. This will interrupt the SMEs' ability to do their normal role, and take
some of the best people out of the day-to-day activities of 'running' the business.

It is always a challenge for the business to take some of their best resources
'out' of the business for a significant amount of time to attend the workshops.
Project team members need to be very sympathetic and sensitive to this, and to
schedule workshops to best suit the business while still delivering the project
to the business within the agreed timeframes. It is important to have the
best people in the workshops, and not just people who are available, if the

project and business are to obtain optimized results. This is why commitment from the business is important.

The workshop schedule should be agreed with the business executives and project sponsor as early as possible, with all necessary rooms and equipment scheduled. Workshop preparation is critical, and must include the following:

- scheduling them well ahead to ensure that SMEs are available
- allowing some contingency in the number of workshops scheduled, as things will always take longer than expected
- specifying the length of workshops (no longer than three hours).

Step 3.2: 'Framing' participants

It is necessary to set the expectations of the project sponsor and participants as early as possible, and certainly well before they walk into the first workshop. If *you* do not set the expectations for the participants, *they* will set their own – and these expectations may not be appropriate for the circumstances.

The format and purpose of the workshops should be discussed and agreed with the project sponsor and/or business owner, an agenda established, and a pre-workshop meeting held with all participants. The project sponsor should chair this meeting with the workshop facilitator.

The project sponsor should inform the participants of the importance of the project, their role, and how important it is for them to attend. The workshop facilitator should outline the broad format of the workshops, the role of the participants, what is expected from them, and the purpose of the workshops, from the project's perspective.

Step 3.3: Conduct the workshops – structured and controlled

Who should attend?

We would recommend that the following attend the workshops:

- the people who actually execute the processes – not the managers who *think* they know how the process works
- team leaders, if they know the process(es) well.

It is always useful for the project sponsor to drop in on the workshops occasionally, so long as the sponsor takes a low profile and listens rather than participates.

Workshop agenda

At the beginning of the first workshop, a presentation should be given to the participants informing them in more detail of the project and how the workshops will be conducted. The agenda, format and suggested presentation outline for the workshop is outlined in detail in Appendix D; however, there are a few points we would like to make here:

1   There is no single correct way to complete process modeling; everyone will have a preferred method. Personally, we like to use a process modeling toolset on a laptop, connected to a projector that can show the model on a screen or wall as it is being created. We have found that using such a process modeling tool promotes discussion, by allowing participants to see and understand the process as it is created in front of them. It also allows participants to become familiar with the tool – in fact, it often gets to the point where the business subject matter experts want to 'take over' the modeling tool. As soon as this happens, you know the business has started to 'own' the process and you have significant buy-in, which is obviously an excellent outcome. We do not plan to cover modeling methods here, as there are many other books on this topic; we will only cover the steps in the Understand phase.

2   Always keep to the scheduled times and timeframe. Completing models for the current processes can be fun, and it is essential to keepto the project plan and ensure that the SMEs do not get bored.

3   Avoid 'the power of one' – the dominance of a single person within the workshops.

4   As mentioned earlier, the Understand modeling should only be completed to the point where you understand what is going on and you have enough information to commence the Innovate phase. What does this actually mean? How much detail should be modeled? This obviously will depend upon the particular organization and goals of the project. The simplest way is to always ask yourself, 'can we stop modeling now?' If the answer is yes, then *stop*.

Case study: End-to-end processes are critical

We were in an insurance organization reviewing the workloads and practices within the finance area. One of the staff commented that a particular process could be 'so much better if only the underwriting area did their job correctly'. We found that in excess of 50 percent of the finance work effort in this process was attributable to 'fixing up' the errors from the underwriting area. Underwriting simply had no idea of the impact it was having on finance. A joint workshop of both finance and underwriting was conducted to model the process (end-to-end), thus enabling the underwriting area to understand the critical nature of key process steps. Once corrected, this significantly diminished the work effort in the finance department.

In this instance, the 'process' of conducting the workshop, to gain a common understanding and realization, was more important than the actual modeling. Modeling was simply a method of demonstrating the impacts of the way specific process steps were being completed.

Message: Always model a process on an end-to-end basis with all participants within the workshops at the same time. Sometimes the 'journey' is more important than the documented outcomes (models).

Don't believe everything you hear. Challenge the information presented to get to the true situation if it does not make sense. People may be tempted to tell you what they think you want to hear, or management may tell you what they 'think' happens. An extremely useful method of understanding the true situation is to take the process(es) modeled within the workshops and validate it in the workplace with 'walkthroughs'.

It is useful to capture the ideas (opportunities) and issues raised during the Understand workshops and log them in an Issues and Opportunities Register. This register should be maintained throughout the project, and a suggested layout of this register is shown in Appendix D.

Step 4: Complete metrics analysis

The purpose of gathering the business process metrics is two-fold:

1   To assist in the understanding of the process(es) and their impact upon the organization, and to provide prioritization for further investigation
2   To provide a baseline for comparative purposes with the Innovate phase of the project. This can assist greatly in the completion of the business case and determination of expected productivity, cost and service level improvements.

Why complete a metrics analysis? Some of the reasons will include the need to:

- assist in the understanding of an organization's processes
- produce an analytical view of the organization
- reconcile the organization's processes costs against departmental budgets to ensure that all major processes are captured or intentionally excluded
- aid the project team members in creating remedial, not just opportunist, solutions
- aid in the prioritization of processes for further investigation during the Innovate phase
- provide a baseline for comparative purposes with any future changes, allowing for the forecast of future potential benefits from any newly designed process environment, and to measure the impact of actual changes
- input into the focus for the redesign effort, indicating areas that have the potential to provide the largest impacts
- allow benchmarking of process data (task times, volumes and costs) between different organizations.

Prior to the commencement of the Understand workshops, a number of initial metrics will be gathered and analyzed. This task will include the following:

- gathering broad costing information – for example, budgets, organization charts and staff listings
- reconciliation of the organization charts and HR staff listings

- restructuring the budget if the budget is for a larger area of the organization than is being analyzed. In this case, the budget must be dissected and allocated to the specific area within the project scope. For example, staff costs could be determined by the number of staff in each department, while the other costs are more likely to be calculated by proportioning the non-productive personnel's staff costs across the productive resources costs.

During the workshops, as many metrics as possible should be collected. At a minimum, the following must be included.

- transactional information – volumes, which role completes the tasks, and the process time
- transactional data to reconcile against the resourcing levels within each process area for reasonability of processing times and volumes, and to identify any additional processes
- direct labor cost per process, which is calculated based on task time, process transactions and labor recovery rates
- IT costs and other overheads allocated to the process, based on daily task time.

A sample costing matrix is shown in Figure 16.3.

The department concerned only processes two types of transactions: receipting and policy updates. The number of transactions per day is shown in Figure 16.3, as is the estimated processing time (in minutes) per transaction (process). The hourly labor rate has been calculated, as has the non-labor hourly allocation. This allows the calculation of the average cost per transaction (process), and the annual cost per transaction (process) based on 250 working days per year.

Depending on the standard day used for calculation, different utilization levels will be acceptable in this reconciliation. For example, based upon a

A	B	C	D	E	F	G	H	I	J	K	L
Process name	Average number of transactions (per day)	Time per transaction (minutes)	Daily time (minutes)	Labor hourly Rate $	Labor costs (Productive labor) $	Non labor hourly allocation (proportioned over processes by daily time) $	Non labor costs (proportioned over processes by daily time) $	Cost (per day) $	Average cost per transaction $	Annual cost (per annum) $	Annual effort %
Receipting	3,000	10	30,000	$25.00	$12,500	$17.00	$8,500	$21,000	$7.00	$5,250,000	55%
Policy updates	3,500	7	24,500	$25.00	$10,208	$17.00	$6,942	$17,150	$4.90	$4,287,500	45%
			(B x C)		(D x E / 60)		(D x G / 60)	(F + H)	(I / B)	(I x 250)	(D / X)
Totals			54,500		$22,708		$15,442			$9,537,500	
			(X)								
Total time available (based on FTE times standard day)			20,000								
			(Y)								
Utilization %			272.5%								
			(X / Y)								

Figure 16.3
Sample simplified costing matrix. (Reproduced with the permission of MPM Group Pty Ltd, trading as TouchPoint Process Management Services.)

7.5-hour day, a utilization level of between 80 and 85 percent could be considered reasonable. If an organization chose a 6.25-hour day, however, 100 percent utilization would be expected. **Note**: be careful with the percentages selected for use in the project, and ensure that they are well socialized and agreed with the business.

Metrics should be collected at all levels, and examples that may be useful include the following (although there is no expectation that all of these will be collected or used).

Process selection matrix level

1   Sales and staffing levels at the business unit level
2   Dissection of the organization (sales $ and volume) across the various segments of the business unit and/or project scope
3   At a process and sub-process level, the percentage split of volumes
4   The cost to the business of transacting this volume of business (for example, annual budgets).

Process level

1   Determination of which part of the process(es) to measure
2   Collection of estimated processing times per process or sub-process – if costs can be contributed to a given process, this is ideal; activity-based costing, if implemented within an organization, can supply a great deal of information
3   Determination of process performance measures, for example, SLAs, KPIs, then sub-process KPIs
4   Details of how the accuracy of the process is currently measured – is there any error tracking?
5   Measurement of wherever bottlenecks occur.

Examples of the types of metrics that may be worth gathering include the following:

*   number of transactions by payment method or region (monthly for last eight to twelve months, to indicate monthly trends or peak periods)
*   process times for major process(es), particularly date-sensitive activities
*   error numbers and types
*   backlog reports, status and volumes (amount and numbers) – trends for last twelve months
*   volumes and values of the various transaction types
*   labor costs for key positions, including labor on-costs
*   overtime/casual/contract hours worked – history for the last twelve months
*   cost per hour, including labor on-costs for overtime
*   complaints register – numbers and trends over the past twelve months, plus a sample analysis
*   extent, percentage of transaction volume, time and labor impact of rework

- value of transactions 'written off' monthly, for the last twelve months
- percentage of time spent on out of scope processes.

Management level

1   Customer satisfaction surveys, which could provide interesting information
2   For quality or effectiveness measures, use:

- efficiency – how much resource is used doing what needs to be done?
- adaptability – how easy is it for the organization to change?
- common denominators, which are time, cost, customer satisfaction
- customer retention rate, by division and/or distribution channel (monthly for the last twelve months, including monthly trends).

3   Productivity trend studies
4   Headcount report by position, matched with the organization chart to discover any discrepancies
5   Copy of management performance measurement reports for the last twelve months
6   ISO and/or audit reports, both internal and external
7   Current provision level for write-offs
8   Staff turnover for the last twelve months
9   Staff length of service.

How are these metrics gathered?

The metrics may be gathered:

- during workshops
- by interviewing management and staff to validate the information gained during workshops
- by various surveys and questionnaires
- from management reports.

If it is difficult to collect process timings during the process modeling workshops, you could complete the process modeling and then hold another workshop or two to go through the models to collect the timing data; alternatively, other people within the organization may have the information. The data can then be extrapolated to ensure that they make sense.

For example, a spreadsheet created to multiply process times by the volume of transactions in order to calculate overall processing times, and extrapolated into the 'expected' number of staff, can then be compared to the 'actual' number of staff currently employed in the processes. In our experience, if this is accurate to within 15–20 percent, it is close enough at this stage. When completing this exercise, make sure that all processes and activities are covered.

It is essential to understand the various executive, management and team leader performance measures to ensure that they are complementary to the process, and not working against it.

Remember, the major purpose of collecting the metrics during the Understand phase is to enable the establishment of a baseline for comparative purposes with the Innovate phase.

Step 5: Root-cause analysis

It is essential to determine the actual 'root' cause of an issue or non-performing process. If you do not fully understand the root cause, you are not in a position to commence the Innovate phase of a process. You cannot be certain that once the redesign has been completed, the reason for the process non-performance has been addressed. It is like a medical doctor treating the symptom and not determining or understanding the actual cause of the disease.

What is the best way to perform root-cause analysis? This will vary from organization to organization. In some organizations the Understand workshops will flush out the root cause; while in other organizations the project team will need to go into the business and analyze the root cause themselves. The latter case will require observation, investigation, analysis, and speaking to the people who execute the processes on a day-to-day basis. Do not forget to talk to people outside the main processing team, because the root cause may be either upstream or downstream of the part of the process currently being analyzed. This is an example of why it is essential to examine processes on a true end-to-end basis, otherwise you cannot be certain that you have covered all aspects of the process. While it is essential to speak to management, it is unusual (depending upon the type of error) that they will know the root cause.

Suggested questions to keep in mind when conducting the root-cause analysis include the following:

- Where are the errors or rework coming from?
- Is this being caused by other process(es)?
- Is the information being received correctly?
- If not, what can be done to rectify the situation?
- Do the staff executing this process have the skills to complete it?
- Could the forms being used be better designed?
- Does the organization have sufficient capacity to complete this process to the desired standard?
- Are staff idle?
- Do the steps in the process add value to the stakeholder requirements and goals of the process?
- Are the steps in the process being completed in the appropriate sequence?

Step 6: Complete people capability matrix

The people capability matrix will provide useful information about both the current and the future environment. It is, however, the future that is the most

Key processes / Knowledge capabilities/ skills required	Ability to sell to customers	Communication skills	Data entry skills	Dealing with difficult customers
Notification	2	2	3	1
Assessment	1	1	3	1
Approval	3	2	3	1
Payment	2	2	3	2
Finalization	2	3	1	1

Figure 16.4
People capability matrix. (Reproduced with the permission of MPM Group Pty Ltd, trading as TouchPoint Process Management Services.)

important. If the future is substantially different from the current situation, then it may not be appropriate to complete the matrix for the current environment other than for understanding the gap between the skills now in the organization and how they will need to change in the future. In some cases, analysis of the current skills can provide useful information about the root causes of particular process aberrations.

This gap analysis is important, and needs to be well documented and understood at a high level at this stage. It is during the Innovate and People phases that this will be analyzed in far more detail and linked to individuals, specific action plans and potential changes to the organization structure.

Figure 16.4 provides an example of how this matrix could be completed. The horizontal axis represents the core skills or competencies required by each of the processes to complete the tasks or activities. The vertical axis represents the end-to-end process model, group of processes or individual processes. These core competencies are then rated on the simple basis of 1, 2 or 3, where 1 is a mandatory core competency and 3 is desirable but not essential.

Remember to:

- look at the current capability versus the future needs
- do it from a 'big picture' level, not at a person level, at this phase of the project
- review role description areas at a high level
- review people core competency enhancement requirements.

Step 7: Identify available information

The purpose of this step is to gain an understanding, within the project scope, of the currently available information within the organization. This step should

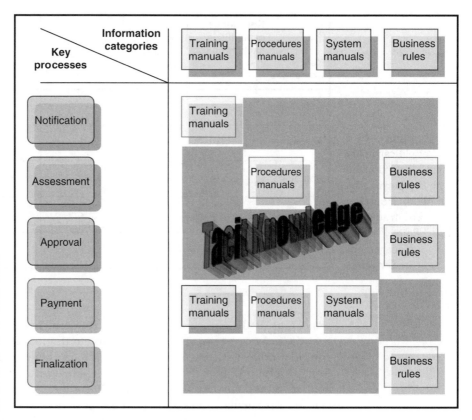

Figure 16.5
Knowledge and information needs map. (Reproduced with the permission of MPM Group Pty Ltd, trading as TouchPoint Process Management Services.)

only be completed if it will be of use within the project. The best way to identify the available process information or knowledge is via a workshop and/or discussions with people within the business, HR and training departments.

Within the Understand workshops, a matrix can be developed in a similar format to the process selection matrix. An example is shown in Figure 16.5.

The key processes for which you wish to complete this matrix are displayed on the vertical axis – in this case, an end-to-end claims process comprising notification, assessment, approval, payment and finalization. The types of knowledge that the business deem to be available or desirable within the organization are shown on the horizontal axis.

Knowledge is usually categorized into two classifications:

1 Tacit human, education, experience (basically, in people's 'heads' and not documented within the organization)
2 Explicit documented knowledge within the organization. Documentation can include the knowledge built into automated solutions, such as workflow or application systems.

The matrix can then be completed in a similar manner to that shown, where the grey areas are all tacit knowledge.

It is particularly useful to identify clearly the knowledge available for the 'identity' and 'priority' processes of the organization; that is, the most valuable processes.

It is equally important to be clear about what type of documentation is needed for the satisfactory delivery of products and services to stakeholders (internal and external). Clearly, the more process knowledge is explicit (documented or systematized) the better it is for the organization, and the less likely it is that knowledge will 'walk' if staff leave the organization.

Step 8: Identify Innovate priorities

Identification of Innovate priorities should be an outcome of the Understand modeling, metrics gathering and root-cause analysis steps. During these steps, it should become obvious which areas of the business, and which process(es), provide an opportunity for improvement and quick wins.

The prioritization should be based upon the analysis completed during the workshops, the metrics, stakeholders' views, and the choices made for each process. These could include the following:

- leaving the process(es) as it is – it is good enough
- improving – which means the process(es) needs 'tweaking' or small changes only
- amalgamating with other process(es)
- redesigning – starting with a blank sheet of paper
- total innovation – thinking outside the 'box' and making radical changes
- outsourcing
- insourcing
- eliminating the process.

In identifying redesign and quick win opportunities, it is essential to ensure that they are consistent with and contribute towards the process goals, organizational strategic objectives and stakeholders' expectations established during the Process architecture phase. Spend some time linking or mapping them back to these goals, objectives and expectations.

It may be necessary to complete a business case (including a cost–benefit and/or economic value analysis) within some organizations before the management grants approval to continue the project. This may be achieved by updating the business case developed earlier.

Step 9: Identify quick wins

As mentioned previously, most organizations insist that process improvement projects are self-funding – so it is essential to find quick wins to implement. It is also highly recommended that some of the suggested quick wins come from the front-line personnel who execute the processes, even if the benefits are not great, because it shows you are listening to them. Ensure that the front-line personnel are given credit in a public way for the ideas and success of these quick win implementations. This contributes towards the change management process essential to any BPM project.

The activities to be performed at this phase of the project are as follows:

- to revisit these quick wins via workshops with the business, to validate them in more detail and to prioritize them for implementation
- to validate the feasibility of implementation; ensuring that the quick wins are cost-effective (that is, the cost of development and implementation does not outweigh the benefits to be gained), and that they will be useful and efficient solutions for the business
- once this has been validated, to document the proposed solution(s) for approval by stakeholders (internal and external)
- after approval is obtained, to finalize and execute a more detailed development and implementation plan.

Consideration should be given to forming a sub-project team to implement these quick wins. This has the advantage of not distracting the core project team from the Innovate phase.

If the quick wins are given to a separate team or the business to implement, the main project team should *not* completely outsource this implementation, nor abdicate responsibility and take no further part in the implementation. The main project team *must* still take ultimate responsibility for the implementation, because if there are any issues regarding not realizing the projected benefits outlined in the business case or quick win documentation, the main team will be deemed responsible – even if this was caused by poor implementation. The main team should set the project scope, assist in the development of the project plans/schedules, quality assure the project continually throughout its life, and ensure that the designated benefits are realized.

Step 10: Understand phase report

At the completion of this phase, the project team should deliver a report to the business and project sponsor documenting the phase outcomes and findings. This report should contain at least the following information:

1 The purpose of the Understand phase
2 The process issues found during the workshops and analysis within the business
3 A list of stakeholders and their relevance to the project
4 Findings:

- current process(es)
- metrics
- identified quick wins

5 A suggested Innovate phase prioritization.

Realize value

Baseline and comparative measurements must be established as part of this phase. For details, refer to Step 3 of Chapter 21, where it is described in the context of realizing value within a project.

Understand phase outputs

The Understand phase will provide valuable input into other phases of the framework (Figure 16.6), including the following few examples:

- knowledge may be gained that will be useful to the process architecture in modifying or enhancing the standards or guidelines for the organization
- certainly there will be input into the Innovate phase – baseline metrics, innovate priorities and so forth
- there will be outcomes that will assist in the potential development of new roles in the People phase, or indications of what may be required in the development of solutions and how a solution may be rolled out across the organization, for example, the people capability matrix.

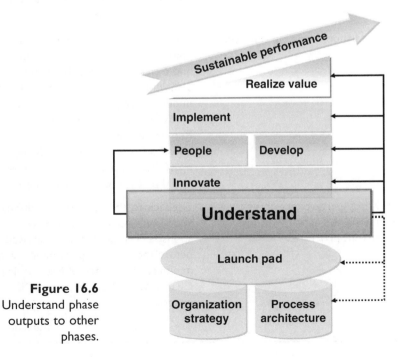

Figure 16.6
Understand phase outputs to other phases.

Understand phase risks

During the execution of the Understand phase there are a number of high-level risks that must be considered. Table 16.1 is not meant to be a complete list; just the beginning of a list of risks that the project team members can use to start their own project risk analysis.

Table 16.1
Understand phase risks and mitigation strategies

Risk	Mitigation strategy
1 Processes are not reviewed on a genuine end-to-end basis	This risks compromising the common level of understanding of a process(es) and the ability to ensure all aspects of a process are covered during the Innovate phase. Ensure that the project scope is for an end-to-end situation, and if in doubt go back to the project sponsor for clarification and amendment
2 The workshops over-run time	Plan the workshops carefully before you commence and keep to the plan. The plan does not need to work perfectly to the minute; however, the overall plan must be achieved. The plan must be constantly reviewed throughout the phase
3 The workshop modeling is in too much detail	The purpose of the Understand phase must always be kept in mind, and modeling must only be in sufficient detail to enable a common understanding and to enable the Innovate phase to commence. Remember always to ask the question, 'can we stop modeling now?' This applies to each process and the entire Understand phase
4 Workshop participants do not understand the actual workings of the current processes	Go back to the business and discuss, and if necessary to the project sponsor. This should be addressed before the workshops commence, to minimize the chance of it occurring. Change workshop participants if necessary

(Continued)

Table 16.1   *(Continued)*

Risk	Mitigation strategy
5 The metrics analysis is completed in too much detail	Again, the purpose of analyzing the process metrics is to provide prioritization for the Innovate phase and a baseline for comparison with the outcomes of the Innovate phase. The project manager (or a delegated person) needs to monitor this and ensure that the metrics analysis does not analyze in too much detail
6 No metrics gathered	This is a critical aspect of the Understand phase to enable the establishment of a baseline for future comparative purposes. If there is push back on the completion of metrics, gain the support of the project sponsor

Chapter 17

Innovate phase

The purpose of the Innovate phase (Figure 17.1) is to make the process(es) within the scope of the project as efficient and effective as possible, to meet stakeholders' current and future expectations. This phase also provides a unique opportunity to quantify further, in a more rigorous manner, the benefits outlined in the original business case.

'Why are we doing this Innovate phase, and to what degree of innovation?' is a fundamental question that must be answered before you can commence. According to Paul O'Neill, Chairman of Alcoa 1991, in a worldwide letter to Alcoa staff in November 1991:

> Continuous improvement is exactly the right idea if you are the world leader in everything you do. It is a terrible idea if you are lagging the world leadership benchmark. It is probably a disastrous idea if you are far behind the world standard–in which case you may need rapid quantum-leap improvement.

Should the project consider automation as part of this phase? There is also a great comment attributable to Bill Gates, CEO of Microsoft, in relation to automation:

> The first rule of any technology is that automation applied to an efficient operation will magnify the efficiency. The second is that automation applied to an inefficient operation will magnify the inefficiency.

Getting the processes 'right' before automation should definitely be a goal, and this was discussed in Chapter 3.

Setting the directions and goals for the Innovate phase is a critical step, and one that needs to be addressed early in the phase. The Innovate phase is like starting a new game – unless you know the rules of the game before you start, it is difficult to play and win. Setting the rules is therefore one of the initial critical steps in the phase.

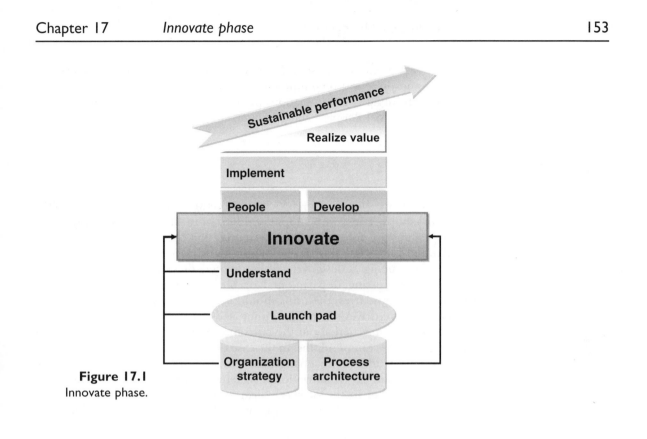

Figure 17.1
Innovate phase.

Results

The various documents that may be created as a result of this phase could include the following:

1   Redesigned process models
2   Documentation supporting the redesigned processes
3   High-level business requirements of the new process options
4   Simulation models and activity-based costing details
5   Capacity planning information
6   Confirmation that the new process option alternatives will meet stakeholder expectations
7   Confirmation that the new process options are consistent with the organization strategy and will achieve the designated process goals
8   A process gap analysis report
9   The project plan in detail for the People and Develop phases
10 Detailed cost–benefit analysis may be produced and be input into the business case
11 An updated business case with more detailed and quantifiable benefits and costs, and assessment of impact on the organization; these should reflect the tangible and intangible benefits
12 A detailed report outlining the steps taken, alternatives and options considered, analysis, findings and recommendations

13 A presentation to senior management supporting the business case and direction recommended
14 An initial communications plan for informing all stakeholders
15 An initial People Change Management Strategy document.

How?

The best way to develop the new process options and alternatives is through the use of workshops. These workshops are different in structure and approach to the Understand workshops, and it is essential that this is understood upfront and planned for in the appropriate way. The workshops need to ensure that the processes being redesigned are completed on a true end-to-end basis. If this means crossing departmental or business unit boundaries, or even organization boundaries, then this should be done. In the case of a 'business as usual', 'in the driver's seat' and 'pilot' scenarios, the Innovate workshops should not be concerned about the current organization structure; if it needs changing, then recommend this. In the case of the 'under the radar' approach, it will be more difficult to change the current organization structure and recommend changes. Organizational structure change should be addressed separately and later in the project, during the People phase; however, there are key analyses required here to support the People phase and provide input into it.

One of the key challenges with regard to providing process innovation to an organization is the mismatch between conventional organization structure (vertical or pyramid basis) and the way 'work' (transactions) is received and processed within an organization.

Figure 17.2 shows the conventional organization structure.

The vertical lines represent the division of the organization into departments, with process workers providing hand-offs to each other across the various departments. Work is processed horizontally, as in Figure 17.3, passing through various departments within the end-to-end process model of the organization.

It is the hand-offs between departments that often provide the greatest opportunities for improvements in processes.

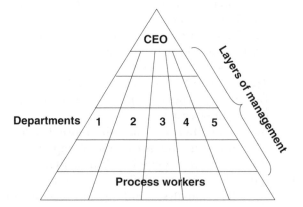

Figure 17.2
Conventional organization structure.

Figure 17.3
Transaction
processing.

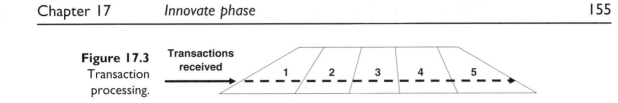

The goals or objectives (key result areas and KPIs) of the various organizational departments, and the transaction passing through them, may be at odds with the efficient and effective processing of the transaction. This mismatch is one of the key challenges for the business and the project team to overcome.

Prior to commencing workshops and the innovation of process(es), there is a critical question that must be asked: How do we know what we have designed and propose to implement is what our customers/suppliers/partners need to achieve a high level of satisfaction *and* effective service? We would like to spend some time looking at this question, because if it is not answered then the project will not have been successful – even if it has achieved reduced costs or increased quality levels.

Figure 17.4 shows how customers' levels of service and satisfaction can be measured. It is important to understand that 'service' and 'satisfaction' are different. A customer can receive a high level of service and still be dissatisfied.

Organizations continually speak of the 'wow' factor, and how they need to 'exceed customers' expectations' and 'surprise' them. This 'wow' factor can come in the form of product features, or an unexpected surprise in the way customers have been serviced. Factors can be extremely effective and build customer loyalty, provided customers are not irritated or annoyed overall. Customer irritation can have far more impact upon how a customer thinks of the organization that does the 'wow' factor.

There is also the area between the irritation zone and the 'wow' zone that should not be addressed by any project or business case if the goals of innovation are increased customer service and customer satisfaction. Spending funds on this area will provide no benefit to the customer, and must be avoided.

Figure 17.4
Customer levels of
service and
satisfaction. Adapted
from Blatter, 2005,
© Citibank,
reproduced with
permission.

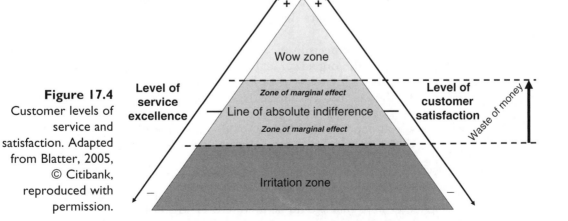

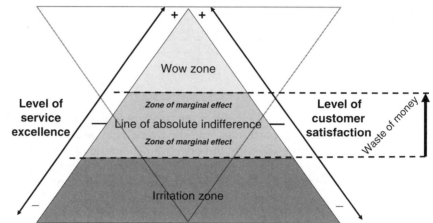

Figure 17.5
Organization effort.

It is interesting that the time spent by organizations on the 'wow' and irritation zones is disproportional to the benefits to be gained from them, as depicted in Figure 17.5.

The inverse triangle in Figure 17.5 depicts the amount of effort organizations traditionally spend upon these aspects of service. Organizations often spend a great deal of time trying to differentiate themselves from other organizations by developing 'wow' factors in their products and services. Conversely, little time is spent upon eliminating the 'irritation' factors of customers. This is the exact opposite of what should be happening.

If organizations spent more time eliminating the irritation factors, they would find that customers would have higher levels of service *and* satisfaction. In general, most of the irritation factors are caused by processes that do not function properly.

When looking at the factors that are critical to a project's success, research must be conducted into understanding the above to assist in the direction of the project and to know that if certain process changes are implemented then customers will have increased satisfaction levels, thus contributing towards customer retention.

Before we move on to the steps associated with the Innovate phase, there are several essential elements that must always be addressed in the workshops. The project must ensure that:

- all disconnects in the organizational functional structure are identified (the organizational relationship map and the list of end-to-end process model(s) assist in this process)
- the new process alternatives are reasonable, practical and simple
- stakeholder expectations are met
- all opportunities for automation are identified
- all interdependencies with other processes or sub-processes are considered and addressed.

To have a successful outcome for the Innovate phase, there is a number of high-level steps that should be followed (Figure 17.6).

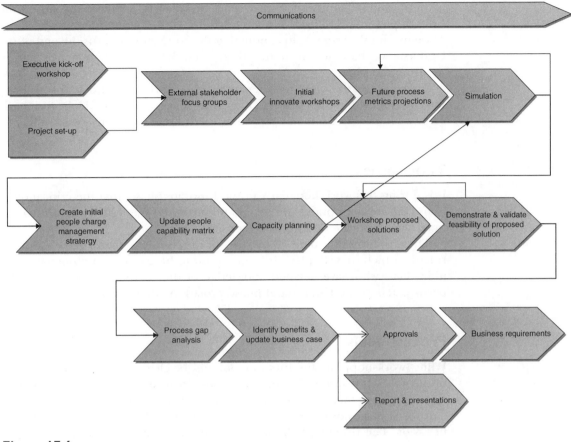

Figure 17.6
Innovate phase steps.

Step 1: Communications

It is important to keep the relevant stakeholders informed about the scope of the Innovate phase, the options being considered, and their status. The communications must ensure that stakeholder input is not lost in the detail, and that stakeholders are always kept informed as to the status of their input. If their suggestions cannot be accommodated, it is important to inform them of the reasons why. This will also assist in them gaining greater understanding of the objectives of, and choices made by, the business on behalf of the project. The development of the initial communications plan will assist with this.

Step 2: Management kick-off workshop

It is necessary to start this phase with a workshop involving the project sponsor and other senior business leaders, to determine and understand the organization's strategy and process goals associated with the project, and the area of the business being redesigned. The information gathered as part of the Launch pad phase will provide some baseline information for this workshop. Thought should be given to conducting this workshop towards the end of the Understand phase, to ensure that there is no delay in the commencement of the Innovate phase.

There is usually one 'key' person in this workshop who is the primary stakeholder within the project. It is this person who should be primarily involved in the decision-making within the Innovate executive workshop.

Timeframes

It is during this workshop, early in the Innovate phase, that the critical questions of Innovate options are asked and answered – questions regarding the timeframes and the options to be considered.

These options are some of the rules of the Innovate phase 'game', and the rules by which we will 'play'. It is important to have one or two open-minded individuals who have detailed knowledge of the current processes and who participated in the Understand phase process modeling workshops.

Process goals

While 'workshopping' the Innovate options, be clear about the establishment of the goals. It is interesting that if the sole focus of the options and phase is cost reduction, then quality often suffers. This is especially so if the reduced cost focus is supported by performance measures that reward cost-reduction behavior. The resulting behavior can result in quality issues as people, team leaders and management focus on driving transactions through the process as fast as possible in order to reduce costs. This is a short-sighted approach, because a drive for 'speed' will result in decreased quality and increasing rework, and thus increased costs. It is important that during this phase, personnel are thinking 'outside the box'. This will provide an opportunity to be better, faster and cheaper by accepting different ways of working. However, the executive management team should list its requirements and the order of priority.

On the other hand, if the focus is on quality, then reduced cost is a likely result as it will reduce errors and rework.

Questions that must be answered in order to determine the process goals include the following.

Strategic:

1   Is this an evolutionary or revolutionary (substantial innovation) project? Do you want to make incremental change, or radical change involving technology, or no technology? The answer to these questions will substantially change the approach to, and expected outcomes from, the Innovate phase.
2   How does the project fit into the organization strategy?
3   How does the project support the plans for the next year or two?

Planning:
1   What is the business rationale for this project?
2   Why are you doing this project?

- to resolve bottlenecks–both current and future?
- to provide an ability to implement new products and services?
- to improve customer service?
- to cut operating costs?
- to decrease customer irritation?
- to improve quality?
- for compliance purposes?

3   What are the specific goals and process performance measures associated with this phase of the project? The customer should be used as the focus for the development of these goals. Compare what the customer and organization think, because they can be at odds – research is critical.
4   Do we have the necessary resources to undertake this project?
5   What do you want to happen as a result of the project?
6   Will it add to the capacity of the organization?
7   What are the 'no-go' conditions?

Constraints:
1   What timeframes should you be working to – three, six, twelve or twenty-four months?
2   What are the barriers and constraints to be built into the Innovate phase (for example, are there allowed to be any changes to the IT systems)?
3   Are there change management or people constraints?

Success:
(Some of the following will already have been addressed in the Launch Pad phase, if this is the case, then update the information with the new knowledge gained.)

1   How will the organization know when you have achieved milestones or completion of the project?
2   What will this involve you doing?
3   What do different stakeholders (internal and external) expect from the project?
4   How will you know when you have been successful? Success criteria should be built in, understood and documented, upfront.

We will provide two examples of the process goals established as a result of executive kick-off workshops. You will note the differences, which are largely attributable to the organizations' BPM maturity (more on BPM maturity can be found in Chapter 27).

Automation

When reviewing the possible future options available to the organization and the project, BPM automation, and especially workflow, is often raised as a possible, or desirable, option.

While workflow can be a significant benefit in the right circumstances, it is not necessarily the most important aspect for improved process performance. The single most important aspect is to focus on people – creating the right culture, motivation, responsibility, ownership, accountability, performance measures, feedback and rewards.

Much BPM hype can lead us to think that workflow and related BPM software solutions can provide the most important benefits. While they can provide an appropriate and beneficial enabler, it is the culture and people aspects that can be significant constraints if not handled correctly, or significant enablers if handled well.

Even though automation can be extremely useful in making processes more effective, the people aspects of a project should not be ignored.

People change management strategy

There will be a need to gain a thorough understanding of the organizations capacity for change, its willingness to change and then agree an appropriate approach. Unless this is clear to the project team, project sponsor and other significant stakeholders before the commencement of the project, it will provide an additional risk factor that could otherwise have been avoided.

Success checklist

Documenting the success checklist is important in determining the scope for the redesign of the business processes. Unless it is clear, it will limit the ability to redesign the business processes and the activities in the People phase scope. For example, the organization may be unwilling to change the current organization structure and this will impact upon the scope and ability to modify the processes. The reason the project team needs to address this now, as opposed to earlier, is that it is usually only at this stage of the project that the project team gains a clearer understanding of the likely changes that the business is contemplating or are required and the magnitude of these proposed changes.

It is essential that the process success evaluation criteria are agreed before the Innovate phase process workshops commence, and that the workshops build on the agreed and defined stakeholder expectations. When conducting the workshops, always ensure that the proposed new process is consistently related back to these stakeholder outcomes, the success checklist, the KPIs and the performance measures.

Management workshop preparation

The preparation for this workshop should include distributing the following information, which will have previously been developed, to all participants:

- the organization process view
- the organizational relationship map
- the end-to-end process model for the business area being examined within the project
- the process selection matrix for the business area being examined within the project
- a list of all the issues and opportunities developed during the Understand phase
- a list of all the processes, by name and function
- appropriate metrics that are relevant to the discussion.

Other useful information to have available includes the business plans and budgets for the current and coming year, and a list of the organization's project portfolio (to review overlapping and related projects).

The workshop should not exceed one day, and should be limited to half a day if possible, to ensure that focus is maintained.

Outcomes

As a minimum, the outcomes of this executive workshop must provide a clear way forward (set of rules) for the Innovate phase. This will include the following:

1 An understanding of how and where the project and new process(es) link with the organizational strategy
2 A documented understanding of the proposed or desired goals for the new process(es) and the associated process performance measurements
3 An agreed list of constraints to be placed upon the innovate process
4 Agreed timeframes for the innovate options
5 An agreed 'width' for the project, and whether it is evolutionary or revolutionary.

Unless you have at least these aspects clear, you place the project outcomes and success at risk. You will have started playing the 'game' when you don't know, or fully understand, the rules (i.e. whether you are scoring points or are heading in the right direction).

Step 3: Project set-up

This step requires a quick review of the current project plan to ensure that, as a result of Step 2, you have the correct people in the Innovate workshops from a project team and business perspective. The different types of people that should be involved in the various Innovate workshops are covered in a later step.

It is necessary to ensure that all the project requirements, as outlined in the project plan (schedule), which can be found in Appendix C, are consistent with the organization strategy and process goals considered necessary as a result of the executive workshop. The agreed timeframes and approach (options) to the Innovate phase may also have an impact upon the project plan. The plan needs to be reviewed and updated as a result of the number of new process scenarios proposed – for example, there may have been a decision to develop new process options for several of the following: three-month horizon; twelve-month horizon; twenty-four-month horizon; automated and non-automated.

Step 4: External stakeholder focus groups

External stakeholders are defined as being 'external' to the business unit/area being reviewed within the project. They will include other stakeholders within the organization but external to the business unit/area, and stakeholders external to the organization.

Prior to conducting the initial innovate workshops, it is often useful to gather appropriate external stakeholders together into a focus group(s) to inform them of the proposed plans and their expected involvement in the process. They should then be asked to input their thoughts regarding the current process(es) (shortcomings and issues) and how they would like to conduct business with the organization, to provide input to the process redesign.

At this early stage, all discussions should be kept at a high level with the detail to come later after the detailed Innovate workshops. The external stakeholders should again be involved at a later stage. The purpose, at this moment, is to gain direction from them and to make them feel involved. It is part of stakeholder management (refer to Chapter 24).

These stakeholder focus groups should also provide input into the earlier discussions regarding customer service excellence and satisfaction.

Step 5: Initial Innovate workshops

This is where the project changes from *analysis* (as undertaken in the Understand phase) to *creative* (synthesis of new ideas, and being innovative). However, be careful: the approach you undertake in the Innovate phase will very much depend upon the outcomes you set. When looking at improving a process, the workshop participants will need to ensure that they do not limit themselves by only looking at fixing the current process problems (unless that is clearly the desired goal). Looking at the current process issues will limit thinking, and the possibilities of process innovation and/or redesign.

The setting of the Innovate options in the management workshop will set the scene for breaking away from this constraint and towards process innovation. The innovate options should not be based upon the Understand phase situation or individual processes.

If you want to improve or redesign your process(es), then synthesizing new creative ideas is important. If, however, the proposed outcome is to implement process innovation, the creativity process should not be limited to internal ideas but should also include external ideas from different industries and quite radical thoughts with regard to the future process structure. Innovation will involve significant questioning of the current paradigm, and thinking outside the tradition for your industry.

Certainly there will be the need to use the knowledge gained from the previous Understand phase, and to rethink the current approach to the process. The obvious question to ask is, is there a better way of approaching/doing this process? The strengths and weaknesses analysis can be useful. This will, at the very least, provide a starting point for discussion.

So what techniques can you employ? Workshops and discussion with the business is definitely the best approach. Employing creativity and innovation techniques by experienced BPM facilitators can be very productive. It is our experience that the use of external facilitators with considerable BPM experience provides the best outcomes in the Innovate phase. (The reason for 'external' facilitators is so that there is no 'baggage' brought to the sessions by people who work in the area being examined. 'External' can mean the organization's internal facilitators who are experienced in BPM and facilitation but do not work within the business area undergoing process innovation, or facilitators external to the organization. Facilitators who are external to the organization can bring experience from other industry sectors.)

During the workshops, concentrate first on getting a quantity of ideas. Don't filter these ideas too much at this stage; this will come later. Initially,

- include divergence of ideas – that is, try to get as many ideas (including radical ones) as possible
- cover right-brain or creative ideas – employ lateral thinking ability
- ensure there is no judgment – it is essential that neither the facilitator nor the workshop participants pass judgment on any idea put forward at this stage; there must be an openness to *all* ideas put forward
- look for opportunities – especially outside the 'square' (traditional thinking)
- look from the other side – view the organization from the perspective of customers, suppliers, partners or competitors.

The question arises, 'how do you get workshop participants to be creative?' Nobel prize winning physician Albert Szent-Gyorgyi is purported to have stated that '*discovery (creative thinking) consists of looking at the same thing as everyone else and thinking something different*' (von Oech, 1990, p. 7). Albert Einstein is also purported to have said that "*we can't solve problems by using the same kind of thinking we used when we created it*" (source unknown).

The challenge for the workshop facilitator and participants is to 'think something different' more often. We are often raised, particularly at school, to believe that we have *mental locks* (von Oech, 1990, p. 10–11). These have been described by von Oech as:

- There is only one right answer
- That is not logical

- Follow the rules
- Be practical
- Play is frivolous
- That is not my area
- Avoid ambiguity
- Don't be foolish
- To err is wrong
- I'm not creative.

All these mental locks need to be broken in order to be creative and 'think outside the box'.

In workshops, the facilitator must establish an environment where the following occurs.

- Ask lots of 'what if . . . ' and 'why this?' questions
- Don't accept what you are told (the first time)
- Look for the second 'right answer'
- The best way to get a good idea is to get a lot of ideas
- The facilitator should regularly change the question and come at it from a different direction. Remember, the answer you get will depend upon the question you ask
- Always challenge the rules
- Always follow your intuitive hunches.

The best starting method is to have the workshop participants model the process from the customers' perspective – how the customer interacts with your organization, because customers do not care what goes on inside your organization, they only care how they interact with you to obtain the product and services they desire. You could also model the customer experience with your competitors and compare them to your own. This can be expanded to include supplier and partners perspectives.

Another mental 'un-locker' is to ensure that, when participants get stuck or run out of ideas, they are provided with a *magic wand* to overcome any blockages and enable them to develop the very best solution, within the bounds of the management workshop scenarios.

The following triggers can be used to start the flow of ideas:

- empower employees to make more decisions themselves and combine logical tasks together, which reduces the waiting time
- build quality control into the process rather than having it as a separate activity at the end of the process
- technology enables information to be available from multiple places, people can be involved in the process without the requirement to have a physical document present
- telecommunication can be more integrated with IT – for example field-staff having access to up-to-date information and making bookings from the client site

- RFID (Radio Frequency Identification) makes it possible to track more economically – for example tracking the progress of an express parcel
- customer self-service – customers can do more things themselves, taking over responsibility for the correctness of information and reducing costs and effort for the organization
- do not create process models that are complex just to handle the exceptions; only look at the mainstream and deal with exceptions separately. For example, a mortgage company was able to reduce the processing time for 95 percent of their mortgages from three weeks to three minutes by separating the odd 5 percent, which require substantial additional checking, from the mainstream straight-through processing
- availability of real-time information – for example pricing of airline tickets is now on the basis of real-time availability of information
- integrate processes with suppliers, partners and clients
- reorganize your processes so that they are much more geared to dealing with customizations – for example Dell has its whole process geared towards customization
- use agent technology to trigger events on the basis of pre-defined situations – for example clients specifying the maximum amount they want to purchase for an airline ticket
- work with multiple vendors to develop a joint solution.

Remember to brainstorm and get lots of ideas first. At a later stage it will be possible to converge to suitable solutions.

Another dimension that can be reviewed, and is often discussed by organizations, is 'best practice'. This can be an excellent starting point for a project if an industry best practice can be found. Some commonly available best practices are the eTOM model (in the telecommunications industry), ITIL (for information technology) and SCOR (for supply chain management). However, be careful, because there will be a need to look at the 'best practice' in its entirety – not just the 'raw' process model or flow. What surrounds a process model can be as important as (or more important than) the actual process flow itself. Surrounding factors include the following: culture, performance measurement, people motivation, people empowerment, business rules, organization policies and so forth. Thus, it is important to customize these reference models and best practice models to the individual objectives and context of the organization. These reference models should have been reviewed in the Process architecture phase.

It can be extremely difficult and highly risky for a project team just to take a best practice process 'flow' and expect it to translate into success for the particular organization.

Once this initial step has been completed, start to bring the ideas together into groups and begin to apply the evaluation criteria developed and agreed earlier. This is where the left-brain logical thinking starts to be applied. As ideas and options are narrowed down, start to gain general acceptance of ideas and options. Start also to look at the feasibility of the options – at least at a high level. Detailed feasibility will come in the following steps. One of the key questions to ask is, how will these ideas meet stakeholder expectations/needs? This is because you must always ensure that the options take into account the ideas and thoughts from the external stakeholder focus group discussions. Obviously, they also need to satisfy the process goals established during the executive workshop.

As the Innovate process workshop is conducted, it can be useful to maintain an 'issues and opportunities' register to record items that must be dealt with, and opportunities to follow up. This register can be populated from the workshop scribe's notes. A sample register is provided in Appendix D.

The number of iterations or options developed for each process will depend upon the timeframes, constraints and width agreed in the executive workshop. Appendix E contains information about the organization of the workshop.

Workshop planning

The timeframes associated with each redesign scenario in the Innovate workshop should have been clearly agreed during the executive workshop.

Where timeframes of three and twelve months have been chosen, the participants in the workshops should be people from the business with the detailed knowledge of the process. Participants in the longer-term, twenty-four-month view, should include senior executives who are able to make decisions relating to more strategic issues, such as changes in the way business is conducted, changes in application systems, whether various methods of payment should be dropped from the payment options, and whether new methods of payment should be introduced, and similarly for the various distribution channels within the organization.

Innovate workshops are often significantly different from Understand workshops, as the discussion moves from recording what currently happens (Understand) to being creative and innovative (Innovate). This means that the workshop participants will generally comprise managers and decision-makers.

For specific details on how to run the Innovate workshops, refer to Appendix E.

Potential results

What results can you expect from these innovate workshops? Obviously, this will depend upon the organization; however, we provide here an example of the results we have experienced.

Once a new process option has been completed (or nearly completed), it is useful to conduct a 'what if?' walkthrough with the business, or even build a prototype if a technology solution is required.

Step 6: Future process metrics projections

Having completed the Innovate workshops and modeled the new processes, it is time to ensure that there is an understanding of the potential operational costs for these new processes and then validate them in relation to the business case. This is also the moment to look and see whether there are additional benefits and opportunities for the business.

This metrics analysis is not about the business case cost–benefit analysis, or the calculation of the cost of implementing the new processes. This is about projecting the potential ongoing operational costs for the business.

One way of approaching this costing is to allocate one or more workshops to the discussion of the expected new process timing for each individual process. This is about reviewing the current process and timing from the Understand phase and, if appropriate, comparing it to the new process to assist in the determination of expected process timings.

If the current process and timings are not applicable, estimates will need to be made of the expected process execution times. Simulation can sometimes be of assistance with this determination. The use of minutes as the common denominator for process metrics measurement will focus attention on the primary objective.

The next step is to extrapolate the expected future transaction volumes. If the option being considered is eighteen months in the future, then the business will need to estimate any increase or decrease in transaction volumes, by process.

The expected process timings can then be multiplied by the future transaction volumes to derive the future total processing minutes. This will be achieved by completing the spreadsheet shown in Figure 16.3 (the costing matrix).

The next step is a review of the departmental budget. The forecast budget is amended to allow costs to be calculated for the various Innovate scenarios selected:

1   Based upon the new resource utilization, the number of FTEs is forecast and a new staff cost calculated (total of salaries for the new number of FTEs). 'Other staff costs' are calculated on an FTE proportional basis.
2   'Other budget' costs are discussed with the business to identify which ones are impacted by a change in FTE count. These costs are proportioned based on the new FTE count. Remaining costs are adjusted according to the business input.
3   The current and the projected IT costs are assessed. An automated BPM solution could increase the IT costs; however, a more streamlined automated BPM solution can actually reduce IT costs. This occurs when inefficient and high maintenance systems can be replaced by better, more cost-effective solutions.

The level of process modeling and the recalculation of transaction volumes and times available will determine the accuracy of the cost allocations.

Thus, a new forecast budget is derived and used in the future process costing metrics analysis.

Step 7: Simulation

Simulation is one method of determining the feasibility and efficiency of the proposed redesigned process options. Simulation can also be used to test the logic and consistency of processes before their implementation.

It requires a significant amount of effort, and should not be underestimated or undertaken lightly. There will be a need to gather the necessary metrics and assumptions to run the simulations. Simulation is a good method to test the various scenarios – What if our demand doubles or quadruples? What if we increase the number of people in one area of the process? Various scenarios should be run to test the metrics and assumptions.

The simulated 'runs' should then be evaluated and, ultimately, activity-based costing and capacity planning estimates completed. This will assist in the determination of performance measurement for the process options.

Options should be narrowed down to the most feasible at this stage, and it is these options that should be 'workshopped' with the various stakeholders in the next step. Simulation allows – even requires – that many assumptions be made (for example, frequency and distribution of demand, effective work rates, number of errors and so on). It is crucial that these assumptions are documented and provided to the stakeholders, including the context in which they were determined.

The suggested solutions, together with supporting evidence, should be documented, and process models completed for distribution prior to the next workshops. A detailed example of how simulation can fit into the Innovate phase is provided in Appendix E's sample Innovate case study.

Step 8: People change management strategy

The completion of this step will significantly influence or direct the outcome of Step 9, as will the outcome of Step 9 influence Step 8 – potentially an iterative process between the two steps.

If, during the completion of this step, there are opportunities identified, then go back to the business to ask them to review the initial people change management constraints provided to the project.

Step 9: Update people capability matrix

Step 6 in the Understand phase discussed the need to create a people capability matrix. The matrix (Figure 16.4) needs to be reviewed, or created, for the future new process(es). This information will then be used in the People phase, to be compared with the matrix of the current people capabilities developed in the Understand phase. A gap analysis will also be completed and linked to individuals, with specific action plans (training or up-skilling), and potential changes to the organization structure.

Step 10: Capacity planning

Capacity planning can be useful from two different perspectives. First, it is about planning to ensure that the right number of rightly skilled people is available at the right time to meet customer and organization needs. Secondly, it will provide input into the establishment of the performance measurements goals to be established in the People phase for individuals, teams and management.

Rather than delve into this here, refer to the sample case study in Appendix E, which shows how capacity planning links with simulation, activity-based costing and work-routing.

Step 11: Workshop proposed solutions

The project team should have narrowed down the process options to a smaller number, and the purpose of the next set of workshops is to gather all the stakeholders together to determine whether the proposed options meet all the stakeholder needs. The stakeholders should include the following:

- business
- external stakeholders (distribution channels, vendors, suppliers, perhaps investors)
- compliance staff
- information technology
- operational risk
- internal audit
- (perhaps) external audit, depending upon the processes.

This is where the documented process options are presented, together with the outcomes of the various simulation runs, the activity-based costing scenarios and other supporting evidence.

All these stakeholders should probably not be involved in the one workshop, due to the potential competing requirements.

There is always a debate as to whether a process should be designed around the audit, compliance and risk requirements or not. We suggest that you should consider redesigning the process to be as efficient and effective as possible, to meet the business and primary stakeholder needs, and then consider the audit, compliance and operational risk requirements in a second pass. Audit, compliance and operational risk should not be driving the redesign, but also must not be ignored: the organization simply has to meet these requirements. Another approach is to outline the basic rules from an audit, compliance and operational risk perspective, and endeavor to include these in the process as it is designed.

We strongly recommended that the business and critical external stakeholders participate in the workshops to ensure that the redesigned processes meet their needs and are not fundamentally changed by other, competing requirements. Only once this has taken place should compliance, operational risk, and internal and external auditors be included.

However, sometimes compliance or operational risk is the initial driving force behind business process projects. We have seen this in several banks, where it has been compliance and operational risk that has provided the initial funding because of external requirements (such as Sarbanes Oxley). Once these requirements have been addressed, the business can then take an interest and expand the original projects to take a BPM improvement direction.

The outcomes of these workshops are the agreement and sign-off of the new process options to take forward to the feasibility step.

Step 12: Demonstrate and validate feasibility of proposed solutions

Further analysis is necessary to ensure that the redesigned options are operationally viable (or feasible):

- Will the new process be able to be supported from an IT perspective?
- Will the business be able to function efficiently and effectively as a result of the new process?

If the new process is to be automated, it is often an excellent idea to build a demonstration or prototype of the proposed process. Vendors often refer to this as a 'proof of concept'. If the process is to be manual, then walkthroughs within the business should be conducted. When conducting these automated demonstrations or walkthroughs, ask the 'testers' to come up with exceptions. Role-playing will assist here. Remember always to go back and evaluate the new options against the process goals agreed in the executive kick-off workshop.

It may be necessary, as a result of this step, to go back to the Innovate workshop step, if you find that some aspects of the process are not feasible or cannot be implemented.

Step 13: Process gap analysis

It is extremely useful to develop a gap analysis between the Understand and new Innovate processes. Waiting until the new process option has been selected during Steps 11 or 12 will save the development of several versions of this document. The purpose of completing this step is to provide a comparison between the new and the old processes for the business, IT department and developers of the training material. This analysis also provides an indication of the magnitude of change. The process gap analysis should cover the following topics for each process:

- a brief overview of the current process
- a brief overview of the new redesigned process
- key changes between the two
- process issues
- relevant metrics
- business and process impact comments
- new (business) opportunities
- required changes (for example, IT changes).

The process gap analysis should also comment upon training, occupational health and safety and organizational structural issues, and will assist in the change management aspects of the project. An example of a process gap analysis is included in Appendix E.

Step 14: Identify benefits and update business case

The initial business case written during the Launch pad phase will have identified some of the estimated benefits. During the Innovate phase of the project, after the redesign options have been finalized, there will be more detailed information available to enable the re-forecasting of the benefits in a more defined manner.

The business case should be able to be far more definitive at this stage because of the work completed during the simulation, activity-based costing and metrics steps: the benefits (for example, improved processes) and the costs (for example, implementation costs) are much clearer. (Sometimes, however, it is difficult to obtain the costs at this stage of the project. Once the new process options have been decided and the project progresses to the Develop phase, the development and implementation costs can be determined more accurately.)

These new costs and metrics will be able to be compared against the metrics gathered during the Understand phase. A comparison between the two (baseline Understand and Innovate) will provide quantifiable benefits for the redesigned processes. This will provide more robust evidence to support the business case. (Refer to Figure 21.5 for an example.)

Furthermore, the business case should aim for a smooth implementation and transition from project to business-as-usual operations. As much as possible, it should also include the known information regarding the proposed new operational situation and the impact upon the people.

Step 15: Report and presentations

This is where the reports and/or presentations are developed, to support the business case, for delivery to senior management for approval. Obviously approval is important, and every effort should be put into the development of the report and/or presentations. This presentation should have been planned and scheduled during the initial communications step, and be directed at the senior management or executives.

The purpose of the report is to provide the project status, outcomes and recommendations of the Innovate phase, and it should be supported by a professional presentation. This is the project team and project sponsor's opportunity to 'sell' the recommendations to the executive for funding (if not already approved).

Step 16: Approvals

This is the step where the organization approves the recommended options. Each organization will have its own process to follow for the approval of a business case, and this should have been clarified and taken into account during the Launch pad phase of the project.

Step 17: Business requirements

The writing of the business requirements is simply the further development of the documentation supporting the process models. This is to be provided to the Develop phase. It may be necessary to provide this to a separate implementation team and/or IT development team if systems development or changes are required.

Each organization will have its preferred method and required documentation, so we do not propose to define it here. Suffice to say, the documentation should be written from a business and process perspective.

In Appendix E, we have provided a detailed case study of how one organization went about substantially changing the way it conducted its business by changing business processes and reducing its operating costs significantly, using the activities outlined in this chapter.

The success of the Innovate phase will be judged not on the standard of the process models (do they follow the organization's agreed process architecture and model conventions?) and not on the efficiency or effectiveness of the process models 'on paper', but on how well they can be translated into implemented processes. Creating new process models can be great fun, but until they translate into implemented, efficient, effective and appropriate processes, adding value to the organization strategy, objectives and all stakeholders, they are just 'interesting' models. (In this instance, 'implementation' means: acceptance by the organization process execution staff, management, customers and all other relevant stakeholders. It means the cost-effectiveness of the implementation.)

Realize value

The benefits mix must be refined and optimized as part of this phase. For details, refer to Step 4 of Chapter 21, where it is described in the context of realizing value within a project.

Innovate phase outputs

The Innovate phase will provide valuable input into other phases of the framework (Figure 17.7), and we list a few examples here:

- knowledge may be gained that will be useful to the process architecture in modifying or enhancing the standards or guidelines for the organization
- opportunities may arise that provide feedback into modifying the organization strategy – for example, in-sourcing for processes where the organization is operationally excellent

- further knowledge of how to structure roles will unfold in the people phase
- innovation is the primary input into the Develop phase, and will provide more ideas on how the proposed changes may be implemented.

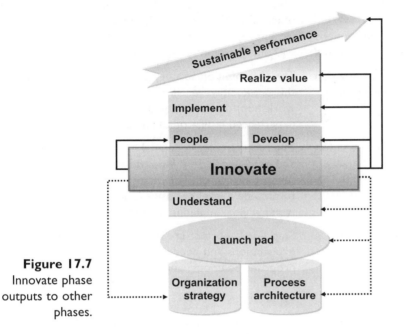

Figure 17.7
Innovate phase outputs to other phases.

Innovate phase risks

This phase provides an opportunity for innovation to occur; however, there are several risks that must be considered and mitigation strategies implemented to eliminate, or at least reduce them. These risks include those listed in Table 17.1.

Table 17.1
Innovate phase risks and mitigation strategies

Risk	Mitigation strategy
1 Unsure where to start	Follow this framework
2 The organization is too ambitious and tries too hard (that is, tries to make too many changes at once)	Step 2 – executive kick-off workshop needs to provide practical BPM process goals and scenarios. Experienced external facilitators can often ensure that the scope is practical without fear of internal conflict
	(Continued)

Table 17.1 (*Continued*)

Risk	Mitigation strategy
3 Too many innovate options are selected – for example, three-, six-, twelve- and twenty-four-month options for both automated and non-automated	Step 2 – executive kick-off workshop needs to provide practical BPM process goals. Experienced external facilitators can often ensure that the scope is practical without fear of internal conflict
4 The organization does not have a vision for the Innovate phase and is unable to establish process goals	The Organization strategy phase provides direction for this phase; however, it is Step 2 (executive kick-off workshop) that provides the detail. Again an experienced facilitator can assist in overcoming this risk
5 The scope for the Innovate phase is too small	The scope is initially defined in the Launch pad phase and is refined for the Innovate phase during Step 2 (executive kick-off workshop). The scope needs to provide a level of business benefits to make it worthwhile completing the project
6 Stakeholder expectations and needs are not considered	Step 4 is important in establishing stakeholder expectations and needs, and Steps 11 (work-shop proposed solutions) and 12 (demonstrate and validate feasibility of proposed solutions) need to revisit these expectations
7 BPM tool (or its vendor) is heading the innovation phase, leading to the business not being optimally supported	The business must lead the process innovation activities, perhaps being inspired by the opportunities that the BPM tool may provide

Case study: Experience from the motor vehicle industry

Examples of traditional and end-to-end process management can be found in the automotive industry process of bringing a new automobile into existence, and how the manufacturing process is conducted.

Traditionally, a simplistic view is that the design department will create the concept design of the new automobile. They then request the engineering department to create a detailed design, and obtain the engine and other appropriate parts. Procurement is then involved in sourcing the parts, and finally the factory manufactures it.

The Japanese (and a few other automobile manufacturers) have adopted a horizontal approach to this process. They have placed one person in charge of the entire process, from the creation to the building of the new automobile. This person has responsibility for the design, engineering, sourcing of parts, manufacturing and so forth, and is truly responsible for the end-to-end process of the new automobile. This individual must work through the 'matrix' reporting structure, while having the responsibility and power to 'make things happen'.

Message: Process management is far more effective when understood and managed from an end-to-end perspective.

Case study: It's the process that matters

One of the authors purchased a laptop computer about a year ago from a well-known, very large computer manufacturer. The carry bag fell apart for the second time, and when the manufacturer was contacted again it exceeded expectations by providing a new leather carry case at no cost as a 'sign of good faith'. However, the fact that he had to wait thirty minutes on the telephone, being transferred multiple times, and was then told that a 'manager' would call back in the next week or so, 'irritated' the author to a far greater extent than he'd been 'wowed' by having his expectations exceeded in getting a leather case for nothing.

Message: The organization must understand the difference between excellent service and customer satisfaction. The 'wow' factor can be easily wiped out by poor service.

Case study: Drive for reduced processing costs

A financial services organization was not meeting its processing SLAs by a long way (achieving less than 50 percent of what they should be), so staff and management were motivated to increase throughput with incentives. To address quality they introduced 100 percent checking, thinking that this would solve any quality issues.

The results were further reduced SLAs and a decrease in quality. An analysis of quality issues revealed the conflict between the need for speed and checking. The processing staff's aim was to process the transaction as quickly as possible, because if there were any errors they would be picked up by the checker. The checkers' view was that the original processor would have processed the transaction correctly, so it would only need a quick check.

These were not complex transactions, and errors should not have resulted from processing. In addition, the supporting workflow system did not have sufficient business rules and built-in knowledge, which only added to the quality issue.

Checking was costing the organization 24 percent of the overall processing costs, and yielding little benefit. There was a general lack of ownership and accountability across the processing staff and team leaders.

Message: By changing the culture to one of ownership and accountability, supported by feedback loops and appropriate performance measurement and rewards, great gains could have been made on quality (and reduced costs) at the same time – thus embedding quality in the process.

Case study: Government department

This organization was on the lowest level of BPM maturity, and unable to envision where it should be in two years time. A six-month horizon was all that could be agreed on and implemented at any one time. It also had no track record in the successful delivery of projects, and therefore lacked confidence in the organization's ability to succeed.

We worked with the organization towards the point of agreeing that workflow and imaging, in a very limited capacity, would be the six-month horizon. This would provide the foundations from which further improvement projects could be made once the organization was comfortable with this implementation and could focus on the next 'vision'.

Message: The options selected must match the organization's BPM maturity and ability to implement.

Case study: Financial services organization with a higher level of BPM maturity

A financial services organization had already installed a workflow system that was used in a very rudimentary manner. During the executive kick-off workshop, the managers understood clearly what a 'full' BPM implementation would entail and how they would benefit from it. They therefore set three scenarios that would potentially assist in building a business case and taking them on the journey to a 'full' BPM implementation:

1   Six months of quick wins with minimal system changes
2   Eighteen months with full BPM and image processing
3   Eighteen months with enhancements to the existing workflow system, no full BPM and no image processing.

The establishment of these three scenarios worked extremely well and, together with significant work on the metrics side, provided excellent information to carry forward and input into the business case.

Message: As the maturity of the organization increases, the options available, and their sophistication, will increase.

Case study: Government department and staff constraint

The organization embarked upon the implementation of a workflow and image processing system. The system was completed, worked well in the testing environment, and was implemented. The staff hated it and refused to use it, and the implementation failed.

There was no effort to involve the staff throughout the project. There was nothing wrong with the software; it was just that the change management issues were not addressed. The staff had never been measured or held accountable before, and they saw the implementation as a threat and refused to use it. The system was abandoned.

Message: If you do not handle the people issues (change management), then the risk of failure will be very high.

Case study: Toyota

Toyota is acknowledged as one of the, if not the most efficient, automobile manufacturers in the world. Many other automobile manufacturers have toured Toyota manufacturing plants, witnessed the 'process flows' and tried to emulate them. So why does Toyota continue to be the best?

It is not just about copying the 'process flow'. Toyota has a complex number of aspects to its production techniques. The company has goals for its customers, employees and itself, which are supported by detailed strategies and continuous improvement programs. This is a way of life for Toyota and its employees, not just a one-time project.

Unless other manufacturers can emulate the 'entire' system and culture, they will not be able to 'copy' Toyota's best practice.

Message: World's best practice is a complex thing, and is not easily duplicated.

Case study: Human touchpoints significantly reduced

This client wanted two scenarios for the Innovate workshops: first, a non-automated and six-month horizon; and secondly, an automated and twelve-month horizon. The end-to-end high-level process model was redesigned to move from a reactive to a proactive basis. The number of processes redesigned was thirteen, and they were consolidated into seven processes during the workshops. In this particular example, the improvements were measured by the reduction in human touchpoints associated with the processes (see table below).

Number of original touchpoints, and reductions achieved

Process	Original	Non-automated	Automated
1	53	23 (57%)	9 (83%)
2	15	15 (0%)	1 (93%)
3	46	46 (0%)	5 (89%)
4	47	18 (62%)	17 (64%)
5	4	4 (0%)	1 (75%)
6	14	10 (29%)	1 (93%)

The reason for using human touchpoints was that the timeframe allowed for the workshops did not provide sufficient time for metrics analysis – which is not an ideal situation. However, the potential reduction in human involvement in the process was impressive.

While we understand that 'touchpoint' measurement need not translate into time and cost savings for the organization, it does show a significant reduction in the handling by the people in the organization, due to the removal of redundancy. Since the people involved in the process were professional, high-salaried people, the costs and customer service did improve dramatically.

Message: Analysis without supporting detailed metrics is very difficult to justify in a business case. An analysis of process 'touchpoints', while indicative, is not enough to justify funding. Always insist on having enough time for detailed metrics analysis.

Case study: Financial services organization

Business drivers for process innovation were the following:

- an inability to meet service levels
- issues with quality
- an inability to provide 'tiered' levels of service.

(Continued)

Case study: Financial services organization (*Continued*)

After following the framework and detailed metrics analysis, the organization understood that a phased implementation towards BPM and image processing would yield a reduction in their annual operational budget of 40 percent and an FTE reduction of 45 percent.

Message: Without the detailed metrics analysis, it would have been difficult to quantify the overall potential for budget reduction and provide sufficient business case detailed analysis (on the benefits side of the equation) to justify the way forward.

Chapter 18

People phase

Why?

The People phase (Figure 18.1) is a crucial phase in any BPM process implementation, and unless it is handled thoroughly and to a high standard, the rest of the project will be put at risk. It is important to understand clearly that this is different from the Implement phase, which focuses on the roll-out of the solution. The People phase will usually be conducted at the same time as the Develop phase of the project. The Develop phase creates the automated (or otherwise) solution, and People phase creates the roles and people measurement solutions.

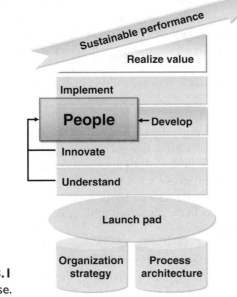

Figure 18.1
People phase.

The purpose of this phase is to ensure that the activities of the individuals who will be executing the new processes are in alignment with the agreed organization and process goals established in earlier phases of the project.

At the end of the day, it is people that will make processes function effectively and efficiently, no matter how much they are automated. If you do not get the people 'on board' with the project and new processes, then they will find a way to ensure that the processes either do not work or do not work efficiently.

(Note: While this statement is true, it has to be balanced with commercial reality, and we will cover this later in Step 4 of this chapter.)

This phase is where business staff and management have their job goals defined and job descriptions redesigned or created. The manner in which their performance will be measured and managed will also be changed or developed to match these process goals and organization structure. It provides the opportunity for the organization to make the roles more interesting and to increase the employability of the people. This relates not only to internal employability (ensuring that the people are capable of performing multiple roles, which means that they can continue with the organization in a variety of roles) but also to external employability (boosting the confidence of staff as well as helping in the transition where retrenchment or outsourcing occurs).

The results of this phase *must* work: failure is not an option. The phase is not a mechanical set of steps that the project just has to work through; it is where the project team needs to spend as much time as is necessary to ensure that the results are successful.

Results

How will you know that this phase has been effective? By the way people react to the change, changed roles, new processes and new role performance management and measurement targets. Sure, there are a number of practical steps and documents to produce during this phase, but at the end of the day it is the people who will show, by their behavior, whether or not this phase has been successful.

Some of the activities and reports that will be produced during this phase include the following:

1   The dissection and amalgamation of the new processes and their component tasks into activities.
2   Redesigned role descriptions and goals that have been discussed and agreed with the people who will be executing them.
3   Performance management and measures for appropriate roles, which have also been discussed and agreed with the people who will be executing them.
4   A plan and set of tasks to enable the organization to 'transform' from where it currently is to where it needs to be. This will include a thorough understanding of the existing and future core competencies and capabilities of the people, at a role level. This will be overlaid on

the process gap analysis produced earlier to enable the appropriate training plan to be developed for individuals and teams of people.

5   A new process-based organization structure for the business area involved in the project.

How?

Many organizations and managers are quick to criticize and blame the people for the lack of performance in an organization. In our experience, this is rarely the fault of the personnel on the 'workshop floor' who execute the processes. An organization should approach an improvement program in the following sequence:

1   *Processes* – get the processes efficient and effective and adding value to the organization strategy
2   *Structure* – get the roles and structure right, or as close to right as you can, to support the new processes
3   *People* – only after the processes and structure steps have been addressed and implemented can you evaluate their performance.

. . . if you put a good performance against a bad system, the system will win almost every time.

(Keen, 1997: 65)

In all the organizations we have consulted with over the years, we have predominantly found that the people executing the processes are good people, doing the best they can with the systems and processes with which they have been provided by management. In many cases, these people do exceptional jobs, putting in long and dedicated hours to service customers. It is management's responsibility to provide these people with the environment and 'tools' (processes, infrastructure, systems) to complete their job in an effective and efficient manner.

At the project level, in order to meet the agreed process goals, the organization will need to design roles to support the processes and sub-processes and ensure that the work environment is structured to enable people to maximize their contribution.

Even if the organization has their structure optimized, people are the ones who execute the processes and make things happen. Without them, you have nothing.

The areas that must be covered during the People phase of the project are the following: a decision on how to execute this phase; the establishment of activities, roles or jobs and performance measurements for the people who are executing the process(es); the establishment of measurements for the people executing the process(es); and taking care that the interface between the process(es) is managed to ensure that there are no 'gaps'. This assumes that you have provided an appropriate level of resources and that they have been allocated appropriately to enable the people to be effective and efficient.

The steps associated with the People phase of the project are shown in Figure 18.2.

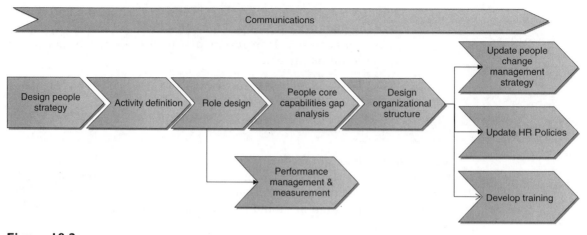

Figure 18.2
People phase steps.

Step 1: Communications

As this phase revolves around the people in the organization, it is clearly best to have them involved and informed of the process. Expect to be asked the following:

- What is proposed?
- How will it be completed?
- How will it affect me?
- What input will I have into the outcomes?
- What if I do not like the outcomes?

These are just some of the questions that will need to be answered. The project team will need to ensure that it has a proactive approach to communicating with the business and the affected people.

Step 2: Design people strategy

While the project team must take accountability for the delivery of this step, the human resources department of the organization should be significantly involved in the strategizing and planning of how the People phase of the project will be approached (the people strategy). However, HR's involvement will be influenced by the BPM project scenario selected. If an 'under the radar' scenario is selected, then the way HR is involved may be impacted. The strategy must take into account the HR work practices and constraints. If the organization is unionized or there is a Worker's Council, this will also have a significant influence on the approach to this phase.

The agreed strategy must then be documented and signed off by the appropriate stakeholders. These stakeholders may include the following: management and leadership, unions, the people themselves, and perhaps even customers and suppliers. It is counterproductive to reorganize in a way that the customers or suppliers will not support.

Step 3: Activity definition

First, let's examine what comprises an 'activity'. An activity may be an entire process or parts (tasks) of a process. Either way, an activity must contribute, or add value, to the process goals established and documented earlier in the project. An activity (collection of tasks) must be clearly defined and communicated to the people who will be executing the tasks, to ensure that they understand what is expected of them, how well they are expected to perform the tasks, and with what aim they are expected to do this (the 'how well' is covered in Step 5).

The process models created during the Innovate phase will show the tasks associated with each process, so reviewing these models is an essential step in creating the definition of the activities.

This step is about collecting process tasks into appropriate activities, as shown in Figure 18.3.

Step 4: Role redesign

Once you are satisfied that the task groupings into activities are correct, then you can start to group the activities into generic 'roles'. We have called them

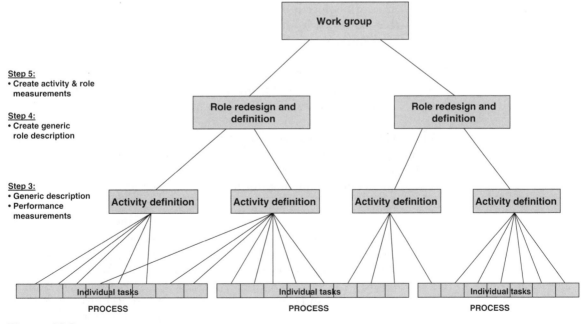

Figure 18.3
Activity, job and structure creation.

roles, rather than jobs, because they are of a generic nature at this point, and the word 'job' seems to imply a specific role for an individual.

At this step of the People phase, a role is defined at a higher level than the individual person or job description; it is a generic role, such as receipting clerk or claims assessor. (Note: We recognize that a particular person's 'job' may comprise several roles, depending upon the size of the organization or department; however, in the example provided we have assumed that this is not the case.)

This may be an iterative process of grouping the various activities into roles, discussing them with management and the people who will be involved in their execution, and then regrouping them, until you and all the stakeholders are satisfied with the outcome of the new role definitions.

Once this has been achieved, you are in the position to write the new role description. Most large organizations have their own templates for a role description, and we will not provide examples here. We will, however, mention a couple of specific process-related considerations.

It is worth taking a few moments to show some of the key components that must be addressed during the creation of activities and roles. The well-known RACI (or RASCI or RASIC) model is a useful method of helping to identify activities, roles and responsibilities during the People phase of a project (www.valuebasedmanagement.net/methods_raci.html, accessed July 2005). This model helps to describe clearly what should be done by whom to make a new process able to be executed by the people.

RACI/RASCI is an abbreviation for:

- R = *Responsibility* – the person who owns the problem or activity
- A = to whom 'R' is *Accountable* – who must sign off (Approve) the work before it is effective
- (S = *Supportive* – can provide resources or other information in a supporting role in the completion of the process or activity)
- C = to be *Consulted* – has information and/or capability that is necessary to complete the process or activity
- I = to be *Informed* – must be notified of the results of the process or activity, but need not be consulted during execution.

These key components (as abbreviations) can be shown in a chart for a particular generic role. Table 18.1 is an example of how five roles interact with the generic role.

The sequence in completing this table is as follows:

1 Identify all the activities as defined in Step 3 (activity definition) of the People phase, and list them on the vertical axis
2 Identify all the likely future roles, list them on the horizontal axis and complete the cells in the table with an R, A, S, C, I for each activity
3 Resolve gaps and overlaps. The situation could occur where there are no 'Rs', multiple 'Rs' or no 'As' for an activity. As a general rule, *every activity should have only one R and at least one A*. These need resolution or completion.

Table 18.1
Sample RASCI model

	Business unit manager	Manager	Business unit head	Team leader	Compliance advisor
Activity 1	R		A		
Activity 2	A	R		S	C
Activity 3	RA		I		I
Activity 4	RA				C
Activity 5	A	R		S	

In reviewing the generic roles of people, the organization has a unique opportunity for management not only to empower staff and make people's jobs more interesting, but also to reward them in more interesting ways (other than financial) and provide promotional opportunities. The more this can be taken into account, the easier it will be for this to be 'sold' to people and therefore implemented.

Most role descriptions must include authority levels, policies and procedures, allocation of responsibilities and environmental considerations. However, a process-related role description must also include performance measures for each part of the end-to-end process or sub-process, which brings us to Step 5.

Step 5: Performance management and measurement

There is a frequently stated comment in process work – 'You get what you measure'. Without measurement you are not managing, whereas if you measure at least the critical parts of the process, and use that information in an intelligent way, then the results will be significantly enhanced.

Performance management covers both the performance of the individual process(es) and the performance of the people. In this chapter, we will be covering the people aspects only, and will discuss the process performance in the Sustainable performance phase chapter.

Louis Gerstner (2002) said that 'since people don't do what you *ex*pect but what you *in*spect . . . you need to create a way to measure results.'

Before you can start people performance management and measurement, there needs to be a clear understanding of the capacity of the business unit or organization. Is the business unit over- or understaffed, or are the staff numbers at the correct level? The reason for completing the capacity planning models, in this context, is to ensure that the performance targets established by management are realistic and do not exceed the capacity of the available staffing levels to deliver. Capacity planning will have been completed during the Innovate phase, and the outcomes should be referenced.

The creation of a performance management system and performance measures throughout the organization is a critical step. If not implemented

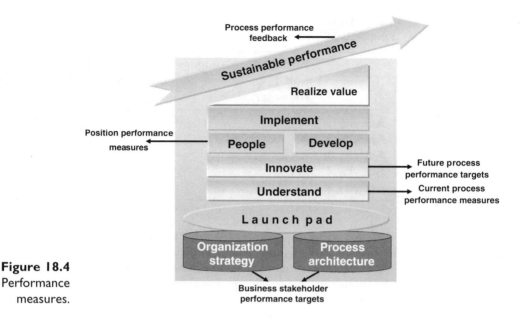

Figure 18.4
Performance
measures.

correctly, BPM will not be as successful as it could have been. The general BPM literature states that it is critical that the performance measures for all people (leadership, senior executives, managers and process execution people) be linked to the organization strategy, targets and process goals. If these links are not tight, then performance and outcomes will become fragmented. In practice, we have found that it is only about the first three levels of management that should have their KPIs directly linked to organization strategy (balanced score card). Cascading the BSC all the way down the organization does not work. The lower levels of the organization staff need simple goals, such as the number of widgets produced per day. Obviously, these can be created in such a way that they add to the organization strategy and objectives.

Figure 18.4 shows that performance measurement is not something that can wait until this phase before it commences; it must be started at the very beginning of a project and considered at every phase, as follows:

- *Organization strategy and Process architecture phases* – obtain a clear understanding of the required outcomes and objectives of the stakeholders. These must be met by the ongoing performance of the people and process(es), and contribute towards these outcomes and objectives. *If the organization's strategy is linked to individual's performance measures, performance bonus' and ability to be promoted, a powerful synergistic relationship is created.* This can be achieved by a BSC approach.
- *Understand phase* – obtain a clear understanding of the current performance measures and how successful they are, and any lessons to be learned from their implementation.
- *Innovate phase* – capacity planning is completed and will contribute towards establishing the future performance targets or goals; targets will be established as part of the process goal-setting.

- *People phase* – all the information collected will be brought together to link to the performance targets established for individual people, teams and management.
- *Sustainable performance phase* – the performance management system will become part of 'what we do around here'. It will become sustainable by continual feedback and improvement.

Our advice is to start performance management and measurement with a few measures only, and to keep them simple. If necessary, the number and complexity of management reports and measures can grow with time and experience. Obviously, these measures must not be in conflict with the goals of other processes and departmental measures. In practice, this is a critical and difficult implementation issue.

Once the new roles and their related activities are understood by the people, you are in a position to set the performance measures. These usually take the form of KRAs and KPIs (Kaplan and Norton, 1996) (KRAs are key result areas and KPIs are key performance indicators).

Measuring role performance is useless unless the organization ensures that people understand why the measures established are important to the organization.

When establishing role description performance measures, you must ensure that they satisfy, and add value to, the process goals and organization strategy. This obviously includes the needs of the various process stakeholders.

It is management's role to create an environment where people can perform effectively. For this to occur, people must have a clear understanding and agreement as to their role and how their performance in that role will be measured. They need to have a written and well-communicated role description, clarity of the performance levels expected from them, and a feedback mechanism. It is management's role to provide these.

We have been in organizations on many occasions where the people do not clearly understand their roles, what is expected of them and how they are being measured. *If you do not understand the rules of the game, how can you be expected to play well, let alone win?!* This seems such a basic and fundamental step, and yet organizations continually fail to complete this well. This can often be a large part of the process problems.

Furthermore, it is also management's role to *listen* to the people who are executing the processes. The people are the experts and knowledge holders who will provide excellent suggestions for process improvement. Management should provide the spark of inspiration for ideas outside the detailed level that the people work in. Management must constantly review processes themselves, or establish mechanisms (internal and external) for this to take place. This will be covered in more detail within the Sustainable performance phase.

It is worthwhile at this point to stop and place all of this in perspective. While consultation with and inclusion of the people executing the processes is essential if the desire is to create a 'process factory', *it is not a democracy.* Management needs to make decisions about 'how things need to get done around here', and people are the ones who execute them. It is appropriate for management to say 'no' to the people who execute the processes – just make sure the people are informed why the answer is 'no', which will provide more insight on what the organization requires. Once management decisions have been made, people are not in a position to wake up one morning and decide that today they are going to execute the process in a different way. This would ultimately lead to process and operational chaos at worst, or ineffective and inefficient processes at best.

After *all* these needs have been established, it is imperative that management uses the performance management and measurement information in the correct way. It should never be used as punishment. It should always be used as a means of coaching and enhancing performance, and improving the decision-making ability, of management and the people.

In fact, ideally managers should not be the ones to provide the performance measurement reporting to the people; it should come directly, or be available, to the people themselves. People must be able to measure their own performance. This will enable them to be able to remedy any situation, in a proactive way, before it becomes a management or business issue.

People should never be surprised with any performance measurement information coming from management.

This performance measurement information should be readily available to all people within the business unit or process team. A little competition, by making the team goals and all individual team members' performance visible, is an important management technique.

The very last question that management should ask is, are the individual people up to the tasks allocated to them? Management should not 'jump to conclusions' about the capability of staff until all the prior points have been addressed.

Example of performance management

Here is an example of how the performance measurement might work within an organization. This example is based upon an actual implementation within a financial services organization.

An organization completed a review of its processes, the competency requirements of the people required to execute them and capacity planning of the business unit. It was decided to create new roles (not more people) to provide more focus on the desired performance outcomes. Two new roles were created: a relationship specialist and a specialist administration role. Previously, a single role had covered both these two roles of relationship and administration activities.

Process activities were examined and new job descriptions were drawn up to reflect the processes to be completed and the desired outcomes. The new suggested performance targets were to continue to be based on a BSC approach that the organization already employed. The targets at the lower levels would add towards the achievement of targets at the next higher level, and cumulatively upwards (for example, administration staff targets would add to team leader's targets; team leader's targets to manager's targets and so forth). Figure 18.5 shows an example of this approach.

The capacity planning assisted management and staff to understand that the targets set for the various roles were realistic and achievable, as the business unit was not over- or understaffed. The performance targets were to reflect throughput and quality, and each of these is discussed separately here.

Figure 18.5
Pyramid of
performance targets.
(Reproduced with
the permission of
MPM Group Pty Ltd,
trading as
TouchPoint Process
Management
Services.)

Figure 18.6
Sample throughput
and service targets.
(Reproduced with
the permission of
MPM Group Pty Ltd,
trading as
TouchPoint Process
Management
Services.)

A suggested structure and approach for the administration role and the associated performance targets is shown in Figure 18.6. This was reviewed to ensure that it was in alignment with the organization strategy and objectives, and departmental objectives and goals. Targets for the administration role included both individual and team targets. The individual targets, for example, would be the number of work units processed within a defined time period. A unit of work (or work unit) was set at fifteen minutes. The reason for using 'work units' instead of a 'number of transactions' completed per time period was that it provided a means of overcoming the difference in processing times between various transaction types – for example, some transactions required fifteen minutes to process, while others took several hours.

The 'work unit' approach required that each transaction type be examined to determine the number of work units of effort to process it. Much of this information was available from the project work completed during the Understand and Innovate phases. For example, process A was 1.25 work units and transaction type B was 2.5 work units. All processes were rounded to the nearest 0.25. Using a standard effective day of 6.25 hours, this equated to 25 work units per day per person. (Staff worked an 8:30 am to 5:00 pm day, which is 8.5 hours; allowing 1 hour for lunch and 0.25 hours for morning and afternoon breaks, and an allowance for bathroom breaks and other activities, the organization settled on a 6.25-hour effective day.)

At a detailed level, in the case study organization, the administration role and team were given the following targets:

- number of work units per week to be achieved = 135. This was 25 per day (6.25 hours divided by 15 minutes) or 125 per week; the additional 10 were established as a stretch target. When the individual was involved in team meetings, training courses and so forth, this time was recorded and counted towards the number of work units.
- there were 10 team members and the team leader established a target of 10 times the 135, or 1350, work units, per week for the team. The team target encouraged staff to help other members of their team who may have been struggling because of inexperience or being flooded with work, and the team to reach its targeted process goal percentage of 90 percent.
- quality targets were also established at individual and team levels. Individuals were initially allowed a small allowance for processing errors per week (this progressed to zero tolerance for errors with experience), but the team as a whole was allowed zero 'external' errors. In other words, team members had to check each others' work to ensure that 'zero' errors reached customers or other stakeholders.

Targets for team leaders included the following:

- the same team targets as the administration role, to encourage the management of the team in a way that benefits everybody (the organization, management, team leaders, team members).
- meeting the process goal timeframes in 90 percent of cases, which ensured that team leaders would manage their teams proactively to ensure that the workload was spread evenly to avoid backlogs
- a target to meet the process goals of the overall department, which encouraged cooperation between team leaders in the same department.

This accumulation and building of targets proceeded up the hierarchy to each level of management.

To raise the level of quality within the organization, staff were to ensure that errors were always routed back to the staff member who caused them in the first place. This would provide feedback to the person on his or her performance. No additional work units were to be credited for the rework.

Team members recorded their performance on a daily basis, and had access to other team members' performance reports and the team performance report on a continual basis.

The team leader and team members also had access to a report that provided information on the number of transactions in the pipeline and any

Transaction type	Brought forward	New transactions	Completed transactions		Carried forward (days left in SLA)				
			within SLA	OOS	OOS	1	3	5	10

Figure 18.7
Process performance report. (Reproduced with the permission of MPM Group Pty Ltd, trading as Touch-Point Process Management Services.)

backlog. This was needed to ensure that the process goals were met. The data needed to measure the above throughput targets were included in the report shown in Figure 18.7.

These data were available for any given time period, by person, team, department and division.

For each transaction type the information included the following:

1   The number of transactions brought forward from the last period
2   The number of transactions received during the period (new transactions)
3   The number of transactions completed during the period that met the respective SLAs (process goals) were Out of Standard (OOS)
4   The number of transactions carried forward into the next period, including the number of days left in the SLA (process goals) or whether it was already out of standard.

It should always be remembered that performance targets only provide benefit if they are recorded, if feedback is provided to all performers, and if the outcome is measured and rewarded.

Step 6: People core capabilities gap analysis

This step is where the project starts to address the capability of the people. The completion of this matrix will have been commenced earlier in the Understand phase, and it must now be updated and finalized. We described the completion of this matrix in Chapter 16, but we will remind you again. The matrix is designed to assist the project team and business in determining the gap analysis between the skills that the people currently have and need for the existing processes, and the skills that are required in the new processes and resulting activities and roles. Obviously the HR department must be intimately involved in this step, as it should in this entire phase.

While the above mentioned matrix represents the capabilities required in the new roles, a similar matrix must also be completed showing the current capabilities of the people executing the processes.

If the selected course of action is to train or provide on-the-job coaching for existing people, do not underestimate how long it may take to change attitudes and behaviors. Considerable effort, time and resource should be devoted to this activity.

Step 7: Design organization's structure

This step is to redesign the organization's structure, and the first activity is to place this in perspective. Organization structures are usually created in one of several ways, and these can be linked back to the selected BPM implementation scenario. The four possible scenarios for the implementation of BPM were described as:

- business as usual
- in the driver's seat
- pilot project
- under the radar.

Only the first and second scenarios are likely to have any immediate impact on the organization's structure; the others are more likely to impact the wider structure of the organization over time.

Figure 18.8 shows how an organization's structure can be created.

It shows that the organization's structure is usually created in two sections. The CEO determines the upper echelons of the organization – his or her direct reports and the areas of responsibility. These areas of responsibility might be broken down by product, customers, distribution channels and so forth. The direct reports then determine the next level down and so on. This component of the structure is about service and reporting lines, and may or may not relate to the organization's processes. It is referred to as being 'top down'.

The lower half of the organization may be created either from the 'bottom up' (based upon a process-centric approach) or from 'middle down' approach (based upon the CEO and their direct reports deciding the structure, usually on a functional basis). The middle-down method is the usual

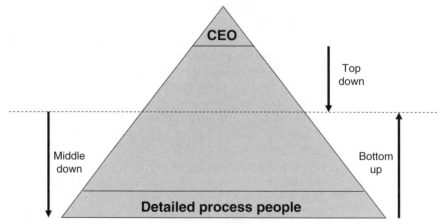

Figure 18.8
Organization's structure creation.

way an organization's structure is created, whereas a process-centric organization will favor the 'bottom up' approach. In the 'bottom up' approach, it is important to start with a decomposition of the processes into activities (as described in Step 3 onwards). There is then a need to distinguish between the 'core' processes of the organization and the 'supporting' and 'strategic' or 'management' processes, with the roles and structure reflecting this split.

Functionally based organizational structures create a tension between various organizational departments or business units, because processes are end-to-end and cross departmental boundaries. To assist in overcoming this tension many organizations today are creating matrix-based organization structures, where functional managers are responsible for the traditional areas of sales, manufacturing, marketing and so on and process managers are responsible for the value chain or high-level end-to-end processes. Where this is the case, there needs to be a facilitated communications process that allows conflicts to be resolved.

Process managers usually have a hierarchy that allocates responsibility from the high-level processes and value chains, down to the sub-processes. The role of a chief process officer is to coordinate all the process managers. Where matrix organizational structures have been created, it is essential that the reward and compensation systems are linked to the structure.

In all cases, the organization's structure is about ensuring that:

- the proposed new structure is designed to support the organization strategy and process goals; and
- process gaps between departments are minimized – they will never be eliminated, but there is a great deal that can be achieved in minimizing them. In a true end-to-end process redesign and process-centric organization structure, these process gaps should be non-existent – or very close to it.

The way to achieve this is to approach organization structure creation as a process. Complete a high-level model and then progressively model the restructured organizational design in more detail. Complete a new organizational relationship model to ensure that the process gaps are minimized as much a possible.

The organizational chart should

- minimize departmental interfaces
- maximize process effectiveness and efficiency
- minimize the layers of management
- most importantly, maximize clarity.

It is important not to get too carried away with getting the new structure perfect. While you should do everything you can to get it right, this is less important than you think, so long as you address all nine components in the Rummler, Brache, Harmon performance framework discussed previously (Harmon, 2003). Organizational structure can, however, be significant in the working of an organization if it is obviously wrong, as it can cause process and management disconnects (from a process perspective). It is more important to get things right at the 'bottom' of the organization's structure, because this is where organization's 'get the work done'.

Remember that structure follows strategy and process redesign. As part of the process of determining the ideal organizational structure, the new redesigned process environment must be considered, including how it is to be measured and managed. In fact, the way the processes are to be measured may well provide the answer as to how the organization should be structured. In an operations area, the management exists to 'manage' the processes and people, requiring the ability to measure both process and people performance.

Process-centric structured organizations are more difficult to manage because the degree of management skill required is higher. Management need to pay substantial attention to performance measurement, motivation, rewards and culture.

There is no one right solution for an organization's structure; it will depend upon the requirements and circumstances of each organization. However,

> there is clearly a wrong solution. The wrong solution places all the power and control with departmental managers and creates incentives for managers based on departmental goals. This almost always results in sub-optimization of overall process improvement and corporate performance.
>
> (Harmon, 2005b)

Organizations have to be adaptable and flexible in order to survive in the long term in the current environment, where change is happening faster and faster. An organization's structure should therefore be fluid and capable of changing in an agile way, continually adapting to the business environment and organization demands.

Step 8: Update people change management strategy

The people change management strategy may require updating as a result of the outcomes from the role design, people core capabilities gap analysis and a redesign of the organizational structure, as undertaken in the previous steps. A change in any of these aspects may require significant consultation and collaboration with the people within the business, and indeed, other stakeholders outside the immediate sphere of influence.

As a minimum, the communications strategy will need updating as well as its execution.

Step 9: Update HR policies

Once all the above details have been finalized, the various policy and procedural manuals, job families/groups (roles), remuneration structures and other HR documentation must be updated or written. When considering how to approach the development of these policies, consider the use of a process modeling tool to attach the new process models to the policies and procedures documentation at the appropriate points. This documentation could then be made available over the organization's intranet. Other documentation that may require updating might include remuneration incentive schemes; these must be tied directly to performance measurement and customer satisfaction.

Step 10: Develop training

During the Understand phase, the organization will have started to identify the information and knowledge needs and to build a capability matrix, which is then extended and completed in the core capability gap analysis step in this phase. These should now be further utilized to develop the training strategy and plan.

It is best to always ensure that, as soon as possible, the training department is engaged in and fully informed of the new activity definitions and role description changes that are taking place. Obviously training and HR need to liaise on a continual basis and should assist in this process.

The activity here is to plan and write the training requirements from a process perspective. The systems training written during the Develop phase will provide input into this step.

To complete the development of the training, the organization will also need to complete the following:

- a training needs analysis
- a training media analysis (how will training be documented and delivered?)
- training material development
- population of just-in-time training vehicles – it is no use training people well ahead of time and then having them forget the lessons learned.

The development of a process gap analysis between the current processes, modeled during the Understand phase, and the new processes, developed and modeled during the Innovate phase, is extremely useful in developing the training requirements. (Refer to Step 13, process gap analysis, in the Innovate phase, Chapter 17, for more detail.)

Activities to consider during the development of the training include the following:

1   How is the training to be delivered –

- by professional trainers?
- by trained 'super' users from within the business (this has benefits because of their specialist knowledge of the business and processes, and will allow the internal trainers to go on to be 'coaches' during the Implement phase)?

- via a pilot(s) training session(s), using this as an opportunity to gain feedback and provide 'train the trainer' skills?
- Training should include the 'gaps' discovered during the people core capability matrix gap analysis.

2 Who should be involved in developing the training –

- project team?
- HR and training departments?
- process staff representatives (those who execute the processes)?
- management?

3 What format should be used –

- classroom?
- on-line computer-based self-study?
- on-the-job training?
- paper-based self-study?

Ensure that the initial training sessions and material include feedback forms that can be used to improve the training as it is rolled out across the organization. Training staff and coaches should also provide feedback.

Realize value

Benefits must be defined in detail in order to gain agreement as part of this phase. For details refer to Step 5 of Chapter 21, where it is described in the context of realizing value within a project.

People phase outputs

The People phase will provide valuable input into other phases of the framework (Figure 18.9), including the following few examples:

- working through the performance measurement could indicate that changes are required in the new processes, which will provide feedback, and possible rework, in the Innovate phase
- how the roles, performance management systems and training are designed will have an impact upon how they are to be implemented; they could also impact how the benefits are to be realized
- the way the performance management systems have been established will impact their sustainability.

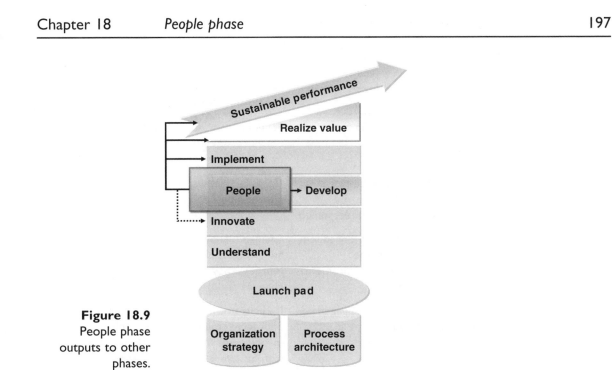

Figure 18.9
People phase
outputs to other
phases.

People phase risks

In this phase there are several risks that must be considered and mitigation strategies implemented to eliminate (or at least reduce) them. These risks include those listed in Table 18.2.

Table 18.2
People phase risks and mitigation strategies

	Risk	Mitigation strategy
1	Communications to people within the organization is not adequate	Communication is the responsibility of the project manager, who should seek the assistance of HR and communications specialists within the organization and the business. People and stakeholders should be fully informed at all times
2	Judging the performance of people within the organization before the process and structural issues have been addressed	Define the processes, new roles, understand and update the people capability matrix, provide appropriate and targeted training and create performance measures and implement them, before the people are evaluated regarding their performance
		(Continued)

Table 18.2   (*Continued*)

	Risk	Mitigation strategy
3	Capacity planning is not complete	Schedule this into the project plan and convince stakeholders and management of its importance
4	Staff performance targets are unrealistic, as the business unit is understaffed	Capacity planning will provide this information
5	People not being consulted or engaged in the performance measurement establishment	Change management is a critical aspect to any project. Unless people are part of the journey, they may refuse to accept the changes and use them
6	HR is not being engaged early enough or at all	If HR is not involved, the impact, rework and delay could be considerable. HR's involvement must be a task in the project plan at a very early stage. Allocate the responsibility for this, and the project manager is to ensure that the task is achieved. Provide as much notice as possible to HR of their required time involvement

Case study: Scope creep results in missing HR component

We were called into an organization that had commenced to make minor adjustment to its processes. We found that while doing this project, the organization had identified more and more improvement opportunities by restructuring and changing the current processes, which it had begun to implement.

Although the proposed changes were excellent improvements, they had completely ignored the people aspects of new processes and increased the scope of the project. As a result, the HR manager was a strong opponent of their implementation because the changes undermined basic principles that had been established within his department for the last ten years. The result was that the new processes had to be redeveloped taking these basic principles into account. Valuable momentum had been lost.

Message: Always involve HR in the new process development prior to implementation, to ensure that all 'people' aspects have been taken into account.

Case study: HR manager support

We undertook a new project to fundamentally review the existing processes in an organization, and conducted stakeholder interviews to obtain stakeholders' points of view and their personal drivers. The HR manager mentioned that his biggest personal driver was to be more engaged with the business on HR issues. He wanted to be able to be more demand-driven by the business, rather than continually pushing his own ideas.

During the Innovate phase, we worked with the various stakeholders and were able to ensure that the new processes related to the required competences. These competences were linked to function, job profile and training programs, as well as the performance measurement. This approach ensured not only that the HR manager's issues were included in the processes, but also that the employees could easily relate to these competences and what was required (including training modules) to perform other tasks.

Message: Integration of all aspects (role definition, training, performance measurement, processes and desired outcomes/objectives) is crucial, and the business and HR departments must work closely together.

Chapter 19

Develop phase

We have stressed in this book that a BPM project need not involve a technology solution in order to be successful, and in fact in Chapter 3 we argued that it is important to improve business processes before automating them. The Develop phase (Figure 19.1) therefore includes the steps necessary to

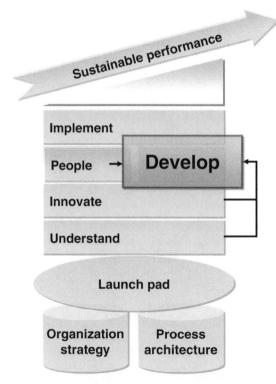

Figure 19.1
Develop phase.

take the newly redesigned or improved processes from the Innovate phase to the Implement phase and deployment. We will not describe the standard development steps in details, as most of these steps will be generally obvious to a project team. We will concentrate here on describing the development of an automated BPM solution (that will have been selected in the previous phases) and the specific topics around an automated BPM solution versus a 'standard' automated solution.

This is the phase where the preparations must be completed and the solution prepared. It is then followed by the Implement phase. It is important to understand that 'develop' in this context should be completed in parallel with the People phase in which the people component is elaborated.

Care should be taken when developing a new system: it should provide sufficient flexibility to meet business changes in the near future and over its lifetime, and to cater for the frequent changes of the business processes. Furthermore, it is important to understand that during the time it takes to develop the BPM system during this phase, the business processes can also change. The development methodology used must be able to accommodate this situation. Unless this is the case, the delivered system will become a legacy system upon implementation, and will seriously hamper the agility of the organization and its business processes.

Case study: The devil is in the detail

A telecommunications organization had an ambitious marketing department that introduced a new bonus incentive, but forgot to inform the systems department. As a result, the manager of the systems department had to read an advertisement in a newspaper to become aware that his department was required to enhance systems to be able to deliver the promises of the advertisement. In an emergency meeting, it was decided that the required changes would be made within 24 hours. The marketing department stated, 'We don't care what it costs, just make the change to enable us to provide the features that we have promised in our advertisement'. A programmer made the changes to the system overnight, and everything seemed to work nicely. However, because of choices made to provide this quick fix, more than half of all the future marketing activities could not be supported by the system – a clear case of organizational sub-optimization.

Message: Reflect on system changes and their impact before making them, and ensure that all stakeholders are involved.

The concept behind a BPM automation solution is that with BPM technology it is now possible for the business rules and process components of an application to be extracted into their own 'layers'. Smith and Fingar (2002) believe that a BPM system comprises three broad areas, as shown in Figure 19.2:

1   *Integration* of internal systems (EAI component)
2   *Automation* of what they refer to as processes (business rules and process repositories)
3   *Collaboration* with external entities – customers, business partners, distribution channels, hubs and business exchanges of information.

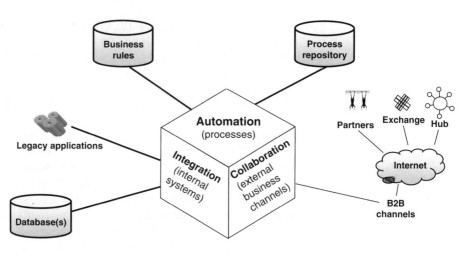

Figure 19.2
Business process
management system.
Adapted from Smith
and Fingar, 2002.

While the individual technology components have been around for some time, it is the integration of these various components, together with the growing process-centric thinking, that have made the difference.

If we could look into the future, it is arguable that the legacy application systems that have served large organizations so well, and yet provided significant constraints on them, will have the potential of 'only' being:

- large data storage and management repositories
- large batch processing modules, for the batch jobs that large organizations require (for example, renewals processing within an insurance organization)
- large batch or volume reporting and printing drivers (for example, again printing renewals for insurance organizations, if they are not already outsourced, or large volumes of reports).

Recent changes in technology mean that it is easier to develop and implement an automated BPM solution than in the past (assuming that it is approached correctly). Furthermore, current technology allows the business to become more directly involved with the development and management of these systems. In other words, the business can drive the automation of a BPM system.

Results

The deliverables for this phase are the following:

1   A high-level overview of the solution
2   Detailed business requirements
3   Finalized software selection documentation
4   Software specification/design
5   Software development/configuration
6   Software test scripts and results

7   Hardware specification
8   Hardware availability
9   Hardware test scripts and results
10   Integration test scripts and results.

How?

There are basically two ways to develop an automated BPM solution: the traditional Software Development Life Cycle (SDLC) approach (specify, develop and test) and the iterative approach of Rapid Application Development (RAD). This chapter will be approached differently from the other phases, as we will provide a few high-level steps (Figure 19.3) that should be considered when implementing an automated BPM solution. Detailed steps for SDLC and RAD are well covered in other publications, and are outside the scope of this book.

Step 1: Communications

During the Develop phase it is important to communicate the scope and proposed extent of the automation to all stakeholders. It is also important to address the main questions that arise in the case of automation:

- Will I keep my job?
- What new skills will I need?
- How will my job change?

Automation might also influence the interaction with suppliers, partners and customers. With web services and service-oriented architecture, it becomes much easier to integrate processes across the borders of the organization. If this is the case, the communication should also extend to the related parties, ensuring that not only the benefits and impact of automation are specified, but also the progress, issues and potential delays.

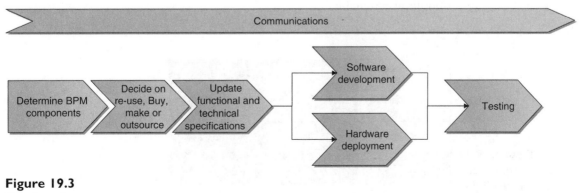

Figure 19.3
Develop phase steps.

Step 2: Determine BPM components

One of the first decisions in the Develop phase is which automated BPM components are required – this is about making a decision regarding the 'tools' that will be required. This may well be a point where it is not so much about making the decision as finalizing it. Several of the tools may already have been purchased for earlier phases of the project (such as, process modeling and management components), and others may have been addressed during the Innovate phase (such as use of business rules and/or a process engine).

An automated solution can consist of one or more of the following components:

1   Process (workflow) engine
2   Business rules engine
3   Integration (Enterprise Application Integration – EAI)
4   Integrated document management system
5   Business Activity Monitoring (BAM).

The other components of an automated solution are a process modeling and management tool, simulation, activity-based costing, and BSC. These components are more concerned with the modeling and configuration of the processes, and will not be dealt with in this chapter. Figure 19.4 shows all the components.

When automating parts of a process, the major challenge that a project will face is obtaining the data that the process requires. These data can be scattered over multiple legacy systems. Based on the ease of gathering the data, the project needs to determine which automated BPM components it intends to use during the development of the solution.

Step 3: Decide on re-use, buy, make or outsource

The next decision for the project is what approach it wishes to adopt with regard to make or buy for the various software components. The following options are available.

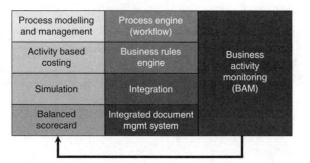

Figure 19.4
Components of an automated BPM solution.

Re-use of an existing system

Main advantages:

- synergy and economies of scale
- the system is known and has proved itself.

Main disadvantage or issue:

- the system might not meet all the current requirements or doesn't provide sufficient flexibility for likely new requirements.

Buy an off-the-shelf product that can be configured

Many BPM vendors are now offering 'skeletons' of applications that are designed to be significant starting points for an organization. They are not expected to provide a total solution, but can supply a simple framework that the organization can enhance (configure) to meet its specific requirements. This can be a significant advantage to an organization (and project) if one is available for the desired application and that predominantly meets the business requirements of the business. Examples of these 'skeleton' solutions include the following: insurance claims processing, various telecommunications applications and loan processing.

Main advantages:

- the chance to obtain a suitable product or starting point
- a solution that meets a specific situation of the organization and marketplace
- product support is available.

Main disadvantages or issues:

- additional costs (although it could end up saving cost)
- it is essential that the initial skeleton configuration predominantly meets the requirements of the organization, otherwise it will become an instant legacy system (configuration of a new package is like pouring concrete – when applying it, it is very flexible, but afterwards it sets rock solid)
- development of a system against immature requirements, which may limit future flexibility.

Develop a new system

This is the development of a bespoke system, and as a general rule should be avoided if at all possible.
Main advantage:

- the system can be fully customized and configured for the organization.

Main disadvantages or issues:

- considerable development cost and time and ongoing operating costs
- project risks include late delivery, low quality and higher costs.

Outsource the application

This is increasingly an option for an organization, and should be seriously considered.

Main advantages:

- makes use of the existing knowledge and processes of the insourcer
- use of economies of scale and synergy.

Main disadvantages and issues:

- cost involved in the handover to the outsourcer
- lack of flexibility.

(Refer to Appendix L for more details on business process outsourcing.)

Number of systems

An automated solution will more than likely involve more than one component – for example, a process (workflow) engine system, an automated business rules engine and a document management system. In a situation with multiple automated components, consideration should be given to the fact that with an increase in the number of systems the number of interfaces increases significantly, and so does the effort required in the development and maintenance of these interfaces.

Step 4: Update functional and technical specifications

There must be a structured approach to the specifications (functional, technical and system or design), development and testing of the BPM solution, and this is shown in Figure 19.5. The V-diagram provides the 'missing links' between the specifications themselves and the specifications and testing. The missing links shown in this figure are often the root cause of why many development projects have failed in the past.

The left-hand side of the figure shows the business requirements and related design documents, and the right-hand side shows the testing to verify that what is produced by the development team conforms with these requirements and designs. The challenge is to ensure that the expectations are fulfilled from a business perspective, and it is the business that decides whether this has been achieved. The boxes above the dotted line relate to the functionality, while the boxes below the dotted line refer to the technical aspects.

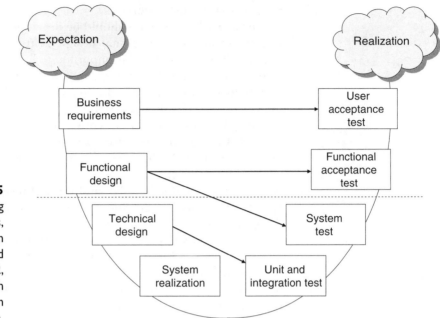

Figure 19.5
V-diagram: linking requirements, system realization and testing. Adapted from Pol *et al.* 2002, published with permission from Pearson Education.

A common problem during the Develop phase is conflict between what the business wants and how the developers interpret the requirements. This is often a function of how these two stakeholders work together and understand the implications of this working relationship.

How many times have we all heard of situations where the business writes a specification of its requirements, technical staff then rewrite this into a technically based functional specification, predominantly in terms that the business finds difficult to understand, and in order to meet the delivery timeframes, gives the business three days to sign it off? The business not only has difficulty in understanding the technical language used, but at the same time has a business to run – and so the three-day timeframe is extremely difficult to meet. To avoid delays, the business signs off on the functional specification without fully understanding the consequences. The development team now designs the new BPM system and delivers it to the business. During the testing phase the stakeholders complain that the system does not meet their expectations, saying, 'this is not what we wanted!' The development team's response is, 'yes it is, refer to page 179 of the signed off technical design specification'. The business then replies, 'well, it is not what we meant!'. The project is then in rework mode, resulting in longer times, greater costs and potential business opportunity losses.

This is the traditional SDLC approach, and it generates a higher-risk situation in a BPM project than is desirable.

These risks can be minimized in several ways, including the following:

1   Perform 'what if?' analysis.
2   Perform simulations.

3 Specify what is out of scope.

4 The business requirements should be developed as part of the Innovate phase and the functional design written during the Develop step. However, it is extremely important to have the business working closely with technical development staff and to write the functional design document jointly. The business needs to be able to sign off on the document, clearly understanding the consequences and ensuring that the requirements are consistent with and add value to the business strategy and objectives. A good way to ensure that the business understands the business requirements is to write them from a process perspective.

5 Separate the functional design and the technical design.

6 Specify and seek agreement on the consequences of the development.

7 As described in Chapter 14, it is important to use the architecture in a flexible way – for example, what do you do if there is an urgent business requirement and the solution does not fit in the architecture? One of the options that could be considered is to allow the requirement to be developed and to make clear rules on how to deal with this exception – such as, the solution should be phased out after x months, or the solution should comply with the architecture within x months. This 'pressure cooker' mechanism is very important, as the ultimate test of an architecture is how it deals with exceptions. Ignoring or rejecting all exceptions may appear to win but will eventually lose the war as people ignore the architecture on an increasing basis.

8 It is crucial to include both the software and the hardware requirements, as in most cases there is a dependency between the two.

Case study: The wrong shortcut

A telecommunications operator wanted to introduce a new system to support its billing and customer care processes, and developed the requirements purely on the basis of its current business model: providing landline services to residents. When we saw the initial specifications, we mentioned that this would make the system very inflexible. From our generic business model, we suggested that the operator should choose to build the system on the basis of a variable set of business parameters rather than hardcoding the functionality into the system. For example, instead of only providing the capability for residential customers it should also allow for other customer types, such as business customers and distributors, and instead of only one role for the organization (service provider) it should allow for multiple types (such as network operator, and distributor). The operator ignored this advice and after two major changes in its strategy, the system was hopelessly constraining its business – to such an extent that they had missed out on an enormous window of opportunity to attract more market share and thus struggled to remain profitable.

Message: Carry out 'what if?' analysis to ensure that your requirements can face expected changes.

An important issue when dealing with software is the use of relevant standards. With the growing technical possibilities, such as XML, web services and service-oriented architecture (SOA), it is becoming increasingly possible to extend process automation possibilities well beyond the boundaries of the organization and to suppliers, customers and partners. This will provide more efficiency and speed.

Currently, the standards discussion for modeling, orchestration, execution and interoperability is still very complex. There is no general consensus on the complete set of BPM standards between tool vendors, although at the moment, BPEL and BPMN are at the forefront. For this reason, we urge readers to be conscious of this fact and to go beyond the discussion and understand if standards really matter in their specific situation.

The following standards are currently leading in BPM:

- BPEL (Business Process Execution Language). This is currently the main execution language that orchestrates business processes using web services, and allows various BPM applications to be linked and integrated.
- BPML (Business Process Modeling Language). This competes directly with BPEL as a meta-language for modeling business processes.
- BPMN (Business Process Management Notation). This is a notation standard (i.e. a set of icons and graphics) for modeling business processes. The primary purpose for this standard is use for common modeling graphics across business process modeling tools and BPM applications, and thus BPMN is complementary to other BPM standards.
- Wf-XML (Workflow XML). This provides interoperability between BPM engines, making it possible to execute long-running business processes that span multiple engines.
- XPDL. This is a business process definition language that describes an entire process, and can be used to integrate BPM components for process modeling, execution and control within their product. XPDL is also widely used in many open-source BPM products.

Step 5: Software development

Basically, any automated BPM solution will have three layers to consider:

1. Presentation layer of the solution to the user
2. Processing layer containing the automated tasks
3. Integration layer to other systems and databases containing the data.

It is crucial to understand that each of these three layers needs a different approach to both development and testing, as it involves different groups of people. The presentation layer is focused on the end-users, and represents their view to the system. Issues to consider are the following:

- is it a view that end-users are familiar with, and does it have a logical look and feel (i.e. is it similar to existing/other systems or does it have a logical flow of the screens)?
- different types of users will have different needs and ways of interacting with the systems (for example, employees, controllers, managers, etc.).

The processing layer deals with the activities that the system needs to perform. This should be completed with people who have a good understanding of the business as well as the objectives of the project. An important issue to consider is the documentation and, with the growing popularity of pilots, RAD and BPM tools development, there is a growing tendency not to document at all, or not in as much detail as is required. The developers' argument is that the documentation is implicit in the configuration of the system and can be reviewed therein. Looking at the system will provide an overview of *what* has been configured, but will not provide the information on *why* this configuration has been chosen. Without the insight into the decisions behind the configuration, it becomes difficult to make changes in the future with any degree of certainty that they will be consistent with the original choices.

The integration/data layer is more technical, as it deals with the interfaces with other systems. A deep technical knowledge is required, as well as a clear understanding of the systems to which the automated BPM solutions link.

One of the most challenging aspects of the software development phase of a project is not just related to the actual development, but also to the migration to the new system. The road to success is scattered with projects that have underestimated the issues involved in migration and interfaces. It looks so easy, but is deceptively complicated.

Migration from a laymen's perspective can look easy, as the business models, processes and data have to be transferred from one system to another and it seems that matching the various fields to each system is all that is required. However, it is critical to ensure that the business models, processes and data in the existing system are correct. Experienced practitioners know that users will have been using the system in different ways, and this will mean that the system (and data) contains far more (systematic) errors than thought at first glance.

Should the organization first migrate the existing system to the new system and then make the changes; or should it make the changes first in the current system and then migrate to the new system? Often the latter is the preferred solution, as many projects and organizations find themselves unable to make changes in the new system once it is populated.

While doing this targeted analysis, it is important to differentiate between the importance that stakeholders put on their various requirements. The MoSCoW approach of the DSDM (Dynamic Systems Development Method, www.dsdm.org) is very practical here. This approach breaks down the priority of the requirements into the following categories:

- **M**ust have
- **S**hould have if at all possible
- **C**ould have this if it does not affect anything else
- **W**on't have (in this release), but would like to have it later.

Option 1: Traditional SDLC approach to development

Figure 19.6 shows the likely steps involved in following a traditional SDLC approach to the development of a BPM project.

While this approach is a tried, tested and proven way of developing solutions, it is not necessarily the best or most appropriate approach for a BPM project. The most appropriate approach will depend upon the scenario, organization and scale of the project.

The traditional SDLC approach requires the project manager to monitor the project at regular intervals to ensure that it is still on track to meet the specified requirements and that the business still supports the original specifications. Too often, the project delivers a software solution after a long period of development and testing, only to find that the business requirements have changed.

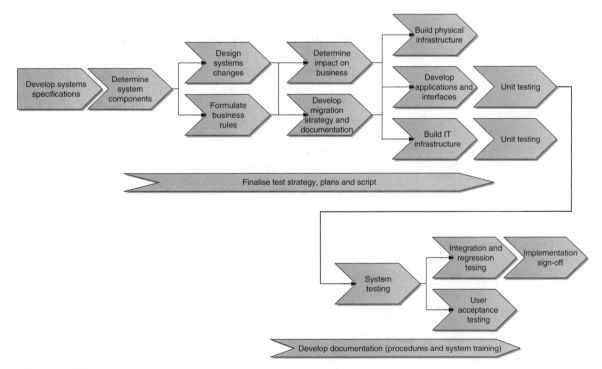

Figure 19.6
Traditional SDLC approach to development of a BPM solution.

Perhaps a more successful approach is the Rapid Application Development approach.

Option 2: Rapid application development

Most automated BPM solutions provide the possibility to configure the processes on a more interactive basis between the business and the technical people. This approach is where the process experts and/or process owners sit with a technical developer and 'model' the automated solution. This is an especially good approach in a pilot scenario, to explore the opportunities that a new BPM solution offers. It will also provide the business with a quick look and feel of the solution. However, when modeling the entire solution it is crucial that proper specifications are still completed to enable testing and documentation for future reference.

It is essential that the business people providing the information on the processes and who are responsible for these processes are fully aware of the configuration, its place within the larger context and the consequences of the choices they made. If this is unclear to them, it will inevitably lead to an IT-dominated system, with the business having insufficient knowledge or influence regarding its development and outcomes.

As BPM technology improves further, this approach will gain significant momentum and business benefits.

Step 6: Hardware deployment

Hardware can include the following aspects: computers for users, servers, networks, and related appliances such as printers, scanners and storage media.
The issues that should be considered include the following:

- compatibility – are all the systems able to communicate with each other, particularly, the interfaces and platforms?
- scalability – can the proposed systems scale upwards to cope with considerable increases in transaction volumes?
- maintenance and support – are all the hardware components assigned to skilled people who can maintain the particular component (including back-up and restore facilities) and provide or arrange for support for users?

Finally, always ensure that the hardware test environment is *exactly* the same as the future production environment. Many systems have tested perfectly in the 'laboratory', only to fail in a production environment because the two were not exactly the same.

Step 7: Testing

Testing is a crucial step in the Develop phase. It is the moment when the developed application systems are compared with the original business

requirements, assuming the test plans and scripts have been developed appropriately. The International Standards Organization (ISO) describes testing
as a:

> Technical operation that consists of the determination of one or more character-
> istics of a given product, process or services according to a specified procedure.
> (Reproduced with the permission of ISO Central Secretariat from the website of
> the International Organization for Standardization, www.iso.org.)

A more appropriate definition for testing of a software application is:

> A process of planning, preparing, executing and analysing, aimed at establishing
> the characteristics of an information system, and demonstrating the difference
> between the actual status and the required status.
>
> (Pol *et al.*, 2002)

Testing becomes more critical in circumstances of fundamental or large-
scale changes than in shorter or smaller development times. Testing is thus
a crucial activity that must be planned appropriately and in detail, and must
not be left too late in the project. Writing test plans and scripts is an activity
that should be completed, in detail, at the time of writing the business and
functional specifications. If test scenarios and test scripts are completed at this
time, it will provide the business and developers with a clearer understanding
of the business requirement. The developers will understand the basis upon
which their new system will be evaluated, which should further diminish the
risks associated with a misunderstanding between the business requirements
and the developers' outcomes.

Important issues to consider include the following:

- It is important to remember that more than half the time involved in
  the testing activities is required to be spent on the preparation and
  planning, and the remainder on the actual execution of the testing.
- It is nearly impossible and highly undesirable to complete a full
  100 percent test, as the costs and timeframes involved will be pro-
  hibitive. It is better to complete a structured approach to testing,
  maximizing the effectiveness and minimizing the effort. The person
  in charge of testing should always specify the extent of testing, the
  number of errors and the 'test coverage'.

We can distinguish between the following types of testing (Pol *et al.*, 2002):

- A *unit test* is a test executed by the developers in a laboratory environment that should demonstrate that a particular activity or step of
  the automated BPM solution meets the requirements established in
  the design specifications.
- An *integration test* is a test executed by the developer in a laboratory
  environment that should demonstrate that a function or an aspect
  of the automated BPM solution meets the requirements established
  in the design specifications.

- A *system test* is a test executed by the developer in a (properly controlled) laboratory environment that should demonstrate that the automated BPM solution or its components meets the requirements established in the functional and quality specifications.
- A *functional acceptance test* is a test executed by the system manager(s) and test team in an environment simulating the operational environment to the greatest possible extent, which should demonstrate that the automated BPM solution meets the functional and quality requirements as specified in the functional requirements.
- A *user acceptance test* (UAT) is a test executed by the users of the system where, in a shadow operational environment, the automated BPM solution will be tested to demonstrate that it meets the business requirements. This is included in the Implementation phase.
- A *regression test* aims to check that all parts of the system still function correctly after the implementation or modification of an automated BPM solution. Regression is a phenomenon to ensure that the quality of the system as a whole has not declined due to individual modifications.

Obviously, the normal testing process should be followed. The usual sequence is as follows:

1   Determine a test objective. Testing always involves a balance between the benefits of testing and its associated costs: 100 percent testing is nearly impsossible and extremely expensive. The TMap® as described by Pol *et al.* (2002) is a pragmatic approach for this.
2   Determine and write a test strategy. This is a strategy regarding how the organization wishes to approach testing. It should include unit testing, user acceptance testing (UAT), integration testing, regression testing and so forth. Consideration should be given to the infrastructure to be employed. **Note**: always do everything within the power of the project to ensure that an exact copy of the live infrastructure environment is used during the testing stage. Many projects have come unstuck where this has not been the case. Also, remember that not all testing relates to application systems. In a process environment, much of the testing will revolve around 'walking' the process through the business and determining that it is fit for purpose.
3   Write a test plan. The organization decides upon the number and type of test cases to be applied. Remember to ensure that all appropriate stakeholders and other project teams are involved.
4   Write the various test cases. The volume of test cases will depend upon the size and complexity of the project. The most important aspect is to cover all the likely scenarios.
5   Execute the testing. The test cases and test scripts are completed.
6   Review the results and decide on how to proceed. The options are to go ahead with the implementation, to stop the implementation until the errors are solved, to go ahead with implementation and ensure that changes can be incorporated along the way, or a combination of these three.

Not all these tests are actually performed in this phase, but they will have to be considered here. The user acceptance testing, for example, is prepared and performed as part of Steps 3 and 5 in the Implement phase.

Realize value

Benefits must be defined in detail in order to gain agreement as part of this phase. For details refer to Step 5 of Chapter 21, where it is described in the context of realizing value within a project.

Develop phase outputs

The Develop phase will provide valuable input into other phases of the framework (Figure 19.7), and a few examples are mentioned here:

- the proposed solution could impose requirements on the people who have to work with the system
- the Develop phase will provide input for the training during the Implementation phase

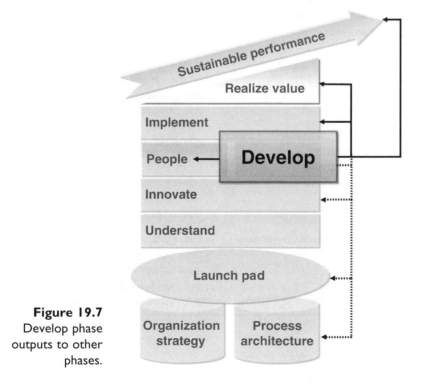

Figure 19.7
Develop phase outputs to other phases.

- the proposed system might provide functionality that gives the business additional opportunities; alternatively, the development might not be able to provide all the requested functionality as specified in the Innovate phase, in which case the same people who prepared the specification after the Innovate phase must be involved.
- the Develop phase should ensure that sustainable performance is created
- the development of software could impact changes in the process architecture (especially the relevant information and technology).

Development phase risks

In this phase there are several risks that must be considered and mitigation strategies implemented to eliminate (or at least reduce) them. These risks include those listed in Table 18.2.

Table 19.1 lists risks and mitigation strategies that must be considered in the Develop phase.

Table 19.1
Development phase risks and mitigation strategies

Risk		Mitigation strategy
1	Developed solution does not meet the business requirements	Ensure that the stakeholders are involved throughout the project and that they fully understand all the decisions made and the consequences, and work on the basis of the agreed process architecture and business case (deviations from both should be agreed with all those concerned)
2	Some applications work, however, the overall solution does not work	One of the causes could be that one or more of the interfaces does not work correctly. Ensure that the initial design takes all interfaces and interoperability into account
3	Testing finds too many errors	Ensure that the requirements (functional and technical design) are explicit and clear enough to be used as bases for the development, as well as preparing the test scripts

Chapter 20

Implement phase

Why?

The Implement phase (Figure 20.1) is the phase where all the designed and developed process improvements will actually be 'brought to life'. It is also the phase where many of the people change management activities come together. Although this is one of the last parts of the framework and project cycle, it needs to be considered at the very start of each project and as early as the Launch pad phase, for it is at the start of the project that the decision should be made regarding how the project will be implemented within the business (see Chapter 15 for details). The implementation decision will impact upon many facets of the project – areas such as how processes are designed or redesigned, how development and testing may be conducted, and so forth. The decision will be continually reviewed during the life of the project, recognizing that the method of implementation may change.

Case study: Implementation too little and too late

We were asked to review a failed BPM project. The project sponsor was surprised that his project had failed: all metrics were established at the start, the technology worked, the main stakeholders received weekly briefings, and the users were informed through a massive poster campaign, email bombardment and extensive training.

We interviewed the users, and they informed us that they were not consulted about the proposed changes, which were built on incorrect assumptions and would not work in practice. When we asked the project sponsor at what stage of the project the users were consulted and informed about the changes, we found that the project only did this after the redesigned processes had been created, with the assistance of an external analyst and internal managers.

Message: Users must be included very early in a project, as indeed must all stakeholders.

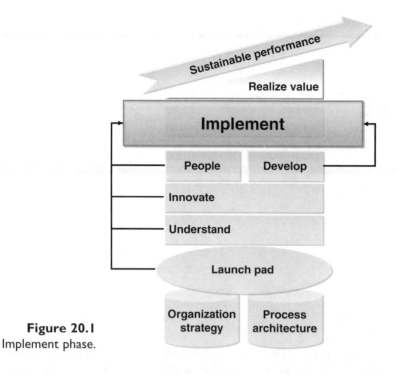

Figure 20.1
Implement phase.

Results

When the Implement phase is completed well, the organization can expect to have

- trained and motivated staff
- improved or new processes that work satisfactorily, according to the identified stakeholders' requirements and needs, and as outlined in the business case.

Case study: The coffee machine test

Involvement of users and stakeholders is frequently spoken about but is not often achieved. We believe there is a test to check (in a simple and non-scientific way!) the involvement of users.

Just ask people at the coffee machine about the proposed process improvements. If you get answers like: 'I have no idea what they are doing', 'they gave a pep talk, but I never heard any more details', or 'they never inform us anyway', you know you have clear signs of user non-involvement and insufficient communication.

We have also seen projects where the people involved in the project did not defend the project when their colleagues were speaking negatively about it. This is often a clear indication of the lack of confidence and pride in the project, which can stem from the non-involvement of these people in its implementation.

Message: It doesn't matter how large the benefits are that you expect to gain from the project; if you don't communicate these benefits to stakeholders and users, they will be difficult to achieve or will not be realized at all.

How?

Projects often fail because implementation is merely restricted to being one of the closing steps of the project, and is mainly centered on one-way communication to inform the users and other stakeholders of the benefits of the new solution for the organization. Moreover, most activities are focused on ensuring that users *can* use the new solution (e.g. training), and not on whether they *want* to use it (e.g. motivation of staff).

The best way to ensure smooth implementation is to start considering implementation issues at the initiation of the project. Only then will the Implement phase of the framework be focused on updating the information and performing the tasks, rather than thinking of last-minute ways to appease the users.

Figure 20.2 illustrates the steps that are applicable in the Implement phase, and these are discussed below.

Step 1: Communications

Good implementation requires good communication, and this involves true two-way communication. Inviting active participation of users in a project will

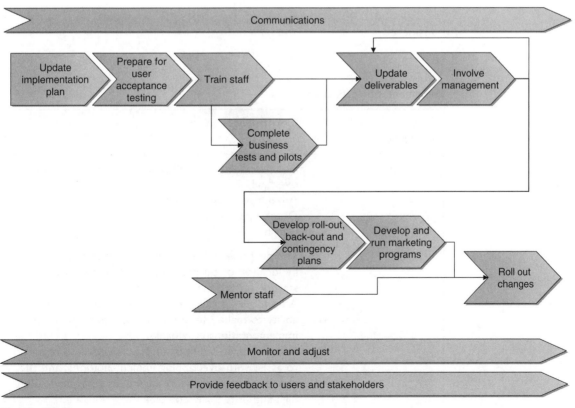

Figure 20.2
Implement phase steps.

lead to excellent suggestions, and it may also lead to some 'interesting' (critical) comments and unsuitable suggestions. However, when users are informed why their comments or suggestions are not contributing to the overall project objective, this leads to more insight on what the project could achieve. It is better to deal with this feedback rather than ignoring it and thus causing disinterest or apathy. It is also interesting and important to understand that some communication actually increases, rather than decreases, the resistance to change – so always monitor your communication methods and activities.

Step 2: Update implementation strategy

At the beginning of the project the implementation strategy should have been determined. When the Implement phase is reached, it is crucial to complete a review of the original implementation strategy because:

- the project team and the organization will have a much better understanding of the proposed changes
- the implementation strategy has to take the current situation into account, and this may (and probably will) have changed since the initial determination of the implementation strategy.

Table 20.1 gives examples of the types of strategies that should be considered.

Table 20.1
Implementation scenarios

Implementation scenarios	Comments
Big Bang	The proposed change is introduced in one major overhaul Advantage – fast to implement Disadvantage – the risk of disruption to the business is high
Parallel	The proposed change is introduced step by step (e.g. by location or business unit), with the next roll-out starting before the previous one is finished Advantage – a relatively fast implementation, and the ability to make use of lessons learned from preceding implementations is valuable Disadvantage – additional resources will be required to assist with overlapping implementations, and the coordination of these simultaneous roll-outs will be high and potentially complex
	(Continued)

Table 20.1   (*Continued*)

Implementation scenarios	Comments
Relay	The proposed change is introduced step by step, with each roll-out only starting once the previous one has been completed Advantage – quality, as the lessons learned from the preceding roll-out(s), can be fully taken into account and the same implementation team can be used Disadvantage – lack of speed, as this implementation could, depending upon the circumstances, take some time to complete
Combination	A combination of the above mentioned implementation approaches – perhaps a small pilot and then building up to larger implementations Advantages – provides the organization with the benefits of tailoring the roll-out to the specific situation; flexible and yet still manageable

Big Bang   Relay

Figure 20.3
Implementation
scenarios.

Parallel   Combination

The implementation scenarios can be modelled as shown in Figure 20.3.

The implementation strategy step is where the various types of users and stakeholders will be once again reviewed and their expectations and involvement are checked.

Step 3: Prepare for user acceptance testing

During this step, if applicable, the test cases for business testing are prepared. The actual business users are required to test the solution in Step 5 (complete business tests and pilots). They will be able to test the completed solution from a 'normal practice' perspective. To this stage in the project the solution will have only been tested against the written specifications of the business requirements, while now the solution must also be tested for integration with the daily routine of the business users, as well as the implicit assumptions and expectations.

Ideally, the preparation for business testing should have started during the design of the new process(es). This could have occurred during either the Innovate or the Develop phase of the project, depending upon the particular circumstances. If the test cases are developed at this early stage, the organization has the ability to compare the test case expected outcomes with the business and technical specifications and design, to ensure that there are no gaps in the requirements. This is an excellent 'checking' activity to avoid costly mistakes being made.

Step 4: Train staff

In the Innovate phase, the new processes will have been designed. The organization will have developed them, and will have defined any changes to the organization's structure, job roles and job descriptions during the Develop and People phases. It is now time to train the people who will be executing these processes.

Just as the test scenarios can be developed based on the redesigned processes, the training materials can be created from the process documentation of the redesigned processes.

Training can take the form of formal courses or on-the-job training (*in situ*). Mentoring and coaching should continue during the business testing, pilot steps and initial implementation.

Obviously, the training materials used should be consistent and the training should not be conducted too far in advance. In fact it is best to train just before the skills are needed, to avoid loss of knowledge (if people learn new skills too early and then do not use them, they will forget the new skills). Suggestions regarding training are

- small doses of just-in-time training
- individual training sessions, ensuring that people know when their session is scheduled (this builds confidence and inclusion)
- test competencies after training
- monitor job performance after an appropriate period of time.

One of the outcomes of the people training step can be the development and training of 'super users' in the new processes. These will be the 'front-line' people that will be available during the implementation steps.

Training should be focused on more than just the key activities or any automated solution; it should also cover aspects such as:

- impacts of the proposed solution
- which existing bottlenecks will be tackled
- any new bottlenecks the participants expect to arise during the implementation period
- the benefits and possibilities of the proposed solution.

Step 5: Complete business tests and pilots

This is where the user acceptance testing test cases are executed by the business. This could range from executing data or transactions through an automated BPM solution to manually simulating the 'processing' transactions through the business. Obviously, the staff will have needed to be trained in the system and or processes prior to commencing the test cases.

It is essential that the organization:

- involves customers and suppliers, where appropriate
- has strong project management of the testing steps
- has a feedback mechanism that is easy to use
- listens and communicates honestly – feedback and listening to the feedback is absolutely essential; there can be a great deal to learn from this step
- has a mechanism to measure and share the results of the tests
- is always prepared to make changes 'on-the-fly' and feed these back into the deliverables (development) cycle
- communicates results of pilots and testing – shows success to stake-holders, especially any wins; however, always be honest about any challenges associated with the testing
- gets testimonials from staff, customers and suppliers
- celebrates success and rewards team members (project team and business).

Step 6: Update deliverables

This covers the feedback from the training and testing steps. It is important continually to update the expected deliverables and ensure that they have stakeholder acceptance and buy-in. The organization must constantly double-check that all stakeholders, management and project team members still have a consistent set of expectations. Also make sure, again, that the roll-out scope is understood and agreed.

Step 7: Involve management

Management must be kept up to date with developments (good and bad) at all times. Honest communication is the only type of communication that is acceptable. Make sure there is plenty of it.

It is the management's responsibility continually to inform staff and external stakeholders of the latest developments on the project. What are some of the means by which this management involvement can be achieved?

- People change management practices (refer to Chapter 25)
- Professional training development
- Off-site workshop retreats (it is best to conduct workshops off-site to minimize distractions for managers); it is often best to have external facilitators to conduct these workshops.

If necessary, include a public relations firm or in-house facilities to assist in this process.

When dealing with management, remember that it is crucial to get the managers through their own personal change first, especially if the proposed changes have a major impact upon them. Only then can the managers help others.

Step 8: Develop roll-out, back-out and contingency plans

Normal project management skills are required, and we will not go into these here other than to say that we suggest taking the following points into consideration:

- complete individual plans for each business unit involved in the roll-out
- develop plans collaboratively with management and staff
- plan for multiple planning sessions, ensuring that the project accommodates mistakes and continually learns and adjusts the plans accordingly
- ensure that individual expectations of people are crystal clear, so there is no room for any misunderstanding
- have a 'dry' run (practice) of the back-out or roll-back and contingency plans, make sure that it works and continue these 'dry' runs until any doubt is removed.

Step 9: Develop and run marketing programs

Think about the applicability of running formal marketing campaigns in the marketplace, specifically targeting external stakeholders. The organization may even wish to publish the innovation program, with the new strengths and competitive advantages that it will bring to the general marketplace. If this latter course of action is chosen, whatever implementation date is announced to the market must be realistic and achieved or the organization risks losing credibility with its stakeholders.

Often individual or small group meetings with key stakeholders can make them feel special, and can result in significant benefits. Plans can be shared, under non-disclosure agreements, with important customers and suppliers as early as possible.

Certainly, whatever method the organization selects, use multiple approaches to marketing and have your top customers informed by senior executives as much as possible.

Step 10: Mentor staff

As mentioned previously in the training step, if selected people are trained as 'super users' first, they may then be used to train the remaining people and provide mentoring during the early period after going 'live'.

It is important that the 'super users'/mentors are available full time during the initial implementation phase, and do not resume their business-as-usual roles until the implementation has settled down to everyone's satisfaction. It is important to provide these people with incentives to break from their daily work and invest time and energy in the project. These incentives should not necessarily be monetary, but could include a new challenging role for these people and a way of proving their ability to handle projects that may lead to a promotion or recognition within the organization.

Step 11: Roll-out changes

Once the roll-out of the new processes has been implemented effectively, you must ensure that the 'old' processes and supporting systems are no longer available to staff. It is also essential that a continuous improvement mechanism is put in place. This is discussed in more detail in Chapter 22.

Reporting relationship and organizational structure changes will also require implementation, as will the initiation of any new roles and incentive schemes based on performance results. Do not underestimate the complexity of this, or the time it will take.

Step 12: Monitor and adjust

During the roll-out of the changes, ample effort should be devoted to monitoring the progress of the roll-out and the progress towards achieving the business results.

It is important to have established performance indicators to monitor progress. Examples of this include the following:

- the number of questions in the first week(s)
- the number of errors in the first week(s)
- the percentage of staff working with new processes
- the level of overtime required to get the work done.

Step 13: Provide feedback to users and stakeholders

During the entire project, and especially in the Implement phase, a great deal is required from the business, business users and stakeholders – their commitment, involvement and participation. Sufficient care should be taken to thank the business, business users and stakeholders for this, and to ensure that they are continually kept informed about the progress of the project and the various lessons learned.

Realize value

Just as in the Develop and People phases, the benefits must be defined in detail in order to gain agreement as part of this phase. For details refer to Step 5 of Chapter 21, where it is described in the context of realizing value within a project.

Implement phase outputs

The Implement phase will provide valuable input into other phases of the framework (Figure 20.4), and we mention a few examples here:

- how the project is implemented will have an impact upon how the realization of the project value (benefits) will take place
- implementation will also provide input into the Sustainable performance phase
- the review and finalization of the implementation approach may necessitate changes to the People and Develop phases – for example, it may not be possible to change immediately to the newly created roles; there may be a need to stage such implementation.

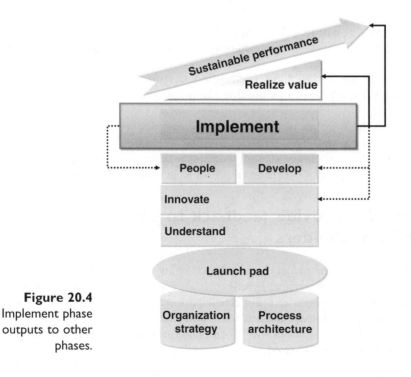

Figure 20.4
Implement phase outputs to other phases.

Implement phase risks

There are several risks that must be considered in this phase, and mitigation strategies are implemented to eliminate (or at least reduce) them. These are listed in Table 20.3.

Table 20.3
Implement phase risks and mitigation strategies

Risk	Mitigation strategy
1 Business testing and/or training becomes a show-stopper	Ensure that the requirements are discussed with the business, key users and stakeholders as early as possible, discussing the expectations and implications of these requirements
2 The core project team is unable to deal with all the problems and enquiries at the start of the implementation and during the early stages	Involve 'super users' and ensure that they are capable (via training), available (full time on the project) and willing (through motivation and involvement). In addition, a flying squad could be helpful, especially for more detailed and technical assistance
3 Stakeholders are not kept informed about the project	Communicate, communicate, and communicate. There can never be too much of it. Ensure that these tasks are allocated to a specific person to coordinate, and that they have sufficient time to complete the task
4 The business does not have sufficient expertise or resources to complete user acceptance testing	The business may need some coaching in how to complete a test plan or write test scripts, and on the execution of these. The project team must take care not to 'take over' these tasks and only provide coaching and guidance. The level of resources required must be discussed and agreed early in the project with the business to ensure that they allocate sufficient people
5 If time is tight on a project, testing is always one of the first things to be cut or minimized	Testing is one of the most crucial aspects of a project, and should never be compromised. If necessary, extend the implementation date, but never cut back on testing; the project and business will pay for it later if it is cut

Chapter 21

Realize value phase

Many project managers and organizations believe that a project is finished after it has successfully gone live and the users are happy. Nothing could be further from the truth. A project is only complete once the reason for its existence has been achieved and it has been handed over to the business in such a way that the business can now sustain the project outcomes.

Why is a project brought into existence in the first place? The business case should tell you. It should contain the business value or benefits that are expected to be achieved at the completion of the project.

Business value doesn't just 'drop out' of projects with no effort. Benefits need to be planned, owned and worked for in order for them to emerge. The realization of this business value (Figure 21.1) rarely happens immediately after the project implementation; sometimes there can be a delay from three to six months, as shown in Figure 21.2.

There is often a transition period where operational costs actually increase for a short period of time after implementation, and then the benefits start to be realized and the operational costs decrease.

There is also an overlap in the project costs and the start of the business value realization, because some part of the project must continue until the benefits begin to be realized and it is handed over to the business as an ongoing activity.

While we have provided steps in each of the other phases that will contribute towards the realization of business value, the purpose of this chapter is to bring all the value realization steps and management framework together to ensure that it is thoroughly understood and the project value is ultimately realized.

If it is discovered during a project that the expected business value cannot be realized, or has gone away, the project should be stopped. If the business case is maintained and updated throughout the project (at each phase), this will become apparent.

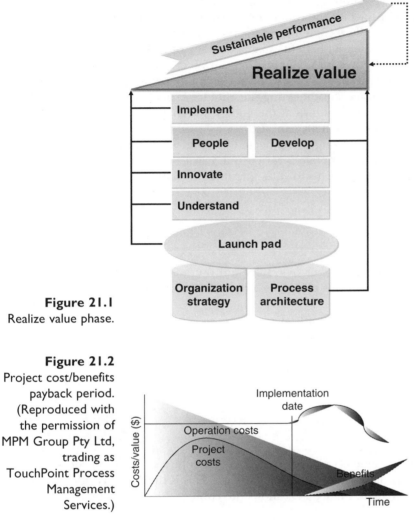

Figure 21.1
Realize value phase.

Figure 21.2
Project cost/benefits
payback period.
(Reproduced with
the permission of
MPM Group Pty Ltd,
trading as
TouchPoint Process
Management
Services.)

In a University of Leeds lecture in 2002, David Vinney (senior lecturer in Information Systems Engineering) stated that:

> Recent research from the Cranfield University School of Management finds that 78 percent of IT-enabled change projects (in large UK companies) failed to deliver business benefits. 47 percent believed assessment of business benefits in business cases was poor or worse and 79 percent said that all the available benefits were not captured during that assessment. 45 percent believed benefits were overstated in their organization to get investment approved.

The United Kingdom government website (www.ogc.gov.uk, accessed 8 June 2005), states that:

> Many business change projects fail to deliver the benefits on which the investment was originally justified. An estimated 30–40 percent of systems to support business change deliver no benefits whatsoever.

These are damning statistics, and can be avoided (or at least minimized) on a BPM project if the framework steps are followed.

The generally accepted term for the control, management and realization of business value is 'benefits management'. Benefits management translates business objectives into benefits that can be measured, tracked and realized.

If an organization chooses not to execute benefits management diligently, the risk of projects not meeting stakeholder expectations is increased. A sample of these risks is shown at the end of this chapter.

Benefits management can also act as a catalyst for further change if the project is not realizing the expected benefits. This can force the project and organization to complete a review that can lead to changes in the approach to the project, and thus to subsequent realization of the expected value.

Results

There will be a number of results and outputs that the business can expect from the steps in this phase, including the following:

- A benefits summary plan
- A benefits milestone network matrix
- A benefits delivery matrix
- A benefits realization register.

How?

If business value is to be realized, there must be a structured process throughout the project and entire organization. This is the benefits side of the cost–benefit analysis. Figure 21.3 shows the context for benefits management.

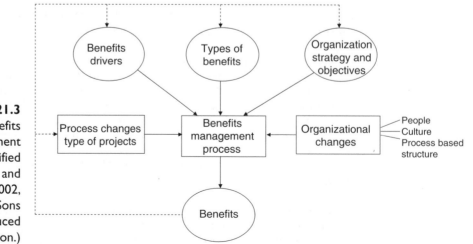

Figure 21.3 Benefits management context. (Modified from Ward and Peppard, 2002, ©John Wiley & Sons Ltd; reproduced with permission.)

The business will have various drivers that are directed by the organization strategy and objectives together with customer needs and the types of benefits that are available to the organization. Another significant influencer is the type of process change project(s) being undertaken within the organization. Are these organizational changes driven by the culture of the organization, people skill levels, or changing from a functional to a process-based structure? These are the critical people change management issues associated with the project.

When executed well, the benefits will be more easily obtained from a project and feed back into the initial business drivers and organization strategies.

According to an article accessed on www.ezinearticles.com on 12 June 2005, 'The challenge of the twenty-first Century is increasingly how to realize end-to-end change across a boundary-less business'. This means that BPM projects have the potential for becoming extremely complex because they may engage multiple sponsors across multiple business units and, potentially, multiple organizations.

It is, however, essential for the project sponsor and project manager to understand that benefits management is not outside the project. It is their responsibility to plan, manage and ensure accountability within the project team, and ultimately to deliver on the business value outlined in the business case.

Realizing business value is a progressive process throughout the project, and the framework shows you how to achieve this by completing the steps outlined in Figure 21.4.

While each of these steps will be described in this chapter, they must be executed in the appropriate nominated phase.

Step 1: Benefits management framework (Process architecture phase)

As indicated earlier, this step is about establishing a benefits management structure for the organization to approach, target, measure and realize project business benefits, and it should be incorporated into the process architecture.

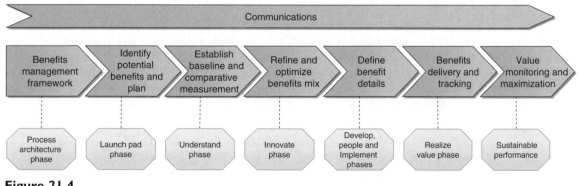

Figure 21.4
Realize value phase steps.

This step is where not only the benefits management structure is created, but also the organization's standards and templates are established and communicated throughout the organization. These standards and templates should include the following:

- how the organization identifies benefits and links them to the organization strategy
- how the organization defines and measures benefits
- benefit roles, responsibilities and ownership
- benefit planning procedures – milestone/benefits network matrices, delivery, assessment and review points, dependencies, risks, business impacts
- the determination of what, when and by whom
- guidelines on how to take advantage of opportunities for unplanned benefits
- identification of any dis-benefits
- identification of who is responsible for baselining and how, and who signs off on the baseline
- a benefits realization register format – What is the benefit? How much it is worth? Who is accountable for delivery? When will it be delivered – timeframe? Where will it impact on the business?

Regular benefits management meetings should be established, with decisions made regarding who should attend and how often the meetings will be held, and a standard agenda set, including the following:

- lessons learned
- benefits realized (Is it enough? Is there more?)
- benefits not realized – why? Adjust plans/mitigation and remediation strategies.

Step 2: Identify potential benefits and plan (Launch pad phase)

The initial business case will have been delivered as part of the Launch pad phase, and will have identified the likely initial benefits associated with the project. The benefits will be further identified and confirmed as the project progresses through subsequent phases of the BPM project framework. The benefits realization register must be used to record, for each identified and defined benefit, the following information:

- a description of the benefit to be achieved
- the person responsible for realizing the benefit
- a description of the current situation or performance of the business process
- the current cost or performance measure of the business process

- the target cost or performance measure of the business process after the planned change
- the target date for the benefit to be realized
- the trigger or event that will cause the benefit to be realized
- the type of contribution to the business
- the assessed value of the benefit or saving
- dependencies
- assumptions
- comments about the assessed value of the benefit or saving
- the organization strategy and objectives supported by the benefit
- how this benefit will contribute to the achievement of the strategic objective.

The benefits may also be summarized in the benefit summary plan (see Table 21.1). This plan records the benefit, who is responsible for the delivery (realization) of the benefits, the expected value, when the benefit will start to accrue and end (if appropriate, as some benefits continue into the future), and any dependencies and risks associated with the benefit.

This step involves documenting and planning for the management of the benefits that are expected to be delivered by the project. These are the benefits that will be monitored throughout the life of the project, and achievement of these benefits will be measured and reported upon at the end of the project. They must also be compared to the business case.

As processes can go across functional areas, this may make the measurement of the BPM benefits difficult to measure. This, however, does not excuse the organization or project from making the measurement.

The project team must take into account that a single project may have both quantifiable and non-quantifiable benefits associated with its implementation.

It should be noted that a productivity improvement by itself does not deliver a tangible cost reduction unless it can be translated into actual savings of staff numbers, avoidance of extra costs, or reduced resource requirements. Savings of small time increments that cannot be aggregated across many staff to provide realizable savings should not be treated as tangible benefits.

Table 21.1
Benefit summary plan

Benefit description	Owner (who)	Benefit amount ($)	Expected benefit realization dates		Dependencies	Risks
			Start	End		

Case study: Don't count incremental savings

We have seen many business cases that were 'justified' on small increments of FTE savings – for example, 0.2 of a person for one task, 0.6 for another and so forth. The CEO wanted to add them all together and save people. This is, in practice, extremely difficult at best, and impossible in reality because the FTE savings can be across various roles and functions.

Message: Only count benefits that can and will be realized. Minor incremental savings are almost never realized in practice.

In consultation with the affected business units, benefit targets should be identified as relevant to the project. The targets should also set a timeframe for achievement, and an outline of the action necessary to reach the targets set. The project sponsor is responsible for the realization of these benefit targets, and for adherence to the timeframes and actions.

A comprehensive plan of action and register of benefits to be achieved should now have been prepared and accepted by the responsible business managers (benefit owners) and approved by the project sponsor.

Step 3: Establish baseline and comparative measurement (Understand phase)

As discussed in the Understand phase, the completion of metrics is an essential step at the time of modeling the current processes, and it is this baseline from which improvements are measured. Therefore, in establishing the baseline, ensure that it is solid and will stand up to scrutiny by others, and that it is aligned with the business case. Ideally, all baseline measurement techniques should be consistent with an agreed institutionalized organization basis that will have been agreed in the process architecture.

Step 4: Refine and optimize benefits mix (Innovate phase)

During the Innovate phase, the processes will be redesigned based upon the criteria determined during the Innovate executive workshop. These newly redesigned processes should have process metrics calculated for them, to estimate their impact on increased processing efficiency.

Confirmation of the benefits should include reviewing the original baseline measures for accuracy and validity, and updating them using the latest rates for business expenses (e.g. salaries) – especially if there has been some delay or time period between phases.

A comparison should then be made between these new Innovate phase metrics and the updated baseline metrics from the Understand phase. In reviewing the various redesign process options, consideration should be given to the 'mix' of options and their impact upon the benefits. Efforts should be

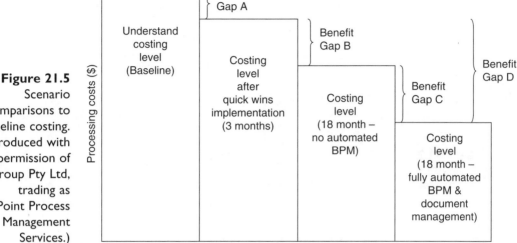

Figure 21.5
Scenario
comparisons to
baseline costing.
(Reproduced with
the permission of
MPM Group Pty Ltd,
trading as
TouchPoint Process
Management
Services.)

made to maximize the benefits by selecting the appropriate process options. As a result of this, process options can be finalized, as can an updated business case.

In the example shown in Figure 21.5, the project has been requested, during the Innovate executive workshop, to complete three redesign scenarios:

1 Three months (what can be implemented without any IT system changes – we would regard these as quick wins)
2 Eighteen months (with no BPM automation; existing application changes are allowed)
3 Eighteen months (with full BPM automation and document management implementations, and changes to existing applications).

The project sponsor has stated that she does not know whether a fully automated BPM and document management system implementation can be cost justified, so she has requested that the project redesign processes be based upon the two eighteen-month options (one automated and the other not automated) in order to determine the additional benefits.

Benefit gap A will show the cost reduction to be gained as a result of implementing the quick wins, and this will assist in their justification. Benefit gap B shows the additional measurable benefits to be gained from the eighteen-month non-automated solution. Benefit gap D shows the measurable cost reduction of the fully automated solution.

It is benefit gap C that the project sponsor is interested in – the additional benefits to be gained from the fully automated solution. It is this gap that needs to be included within the business case to justify the potential additional costs associated with the BPM and a document management solution.

(A note of caution: a fully automated BPM solution should not only use the measurable benefits as justification; there are many non-financial benefits to implementing this type of solution, such as business agility, increased staff satisfaction and an ability to interface with suppliers and customers.)

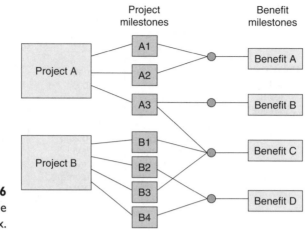

Figure 21.6
Benefit milestone
matrix.

This comparison will prompt the following question for the project steering committee: Do the calculated benefits meet the expectations outlined in the business plan? If the answer is no, then the project should either be terminated or go back to the Launch pad phase, where a different set of processes will be selected for the project.

Once all of the above analysis has been completed, the benefit milestone matrix (Figure 21.6) can be finalized.

This network matrix shows the relationship between various projects, project milestones and specific benefits. Unless you can show this relationship continuously throughout the project, linking milestones directly to benefits, the benefit may have gone away and the project, or part of the project, should be stopped. All project team members and business people must understand this relationship – especially the project sponsor, project manager and business owner.

It is necessary to ensure that business change issues are identified so that their progress can be monitored in terms of benefits realization. Some of these will have been identified in the benefits realization plan, whilst others will emerge as more detailed people change management plans are developed. Equally, hidden benefits identified during implementation should also be incorporated into the benefit realization plan. It will be necessary to develop milestones and targets for benefits realization associated with the people change management activities so that it will be possible to monitor the progress of benefits realization amongst these change activities.

Step 5: Define benefit details (Develop, People and Implement phases)

At the commencement of the Develop phase, after updating project plan, the benefits delivery matrix (Figure 21.7) must be completed. This matrix shows the relationships of the project milestones and benefits as outlined in the benefits milestone matrix. The difference here is that the milestones and

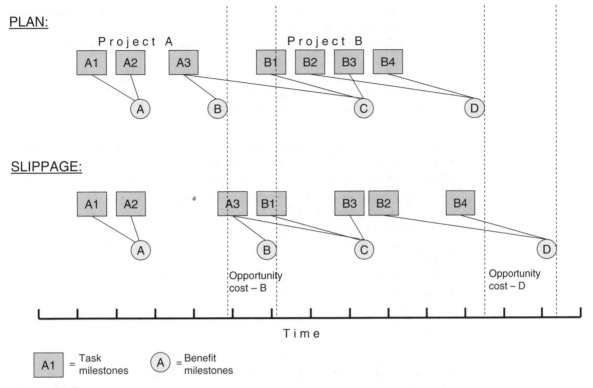

Figure 21.7
Benefits delivery matrix.

benefits are time-lined and then adjusted on a continual basis for changes in the delivery dates for the project milestone tasks. Note that there can be a delay between a milestone being completed and the realization of a benefit such as benefit D in Figure 21.7.

In this example:

- milestones A1 and A2 have been delivered according to schedule, resulting in benefit A being realized on the planned date
- milestone A3 has slipped while B1 and B3 are on schedule, which has resulted in benefit B being delivered late and benefit C being on time; the slippage of benefit B will have a cost associated with the delay
- both milestone B2 and B4 are late and have caused the slippage of benefit D, which also has a cost associated with the delay.

It is important to track slippages, as the impacts on the organization can be several-fold. A few of the impacts are as follows:

- the least cost is the cost of funds associated with not releasing the cash benefit earlier, such as interest and cash flow impact
- missed business opportunities (unable to capitalize on a business opportunity because of the non-delivery of a project or project

milestones on time); some business opportunities have a limited window of opportunity

- additional cost of the project, including the cost of resources for a longer period of time
- missed profit targets for the organization (may slip from one financial year or quarter to another)
- lack of capacity for a new contract.

Understanding the relationship of milestones and benefits, when a slippage is looming, will direct the business and project team as to where to place resources to yield the maximum benefits for the organization. Perhaps resources should be taken away from other tasks or projects (whose benefits are of less value) and placed on tasks with high benefit value.

Monitoring of progress against benefits realization milestones should be an integral part of project reporting, and incorporated as a segment in the regular reports to the project sponsor and Project Steering Committee.

The benefit milestone matrix and benefit delivery matrix must continue to be updated during the development phase, and taken into account during the completion of the People phase.

Step 6: Benefits delivery and tracking (Realize value phase)

It is the responsibility of the benefits owner to ensure that:

- all activities identified in the benefits summary plan are realized
- the appropriate control structures necessary for benefits realization are in place.

People change management planning is regarded as a crucial element in project success; it should be undertaken in parallel with project implementation planning and, in fact, the entire project. The project sponsor and benefits owner should ensure that any dependencies between the project implementation, the people change management and the benefits realization activities are in the plans.

Once benefits are realized, obtain a formal sign-off, put them in the register and 'tell people' (celebrate).

Step 7: Value monitoring and maximization (Sustainable performance phase)

As the achievement of some benefit targets will rely on activities occurring after project completion, it will be necessary to ensure that post-implementation reviews check that the benefits targets are being realized and continue to be realized. Checks should include the following:

- an internal audit of compliance against benefit targets in the benefits realization register
- a review of project plans and registers to ensure all the benefits realization-related activities were successfully completed
- a review of benefits realization related to major people change management activities.

This does not mean that the project should wait until the completion of the project to commence monitoring the realization of the value expected from it. Monitoring, via the various matrices outlined previously, together with compliance or project office audits, should take place during the project lifecycle.

At the completion of the project, a full report on the achievement of benefits should be provided to the project sponsor and business project owner. Where benefits were fully achieved, or targets exceeded, it will only be necessary to record that occurrence. Where benefits failed to reach targets by a margin of greater than 10 percent, the report should analyze the circumstances that caused the shortfall and recommend whether remedial action is appropriate. A full analysis will facilitate more accurate benefit estimates and will provide input into the Launch pad phase for future projects.

These areas should be followed up with the responsible business managers to validate the findings and identify areas where remedial action may be appropriate. Where the business managers identify that benefits may still be achieved, new targets should be established in consultation with them.

For each of the benefit areas where new targets have been agreed, an action plan should be developed in conjunction with the responsible business manager. Responsibility for the implementation of this action plan should be assigned to the business manager in charge of the area in which the benefits will be realized. The benefits realization register should be updated, subject to approval by the project sponsor, to reflect the newly agreed benefits targets.

The organization should be confident that it has achieved the maximum possible benefit from the investment it has made. If this benefit has fallen short of the original expectation, there should at least be an understanding of the causes and possibly a plan for future remedies.

Step 8: Communications

This is the step where the project team and the business communicate to the wider organization and appropriate external stakeholders. The communication will inform them of the success of the project and the benefits that have been realized.

This communication should also include information regarding how these benefits will be sustained across the organization in the future, and the effort and activities required to ensure that this is permanently achieved.

Critical success factors

How does an organization ensure that it maximizes the benefits from its projects? We have outlined an approach within this chapter, and list some of the critical success factors below:

- an understanding that the realization of value needs to be intricately intertwined with, and a critical part of, the project and organization culture
- it is necessary to plan benefit delivery – timeframes and costs
- there must be agreement of the roles, responsibilities and account-abilities associated with the realization of value
- there must be complete identification of the risks associated with the non-delivery of the value, and appropriate remediation strategies
- the staff involved in the realization of the value must be trained in benefits identification, analysis and review
- relevant measures and management must be in place to track and act on the results
- unexpected benefits must be recognized and recorded
- if it is possible to benchmark against other organizations within your industry, or appropriate other industries, then do so
- never underestimate the importance of the people change manage-ment aspect of the project on realizing value; if you do not have the support of the people, it will be extremely challenging to meet the project benefit expectations.

Realize value phase outputs

The Realize value phase will provide valuable input into other phases of the framework (Figure 21.8), and we provide a few examples here:

- feedback may be provided to suggest changes in the way implemen-tation is completed to maximize the future benefits; this could assist where a staged roll-out is being completed, to ensure that subsequent roll-outs are changed to maximize the benefits
- changes to the people change management could also be suggested
- it may be realized that changes are needed in the way the new pro-cesses have been designed and developed to again maximize benefits
- knowledge will also be gained that will contribute towards ensuring the sustainability of the project outcomes.

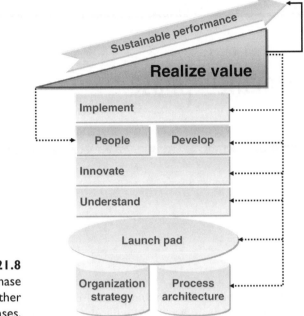

Figure 21.8
Realize value phase
outputs to other
phases.

Realize value phase risks

An overview of the high-level risks that must be considered during the Realize value phase is given in Table 21.2.

Table 21.2
Realize phase value risks and mitigation strategies

Risk	Mitigation strategy
1 Business may not commit to the realization of the benefits	Project manager, process architecture team and project sponsor are responsible for the benefits management system
2 Lack of focus on realizing the business value as outlined in the business case	Project manager, process architecture and project sponsor are responsible for the focus
3 Unrealistic benefit expectations, making it difficult to realize with any level of certainty	Only record realistic benefits in the business case and reporting matrices
4 Lack of a structured approach to the realization of the business value (benefits)	Establish a benefits management system as part of process architecture of the organization

Chapter 22

Sustainable performance phase

This chapter describes the Sustainable performance phase (Figure 22.1), the last phase of the BPM framework, which relates to the need to move from a project-based to a business-based BPM environment. While this is the last phase of the framework, it is the first phase of BPM as a business-as-usual activity. As Stephen Schwartz of IBM is purported to have said,

> We had improvement programs. But the real difference came when we decided it was no longer a program, it was a business strategy.

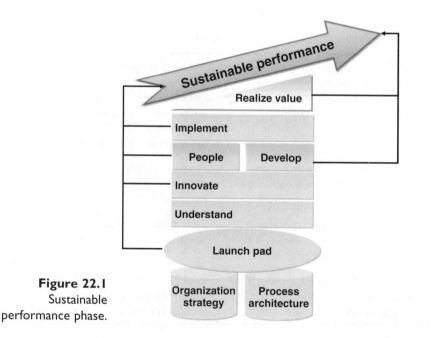

Figure 22.1
Sustainable
performance phase.

Why?

Process improvements without sustainability is arguably not worth the effort, as the improved practices quickly fade away as the business grows and changes. In addition, the expectations that have been built with the stakeholders will not be met over the long term, which in turn will make it more difficult to obtain their commitment and trust for future projects.

The purpose of this phase is to ensure the ongoing sustainability of process improvements and make it part of business-as-usual. The considerable investment made in any project must be maintained and enhanced over time – certainly not diminished or depreciated. The organization must understand that processes have a limited life and can continue to be improved after the project's targeted improvements have been realized.

Sustainability is determined by an organization's ability to create and deliver value for all stakeholders on a continuing basis. It is about understanding what customers value, now and in the future, which will influence organizational strategy, design and call to action. Processes must continuously be improved and redesigned to reflect this call to action. If this doesn't happen, the organization will simply be running its processes in a sub-optimal fashion.

In other words, sustainable performance is about the continual management of processes aimed at achieving the specified objectives. This chapter will specify how processes can improve autonomously, by evaluating the way the work is done and looking for improvements that can be made. The autonomous improvements are normally smaller steps and have a limited scope. If the scope increases, then a project with a clear business case is the best approach and the described framework in this book is the best guidance.

Results

The results that will be delivered during this phase are the following:

1. Mechanisms (a set of practical steps) to manage business processes, and identify and realize opportunities for process improvements
2. Managed and improved processes.

How?

The steps involved in the Sustainable performance phase are shown in Figure 22.2.

Step 1: Evaluate project results

During this step, the initial business case (along with any modifications) should be compared to the actual outcomes of the project (which will include the

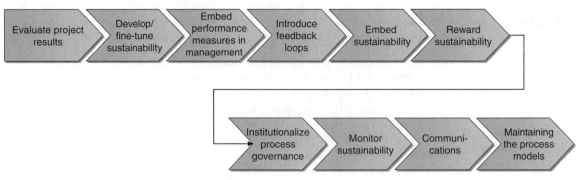

Figure 22.2
Sustainable performance phase steps.

value that has been realized). The original baseline is reviewed to determine the following:

- how much faster the processes are executed
- by how much errors, rework and backlogs have been reduced
- how efficient the processes being performed are
- how much customer satisfaction has improved
- how much employee satisfaction has improved
- the overall cost–benefit analysis for this project
- whether the benefits have started to flow as expected.

The results of this evaluation have two purposes:

1   To make the necessary changes to the current environment to correct any shortcomings
2   To include lessons learned from the project in the relevant aspects of the Organization strategy, Process architecture and the Launch pad phases for later projects – in other words, to see process improvement as a process to improve the execution of the BPM projects.

Step 2: Develop/fine-tune sustainability strategy

The project must contain tasks to create a mechanism for continual process optimization and management. This continual optimization and management must be established within the project, and handed over from the project team to the business in a controlled manner.

Many organizations that have engaged in BPM projects have failed to realize the expected benefits, due to a lack of monitoring and analysis of the way the new processes are operating. This can result in the loss of a large part of the investment the organization has made in the project.

The organization's, customers', suppliers' – in fact, all stakeholders' – expectations and needs change over time. The organization's sustainability strategy must establish several formal mechanisms to ensure that it will not only maintain the investment made in these processes, but also continually review the applicability of the processes to the current, and expected future, operating environment.

The organization must continue to reassess the relationship between the business and process stakeholders, and the organization's evolving strategies and plans, and understand the gaps as they emerge. The mechanism must then be available to fill these gaps and adjust processes and handle the change management issues arising out of these gaps.

Sustainable performance should have already been addressed in the process architecture as well as the business case and project plan/schedule. The sustainable performance strategy should answer questions such as:

- What are the objectives of sustainable performance?
- What is in the scope of sustainable performance and what is out of scope?
- What are the roles and responsibilities regarding sustainable performance?
- How are people rewarded for their contribution towards a sustainable environment?

Step 3: Embed performance measures in management

In order to achieve sustainable performance it is crucial that processes are managed, and managing processes requires continuous measurement of their performance.

Measuring should ideally be linked to a higher-level organization objective to ensure that the processes are geared towards and evaluated by their contribution to this objective. Furthermore, measuring processes should also relate to evaluating the performance of the people involved. In other words, good process performance should be rewarded.

The BSC is an excellent way to measure the processes, as it not only deals with the short-term financial aspects but also covers the customer perspective and the internal view. In fact, it is important that all stakeholder needs and expectations are covered in any score card that is established. Another benefit of the BSC approach is that it explicitly links the performance of the processes to the objectives of the organization, as well as linking initiatives to the specified objectives. This highlights the importance of carefully selecting the score card indices.

The BSC approach should not be cascaded all the way down the organization. It is an extremely useful mechanism for the first three or so layers within an organization, but once the lower echelons are reached, the performance measures need to be simple (and able to be clearly understood by people) and not necessarily directly linked to higher-level objectives. These people performance measures should have already been established during the People phase of the project.

Remember that when process performance measures are determined there are several components to be taken into account. These include effectiveness (including quality), efficiency (including cost and time), adaptability, risk, customer satisfaction and many more. There will be different drivers in different parts of the organization.

Continual measurement must be a key component in the establishment of process measures and performance targets. The targeted measurements must be capable of being compared to the actual outcomes of the process. There are, however, several ways or levels of measurement, including the measurement of:

- stakeholder visions and expectations
- management expectations (although 'management' is obviously a stakeholder, it is a 'special' stakeholder and its needs must be met). Management's expectations, however, must be articulated in quantitative terms, and the usual way of expressing this is via KPIs. Qualitative measures can also been measured through KPIs.

The measures, once established, should allow the organizations' supervisors, team leaders and area managers to act in a proactive way, changing staffing levels, redirecting staff and resources to immediately eliminate bottlenecks, and providing input into process changes that are necessary.

Other measures that can be made are the following:

- comparative measurements within the organization's industry, against competitors, and outside the industry, where this can be sensibly achieved and meaningful measures obtained
- ensuring that the process owners understand their role in detail and have accepted it (remember, not every process needs to have an owner; some are too small and others are simply not important enough to warrant an owner)
- providing the process owners with written job descriptions and KPIs
- ensuring that the people change management process has empowered the people for change
- centrally monitoring, in detail, that this continuous improvement strategy is working
- adjusting the approach from the lessons learned
- continually re-evaluating the applicability of the performance measures established, as the business changes and moves on, which will lead to a change in the way of measuring.

Benchmarking

When organizations start measuring the performance of their processes, they often wonder how they compare across business units within their organization or with competitors. Benchmarking processes allows this comparison to take place. Before comparing figures with other organizations, it is crucial to understand all the considerations and definitions used in the comparison to ensure that the figures are comparable. Too often organizations compare figures without understanding the difference in scope, complexity or culture.

Benchmarking can be related to throughput times, processing times, costs, quality, customer satisfaction, and profitability. Benchmarking can also be completed at different levels, such as product level, process level, business unit level and organization level.

Step 4: Introduce feedback loops

We have stated previously that BPM is about the management of business processes and, at a simplistic level, there are two elements: the processes themselves and the management of the processes (Kramer *et al.*, 1991). For the organization's management to be able to manage the relevant business processes, the following should be in place:

1   One or more performance measures must be specified. These measures include the effectiveness criteria upon which the process will be evaluated, and should include quantity (e.g. financial target) and quality measures (e.g. customer satisfaction). The BSC will assist with this.
2   Management should have a model of the underlying end-to-end processes which will enable managers to understand the effects of the selected management activities. This will be partially documented (e.g. the process models) and partially implicit (e.g. lessons learned from previous projects or measurement attempts). Always be careful that the performance measures selected generate the behavior that management wishes to foster or create.
3   Management should have sufficient information about the state of the process – this does not only relate to the output of the processes, but also to process characteristics such as errors, major issues, work in progress and rework.
4   Management should have sufficient management measures to deal with the related level of uncertainty and changes. The available management activities should be sufficient to deal with the expected variance in circumstances.
5   Management should have sufficient information regarding processing capacity to absorb the generated information and be able to verify this information (e.g. be able to detect 'noise' and inconsistencies in the data). This requires that management has sufficient capability and time to understand the data and take the necessary action.
6   If the outcomes seem to be difficult or impossible to achieve, management should defer to higher levels of management and discuss how to proceed in this situation.

The organization should also understand that the various levels of management within the organization will approach the management of process in different ways:

• At the strategic level, there is a higher level of change and uncertainty, but managers also have more variables at their disposal – process improvement, re-engineering processes, collaboration, migrating to another business model or even outsourcing. At the operational level, there is less uncertainty and changes and fewer managing variables – for example, more or less resources and ability to escalate.

- Managers who are responsible for the organizational strategy will have a broader scope and be subject to more fluctuations in their view than the operational management.
- The objectives of the lower-level management are set by the higher-level management.

Once measures are put in place, it is critical to create feedback loops to enable the continuous improvement of processes. Deming introduced this mechanism in his Plan–Do–Check–Act approach (Walton, 1986), shown in Figure 22.3.

Management not only obtains information from the processing itself, but also prior to the processing (feedforward) and after the processing is complete (feedback).

In *feedforward* (Figure 22.4), prior to the processes commencing their execution cycle, relevant influences and factors should be available to allow management to anticipate the impact of the processes and enable appropriate

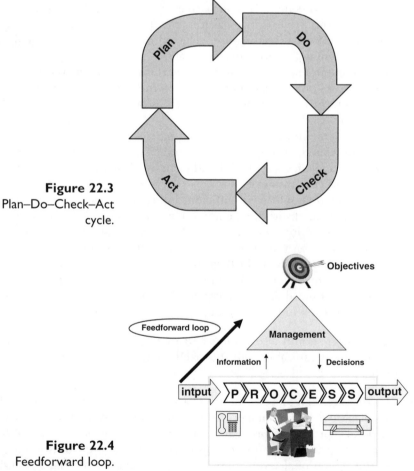

Figure 22.3
Plan–Do–Check–Act cycle.

Figure 22.4
Feedforward loop.

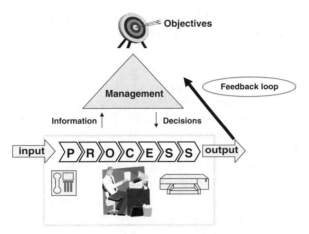

Figure 22.5
Feedback loop.

action to be taken (for example, if the volume is higher than anticipated, management will need to bring 'on-line' more people for process execution). It is important to understand and anticipate the impact that the feedforward can have on the organization's ability to reach its objectives – for example, the introduction of a new product could lead to more questions in the call center, which could impact the call center's ability to meet the objectives specified for response time.

In *feedback* (Figure 22.5), the actual end results of the measurement process will be compared with the process targets or objectives (for example, a thermostat adjusting the heating or cooling depending on the discrepancy between the actual temperature and the desired temperature). It is important to understand how the process needs to be adjusted to ensure that the next time it is executed, the process is better geared towards meeting the processing targets or objectives. This may require the adjustment of the process itself, or it could require the adjustment of resources available to the process – for example, there may be a requirement for more people to be available or it may require that transactions are routed to more or less skilled people.

The advantage of a feedforward loop is that it anticipates new situations. The disadvantage is that it is difficult to obtain all the necessary information and then determine the impact on the processes.

The advantage of a feedback loop is that it can accurately measure the extent to which the process is meeting the targets or objectives. The disadvantage is that it only provides information after the process is completed, and this may be too late to meet the process targets and objectives.

It is clearly better to combine both forms of information loops to enable anticipation, monitoring, managing and correction. It is crucial that the feedback loop information allows management to consider not only the process-related issues, but also the measures that have been put in place to monitor the loops. This will provide better insight into how the process is being impacted by changes in circumstances and/or the related management measures.

Feedback should not just be restricted to a particular process step, as it is associated with the end-to-end perspective of a business process. Most errors, delays and frustrations occur on an end-to-end process basis, especially when the people causing the problem and the people affected by it do not know each other or are not aware of each others' activities. This can be addressed as follows:

- feedforward – if at the beginning of the process there is a change to the normal practice (for example, an increased number of applications have been received), future process steps can be informed of this fact and they can take anticipatory measures
- monitoring – the end-to-end process owner should monitor the flow of the process and ensure that it flows as smoothly as planned; any issues need to be addressed
- feedback – if at the end of the process the target or objective has not been met (e.g. turn-around time for customer requests), the relevant people should be informed.

The critical element is that the feedback loop reaches the correct person. Often the feedback relating to process improvement is provided to the previous step in the process, which will only lead to process sub-optimization unless it addresses the end-to-end process.

Case study: Feedback in end-to-end processes

A bank had an increasing number of errors in mortgage processing. The traditional approach of informing the people involved in the previous process steps did not provide any results. We then invited all relevant people in the end-to-end process (from requesting a mortgage quotation to producing the quotations) to a workshop. The high-level process was then modeled, and every person was invited to indicate his or her main problems with the process. It became clear to all involved that many of the errors were caused early in the process. At the same time, the people involved in the early part of the process did not realize the importance, relevance and impact of some of the data entered and the decisions they were making. With the visibility and sharing of this knowledge, the number of errors decreased significantly. Just as importantly, everyone understood the end-to-end process and was able to meet the other people involved in the process for the first time. This allowed them to feel comfortable, when new problems arose, in contacting each other and resolving issues.

Message: Feedback should be related to the full end-to-end process and not limited to the previous process step.

Feedback can occur at several levels and for different people:

- personal feedback – for example, the claims officer is informed that his decision on the claim is not correct, including the reason and the correct solution
- management feedback – for example, the claims manager is informed about the number of claims that require rework, due to incorrect initial assessment

- process feedback – for example, the claims process is reviewed if too many errors are detected. This will include the process documentation and training material. This could result in changes either to the documentation (such as making it more clear) or to the process itself.

Step 5: Embed sustainability

Sustainability of process improvement can only be achieved if people keep on using the improved processes in the correct way. After new processes have been implemented, people can revert back to their old ways of working unless there has been sufficient communication and conviction regarding the benefits of the new improved processes. Another reason can be a lack of in-depth training or implementation support, causing the people to forget the details of the new processes. This can mean either reverting back to the old ways or processes, or people may 'create' their own new unique processes 'on the fly'.

One method to support and guide people during the execution of the initial stages of the new process is to publish them on the intranet with all the necessary supporting information (such as what the triggers are, what activities have to be performed, which output has to be achieved, which guidelines to comply with, who the process owners are, which documents and systems are involved, and so on). This could be supplemented with additional and supporting information, such as the forms to be used, documents to be taken into account, websites to consult or even applications to use. Using the process models as a key to find all this information has two main benefits: first, people will actually consult the processes, and secondly, everyone always has access to the most up-to-date version of the documentation.

Sustainability of BPM can only be achieved when the processes are kept up to date. This point cannot be overemphasized. When process modeling workshops are commenced, people often say, 'Why are we modeling our processes again? We did it last year!' When you ask them for the results of the previous exercise, it is amazing but true that in many circumstances the process models cannot be found, let alone actually used by the business! The best way to keep the processes and related information up to date is to publish them on the intranet and make it easy for people to provide feedback on the process steps and provide ideas for process improvements.

When putting processes on the intranet, it is crucial to have a user-centric approach: what do the users of the information want to see, and how can this best be achieved? Process models and all related information should be placed in a repository, and it should be possible for different types of users to obtain different views, types and details of information. For example, process analysts will be interested in which tasks must be performed; IT staff will be more interested in how the systems, processes and documents are related; and the finance department will be interested in the financial processing and the segregation of duties. Consideration must also be given of how much information should be made available to the various types of users – for example, information on risks and issues relating to processes may not be appropriate for all employees.

Should the processes be published on the web for the benefit of customers, suppliers and partners? This could provide them with insights into the steps that the organization must perform and allow them to track the process progress through the organization. Care must also be taken about the information that should be made available from confidentiality and privacy perspectives.

Publishing process models and information on the intranet, as outlined above, will require an appropriate process management and monitoring tool.

A good way to embed sustainability of BPM at the end of the project is to establish a central Center of Business Process Excellence which serves the business units. More details of this can be found in Chapter 28.

Analyzing processes, identifying bottlenecks and points of improvement, and acting upon them should be embedded in the organization as 'a way of life'. People who execute the processes often know what the problems are, but are unable or unwilling to communicate this to 'someone who cares' (or should care). Cultural empowerment must be created to allow this to occur. The identification and publication of the process owners will also identify the 'someone who cares'.

The *Kaizen* approach is a good way to include process thinking in everyone's job profile. *Kaizen* is a Japanese concept indicating continuous step-by-step improvement at the following three levels: management, teams of employees and the individual employee. '*Kai*' means 'to change' or 'to modify', while '*Zen*' means 'good' or 'right'. The management aims to improve the systems and procedures, teams of employees concentrate on the improvement of processes (feedback loops) and the related targets, and individual employees aim at improving their direct work environment. This allows continuous small process improvements, and should be dealt with at the 'workshop' floor level. Suggestions for major changes should be brought to the attention of the process owner. The advantage of making small improvements is that they are normally quick and easy to implement, with visible results. This also provides the employees with a feeling that they are making a difference and a contribution to the organization.

Step 6: Reward sustainability

Unfortunately, process improvements and better management of processes within an organization are either insufficiently rewarded or not rewarded at all. The best way to provide rewards is to base them on results, which should include more than just financial and volume-based indicators; however, in a start-up phase it may be better to reward initiatives and once BPM has taken off, the management can then switch to a more outcomes-based performance reward system. The reward system adopted must not be short-term focused, to achieve this month's or quarter's bonus, without undertaking the necessary effort to provide the fundamental steps required to achieve lasting results (this can obviously require a longer reward cycle). We have all seen that successful BPM initiatives include a component of rewards for the people involved. Jack Welsh, of General Electric, is known to have made a large part of the bonus for his managers dependent on their achievements in the implementation of Six Sigma. Other organizations have process training or certification as a requirement for employees to be eligible for a promotion.

Case study: Rewards bring success

A telecommunications organization tried several times to improve processes and related systems, but all of these attempts failed to deliver the expected outcomes. Evaluation of the efforts revealed that the proposals and the approach to implementing them were correct. However, further evaluation revealed that the management showed involvement during the initiation of the project, but didn't follow through with the implementation. The work had to be done by employees who were evaluated and rewarded on their 'normal' business-as-usual work, and were expected to assist the project on the basis of their own goodwill. This explained the rapid dwindling of support for the improvements.

Each business unit was provided with a process coach, and bonuses were realigned so that a large part depended upon the success of the process work while the remainder was dependent on their 'normal' work. As a result, the people in this project did not just continue their involvement in the project but actually increased their commitment to the results.

Message: Focusing people with a meaningful reward system gets results.

Step 7: Institutionalize process governance

Governance has become a major requirement in most organizations and business communities. We would define the governance of processes as 'the managing, controlling and reporting of processes within an organization'. Governance forces organizations to consider all the relevant stakeholders, such as employees, financers, shareholders, government, customers, suppliers and the community at large.

Governance is not a new phenomenon; it has been around for many years within organizations. However, it is shifting radically from being voluntary (as in a voluntary code of conduct between organizations or an industry) to becoming more rigid and far-reaching legislation (such as the Sarbanes Oxley Act of 2002). This has been accelerated by the recent collapse of large billion-dollar organizations, which has shown that self-regulation is difficult for organizations. Furthermore, an increasing number of organizations are adopting good governance practices, even though they are not legally required to do so, or voluntarily regulations such as EFQM and ISO.

What is the impact of governance on BPM? There are two levels of impact: the impact on the processes, and the impact on the management of the processes.

Impact on the processes refers to the increasing rules and regulations applying to processes. The best way to address this is to ensure that governance is included within the process architecture (which is the foundation for the design of new processes and the reviewing and assessment of the existing processes). The process architecture must ensure that the processes are

- transparent
- accountable for all individual process steps and for the entire end-to-end process
- able to produce the required reporting.

Impact on the management of the business processes refers to the fact that governance forces organizations to take all the necessary measures to ensure that the processes are managed and under control, and that they are properly administered. This could include the following:

- ensuring that the processes are properly followed
- ensuring that exceptions and undesirable outcomes are identified and dealt with by the process manager
- ensuring that the reporting and audit trail of the actions taken by process managers are properly recorded
- identifying the non-compliancy, risk and weak points in the process and taking appropriate measures.

When completing a BPM project, the project manager must ensure that governance is taken into account at each of the framework phases – thus further embedding governance as part of the organization's process management approach.

From a governance perspective, the following points should be considered (Bloem and van Doorn, 2004):

1 *Keep measuring.* This involves the cycle of ensuring that the expected outcomes are specified at the start of the project, measuring the progress in achieving the expected outcomes, and evaluating the extent to which the outcomes have been achieved. Lessons learned should also be evaluated and applied to future projects. Remember, measuring only makes sense when management applies what is learned from the measures and ensures that the roles and tasks are properly allocated to apply these lessons.

2 *Divide the leadership.* Many managers strive to have all aspects of a process fully under their control; however, many of these managers fall into the same trap – the more they want to control, the more time it takes and the less effective they are, so they become more and more their own major bottleneck. Managers should move to a form of distributed leadership (delegated responsibility), ensuring that all aspects of a process are taken care of, rather than having to understand every detailed aspect. Thus, only when everyone understands what is expected of them in a process and what they are accountable for can the managers really manage a process.

3 *Almost any governance structure is good.* The most important thing is that a governance structure is selected and used. It is not important to select the most complete or recent model; what is crucial is that it fits with the organization, meets the organization's objectives and is consistently applied.

4 *Encourage the desired behavior.* Ensure that the people are supported and encouraged to do the right things correctly. Management has a large range of measures which can be used to achieve this, from incentives to sanctions. Senior management has the important role of setting the right example. Furthermore, the right behavior should be included in performance reviews.

5   *People are allergic to excessive control.* Excessive control does not improve the performance of people. Appropriate control measures should become an integral part of everyone's working environment, and should also be delegated just like leadership.

6   *Keep it simple.* Management often falls into the trap of preparing models that are too complex, which inevitably leads to complications. If a control model is too difficult to understand, it becomes less effective.

Step 8: Monitor sustainability

It is not only processes that should be monitored; the execution of BPM programs should also be measured and monitored. In other words, 'practice what you preach'. The best way to achieve this is to establish upfront targets that can be achieved. Potential measures could include the following:

- customer, partner and employee satisfaction with the internal BPM programs and services (via a survey)
- the number of times process models are consulted
- the number of complaints from people that the process models are not up to date or correct
- the number of process model descriptions that have not been reviewed or modified in the agreed time period
- the turnover of staff (internal and external)
- the percentage of projects that have achieved their targets and were completed on time and on budget
- the availability of process models
- the turn-around time for process modeling.

The BPM proponents within the organization must realize that the main emphasis is now on the correct execution of the processes. New initiatives should be started only when there is a strong business case and the business and/or management is eager for this to occur. New initiatives should not be started just because BPM resources are available. Process changes must never occur without business involvement.

Step 9: Communications

When the project moves from the project phase to business-as-usual, it must focus its communication on the actual benefits that have been realized and motivate people to identify other areas to explore, as well as ensuring that people work according to the new process(es). It is important to emphasize that each completed project should bring the organization one step closer to a more process-centric way of thinking and working.

Step 10: Maintaining the process models

Processes are not static but dynamic, as they adjust to new internal and external circumstances. Process descriptions therefore need to be modified to reflect these changes.

Any process changes should be treated as a change request and follow the following path:

1   Register the change (for example, who requested the change)
2   Determine the type of change and the drivers for change
3   Prioritize changes
4   Determine impact assessment
5   Obtain approval for the change
6   Plan realization of the change
7   Implement change
8   Review implementation of the change.

Realize value

Value must be monitored and maximized as part of this phase. For details refer to Step 7 of Chapter 21, where it is described in the context of realizing value within a project.

Sustainable performance phase outputs

The Sustainable performance phase will provide valuable input into other phases of the framework (Figure 22.6). The main outputs will be to the

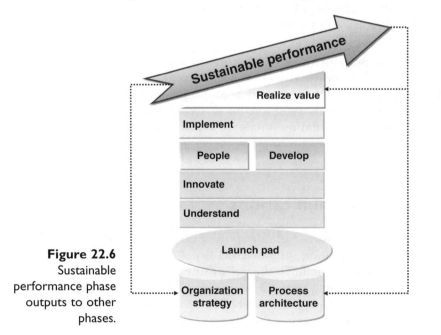

Figure 22.6
Sustainable performance phase outputs to other phases.

Organization strategy and Process architecture phases, with lessons learned being taken into future Launch pad phases. The knowledge gained from the ongoing business activities will provide information that could change both these phases for subsequent projects and the further business-as-usual activities.

Sustainable performance phase risks

Table 22.1 highlights the most common risks involved in ensuring sustainable performance.

Table 22.1
Sustainable performance phase risks and mitigation strategies

Risk	Mitigation strategy
1 No one takes ownership of the processes and the management of the processes	Discuss with senior management, as ownership has already been specified at the launch – this is the most critical success factor in BPM
2 People are not following the new way of working	Find out why people are not working in the new way and address the issue. If people are not motivated, 'sell' the benefits to them. If people have forgotten how to use the new way, provide additional training and guidance
3 Processes are not updated	Ensure that people are using the process models and can detect any issues that are outdated, and ensure that processes are reviewed on a regular basis
4 No further process improvements are identified or initiated from employees and line management	Encourage employees and line management to provide suggestions. Explain what happens to their suggestions, explain why certain suggestions are not viable, and communicate successes initiated by employees
5 Difficulty in keeping up with the pace at which governance requirements are formulated	Approach governance holistically, rather than piece by piece

Chapter 23

Essentials introduction

The ten specified phases are not sufficient to ensure the success of a BPM project, as a BPM project requires many aspects and facets to be covered. We have therefore defined the three *essentials*: project management, people change management and leadership.

The Cambridge Dictionary defines the word *essential* as: 'necessary; needed; a basic thing that you cannot live without'. We believe that a BPM project cannot 'live' without these three essentials.

An *essential* is an aspect of the project that is considered extremely important, in fact crucial, to ensuring the success of the project, but it does not occur as a sequential activity or at a certain time within a project. An essential occurs on a continual basis throughout the entire project, and this is why we have depicted essentials differently in Figure 23.1.

Figure 23.1
Project phases and
essentials.

While the ten phases of the framework are not rigid sequential activities either, as they overlap and intertwine, they *predominantly* occur in the sequence we have shown. The method of approach and scenarios described throughout Part II provide examples of how the framework could be used and sequenced.

An *essential* is considered to be fundamental to the success of the entire project, and an aspect that permeates and occurs throughout every phase. Essentials are the foundations upon which any successful BPM project rests. When executed well, these foundations will be rock solid; when executed poorly, they will act like quicksand and the BPM project 'stool' (see Chapter 11) will tilt, sink or collapse.

Project management, people change management and leadership are topics that have been written about in significant detail in countless articles and books. We will not describe all the aspects of a successful project management methodology, or the framework of how to complete an organization-wide people change program, or what makes a great leader. We will, however, describe the aspects of each that are considered *essential* to a BPM project – the aspects that, if missing or executed poorly, will have a significant impact on the success of BPM projects. We will cover the parts of each of these that the business and project team must address during a project to ensure success.

Chapter 24

Project management

This chapter is not intended as a guide to project management. It is assumed that project management discipline is already understood. The intention is to focus on the aspects of project management that require particular attention in a BPM project in order to increase the chances of delivering a success.

Project management is considered to be one of the three *essentials* in the BPM project framework (Figure 24.1). Without excellent project management, an organization and project team cannot deliver a successful project. Is being

Figure 24.1
Project management essentials.

a good project manager enough? We would say no. Being a good project manager is no longer about having the skills and knowledge inherent in using traditional project management methodologies. BPM project managers must include in their repertoire significant skills with regard to:

- people change management
- stakeholder management
- in a BPM project, in-depth knowledge and experience in the implementation of BPM projects.

It could be argued that good project management has always required the first two of these skills; it is just that BPM projects require this knowledge to be deeper and better executed than in the past. Traditionally, projects delivered under project management methodologies have targeted the technology-based or low-resistance business changes. This enables a certainty of delivery that project sponsors like to have. BPM changes are different in one very important aspect: they almost always require a large element of people and/or cultural change.

Why is this? Consider any manager in a large organization in control of inefficient processes. Nine times out of ten the manager is well aware of the inefficient operation – as indeed are his or her superior managers and most of the process workers. Once a BPM practitioner is brought in to improve the situation and recognizes that stakeholders understand that the processes are inefficient, the obvious assumption to make is that the implementation job will be easy. This, of course, is not the case. The difference with BPM projects is the people and cultural impact of process changes. The underlying causes, interests and agendas that require the operation to change are often not recognized, understood or addressed. We are now deep in territory where a traditional project manager does not want to be – this world is uncertain, high risk and not easily controlled. A BPM project manager needs to be skilled enough to succeed in this type of environment. Table 24.1 provides some guidelines for this.

The question is, can a normal application or business project manager implement a BPM project and be successful? The answer is a qualified yes (probably), but nowhere nearly as well as an experienced *BPM* project manager. With an inexperienced BPM project manager, or a project manager with limited BPM experience, the project risks will simply be significantly higher and the organization risks foregoing potential benefits that can be achieved via BPM.

It is important for the organization to appoint its own project manager with overall responsibility for the entire project, even if the project manager is inexperienced in BPM implementation. If this is the case, it is crucial that the project manager is a business person and not an IT appointee; IT, vendor and all other project components must report to this business BPM project manager. To support an inexperienced BPM project manager, a senior and experienced BPM consultant (internal or external) is required to coach the

Table 24.1
Traditional verses BPM project management

Traditional project management	BPM project management
Ensure scope provides certainty for delivery	Ensure scope delivers the business objective required by improved processes
Stakeholder management to deliver implementation only	Stakeholder management to deliver implementation and long-term behavioral change and sustainability for the business
Contingency planning is only for recognized and easily defined risks	Cultural change hurdles (sometimes up to 50 percent of total effort) and contingency for unrecognized and difficult to define risks must be built into the plan
Works with sponsor/steering committee/project board to deliver certain outcomes	Works with the sponsor, steering committee, project board, business and users to manage uncertainty and deliver uncertain outcomes while delivering to meet the organization's strategy and objectives
Project success criteria are driven by quantifiable goals only	Project success criteria are driven equally by quantifiable and qualitative goals

project manager through the project. In addition, the consultant can add value to the project by:

- objectively managing situations when process compromises need to be made during the course of the project (as they inevitably will be); such decisions can have very serious repercussions, and a BPM specialist should be able to manage these risks appropriately to prevent the BPM project turning into an expensive, small incremental improvement project
- ensuring that the BPM project remains focused and as self-funding as possible, and continues to deliver real business value
- ensuring that the required people change management and cultural elements are correctly built into the project plan and managed as an essential part of the project
- adding value to stakeholder management and providing the expertise necessary to ensure that stakeholders remain continually engaged, have their needs met and are focused towards a successful BPM delivery.

Can a person without significant project management experience implement a BPM project? The answer to this question is easy – no. Project management is a fundamental skill or requirement for any project, and a BPM project is no different – in fact, the requirement is even greater because of the increased complexity.

Results

When project management is executed well, the risks of the project are significantly diminished and the likelihood of achieving the organization's project objectives and realization of the benefits is enhanced.

All projects must be subject to the normal organizational project governance requirements throughout their life, and these will be covered in the project methodology used by the project manager.

How?

There are many project management methodologies, and there have been many books written on it, so we do not propose to outline a new methodology here. We will, however, examine two key aspects of project management from a BPM perspective. These two key aspects are as follows:

- that there are several key 'gates' that must be passed satisfactorily if your BPM project is to be a success or indeed continue
- stakeholder management.

Project 'gates'

A project 'gate' represents a critical checkpoint or milestone in the journey of the project. When this milestone is reached, the gate is always assumed to be closed until the project manager and project sponsor are satisfied that there is sufficient information available to 'open' the gate and continue the project. If the gate is to remain closed, because the available information is not satisfactory, then the project should be stopped until information is available to allow the gate to be opened. A partially closed gate means that the information is incomplete and the project should be paused or slowed down until more information is gained in order to open or close the gate fully.

We will outline a few of the possible gates that the project may encounter along the project journey. We cannot and do not propose to mention all the possible gates that a project may encounter, as each project is unique and will encounter its own unique set of gates. Critical gates should be identified as early as possible in the project planning, and should be

- at points where the business can exit or pause the project, if necessary, with reduced risk and costs to the organization; exit strategies should be planned and agreed when gates are identified
- placed strategically to ensure that value has been created for the organization up to this time, regardless of the exit point.

We have numbered the gates here so that we can refer to them. The reader should not interpret the numbers as an order of occurrence within a project.

Gate 1: Stakeholder analysis

One of the first steps in a project should be the identification and subsequent analysis of the project stakeholders. The analysis should include the following:

- leadership styles of the stakeholders (refer to Chapter 26 for a more detailed examination and categorization of leadership styles)
- an understanding of where the internal stakeholders are placed within the organization and the organization hierarchy
- an understanding of the internal stakeholder's business (organization) and personal drivers – the business drivers are usually reflected in the individuals key result areas and key performance indicators; however, the personal drivers (ambition) of the internal stakeholders can be an extremely important motivator for an individual.

This gate is often closed until the stakeholder environment has been assessed and is deemed to be in alignment with the project goals. Are the stakeholders generally aligned to the proposed changes (project)? Is there misalignment? Are most of the stakeholders aligned, but not the major decision-makers or influencers? This is also related to the BPM maturity of the individual(s) and to organization BPM maturity. If the change is large and the stakeholder environment is not fully aligned to support the change, the project is unlikely to succeed.

This gate is often opened by:

- confirmation that the stakeholder environment, BPM maturity and BPM project objectives are consistent (aligned) with achieving a successful outcome
- planning the steps necessary to achieve stakeholder alignment so that they are adequately completed and under control. This may mean additional time, cost, multiple project checkpoints and the creation of additional gates.

This will be covered in more detail on the next section of this chapter (Stakeholder management).

Gate 2: Understand magnitude of change

The level of change and alignment of the stakeholders will, to some extent, be linked to the implementation scenario. In a 'business as usual' scenario, the expectation would be that all the stakeholders are aligned. The 'in the driver's seat' scenario will, in all probability, require a higher level of change and alignment than will the 'pilot' and 'under the radar' scenarios.

In the early planning stages of the project, during the Launch pad phase, the project team will need to determine and document the magnitude of change and stakeholder alignment required during the project – as known at that stage. The magnitude of change will be further refined during the Innovate phase, once there is knowledge of how processes are to change, and once the people capability matrices have been completed.

There needs to be a very clear understanding of the magnitude of change required by the organization. Until this is understood the project should not proceed, because an understanding of this leads directly into the next project gate – the capacity of the organization to change.

This gate is often closed because:

- the scope of the change is not understood by the business and/or project team, owing to unclear baseline processes, lack of information regarding organizational operations, differing stakeholder needs and so on.
- the total impact to the organization is unknown: that is, the size of the immediate change is understood, but the impact to related processes and to the organization is not.

This gate is often opened by:

- scoping agreement
- impact assessment.

The difficulties with scope can often be because the business problem that the organization is trying to resolve has not yet been adequately defined and agreed upon by the business and stakeholders. This is a critical step, and one that must be addressed and agreed upon before the business case can be finalized.

Case study: Business problem definition

An organization was planning a multimillion-dollar project to implement a CRM (to address Call Centre issues), a data warehouse, data mining, a major data cleansing operation for data integrity reasons, and a document management system.

A stakeholder workshop was held for the primary purpose of defining the business problem the project was expected to resolve. After three hours, the problem could not be defined by the stakeholders. The

(Continued)

Case study: Business problem definition (*Continued*)

stakeholders (management) simply wanted the new 'system', and external consultants had recommended it. It was a technical solution looking for a problem.

It was recommended that the project be broken down into smaller components and a business case be built for each component.

This advice was ignored, and the project manager spent the next year canvassing the stakeholders and trying to build a business case. The project did not proceed.

Message: Workshop, with all relevant stakeholders, the reason for the project and the business problem that it will solve prior to building, or at least finalizing, the business case.

Gate 3: The organization's capacity to change

The nature of a BPM project is such that it will no doubt cause change within the organization. The level of change can range from small to significant; however, in most BPM projects the level of change will be from the middle to the high end of the change scale.

An organization's ability to (and capacity for) change will be put to the test in a BPM project. This ability and capacity for change within an organization needs to be determined very early on in the project, because if the project requires significant change and the organization maturity is unable to cope with the level of change required, the project is doomed to failure from the outset. In this instance, the project manager should go back to the project sponsor to discuss and decide upon a course of action. This could mean walking away from, or stopping, the project. It is far better to establish this at an early start in a project than to spend time and money, only to discover later that the organization is incapable of changing to the extent necessary.

Chapter 27 will assist the project sponsor and project manager to gauge the organization's maturity to cope with change.

This gate is often closed because of:

- overconfidence – organizations tend to have an insatiable appetite to 'want the universe', and yet they are only capable of changing their world at a limited rate. BPM project managers need to identify the gap between an organization's desire for change, and reality
- lack of confidence – an organization may not clearly understand its capability to change and tend to underestimate its capacity to absorb change.

This gate is often opened by:

- assessing and understanding organizational BPM maturity
- assessing capacity for change (reviewing similar past projects may assist in this regard)

- planning for the rate of change. Ambitious objectives can often be broken down into smaller stages – that is, instead of one large step change, you may plan for a smaller step change with specific milestones, followed by further incremental improvements, followed by another smaller step change, followed by further incremental improvements, and so on.

Gate 4: Organization's acceptance of BPM

Organization BPM maturity also relates to the organization's understanding of the importance of processes and how process improvement can make a substantial difference in meeting the organization's strategy and objectives.

It is a combination of organizational BPM maturity and executive understanding of BPM, and the executive's attention to process, that will determine an organization's process-centric view.

This gate is often closed because:

- executives are too busy 'fighting fires'
- executives do not understand the importance of processes to their organizational effectiveness.

This gate is often opened by:

- market pressures forcing organizations to look at cost reductions, and thus focus upon processes
- growing maturity and successful case studies of BPM implementations within other organizations
- just one executive within the organization implementing a 'pilot' or 'under the radar' BPM project that is successful; this is sometimes enough to demonstrate the benefits of BPM to the organization.

Gate 5: Technical review

Where a BPM project is to involve automation and interfacing to existing infrastructure (hardware, networks, legacy application systems), there needs to be a technical review conducted early in the project to ensure that the selected BPM solution can indeed interface with the required infrastructure. This can be a 'show-stopper' if it either is not technically possible or will involve significant expenditure to achieve.

This may seem obvious; however, it is disappointing how often a review of this nature does not occur early in a project.

This gate is often closed because:

- the existing technical infrastructure is unknown, poorly documented, the interfaces are not understood, technologies are incompatible and so on.

This gate is often opened by:

- technical analysis at an early stage
- consideration in the selection of the BPM automation toolset (and a vendor 'proof of concept' demonstration during the selection process).

Case study: Infrastructure 'show-stopper'

We were managing an automated BPM project implementation for a client who had an infrastructure that had grown piecemeal with the incredible growth of the organization. This left some interesting challenges with regard to the existing infrastructure.

We informed the client that the project should temporarily pause to review and pilot how the selected BPM solution was going to interface with the existing infrastructure, as there were concerns that the legacy applications may require substantial changes to accommodate the BPM solution. The client ignored this advice and insisted on proceeding because of business imperatives to implement.

A couple of months later the project was *forced* to halt because the infrastructure could not be interfaced without significant rework. Had the project paused when originally suggested, the rework could have taken place in parallel with other aspects of the BPM project – thus avoiding the delay and costs.

Message: If there are potential major issues with infrastructure, address them early in the project to ensure that the impact is known and understood, to save time and money.

Stakeholder management

First, let's consider who is a stakeholder. A stakeholder is an individual, or group of individuals, who have (or believe they have) a 'stake' (positive or negative) in the project. They can be as diverse as: individual managers, staff, vendors, other internal business units, suppliers, customers, distribution channels, the community, the environment and the marketplace.

Stakeholder management is important – in fact we would suggest crucial – in a BPM project for a number of reasons:

1   Without key internal stakeholders, the project will not have funding.
2   In the Understand and Innovate phases, we have suggested that processes need to be examined on an end-to-end basis – which means that in all likelihood they will cross departmental and organizational boundaries. Without key stakeholder support, both internal and external, this cannot be achieved in any meaningful way.
3   Without stakeholder support it will be extremely difficult to realize the business benefits set out in the business case.

4   There are many parties to a BPM project – the business, project team members, vendors, suppliers, customers, and so forth – and without their support and enthusiasm, the project simply becomes more difficult.

5   Certain external stakeholders can be crucial to a BPM project, and these must be identified.

Communications must be targeted specifically to the various groups.

Case study: External stakeholder involvement

We were engaged in a BPM project where the majority of the organization's business was distributed via intermediaries. We were asked to assist the organization redesign processes that were generated by these intermediaries.

When we suggested that a small number of stakeholder focus groups should be established to inform the intermediaries of what the organization wished to achieve, to listen to their concerns and ensure that the intermediaries would ultimately use the new processes, we were met with resistance by the sales team and a belief this was simply not necessary.

Once the client understood the opportunity and need for the meeting, it proceeded to engage the intermediaries and the outcomes were excellent.

Message: If external stakeholders of processes are not involved in their creation, how can you expect them to use the processes once introduced?

Stakeholder management is all about relationship management. It is a structured process approach for handling the necessary relationships involved in the project. Owing to the complexity of BPM projects, this stakeholder management needs to be a more formal process than in traditional projects.

How do you create this more formal stakeholder management structured process?

There are two types of stakeholder management usually required for successful BPM projects. The first is called 'managing stakeholders for successful delivery'. This is a more formal method of ensuring that stakeholders do the tasks asked of them to ensure delivery of the project. This is based on more traditional project management delivery-focused techniques. It is adversarial based, and recognizes that most organizations are still an adversarial environment. It is a 'get things done' environment. This approach will assist with delivery; however, it is unlikely to effect any long-term behavioral change, which can influence the people change management aspects of a project.

The second is 'interest-based' stakeholder management, and this is based on cooperative problem-solving techniques. This is where relationships are made and maintained that progress towards permanent change in individual and group behavior – more conducive to cultural change.

Both techniques will need to be used for the significant organizational change that is necessary for BPM projects. For small changes or large projects with minimal cultural change impact, the key technique to use is 'managing stakeholders for successful delivery'.

The topic of managing stakeholders and the detail of the theories and these techniques is too vast a topic to discuss in this book. We will provide a summarized practical stakeholder management framework of how to utilize these techniques within a BPM project.

Managing stakeholders for successful delivery

The steps are as follows:

1   Establish the internal project or business team to build the stakeholder management structure, plan, engagement and execution.
2   Identify all stakeholders and their relationship to the project.
3   Profile the role key stakeholders will play in the project.
4   Map stakeholders to determine the individual stakeholder requirements or the outcomes that they need from the project.
5   Determine the best strategies to engage and manage each stakeholder, to satisfy their needs and ensure a safe delivery of the project.

Each of these steps is discussed here in more detail.

Step 1: Establish the internal stakeholder team

In this step, it is essential that the project manager involves the business owners to ensure that they are fully engaged in the building of the stakeholder management structure (the how are we going to do this step), and the detailed planning, engagement and execution.

Who from the business needs to be involved? Usually this includes the project business owner, the project sponsor and all other business stakeholders who have to advise or propose a final solution.

The project manager and business stakeholder leader will have overall responsibility for stakeholder management, and need to be people who:

- are well respected by the executives across the organization
- have credibility throughout the organization
- are comfortable in speaking their mind, even if it goes against the organization's culture
- are able to deliver both good and bad news in a sensitive and yet honest manner
- are considered to be agents for change within the organization
- are able to get things done.

It is the responsibility of the project manager to 'move' stakeholders to where they need to be in supporting the project, and to control and manage the stakeholder relations. The project manager will need to have confidence that he or she has the support and assistance of the project sponsor, and that the two of them can have confidential conversations about stakeholder management issues.

The project manager will need to provide project team members with the messages to deliver to specific stakeholders to assist in gaining individual stakeholders' support. The message needs to be delivered consistently by all project team members.

Activities need to be allocated by the project manager to other key project and business team members. These activities will be developed during the next steps.

Step 2: Identify all the stakeholders and their relationship to the project

A detailed list of stakeholders needs must be compiled. The starting point for this list will be the list of stakeholders compiled during the Launch pad phase Step 4 – Stakeholder identification. A sample list of stakeholders identified during this step of a small BPM project includes the following:

Internal:	**External:**
Staff	Intermediaries
Management	Clients
Finance	Funds managers
Facilities management	External audit
Compliance	Vendors
Risk management	Legislative bodies
Information technology	Partners
Human resources	
Internal audit	
Business development	

As can be seen from the above list of possible stakeholder groups, there maybe many stakeholders to manage – probably more than you have time for, or it is appropriate to manage, within the project. The above are stakeholder groups, and it will be necessary to identify individuals within these groups who are important stakeholders. It is essential for the project team to understand that the organization's staff are one of the key stakeholders, and without their support and enthusiasm the project will either not be a success or be severely challenged. Refer to Chapter 25 for a more detailed discussion on this aspect.

In order to determine which stakeholders to manage, the project manager and business stakeholder leader should complete one or both of the matrices in Step 3. Both these will assist in the identification of which stakeholders it is appropriate to manage. It should be updated, as required, after each stakeholder meeting.

Step 3: Profile the role key stakeholders will play in the project

Once stakeholders have been identified, the project manager needs to profile them. A form such as that shown in Table 24.2 can be used effectively for each key stakeholder. The individual stakeholder analysis should be reviewed by the

Table 24.2
Individual stakeholder analysis

Name:	Position:
Ability to Impact Project:	**View of Project (commitment level):**
High —|—|—|—|—|— Low (circle position on the line)	Positive —|—|—|—|—|— Negative (circle position on the line)
Risks: *(What risks does this stakeholder bring to the project? What risks are associated with the stakeholder?)*	
Strengths: *(What strengths does this stakeholder bring to the project?)*	
Weaknesses: *(What weaknesses are associated with this stakeholder being involved with the project?)*	
WIIFM *(What's in it for stakeholder?)*	
What turns him/her off? *(What does the stakeholder like/dislike about the project, their role, organization, personal interests, and so forth)*	
What actions do I need to take?	
Action:	**Timeframe:**

Table 24.3
Stakeholder analysis matrix

Type	Name	Power today		Power after implementation of project		Ability to influence project and other stakeholders	View of project (interest level)	WIIFM
		Source	Relative strength	Source	Relative strength			

project manager and/or business stakeholder leader prior to meeting with a stakeholder, to provide a reminder of the issues regarding the stakeholder and what the project wants to achieve with that particular stakeholder's assistance.

In order to identify key stakeholders and to facilitate the stakeholder mapping step, it is often useful to document further stakeholder information in a matrix as in Table 24.3. Do not interpret from the perceived sequence that one of these tables should be completed before the other; often both will happen concurrently and are constantly maintained throughout the project.

Table 24.3 shows similar summarized information for all identified stakeholders.

The first step in the completion of this matrix is to categorize the stakeholders by type or group and individual name. The next step is to distinguish between the power the stakeholder has now, in relation to the project, and the power the stakeholder will have after the completion of the project implementation. It is essential to distinguish those stakeholders that are critical to the progress of the project from those that simply have an interest in the project. Use Table 24.2 to assist in understanding the categorization.

A brief explanation of the columns of Table 24.3 follows (except where the columns are self-explanatory).

- *Power today, and Power after implementation of project*: *Source* refers to position, personality (aggressive, charismatic), knowledge or expertise (maturity) regarding BPM, resource control (ability to grant or withhold resources to the project), and whether the stakeholder has the power of veto over the project. *Relative strength* should simply be ranked as high, medium or low.
- *Ability to influence project and other stakeholders*: there is a need to understand how great the influence or power is that the stakeholder can exert over the project and other stakeholder(s). Who is able to influence whom, and how is this achieved? As the project is executed, will the reaction of stakeholders change – and how? In Chapter 25, we mention the 'gatekeepers' of change. These are the people who potentially 'filter' information before it is passed on to other stakeholders or stakeholder groups. It is necessary to understand whether a stakeholder is a 'gatekeeper' or not and, if so, how the stakeholder will behave and possibly filter information onwards. The impact this could (or will) have on the project must also be understood.
- *View of project (interest level)*: not all stakeholders have a view on or interest in the outcomes of the project; some are only interested in what happens during the execution of the project. However, it is important always to be vigilant and on the lookout for new stakeholders; some may only start to pay attention to the project once it starts to have an impact upon them. These stakeholders need to be identified and managed as early as possible.
- *WIIFM*. 'What's In It For Me' is a critical area to understand. If you do not understand what is in it for a particular stakeholder, how can you direct communication and outcomes? WIIFM is not only about the impact of the immediate outcomes of the project, but also about the impact of the project on the future of the stakeholder and what they get out of it at a personal and a professional level.

Case study: Stakeholder no longer has a role as a result of the project

We commenced a BPM project with the usual Launch pad phase. By the time we had completed the Innovate report, a significant recommendation of the project was the reorganization of the department's structure. The recommendations were that the department staff numbers decrease by half, and that there be a reduction from one departmental manager with four sub-managers to one manager for the entire department. Our project sponsor was the departmental manager, so the project sponsor could potentially end the project without having a role within the organization. Without careful and sensitive stakeholder management, this could have resulted in a difficult situation.

Message: Always complete stakeholder analysis and understand the possible future impacts for key stakeholders, and handle this with care and sensitivity.

Predicting outcomes is part of stakeholder analysis and management. The likely impacts must be maintained on a continual basis throughout the project.

We understand that some of this information will be difficult to obtain, will be subjective, and could be extremely confidential and sensitive. The culture and maturity of the organization and individual stakeholders will determine how open the project manager can be with this information. There is an emerging trend in some countries to be far more open about stakeholder management and individual stakeholder positions on projects. It is based upon an understanding that stakeholder management is not 'manipulation', but openly influencing them with an integrity that endeavors to understand the stakeholders' underlying interests and address these interests. This approach will build trust.

However, openness is not always possible in all organizations due to the level of organizational maturity and the maturity of individual stakeholders. Where this is the case, the project manager must respect this information and keep it absolutely confidential. Great care must be taken regarding where this information is stored in project documentation and to whom access is given.

Step 4: Map stakeholders

Taking the information gathered so far, we suggest the next step is to map the stakeholders onto two separate matrices that bring out subtle differences which will enable decisions to be made as to how to engage with the stakeholders. The purpose of mapping is to determine where your stakeholders are now, and then to understand where they need to be, from a project perspective.

The first matrix (stakeholder project impact and view analysis – Figure 24.2) will show the project manager a stakeholder's ability to impact the project, and view of the project.

The 'ability to impact project' axis refers to the power a stakeholder may have over the project. The stakeholder may have the power of veto or approval. Stakeholders can also overtly or subtly have significant power and impact over a project, at the project commencement, during the project and at the implementation stage.

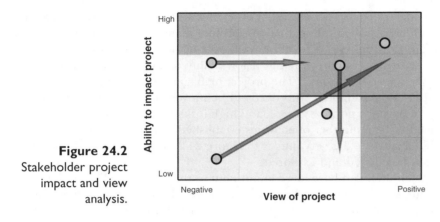

Figure 24.2
Stakeholder project
impact and view
analysis.

Coupled with this impact is the 'view of the project' axis. Stakeholders may be vitally interested in the project, as it will have a positive or negative impact upon their ability to meet their business and personal objectives, or they may have no view or interest at all. It is important for the project manager to recognize that individual stakeholders may also develop a 'view' during the project as they come to realize the project impact upon themselves. This new view may be as a result of the project manager's stakeholder management, or stakeholders may have more information and come to the conclusion themselves; either way, the project manager must recognize this, re-map it and manage it.

The circles in Figures 24.2 and 24.3 represent the current position of an individual stakeholder, and the arrow indicates the position to which the

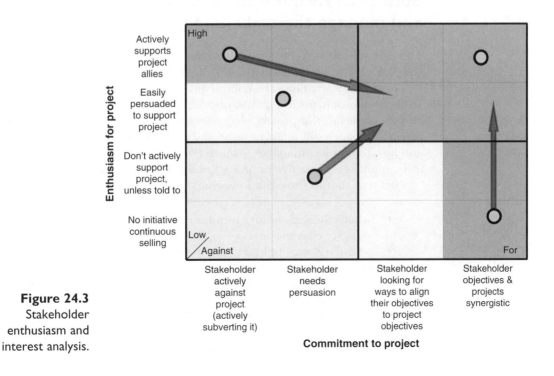

Figure 24.3
Stakeholder
enthusiasm and
interest analysis.

stakeholder needs to be moved. The circles without arrows mean that the stakeholder is in a position that the project manager thinks is correct and therefore does not need to be moved. As can be seen in Figure 24.2, one of the stakeholders currently has a low ability to impact the project and a negative view of the project. The project manager has determined that this is an important stakeholder who needs to be moved from the current position to one of having a positive view of, and high influence over, the project. There will need to be a number of activities established to make this occur.

While Figure 24.3 is very similar to Figure 24.2, there are subtle differences than can be elicited and explored.

A stakeholder can have low commitment to the project and yet a high level of enthusiasm. Equally, a stakeholder may have a high level of enthusiasm for the project and yet it could be at odds with their business or personal objectives, and therefore their commitment level is 'against' it (the organizational silo effect).

If movement of a stakeholder is to take place, the project manager will need to develop a strategy for each arrow in these two figures. The strategy will be a set of activities that will, once executed, move the stakeholder to the desired position on the matrices. This brings us to the last step to be completed in gathering stakeholder information before planning the stakeholder strategy and engagement. This is the need to document the outcomes or objectives that each stakeholder will want from the project, and map these to the actual project outcomes and objectives. This will provide obvious evidence of where the objectives are synergistic or otherwise.

Step 5: Determine the best strategy to engage and manage the stakeholder

This last step in stakeholder management is about creating a strategic plan (or pathway) towards successful stakeholder engagement.

The strategic plan must be completed at project and individual stakeholder levels, and must provide a pathway from the individual stakeholder's objectives and outcomes to the project objectives and outcomes. It must show how the project manager will manage those stakeholders for and against the project, and how the project manager plans to encourage low-enthusiasm stakeholders to be highly enthusiastic (or at least neutral) towards the project.

The plan should show the following:

- where the stakeholder is in his or her thinking with regard to project delivery effectiveness
- where the stakeholder needs to be in order to contribute to successful delivery of the project
- using identified stakeholder drivers, how the project manager will move stakeholder interests to support project delivery appropriately
- continuous review periods – this should be every time a project manager meets a stakeholder, whether it is in a formal meeting or for an informal chat in a hallway.

This stage should link with the communications plan developed as part of the project. It should also link with the aspects discussed in Chapter 26.

'Interest-based' stakeholder management

Managing stakeholders to deliver projects can create adversarial conflict, which can not only damage relationships but also ensure only short-term behavioral change. Here, once the project is closed, behavior reverts back to previous patterns and potential benefits to the organization can be lost. If this is the case, it is very important to use other techniques that ensure the maintenance of relationships throughout the ups and downs of project delivery pressure and also to ensure that behavior change is an ongoing and permanent outcome of the project. The best way to achieve this is to utilize interest-based stakeholder management, which involves cooperative problem-solving techniques. The process of interest-based stakeholder management is detailed in Figure 24.4.

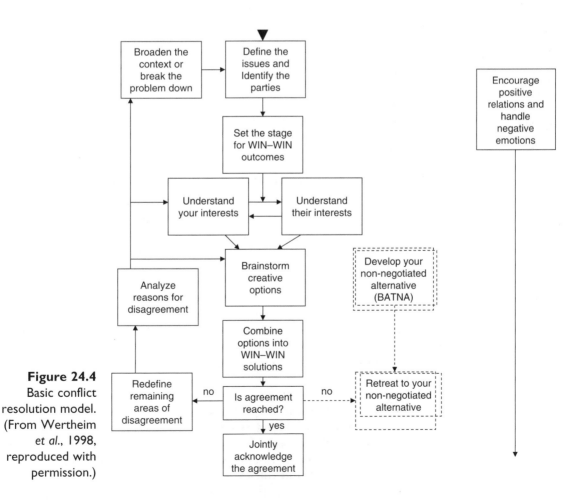

Figure 24.4 Basic conflict resolution model. (From Wertheim *et al.*, 1998, reproduced with permission.)

Interest-based stakeholder management is about:

- assessing the problems, defining the issues and setting the stage for win–win solutions – these are necessary steps prior to identifying individual underlying interests
- the underlying interests that need to be identified, which are those that cause individuals to take positions relating to the problem
- analyzing any areas of disagreement, using techniques such as brainstorming to develop win–win solutions. BATNA is one such negotiation technique, where you determine your Best Alternative To a Negotiated Agreement. This allows you to understand your negotiating boundaries and reduces the chances of holding an entrenched position to the detriment of all concerned.

The skills required for cooperative problem-solving, as described by Wertheim *et al.* (1998), are the ability to:

- identify underlying interests in relation to needs, wants, concerns and fears; this is done by understanding why you are taking a certain position in the conflict
- examine all interests, including the use of empathy
- listen actively, using skills such as reflection, communicating by taking turns, utilizing attentive body language and not behaving defensively
- separate the people from the problem
- brainstorm
- find creative new alternatives
- assess whether the solution satisfies the resolution of all the underlying issues.

Multi-party interest-based stakeholder management

The same principles used in cooperative problem-solving between two parties can also be used for organizational multi-party problem-solving. The resolution process must take into account the organizational structure, and be aware of dealing with coalitions, factions and alliances of stakeholders in addition to individuals. The principle is still the same, whereby win–win solutions are sought to resolve underlying issues.

An example of this is described by Gray (1989), who explains a collaborative approach to multi-party conflict resolution. This approach seeks to explore the differences between stakeholders over an issue in order to create new solutions to solve the problem. The skills required to apply this collaborative approach to conflict resolution include the ability to:

- define the problem
- commit to solve the problem
- identify all stakeholders impacted by the problem
- assess stakeholder interests
- identify available resources to solve the problem
- establish ground rules

- set agendas
- organize sub-groups working on the problem resolution
- share information
- explore multiple options
- reach agreements with other stakeholders
- implement the agreement.

Third-party intervention

Third-party intervention takes into account mediation, conciliation, arbitration and adjudication. These approaches are a mixture of adversarial and cooperative approaches to managing stakeholders, and involve the introduction of a third party with a specific role in order to guide parties in conflict towards some sort of agreement or settlement. The skills required when using these methods are the ability to:

- know when to introduce a third party into a conflict resolution process
- define clearly the role of the third party
- agree the process for resolution under these approaches
- agree to the final outcome of the process.

Putting it into practice

Stakeholder management during a project is often handled on an intuitive (rather than formal) basis. While project managers often speak of the need for stakeholder management and spend a great deal of time on this aspect of project management, it is rarely systematically analyzed, planned and executed and yet relationships are the basis for everything we do.

The critical aspects of stakeholder management are to:

- understand who the stakeholders are
- understand their relationships to the project and each other
- determine what role they are playing, or will play, in the project
- determine their requirements from the project
- determine how best to engage with them to satisfy their needs.

It is best if the business owners (project sponsor and business owner) are engaged in and actively support the stakeholder planning, engagement and execution processes.

It is important for the project manager and sponsor to recognize that stakeholder management is about dealing with people, and because of this there are no guarantees of the outcomes. The project manager can complete the stakeholder management to a very high standard and still not achieve the desired outcomes, because a stakeholder has either provided the wrong signals (on purpose or unintentionally) or simply changed his or her mind.

Project management risks

In this essential part of the project, there are several risks that must be considered and mitigation strategies implemented to eliminate or at least reduce them. Table 24.4 shows some of these.

Table 24.4
Project management risks and mitigation strategies

Risk	Mitigation strategy
1 All 'gates' are not identified and managed	During the Launch pad phase, and continually throughout the other phases of the project, potential gates must be identified and managed as early as possible in the project. Stop or pause the project if a gate has not been satisfactorily addressed
2 Stakeholder analysis and management are not addressed thoroughly	Ensure that the stakeholder management steps are included in the project plan and continually addressed proactively throughout the project
3 There is no appointed business project manager	BPM is a critical activity for the business and one that has the potential for substantial risk. The business project manager is *not* the business expert, and needs to have both substantial project management *and* BPM experience
4 Insufficient BPM expertise is available to the project team	Ensure that the project has both specialist BPM project management and and process analyst skills available

Chapter 25

People change management

Good companies react quickly to change;
Great companies create change.
Move before the wave; change before you have to.

(Hriegel and Brandt, 1996)

Opinions on the importance of people change management vary enormously. Various writers and leaders have stated differing views, such as:

. . . transforming the corporation is not just a dream but an urgent necessity.

(Keen, 1997: 15)

There is no such thing as luck in business. If you are in the business of continuous change you must have a process, applied in a very disciplined way, that tells you where you are heading. You need to understand what you are trying to achieve and make sure that when you do it, you do it right.

(Don Argus, Former CEO, National Australia Bank, in Cavanagh, 1999)

Jim Collins' (2001) research led him to state that:

The good-to-great companies paid scant attention to managing change, motivating people, or creating alignment. Under the right conditions, the problems of commitment, alignment, motivation, and change largely melt away.

The interesting phrase in this last quotation is *under the right conditions*. It is the responsibility of the leadership of the organization to 'create' the right conditions, and these do not happen by accident. As Don Argus said, 'you must have a process and apply it in a disciplined way'. This is why people change management is one of the three essentials of a BPM project (Figure 25.1). It is the process of applying the changes planned for in the project.

During a BPM project, unless it is an extremely small and isolated project, culture will need to be dealt with, especially as part of the People phase. However, be careful not to have the people within the organization who use

Figure 25.1
The People change management essential.

culture as an excuse and tell you that this is 'just the way we do things around here', or this is 'just the way things are'. If culture needs improving, then it will always be as a result of some part of the organization's processes, structure or people management systems (including leadership) not functioning as they should. It could be incorrect role descriptions or performance measurement targets; lack of appropriate management reporting or structure; lack of skills or capacity; inappropriate leadership style; or external forces imposing change on the organization and the organization's processes, structure or people management systems not responding or changing as required. These issues are usually the root cause, and the culture is the outcome.

Within a BPM project, always remember that the project outcome is the goal, and any cultural change that may be necessary is a result of the project goals. Some cultural change is essential as part of a successful project; however, cultural change is not an end in itself.

In this chapter, we will look at the importance of the change process as it specifically relates to the implementation of a BPM project. BPM projects are about changing the processes and the way business is conducted within an organization and, if you think about it, cultural change is 'just' another process itself. We will discuss this 'process', how it can be implemented and, most importantly, how it can be sustained over time.

People change management is a core essential of successful BPM projects, and an area that must be focused upon throughout the entire project. It is not usually possible to identify, upfront, all of the change steps and issues that will be required during a people change program, so it is critical to have a clear mechanism to lead the project through this process. Figure 25.2 provides an example of this mechanism.

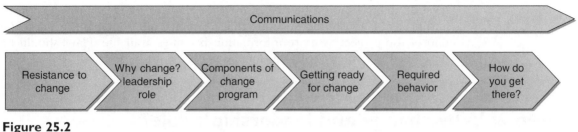

Figure 25.2
People change management steps.

> Change is personal . . . Forceful leadership can accomplish only so much. The shift from machine-age bureaucracy to flexible, self-managed teams requires that lots of ordinary managers and workers be psychologically prepared.
>
> (*Fortune*, 27 August 1994)

This chapter is about providing a 'process' of how to assist these 'ordinary managers and workers' to become prepared for, and accept, change.

The communications step has not been described separately but is discussed throughout the various steps, especially Step 3.

Step 1: Resistance to change

Mark Twain is purported to have said that 'the only person who likes change is a wet baby', and you know, he is probably right.

If Mark Twain is correct, why do people dislike change so much? Some of the reasons include the following:

1 *Fear.* This is the most common cause of resistance, and one of the most powerful. This is often because change is uncertain, uncomfortable, unpredictable and unsafe. Communication and honesty are powerful ways of overcoming this fear factor.
2 *Feeling powerless.* This is often because the project team and business management have not involved the people enough. Provide people with the opportunity to participate and feel they have power to influence the change process.
3 *Too much effort and pain is involved.* It takes a great deal of effort and often pain to achieve change, and then to become comfortable with it. Most people will avoid pain and move towards pleasure, and in this instance pleasure equals the *status quo.*
4 *Absence of self-interest.* People need to understand what is in it for them, or that they will not be any worse off. If it is the latter, then they will ask, 'Why change?' and this needs to be clearly articulated. In Step 2, we will discuss why people should understand the need for change.

Resistance must be anticipated as much as possible, and research, via surveys and questionnaires, should be conducted. An understanding of the type and level of change should be determined for the project. The project sponsor and project team should be aware that resistance often increases towards the end of the project as more information becomes available. Plans should be developed to contend with this increase.

Step 2: Why change and leadership's role?

In traditional BPR projects, 'the focus of change is on work processes, new technology . . . and decentralized service rather than on the people who must implement change (Goldsmith, 1995).' As Michael Hammer stated in 1993, 'coming up with the ideas is the easy part, but getting things done is the tough part. The place where these reforms die is . . . down in the trenches' – and who 'owns' the trenches? People.

It is the 'people' who are the gatekeepers of change, and Michael Hammer expressed it well when he said that people are 'the most perplexing, annoying, distressing, and confusing part' of BPR (Hammer, 1995). Whether or not people are annoying and distressing does not matter; the fact is, they are a critical part of the success of any BPM project, and if you do not get this part of the project right, the project will either fail or have only limited success. The project team can create the best processes and BPM systems, but if people refuse to use them, or use them poorly, then the project will not be successful.

Case study: Workflow and image implementation

We were involved with an organization that was extremely conservative. In assisting the organization in building a business case for the implementation of a workflow and imaging system, we were told that it would not work!

When we asked why, we were told that the organization tried it five years ago and it was a failure, and management was nervous about trying again. Further investigation revealed that no people change management had been included in the project.

The organization's people were extremely fearful of the new system, and when it was implemented they simply *refused* to use it. Management had to de-install the system and go back to the old, costly, manual processes.

Message: If you expect a change in people's behavior, then they must be listened to and included within the planning for the change process.

While we will cover the more detailed role of leadership in Chapter 26, it is important to state here, briefly, the function that leadership must play in the people change management events.

People do not like change and will not implement or participate in a change program, *unless* they believe it is necessary. Simplistically, there are two methods of convincing people to change. The method selected will depend upon the organization, the particular situation, and the leadership style of the leader.

The first method suggests that:

> there must be a crisis, and it is the job of the CEO to define and communicate that crisis, its magnitude, its severity, and its impact. Just as important, the CEO must also be able to communicate how to end the crisis – the new strategy, the new company model, the new culture.
>
> (Gerstner, 2002)

In communicating the crisis, or the reasons why change is necessary, it is imperative that the CEO or change leader formally informs the people that *no change is not an option*, so that they are fully aware that the change program *is* going to take place and it is their role to decide how and when to come on the journey. If a crisis exists, then openness, honesty and the maintenance of integrity is essential in communicating the crisis and way forward. If a crisis is 'manufactured' to instigate change, then this has the potential to conflict with the required honesty and integrity required of leadership.

The second method is more subtle, and requires leadership to have people understand that there is a 'problem' and inform them of the magnitude of the problem and why it is essential to change. People will need to understand the impact upon the organization and themselves if the problem is not addressed.

The people within the organization do not need 'rah-rah' speeches; they need leadership – direction, consistency, momentum and persistence. They want leaders who will focus on solutions and actions. If there are hard decisions to make, as there often are in any change program, make them as early as possible in the program, and make sure everyone (management, staff and stakeholders) knows about it and why it was necessary; then implement it.

As one unknown person purportedly stated, 'Reengineering is like starting a fire on your head and putting it out with a hammer' – that is, it's painful and boring.

While the CEO does not, and should not, need to be the leader of all people change management programs, especially if a 'pilot project' or 'under the radar' scenario is selected, the program does need to have a primary leader or sponsor who will guide the change process. This person's role will include providing the answers to the following questions, always remembering to keep this within the bounds of your BPM project:

- What is the change intended to achieve?
- Why the changes are necessary?
- What will be the consequences of these changes to both the organization and the individuals? (Scheer *et al.*, 2003: 26)

The latter point must cover not only outcomes of the change process, but also what will happen if we do not change.

Change takes a great deal of time and considerable commitment by leadership at all levels within the organization and project team. It cannot only be led by the CEO – we will cover the three suggested levels of 'leadership' in Chapter 26.

When leadership commences the communication process of motivating people for the change, leaders must show them the way forward – the 'reality' of the situation. Truth, however, is critical in showing and telling people the facts.

If the leadership and management of the organization say they do not have time for this, they need to understand that this *is their job!* It is they who must change first and then be the role models for the rest of the organization. In other words, *walk the talk* for everyone to see.

While it is not the leadership's role to provide a detailed project plan of the people change management steps, the leadership must ensure that the project manager has taken responsibility for this. The project manager needs to work with the project sponsor, organization leadership and the human resources department to ensure that all the steps are addressed and the project plan is completed and implemented.

Leaders, and in this context we are referring to anyone providing a role model for others, need to understand that people are different and take different amounts of time and effort to change. Some will change fast and get on board, others will be slower, and still others will never change and will need to be accommodated in an appropriate way. It is the leader's role to understand this and to provide people with the necessary time and support.

Successful change programs have three important qualities: passion, enthusiasm and intense excitement. It is the leader's responsibility to ignite each of these and find others to keep the 'fire burning'.

The crucial element for this, and the bottom line for any people change management program, is 'communication squared' – you can *never* do too much of it. This will be discussed further in Step 3 (components of the change program).

Step 3: Components of the change program

Before we launch into the components of a people change management program, it is important to make it clear that it is the responsibility of the BPM Project Steering Committee, together with the project manager and business sponsor, to deliver the results of this program. It cannot be outsourced, or totally (or significantly) delegated to any of the following:

1   Another area. Sometimes there can be a temptation to 'hand it over' to the human resources department. While there is no question that HR should be intimately involved in the program, the coordination of activities is such that the project manager needs to involve all aspects of the BPM project – for example, the People phase will have a significant impact upon and input to the people change management program.

2   Consultants. This is an 'inside job' that cannot be given to an outside group to complete. Certainly, consultants can contribute ideas, structure and learning from their other engagements, but the responsibility must lie with the project manager and business to plan, execute and deliver.

We would suggest that the essential components of a change program include the following:

1   Planning a detailed project plan
2   Selection of key personnel to be involved in the program
3   A clear understanding of the program's links to: strategy, culture, structure, new people roles, new processes and the overall BPM project
4   A detailed communications plan, outlining the way information will be delivered to all stakeholders.

We will take each of these and briefly describe its role in the change program, and the important issues to consider.

Planning

The people change management program can be a significant program of effort in its own right, and will have many activities and tasks that must be integrated with and form part of the overall project plan. The plan should obviously contain all the steps involved in the change program, responsibilities, and deliver dates. It must include steps specifically designed to show how the organization or business unit proposes to unfreeze, move and refreeze the organization.

Unfreezing is about creating the awareness and need for change, and creating a climate that is receptive for change. *Moving* the organization focuses on the changing forces and changing behavior from the old to the new. *Refreezing* is the reinforcement process that occurs, leading to the institutionalization of the change making it sustainable and part of 'business as usual' (Lewin, undated).

The basic questions of who, what, which and how need to be answered. Examples of these questions are as follows:

1   Who will be involved in the change program – customers, suppliers, investors, management, people within the organization (organization-wide or localized to one or more departments)? Obviously, this will depend upon the BPM project scenario selected.
2   What is going to change and what new information will be needed or produced?
3   Which new deliverables or outcomes can be expected?
4   How do the changes fit together and influence the new expected state for the organization?

These questions need to be answered before the planning process can be completed.

Selection of key personnel

This refers to the selection of the change champions – those members of the organization who will be the leaders of the change program. These people will come from all levels within the organization and project team. Chapter 26 will outline three levels of 'leadership', and the change champions should be carefully selected from all of these levels.

Understanding of links

The change program will impact, and be impacted by, all phases and aspects of the BPM project. We have discussed many of these links throughout the book, but they include links to:

- organization strategy
- culture of the organization
- any proposed new organization structure, people roles and processes.

As described in the introduction to the essential aspects, these links are why people change management is shown as an essential in the framework and not as a phase.

Communications plan

The completion of a communications strategy and plan is an essential aspect of any change program. It needs to be thought through in a thorough way, and continually adjusted throughout its life as feedback is received and an understanding of what has worked well and what could have worked better is obtained.

Here follows an outline summary of general guidelines regarding how to go about the construction of a communications plan, and what should it address (Scheer *et al.*, 2003: 7–8).

Preparation

1　Segment the audience or different groups who will be receiving the messages.
2　Plan to use multiple channels for the delivery of the messages, ensuring that all personal communication modalities of people are addressed – visual, auditory and kinesthetic.
3　Use multiple people to deliver messages – different people will have different styles; however, you must ensure that the message is consistent and never contradictory.
4　Be clear and communicate simple messages, always ensuring that the change program is setting the expectations and never leaving expectations to be set by the recipients.

5   There should be a small number of key, simple messages for the entire program. People will not remember, nor want to hear, a large number of complex reasons or messages. The more senior the manager, the more simple and consistent the message needs to be.

6   Honesty is the *only* policy – sooner or later people will find out the truth anyway, and the program and deliverer will then lose all credibility if an honest approach has not been adopted.

7   Play to people's emotions; logic alone will not be accepted, nor will it work.

8   Empathize and acknowledge that change is difficult, for the problem is not so much the new state of where you expect people to end up, but the pain of the transition to get there.

9   Make the message tangible and simple – tell people how and what will change specifically for them and their work area (team). Change must address the specifics of how it will affect individuals.

10   Match key project plan milestones to communication events.

11   The most crucial aspect is *Listen, Listen, Listen* – and learn from and react to what you hear.

Target stakeholder group segmentation

Segmentation will allow the targeting of messages to a specific audience by meeting that audience's particular requirements. The following questions will help in targeting messages.

1   What are the segments, and who is in them?

2   How will people be affected? Remember to be specific.

3   What reaction will they have? Anticipating the likely questions that will be asked and having prepared answers for them will be important. Managers should not have to answer questions 'by the seat of their pants', and preparation will ensure that the messages are consistent across the organization, thus avoiding confusion and potential conflict.

4   What behavior will we need from the recipients?

5   What shall we communicate to them? The how and what may vary according to the recipients. The selection of communication channels will be critical, and must be varied and tailored to specific segments. Channels could include the following:

- regular newsletters
- the intranet
- frequent contact via email updates
- a poster campaign
- videos
- personal presentations and briefings
- project and program updates (drop-in sessions)

- workshops with people to gain feedback and jointly work through issues
- reminder pop-up messages on people's PCs.

6   How will we tell them?
7   Who should tell them?

In all communications there must be an agreed and established 'uniform language' used, with standard graphical models and diagrams; these will all contribute to the consistency of the messages.

Remember, you will need to tell communicate, communicate, and communicate some more. However, be aware of the law of diminishing returns. If you do not have news, do not make some up for the sake of justs communicating.

Step 4: Getting ready for change

Simplistically, getting ready for change falls into two categories:

1   Create an environment that will allow and encourage people to change.
2   Ensure that there is feedback regarding performance and the change program.

Create an environment

There are essentially three broad components involved in creating the environment that allows people to change: trust, caring and ownership.

Trust is critical. People must feel they can trust their leaders and the environment within which they function, at all levels within the organization. They must believe that leaders are honest with them, have high levels of integrity and are reliable and open. People must believe that they can ask any question and get an honest answer. Table 25.1 shows a number of actions that do and do not fulfill these criteria.

Caring is about respect and empathy for others. It is about acknowledging and thanking people for their contribution and effort. Respect includes many of the trust builders mentioned above. People will feel they have respect from leaders when the leaders always tell the truth, keep their word and respect each other.

Ownership is about providing people with as much control over their own destiny as is possible. It is about empowering people with information that will allow them to be responsible for their own decisions and actions, and to be held accountable for them. Clarify expectations (what the organization expects from its people) and responsibility (how the organization expects its people to be responsible in their actions and behavior) – don't delegate, elevate. Provide a sense of ownership by providing people with access to feedback (performance reporting) before the boss gets it, thus allowing people to make corrections themselves before the boss provides the feedback. This leads us to the next point.

Table 25.1
Trust builders and busters (Hriegel and Brandt, 1996: 161–169)

Trust builder	Trust buster
'Walk the talk' – that is, attitudes and actions are consistent with the words spoken or written	Talking, but not 'walking the talk'
Openness and honesty – there is no substitute for communication, communication, communication, as long as it is 'open and honest' communication. Always ensure you address the 'grapevine talk'	Not telling the truth (if communication is poor, then the organization 'grapevine' will create rumors and meaning that may have absolutely no resemblance to the truth). How important is telling the truth? In the 1980s, AT&T confided to Wall Street analysts that there would be retrenchments. Obviously word leaked out, and some employees even read about it in the news-papers. Work almost came to a standstill while employees worried about their future. At least two employees killed themselves (Fortune, 18 October 1993: 67). Change and the truth is a serious thing. It may hurt, but people deserve and have the right to the truth
Use the word 'we' and not 'me' – create a team environment	A superior who takes the credit stealing an idea from a staff member and taking credit for it or, conversely, blames another for his or her mistakes. Nothing will demotivate people and break down trust and teamwork faster than these activities
Overcommunication goes a long way towards eliminating gossip	'Loose lips sink ships'

Provide performance feedback

Leadership cannot expect behavior change until people have been provided with an appropriate environment for work (systems and processes, as well as the human environment), and until they are provided with feedback on their performance via appropriate performance measurement systems linked to rewards. This was covered in detail in Chapter 18.

Case study: How useful is staff training?

An organization told us: 'We trained the staff six months ago in customer care and telephone skills to increase service levels and we have not changed much at all.'

We asked, 'What measures do you have in place to provide feedback to staff and management on the level of customer service and telephone calls informing customers of the status of their processing?' The reply was, 'We monitor it by the customer complaints register.'

As we have said earlier in this book, 'since people don't do what you expect but what you inspect . . . you need to create a way to measure results' (Gerstner, 2002). We worked with the client to establish a set of simple people performance measures to provide immediate feedback to people and change their behavior.

Message: You cannot expect people to change unless you provide them with performance feedback measures and link the achievement of these measures to rewards.

Step 5: Required behavior

Having discussed why we must change, why people are resistance to change, leadership's role in the change process, the various components of the change process and how we should get ready for it, what exactly is it?

What behavioral changes does the organization expect and demand from its people?

Case study: Increasing a division's ranking in an organization staff survey

The division was not performing well in the annual corporate staff cultural survey, and we were asked by the head of the division to investigate why and to ensure that the ranking increased at the next survey. We conducted one-on-one interviews with direct reports and focus groups for 25 percent of the divisional staff. Confidentiality was insisted upon by us and promised to the staff.

The first step was to establish a baseline understanding of where the division was currently (the survey did not provide this in enough detail), what the staff saw as the issues, and where the staff and management wanted to be in two years' time.

A pathway was devised with in excess of thirty recommendations regarding actions required in order to achieve the desired outcome.

Message: Unless people are listened to and included in the process of creating their own pathway to a changed environment, you cannot expect them to participate passionately.

There is much talk in management literature of corporate culture and the role it plays in an organization. What type of culture is best, what type does your organization want or already have, and do you wish to change it?

Louis Gerstner (2002) made a very profound and practical statement with regard to culture when he said: 'I came to see, in my time at IBM, that culture isn't just one aspect of the game – it is the game. In the end, an organization is nothing more than the collective capacity of its people to create value.'

What he is really saying is that we all must make the culture we want in the organization into part of the organization's DNA.

How much influence will the BPM project have over the organization's culture? Obviously, this will depend upon the implementation scenario selected. From within the 'under the radar' and 'pilot' scenarios, it will be difficult to influence or create large cultural reform. The 'in the driver's seat' scenario will be capable of being more influential. However, never underestimate the impact a reasonably small-sized project team can have on the culture of an organization.

Case study: The impact of a small project on the organization-wide culture

Many years ago, we were involved in the implementation of a banking system into a multi-branch building society. The organization, now privatized, was still emerging from its government bureaucratic heritage.

The organization's staff on the project had relatively low productivity and motivation compared to similar organizations in the private sector. We instituted a 'fun' and 'empowering' environment within the project team. Not only did the project staff productivity increase to 200–300 percent above the norm within the organization; the culture also started to permeate the rest of the organization in a positive way.

While this BPM project team involved a comparatively small number of people, it influenced the entire organization.

Message: You cannot *not* influence other people with whom you come into contact.

There are three simple steps that, if published widely, can assist the people change management process:

1   A short, clear uncomplicated message needs to be developed. 'Win, execute, and team' (Gerstner, 2002) provides an example of how short, clear and powerful this message can be.
2   A behavioral charter needs to be developed showing the behavioral change required for change from the current to the new behavior
3   A set of *principles* that we will all live by within the organization must be developed.

It is essential that these are documented and widely communicated to all the people within the organization.

Step 6: How do you get there?

Many of the 'how to's have been explained in earlier steps in this chapter, and we will not repeat or summarize them all here. We will, however, briefly revisit or explain some of the critical elements.

Before we start, it is important to understand that you should never underestimate the time and effort involved in a change program. The project scenario selected will impact the role of the leaders. If the scenario is 'business as usual' or 'in the driver's seat', it could take hundreds of hours of the leader's time to personally 'get down in the trenches' and visit people throughout the organization, telling them of the vision, principles and behavioral charter, and then continuously and consistently to 'walk the talk'. Even then it will take a minimum of three years for a smaller organization, and five-plus years for a multinational-sized organization, to 'move' culture, and there are no guarantees. While the leader plays a pivotal role, imparting the consistent message applies to all senior management, team leaders and people within the organization.

Consistency, persistency and communication are the bywords of an organization cultural change program.

Table 25.2
Summary of the decisions and outcomes of a change program (Stace and Dunphy, 1996)

Radical delegation	Fewer levels of hierarchy Greater decision-making More delegated authority More trust
Freedom and responsibility	Empowerment Fewer rules Clear vision and understanding of team goals
Broad skills and learning individuals	Multi-skilling of people Technical skills within each team Continuous training and learning Higher skill levels, progressing to . . .
Relentless improvement	Productivity programs must be emphasized Provide feedback on performance Link to process improvement
Reward for skill and performance	Link to performance measurement and rewards
People as the core of the business	Emphasize occupational health and safety issues Provide people with the 'tools' needed to perform their roles Process redesign and role redesign by team members themselves.

The first step is to analyze the needs of the BPM project, based upon the project scenario selected, because deciding what and how to change is critical:

- Does the project require the entire organization to change, or only parts of it?
- Once this is agreed, determine the depth and breadth of the change program.
- Always have 'depth' rather than a 'shallow' change effort; understanding this will take longer and require more effort, but will yield significantly better sustainable results.
- Always match the change program to the various aspects of the People phase of the framework.

Stace and Dunphy (1996) provide an extremely useful summary of the decisions and outcomes of a change program, and this is shown in Table 25.2.

In looking at and evaluating the actions to be executed during the people change management program, always test the tasks and proposed actions against both the project scenario selected and the following rule:

If it doesn't:

- add-value to a customer
- increase productivity or
- increase morale

then don't do it.

Chapter 26

Leadership

Why is leadership (Figure 26.1) one of the essentials to a successful BPM project? This is an important question. The answer partially lies in the BPM project scenario selected by the business.

The 'business as usual' and 'in the driver's seat' scenarios will require a high level of BPM understanding and support from leadership. Without this level of support the project will struggle to obtain funding and commitment from the organization and business. Projects under these scenarios tend to be high profile and have the potential to have a high business impact. Leadership must not allow projects of this nature to proceed unless they support them.

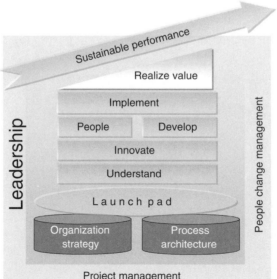

Figure 26.1
The Leadership essential.

The 'pilot project' and 'under the radar' scenarios generally do not require the same level of understanding and commitment from leadership. By their very nature, these projects will have a lower profile within the organization. These projects will obviously need some level of support and understanding from leadership, but they will usually (but not always) be lower-level leaders than the first two scenarios.

How?

We will not be completing a series of steps for this BPM project essential, as it is not appropriate. Instead, we will discuss the following topics:

* what leadership means in the context of a BPM project
* leadership's sphere of influence
* how organizational strategy and leadership are related
* six leadership styles and how they will influence a BPM program
* the importance of communications and the role leadership plays
* relationships – leadership at all levels within the organization is all about relationships.

We will then bring this all together into a leadership levels and components table.

> Leaders should lead as far as they can and then vanish. Their ashes should not choke the fire they have lit.
>
> (H. G. Wells)

What is leadership in the context of a BPM program/project?

The essence of leadership is captured in this simple statement:

> The yardstick to measure good leadership is the culture of enduring excellence which a leader leaves behind after he is gone from the scene.
>
> (Chibber, undated)

An initial reading of this quotation leads you to think of the leader as the CEO; however, when you read it again, it can apply to any level of leadership within an organization. For the purpose of discussing leadership in the context of a BPM program or project, we have devised three levels of leadership:

1. Chief executive officer (CEO), senior executive or business unit manager
2. Program/project sponsor, program director and project manager
3. People (project team members and business staff). It is important to understand that this group of people provides leadership to each

other and to other stakeholders. They are role models and leaders of change within smaller parts of the organization than are the higher-level leaders, but they are leaders just the same.

The role each leader plays will depend, as stated previously, upon the BPM project scenario selected.

Sphere of influence

The leadership levels can have varying degrees of influence over a BPM project, the organization, people and their environment. Figure 26.2 shows the sphere of influence of leadership in general terms.

The three levels of leadership described earlier will have varying degrees of influence over the components of Figure 26.2:

- *Level 1 leaders* (CEO, senior executive or business unit manager) will have a sphere of influence over all or most of the various components of Figure 26.2.
- *Level 2 leaders* (program/project sponsor, program director and project manager) will have a sphere of influence that will vary depending upon the size and scenario of the project being undertaken by the organization. This influence will range from within the business unit only to across most of the organization and perhaps several of the external stakeholders within the market and resources groupings. It is unlikely that they will have much influence over the environment and investors or competitors, although a large BPM program could impact upon the value of the organization and have

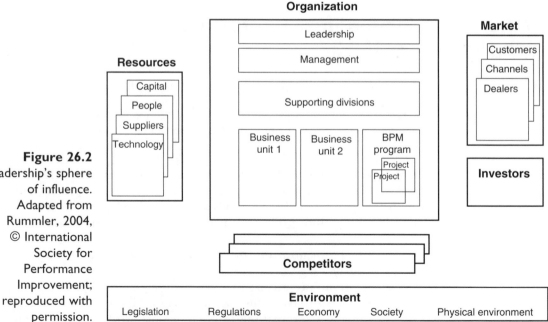

Figure 26.2
Leadership's sphere
of influence.
Adapted from
Rummler, 2004,
© International
Society for
Performance
Improvement;
reproduced with
permission.

an impact upon investors and competitors. Some Level 2 leaders can have an extensive network within and outside the organization due to their personal networks and/or length of service with the organization.

- *Level 3 leaders* (people – project team members and business staff) will invariably have a sphere of influence either within their business unit or confined to the organization.

No matter what your level of leadership, it could be argued simplistically that the most important quality of a leader is to have *passion*, closely followed by *honesty* and *integrity*, and the ability genuinely to *listen*. This is true of all levels of leadership, but obviously magnifies with seniority within the organization.

According to Hawley (1993):

> One of the hardest things I have come to realize as a general manager is that my state of mind is really my primary tool . . . My everyday life is spent dispensing energy, and keeping a mental focus is a full-time effort.

Passion is about 'the emotions as distinguished from reason; intense; driving, or overmastering feeling of conviction'. Synonyms include enthusiasm and zest ('energetic and unflagging pursuit of an aim or devotion to a cause' – *Merriam–Webster online dictionary*). We believe that leadership, in this context, also includes *attention* to the various tasks at hand. If a significant BPM program or project does not have the attention and the passion of the leadership of the organization, then do not do it – it will be a battle all the way to completion, which will place the project at signifi cant risk.

It is critical to understand and address the sphere of influence of Level 1 and Level 2 leaders. An example is the statement by Stephen Covey, when he said that 'the key to the ninety-nine is the one . . . how you treat the one reveals how you regard the ninety-nine because everyone is ultimately one' (Hawley, 1993). This comment refers to the need for leaders and all levels to 'walk the talk' – people pick up in an instance on a mismatch between what has been said by someone and his or her subsequent behavior. This lack of congruency is a mismatch of integrity and honesty. Whenever leaders at all levels complain of the lack of commitment of people within the organization, it is usually as a result of the commitment the leaders have to their people. The need for leaders at all levels to 'walk the talk' is essential.

Case study: BPM, another project

We were once 'selling' the benefits of BPM to a senior executive, who said that he had just been on a two-day planning session with his people and they had listed sixty-seven projects for the next year. He was so impressed with the potential benefits of BPM for his organization that he was seriously going to consider making this the sixty-eighth project.

Our suggestion was that he didn't, because it would not have his 'attention'.

Message: Ensure that the BPM project is one of the top priorities of the key person. If a CEO cannot provide sufficient attention for this, then consider an 'under the radar' or a 'pilot project' scenario with a middle manager.

Organization strategy

This is about Level 1 leaders' developing a strategy for the organization. As stated in the Organization strategy phase, we will not provide mechanisms or techniques for strategy creation; we do, however, think it is worth taking a few moments to understand what constitutes a strategy, and what use it is to an organization and, therefore, a BPM project.

A strategy is not a plan, 'it is a purposeful process of engaging people inside and outside the organization in scoping out new paths ahead' (Stace and Dunphy, 1996). There needs to be a link between the strategy and how it is to be implemented and 'sold' to the people in the organization.

According to Blount (1999):

> Leadership is about 'bringing everyone along' in a balanced way, not just in their minds so they understand it, but emotionally as well, in their hearts, so they are really energized and identifying with it, and they themselves take part in the leadership.

A compelling strategy or vision rarely motivates people. People move away from pain and towards pleasure. Confronting reality can provide the pain to move. A leader must create a climate where 'the truth is heard and the brutal facts confronted' (Collins, 2001).

As discussed in Chapter 25, looking at it simplistically, there are two methods regarding how people can be convinced to change. The method selected will depend upon the organization, the particular situation and the leadership style of the leader.

The first method was used in turning around IBM in the 1990s, where Lou Gerstner (2002) stated that:

> If employees do not believe a crisis exists, they will not make the sacrifices that are necessary to change. Nobody likes change. So there must be a crisis, and it is the job of the CEO to define and communicate that crisis, its magnitude, its severity, and its impact. Just as important, the CEO must be able to communicate how to end the crisis – the new strategy, the new company model, the new culture.
>
>   All this takes enormous commitment from the CEO to communicate, communicate, and communicate some more. No institutional transformation takes place, I believe, without a multi-year commitment by the CEO to put himself or herself constantly in front of employees and speak plain, simple, compelling language that drives conviction and action throughout the organization.

The second method is more subtle, and requires leadership to enable people to understand that there is a 'problem', and to inform them of the magnitude of the problem and why it is essential to change. People will need to understand what the impact will be upon the organization and themselves if the problem is not addressed.

Communication is not just with the people within the organization; the strategy must be 'sold' to all stakeholders continually until it becomes inculcated in the culture of the organization. People need to take it up with a level of *urgency* and *passion*.

Having set the organization strategy and vision, and continuing to communicate it until it is inculcated within the culture, it is critical to review it continually along the journey. Rarely will a CEO 'dream up' a strategy that is perfect, or indeed dream up the strategy on his or her own. Strategies usually provide a vision or broad way forward, with the detail being determined and implemented further down the organization's hierarchy. According to Stace and Dunphy (1996):

> Strategy is the search for directions which energize the life of an organization; structures provide the social organization needed to facilitate the strategy . . . Strategy and structure need to be constantly re-examined and realigned to be effective.

However, having said how important strategy is, it must be seen in context – for it is important to understand that as a leader 'your state of mind is more important than your well-knit strategies and perfectly laid plans' (Hawley, 1993). It is better to have a leader who exhibits great passion, honesty, integrity and an ability to listen, with no strategy, than the opposite of this.

Leadership style

Which BPM project scenario should be selected by the organization or business unit will be influenced by the leadership style of the organization. Leadership style 'is not a strategy but an approach to strategy: it is defined by the role of a firm's leaders' (Keen, 1997).

Keen has identified six leadership styles (he calls them 'strategic styles') that we have found to be consistent with the leadership styles in the organizations we have engaged with:

1   Transformational leadership
2   Delegated mandate
3   Reactive urgency
4   Individual initiative
5   Sustained improvement
6   Opportunism.

(Keen, 1997; ©Harvard Business School Publishing, reprinted here with permission.)

We will briefly describe each of these, relating them to the likely BPM implementation scenarios.

Transformational leadership

This type of leadership style requires a unique leader who will be either a hero or a villain at the conclusion of the transformation. The leader (Level 1 or 2) will personally lead the change program, selling it to all stakeholders, internal and external, and it is a high-risk activity. Don't underestimate the time for transformational change; it can take from five to ten years. The Level 2 project sponsor or project manager could provide this leadership style to the project, as long as this person has a strong enough personality to be able to 'sell' the project/program to the rest of the organization.

For example, an Australian bank undertook such a program. The CEO initiated a $1.5 billion spend over three years to transform the operational processes of the bank to make it more customer-focused and efficient. He personally took the 'driver's seat' in selling this program to the management, staff and investment community. At the time of writing, the program is halfway through its life and yielding results; however, in the initial phases the CEO came in for a great deal of criticism from the financial press and staff. The outcome is perceived by the investment community and financial press as being a success.

The scenario adopted would most likely be the 'in the drivers seat', because the expectation for change is high and the mandate is clear.

Delegated mandate

Keen says that this leadership style is seen in about one-third of organizations. This style is where the leader (CEO) provides a clear mandate for the need for change but the strategy is only communicated in generalist terms – for example, 'we need to be more customer focused', 'we need to be more competitive and therefore, need to cut our costs by $xx million'.

The details of the execution are left up to the lower management levels. This can result in unclear messages and doubt regarding how to execute the strategy. For Level 2 leaders, this could equate to the project sponsor or project manager telling the project team, in broad terms, what the desired outcome of the project is expected to be, and leaving it up to the project team leaders and members to deliver. The difficulty with this situation is matching the activities to the desired project goals, and the coordination between the various project team leaders – especially as the project manager has to ensure that the project's goals are met.

This style usually results in incremental programs and projects, such as BPR. The scenarios adopted are either 'pilot project' or 'under the radar', until a clearer understanding of the direction is available.

Case study: What do we do?

We witnessed a CEO initiating a multiple-year program with the outcome to be a reduction in the cost level of the organization of $25m per annum. He launched this to the organization and told his direct reports to 'go and make it happen'.

The response, away from the CEO, was one of disbelief and confusion. They were confused as to the expectations – did he want just cost reduction, which could have happened simply by retrenching staff, and cutting other costs? This obviously would have impacted growth, service levels and future business opportunities.

The program limped along for eighteen months before, through trial and error, the direct reports gained an understanding of the CEO's expectations.

Message: A more transformational leadership style would have provided a common vision which would have allowed the organization to gain momentum much faster, with resulting benefits to the organization.

Reactive urgency

This is crisis management, and the most common leadership style. It is usually initiated as a reaction to competitor or market conditions. Reengineering, cost-cutting and downsizing are the typical approaches, and these are typically led by a tough senior executive with a reputation for 'getting things done'.

While a crisis can focus an organization and get results, it is far better to be proactive or predictive than reactive.

The BPM implementation scenario chosen will be 'in the driver's seat' if the senior leadership is convinced of the benefits to be gained from a BPM implementation, or 'pilot project' if the commitment to, and understanding of the benefits of, BPM is not quite mature enough. Either way, the implementation will have a significant urgency about it and the expectations will be for immediate results, which can sometimes be a challenge, or unrealistic.

Project management (Level 2) and project team members and business staff (Level 3) acting in crisis mode can be counterproductive and compromise project outcomes, or at least add significant risk to projects, as too much pressure or urgency can lead to errors and omissions.

Individual initiative

This leadership style relies on a well-meaning leader who is in a position to make a change. It is usually started by the leader finding a 'solution' that he or she thinks will be extremely useful to the organization, and then going looking for a problem.

The scenario is usually 'under the radar' until it is proven. When successful, the leader will be seen as having great initiative and the solution will start to spread throughout the organization. Never underestimate the impact that this style can have on an organization.

Level 2 and Level 3 leaders can also initiate activities that lead to benefits (and risks) for the organization; the extent will simply be smaller the lower the level of leader.

Sometimes, when the time is right, the slightest variation can have explosive results within an organization. Part of a leader's role is to create an environment where this can take place – where an individual can take initiative, be empowered and be allowed to fail without recrimination.

Sustained improvement

This type of improvement program can only be tolerated if the organization is best in class (the world leader). Paul O'Neill (1991), Chairman of Alcoa, made a great statement, which we quoted in Chapter 17; it is worth repeating here:

> Continuous improvement is exactly the right idea if you are the world leader in everything you do. It is a terrible idea if you are lagging the world leadership benchmark. It is probably a disastrous idea if you are far behind the world standard – in which case you may need rapid quantum-leap improvement.

Toyota is another great example of the sustained improvement program proponents. These organizations never rest on their laurels; they continuously work hard at getting better and better.

Unless you are a world leader, then this is not the strategy style that should be adopted. In this case, it is not good enough to be better than you were last year, or even better than your competitors; there needs to be a significant leap forward in your productivity. It should be in either the 'in the driver's seat' scenario or at least the 'pilot project' scenario (to test and learn from rapidly) followed rapidly by 'in the driver's seat'.

This leadership style should be adopted by all leadership levels within the organization. All people must contribute, on a continuous basis, towards sustained improvement of the organization.

Opportunism

This can be an extremely successful strategy for some organizations. It is not crisis management, like the 'reactive urgency' style; however, it is also not predictive, and nor is it a sustained improvement strategy. Leaders who adopt this style tend to be proactive in the prevention of crises, but do not lead the industry or get too far ahead of their competitors. They can be a bit trendy, in the sense of trying the latest management fad (TQM, BPR, Six Sigma, BPM).

They would be more inclined to adopt a 'pilot project' scenario, to try an approach out, or, if they are confident of the technology and their ability to manage it, the 'in the driver's seat' scenario.

Again, it is the responsibility of all levels continually to be on the look out for opportunities for the organization. Level 1 and Level 2 leaders must ensure that the culture of the organization promotes and encourages ideas from all people.

It is fair to say that leaders should adopt different strategy styles at different times within the organization. Sometimes a BPM program needs to be incremental, and at other times it should be radical. Both can be appropriate at the same time within different business units. Organizational transformation is difficult and complex, and there is no single right way of doing it.

Communications

Even if a leader sets and communicates an excellent strategy, unless the leader can get the majority to follow, it is useless. People are therefore a critical component. As Jim Collins said, 'the old adage "people are your most important asset" turns out to be wrong. People are *not* your most important asset. The *right* people are' (Collins, 2001). Get the 'right' people on board and get the 'wrong' people off, and then the 'right' people can help build the strategy. There is nothing like involvement to get buy-in, ownership and commitment.

Thus, do the *who* first (get the right people), and they will figure out the *how* and *what*.

Leadership is about 'infecting' people with an exciting way forward, and a desire for results and a pride in attaining these results.

Great leaders understand the difference between providing people with an opportunity to be heard and providing them with an opportunity to have their say. Hierarchical organizations have difficulty in allowing people to have an opportunity to be heard. The 'I am the boss' syndrome gets in the way. These days, you would expect this to be less of a problem – but is it? Not, unfortunately, in our experience.

Case study: Hierarchical management style

An organization had an extremely egalitarian culture and management style. The CEO regarded himself as simply having a different role to the people, and the culture allowed all personnel to be heard and respected. The organization grew rapidly, and consistently achieved a compounding 35 percent growth rate.

With a change in leader came a change in the leadership style, so that it became more hierarchical and command-and-control. When decisions were made that the majority of the people disagreed with, and spoke out against, they were told just to worry about doing their job and to leave the running of the organization to those responsible for running it.

Growth suffered for many years, and in fact the organization shrank in size and underwent retrenchments. It took several years for the leadership to change and the organization to begin to recover both its culture and growth.

Message: It takes a long time and dedication, with a persistent and consistent approach, to implement the 'correct' culture for an organization. Unfortunately, it is very easy to lose the 'correct' culture by a change in leadership (at all levels within the organization).

> If organizations are machines, control makes sense. If organizations are process structures, then seeking to impose control through permanent structure is suicide. If we believe that acting responsibly means exerting control by having our hands in everything, then we cannot hope for anything except what we already have – a treadmill of effort and life-destroying stress.
>
> (Wheatley, 1994)

We should be looking for *order* rather than *control*. However, we must understand that '*disorder* can be a source of *order*, and that growth is found in disequilibrium, not in balance' (Wheatley, 1994). Disequilibrium is extremely uncomfortable for people in general – even for some leaders. The normal reaction is to do whatever is necessary to quell the disturbance.

Some leaders create an overload and confusion on purpose (taking people outside their comfort zones), because they realize that from confusion emerges order and new and interesting ideas and possibilities that would rarely come from any other activity.

The important constant in this is for the leader (CEO) to have established a compelling vision or strategy that other internal organizational leaders can use as a reference point to maintain the focus.

From this *disorder* or *chaos* will come surprises, and while as consultants we were always told there should be *no surprises* for our clients, this is not true in a leadership role. 'Surprise *is* the only route to discovery' (Wheatley, 1994), and in order to discover, leaders need to create an environment where mistakes are tolerated. Human beings learn by their mistakes, and unless we are allowed to try and fail we will simply stop trying. This applies to all three levels of leadership, from the CEO to team leaders within the business.

Relationships

Wheatley (1994) would argue that *relationships* are the basis for everything we do:

> With relationships, we give up predictability for potentials. . . . None of us exists independent of our relationships with others. Different settings and people evoke some qualities from us and leave others dormant.

According to Chibber (undated), 'Twelve percent of "effective management" (which is the management terminology for leadership) is knowledge and eighty-eight percent is dealing appropriately with people.'

So what has the more important influence on behavior – the system or the individual?

Rummler (2004) would say 'Put a good performer in a bad system, and the systems will win every time'. The converse is also true – poor performers will still perform badly with a good system (although hopefully less so). Wheatley would argue that 'It depends . . . There is no need to decide between the two. What is critical is the *relationship* created between the person and the setting' (or system) (Wheatley, 1994).

Obviously, if the reward and performance systems are aligned with the strategy, the synchronicity adds significant impetus to the execution and drive. However, while rewards are important, they will not achieve the results. Once you have the right people, they will infect the rest of the 'right' people (a chain/change reaction) and pride in achieving will be a motivator. It is nice to receive rewards and recognition, and these will help in the sustainability over the longer term.

If you need rewards and compensation to get the 'right' people, then you have the 'wrong' people. The right people will not settle for second best; irrespective of the reward system, they will have a need to build something great.

So what should leaders do in relation to the implementation of BPM into their organization?

First, leaders such as the project sponsor should facilitate relationships between the project manager, stakeholders (internal and external) and himself or herself.

Secondly, how should they start? We like the saying, 'eat the elephant one bite at a time'. Other more common suggestions are as follows:

- think globally, act locally
- think big, start small.

Case study: Rewards can motivate incorrectly

We have all seen examples where a senior leader within an organization is *solely* motivated by his KPIs and the linked bonus to them. This certainly means that the targets set by the CEO are achieved, even if they are not in the long-term interests of the organization.

In one case, there was a large legacy system being replaced (the entire business ran on this system). The planned implementation effort was underestimated (which was nobody's fault, as the organization had no experience in this). A 'go live' date was set, but as the underestimation became apparent there was clearly a need to delay the implementation by three months.

The CEO insisted it go live on the original date, which it did. This caused untold chaos to the operations area of the organization.

It was later discovered that the CEO had a huge component of his bonus attributable to meeting the original date.

Message: The linkage between reward and performance, while important, needs to be an appropriate link.

Certainly an enterprise-wide implementation of BPM is a very rare, and probably far too ambitious for most organizations. As we suggested previously, there are four likely scenarios to start with: 'business as usual', 'in the driver's seat', 'pilot project' and 'under the radar'. These are all methods of acting locally by starting small, building confidence, experience and a self-funding basis for further implementations.

Do not underestimate the impact of creating an incremental change environment within the organization. Many extremely successful large programs start small and progress to change an entire organization.

Summary

In Table 26.1, we have brought the three leadership levels and the six components together to show the impact each level of leadership will (or can) have within a BPM project.

Table 26.1
Leadership levels and components table

Leadership level	Leadership component	Roles and responsibility
Level 1 – CEO, senior executive, business unit manager	Sphere of influence	• The entire organization and all its people and management • All components of the leadership sphere of influence (Figure 25.2) • The strategy can and will impact resources, markets, competitors and the environment
	Organization strategy	• Responsible for strategic direction • What is strategy? Consistent direction, provides focus • Why it is important? • How does it contribute to a BPM program/project?

(Continued)

Table 26.1   (*Continued*)

Leadership level	Leadership component	Roles and responsibility
		• Strategic alignment – keep communicating the message of how the project is aligned with the organization strategy – how it fits with and contributes towards the strategy • Allocation of process owners • Allocation of funds to the project(s) • Creates project(s) for strategy execution • Responsible for selling strategy message throughout the organization and to all stakeholders
	Leadership style	• This is a personal thing. The CEO's style will probably come from the options provided in the Leadership style section of this chapter • Aware leaders adopt the leadership style for the particular occasion and change their style as the organization changes
	Communication	• Can never do too much of it • 'Walk the talk' • Continually promote the strategy • Use formal and informal methods • Be receptive to feedback • This is covered in detail in Chapter 25
	Relationships	This will vary depending upon the role *CEO*: • Direct reports, management and rapport and trust from all people within the organization • Market, resources and competitors as defined in Figure 25.2 • Policicians, regulators, legislators, media and appropriate members of society *Senior executives and business unit managers*: • Direct reports, management and rapport and trust from all people within the organization • Market, resources and competitors as defined in Figure 25.2
Level 2 – program/project sponsor, program director and project manager	Sphere of influence	• People within the area of the project – this covers the end-to-end process(es), so it could and probably will cross business unit boundaries • Level 1 and 3 leadership levels – leadership and management • Stakeholders involved in and near the project • Supporting divisions within the organization • Market – customers, channels and dealers • Resources – people, suppliers and technology • Perhaps competitors

(*Continued*)

Table 26.1   *(Continued)*

Leadership level	Leadership component	Roles and responsibility
	Organization strategy	• Need to understand how the strategy was created and why • Provide feedback on the strategy • Provide detailed implementation plans for strategy execution • Responsible for delivering projects • Need to help 'sell' the strategy to people (project, business and stakeholders)
	Leadership style	• Work with the leadership style of the CEO and other senior Level 1 leaders – understand it and accommodate it • Be passionate about the delivery of the project(s) • Deliver project(s) on time and budget • Ensure value is realized from the project(s) • Be accessible to project team members and business staff
	Communication	• Can never do too much of it • 'Walk the talk' • Continually promote the project strategy and outcomes • Use formal and informal methods • Be receptive to feedback • This is covered in detail in Chapter 25
	Relationships	• Level 1 leaders • Project sponsor, project director and project manager need to have a solid, trustworthy and honest relationship • Project team members • Business units members related to, and involved with, the project • Suppliers and vendors • Project stakeholders (customers, suppliers and business stakeholders)

Level 3 – people (project team members and business staff)	Sphere of Influence	• Fellow employees
		  • Level 2 leadership
		  • Customers, suppliers and other stakeholders

	Organization strategy	• Need to understand the strategy and why it is important to the organization • Need to be passionate about implementing the strategy via project(s) and other means

(Continued)

Table 26.1   (*Continued*)

Leadership level	Leadership component	Roles and responsibility
	Leadership style	• There will be an individual style for each person
	Communication	• Ask questions • Provide feedback
	Relationships	• Level 2 leaders • Fellow employees and workers of the organization • Customers, suppliers and business stakeholders within their sphere of influence

Part III

BPM and the organization

This part of the book is aimed predominantly at the executives of an organization, although project manager and team members will find that it contains useful and important information. It provides insights into how to determine the BPM maturity (BPMM) of the organization or business unit and how to embed BPM within an organization to ensure a continuous business process improvement culture.

Chapter 27 (BPM Maturity) is jointly written by Professor Michael Rosemann and Tonia de Bruin of the Queensland University of Technology, and Brad Power, the Executive Director of the Process Management Research Center at Babson College in Boston. Tonia is a former consultant who, at the time of writing, was undertaking her PhD and is working with Michael and Brad to develop a BPMM model that can be used as a global standard.

The chapter provides a brief overview of the model and their research findings to date. While many individuals and organizations have developed BPMM models, this one is more sophisticated than its predecessors and addresses-specific BPM complexities in a highly practical manner. The chapter will allow readers the opportunity to estimate their level of (BPMM) and develop a rudimentary roadmap forward.

Chapter 28 takes the information learned from the framework and maturity model and suggests ways of embedding BPM within the organization, depending upon the level of process understanding and acceptance within the organization. The aim is to develop a business operational state that will continuously observe and improve business processes; to create a culture that has process improvement at the forefront of business and people initiatives; to provide organization agility, continuous improvement and business opportunities that may not otherwise be available.

Chapter 27

BPM maturity

Michael Rosemann, Tonia de Bruin and Brad Power

Introduction

As this entire book outlines, BPM is a holistic organizational management practice that requires top management understanding and involvement, clearly defined roles and decision processes as part of BPM governance, appropriate BPM methodologies, process-aware information systems, educated and well-trained people, and a culture receptive to business processes. BPM has its roots in a number of approaches, including BPR, quality management (e.g. TQM, Six Sigma), operations management (e.g. MRP II, CIM, Kanban), business process modeling and process-aware information systems (e.g. workflow management systems, service-oriented architectures). It is widely recognized as a foundation for contemporary management approaches as the analysis of business processes drives understanding to the roots of an organization. The popularity and significance of BPM leads to the question of how advanced different organizations are in their BPM development. The notion of 'maturity' has been proposed for a number of management approaches as a way to evaluate 'the state of being complete, perfect, or ready' or the 'fullness or perfection of growth or development' (Oxford University Press, 2004). This chapter describes a new business process management maturity (BPMM) model that has been developed for the evaluation and advancement of BPM effectiveness across organizations.

The structure of this chapter is as follows. The second section looks at the value proposition of a BPMM model and how different maturity stages can be represented within such a model. The third section presents a new maturity model developed specifically for BPM, and details the objectives and core framework of this model. A focus of this section is on the major characteristics of the model as represented by six critical success factors and their underlying capability areas. The fourth section discusses how this

BPMM model can be applied within an organization to drive improved operational performance, whilst the fifth section provides the justification and support for the model development. The final section concludes with a brief summary.

Business process management maturity

Business process management is a complex management practice that many organizations find difficult to implement and progress to higher stages of maturity. This is supported by research indicating that 97 percent of European organizations surveyed considered BPM to be important to the organization and only 3 percent had not commenced BPM practices. Despite this importance, 73 percent were considered to be only at the early stages of adoption (Pritchard and Armistead, 1999: 13). A recent review of CIOs by Gartner (Gartner, 2005) confirmed the importance of BPM, with the top issue identified for 2005 being BPM. For BPM practitioners, therefore, one concern is that the complexity of BPM may result in organizations being unable to achieve desired benefits of BPM.

Maturity models are used as an evaluative and comparative basis for improvement (Fisher, 2004; Harmon, 2004; Spanyi, 2004), and in order to derive an informed approach for increasing the capability of a specific area within an organization (Ahern *et al.*, 2004; Hakes, 1996; Paulk *et al.*, 1993). They have been designed to assess the maturity (i.e. competency, capability, level of sophistication) of a selected domain, based on a more or less comprehensive set of criteria. Therefore, a BPMM model is a tool that can assist organizations in becoming more successful with BPM, resulting in the achievement of greater operational and business performance benefits. In addition, the increased success of BPM adoptions will contribute to positioning BPM as an enduring management practice. In particular, maturity models can be used for three purposes:

1   As *a descriptive* tool enabling an 'as-is' assessment of strengths and weaknesses.
2   As a *prescriptive* tool enabling the development of a roadmap for improvement.
3   As a *comparative* tool enabling benchmarking to assess against industry standards and other organizations.

Unlike other existing models, the BPMM model discussed in the following sections has been developed to enable each of these three purposes.

A typology of BPMM stages

Paulk *et al.* (1993: 5) stress that improved maturity results 'in an increase in the process capability of the organization'. Consequently, it is not a surprise that recently a number of models to measure the maturity of different facets of BPM have been proposed (Davenport, 2005). The common base for the majority of these models has been the Capability Maturity Model (CMM), where the most popular way of evaluating maturity is a five-point Likert scale with '5' representing the highest level of maturity. Among others, Harmon (2004) developed a BPMM model based on the CMM (see also Harmon, 2003). In a similar way, Fisher (2004) combined five 'levers of change' with five states of maturity. Smith and Fingar (2004) argue that a CMM-based maturity model that postulates well-organized and repeatable processes cannot capture the need for business process innovation. Further BPMM models are offered by TeraQuest/Borland Software (Curtis *et al.*, 2004) and the Business Process Management Group (BPMG). In addition to dedicated BPMM models, a number of models have been proposed that study single facets of a BPMM model. Examples are Luftman's maturity model for strategic alignment (Luftman, 2003) and McCormack's maturity model for process orientation which focuses on process performance (McCormack, 1999).

An attempt to divide organizations into groups depending on their grade and progression of BPM implementation was made by Pritchard and Armistead (1999). Whilst trying to define maturity of BPR programs, Maull *et al.* (2003) encountered problems when attempting to use objective measures. They tried to define maturity using two dimensions; an objective measure (time, team size, etc.) and a 'weighting for readiness to change' (Maull *et al.*, 2003). However, this approach turned out to be too complex to measure. Therefore, they chose a phenomenological approach assessing the organization's perception of its maturity, using objective measures as a guideline. Another example of how to define maturity (or, in their case, 'process condition') is provided by DeToro and McCabe (1997), who used two dimensions (effectiveness and efficiency) to rate a process' condition.

The comparison of low and high maturity in Figure 27.1 helps to clarify the comprehensiveness and range of BPMM. The idea of comparing low and high maturity derives from Paulk *et al.* (1993), who presented such a comparison to facilitate the understanding of the concept of process maturity.

The proposed BPMM model adopts the five maturity stages of CMM in an attempt to differentiate various levels of sophistication of a BPM initiative.

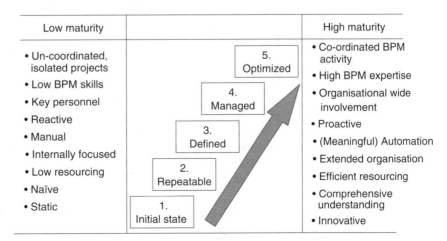

Figure 27.1 Comparison of low and high maturity and the five maturity stages.

Stage 1: Initial state

An organization with a BPMM at Stage 1 will have made either no or very uncoordinated and unstructured attempts towards BPM. Typically, such an organization may display some combination of the following characteristics:

- *ad hoc* approaches
- individual efforts (IT or business)
- various and non-consolidated approaches to methodology, tools and techniques
- limited scope of BPM initiatives
- minimal employee involvement
- low reliance on external BPM expertise
- high levels of manual interventions and work-arounds.

Stage 2: Repeatable

An organization with a BPMM at Stage 2 will have progressed past making first BPM experiences and will be starting to build up BPM capability and increasing the number of people who look at the organization from a process perspective. Typically, such an organization may display some combination of the following characteristics:

- first documented processes
- recognition of the importance of BPM
- increased involvement of executives and top management
- one main purpose for exploring BPM
- extensive use of simple process modeling with simple repositories
- first attempts with a structured methodology and common standards
- increased reliance on external BPM expertise.

Stage 3: Defined

An organization with a BPMM at Stage 3 will experience increased momentum in its quest to develop BPM capability and expand the number of people looking at the organization from a process perspective. Typically, such an organization may display some combination of the following characteristics:

- focus on the management of the early phases of the process lifestyle
- use of elaborate tools (e.g. dynamic modeling, server-based applications, multiple and distributed users)
- a combination of different process management methods and tools (e.g. process redesign, workflow management and process-based risk management)
- more extensive use of technology for delivery and communication of BPM (e.g. process designs available to users via an intranet site)
- comprehensive and formal BPM training sessions
- less reliance on external expertise.

Stage 4: Managed

An organization with a BPMM at Stage 4 will enjoy the benefits of having BPM firmly entrenched in the strategic make-up of the organization. Typically, such an organization may display some combination of the following characteristics:

- an established Process Management Center of Excellence that maintains standards
- exploration of business process controlling methods and technologies
- merging of IT and business perspectives on process management (e.g. workflow management and activity-based costing)
- formal, designated process management positions
- widely accepted methods and technologies
- integrated process management purposes
- process orientation as a mandatory project component
- continuous extension and consolidation of process management initiatives
- minimal reliance on external expertise.

Stage 5: Optimized

An organization with a BPMM at Stage 5 will enjoy the benefits of having BPM firmly entrenched as a core part of both strategic and operational management within the organization. Typically, such an organization may display some combination of the following characteristics:

- process management is a part of managers' activities, accountabilities and performance measurements
- wide acceptance and use of standard methods and technologies
- one organization-wide approach to BPM that incorporates customers, suppliers, distributors and other stakeholders
- established business process lifecycle management
- Business Process Management Center of Excellence reduces in size as process management becomes simply the way business is done.

The BPMM model

Our BPMM model extends and updates earlier maturity models by addressing the requirements and complexities identified within BPM in a more holistic and contemporary way.

Objectives and framework

The development of our model was driven by the following requirements:

1 We wanted to develop a model with a *solid theoretical foundation*. Consequently, we carefully studied previous research on BPM and

the development of maturity models across a range of domains. Our proposed model has been heavily influenced by the consolidation of these previous research outcomes.

2   We wanted to design a *widely accepted global standard* rather than providing yet another competitive maturity model. As such, we approached authors and developers of previous BPMM models for collaboration. Over a period of six months, we conducted a series of Delphi studies designed to incorporate input of recognized thought leaders in the BPM domain. Each Delphi study related to a single factor of the model and used a moderated survey method, utilizing three or four rounds per factor to derive consensus on a number of issues (Rosemann and de Bruin, 2005). The proposed model is now not only a result of merging three reasonably advanced models, but also includes the contributions of more than twenty BPM thought leaders.

3   We were interested in developing a *holistic model* that captured the entire scope of BPM. The extensive literature review that provided us with a solid theoretical foundation also provided insights into the success factors of BPM including perceived barriers to BPM success and details of various implementation approaches for BPM initiatives. Thus our model incorporates factors covering such diverse areas such as strategic alignment, information technology and culture.

4   We wanted to balance the theoretical rigor of the model with *high applicability*. As a consequence, over the last two years our model has been applied, at different stages of its development lifecycle, to a number of organizations in a range of industries. The continuous industry feedback has been used to ensure an industry-oriented structure and terminology throughout the entire model.

5   A main design paradigm was that the model should *support the individual information needs of different stakeholder groups*. As a consequence, the model has three levels: Level 1 – the six success factors; Level 2 – capability areas within each of these factors; and Level 3 – detailed questions to measure each capability area. Essentially these levels form a tree structure that can be expanded based on the reporting and analysis requirements of the individual stakeholder.

The resultant model is multi-dimensional, including a number of distinct components: factors, stages and scope (organizational entity and time). The underlying assumption of the theoretical model is that the factors (based on identified BPM critical success factors, barriers to BPM success, and implementation approaches for BPM initiatives) represent independent variables, and the dependent variable is BPM success. A further assumption is that higher maturity in each of these factors will be reflected in higher levels of success in the BPM initiative. Finally, the notion of 'process success' has to be translated into relevant, BPM-independent success measures for the entire organization – that is actual business success (Figure 27.2).

The focus of our model is on the independent factors for two reasons. First, they provide insights into how process performance can actually be improved rather than measured. Secondly, a number of models and solutions are already

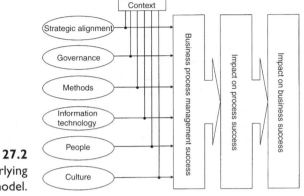

Figure 27.2
The underlying
model.

available for the measurement of process performance (e.g. IDS Business Process Performance Measurement). A brief overview of the dimensions of our model, including definition, origin and purpose, is included in Table 27.1.

Factors are considered to be the primary dimension, as they represent the elements within organizations critical to the success of BPM. (Further insights into the detailed elements of the model can be found in Rosemann and de Bruin, 2004.)

It will be important in our future research to identify relevant contextual factors – for example, process-oriented incentive schema might be an indication for a mature organization, but such schema cannot be applied to public organizations. This leads to the important aspect that there is (most likely) not a common set of BPM best practices that are equally valid for all organizations. Consequently, we define the highest level of maturity (level 5) as the most sophisticated level of conducting BPM, which is *not* necessarily identical with the best way for all organizations. It is a case-by-case challenge to identify the most appropriate BPMM level for an organization, based on context, underlying objectives, related constraints, possible business cases and so on.

The six factors of BPMM

The consolidation of related literature, the merger of three existing BPMM models and the subsequent Delphi process led to the development of our maturity model, which contains at its core six factors. Each factor represents a critical success factor for BPM – that is, this element has to go right in order for the organization to be successful with BPM. Each of these six factors has been expanded to a further level of detail, derived from the Delphi study. Our aim with using the Delphi technique was to access views on contemporary global BPM issues not easily identifiable through a review of existing literature. We call the resultant sub-elements of the factors *capability areas*. Table 27.2 shows the demographics of thought leaders that contributed to the Delphi studies.

Whilst the following sections provide further insights into each of the factors, Figure 27.3 provides an overview of the model incorporating the capability areas that were derived through the Delphi studies.

Table 27.1
Dimensions of the BPMM model

Dimension	Definition	Origin	Purpose
Factor	A specific, measurable and independent element that reflects a fundamental and distinct characteristic of BPM. Each factor is further broken down in a 1-m hierarchy	Current factors have been derived from an extensive literature review of BPM critical success factors and barriers to successful BPM implementations	• To cluster important components of BPM and allow a separate evaluation of these factors, that is to enable identification of strengths and weaknesses within the organization that are most likely to impact on BPM success • To enable organizations to tailor specific BPM strategies with a view to improving BPM success • To enable future research into relationships and correlation between factors to improve understanding of BPM issues
Maturity stage	A pre-defined maturity stage ranging from 1 (low) to 5 (high)	Levels and names are based on those used in CMM	• To quantify and summarize evaluations in a consistent and comparable manner
Scope: organizational entity	The organizational entity which defines the unit of analysis and to which the model is being applied, for example a division, a business unit, a subsidiary	The organizational entity is defined on a case-by-case base by the participating organization	• Acknowledgement that in reality BPM does not conform to any one implementation and adoption route • To enable internal comparison and assessment between entities • To enable specific strategies to be implemented

(Continued)

Table 27.1   (*Continued*)

Dimension	Definition	Origin	Purpose
Scope: time	The point in time at which the model is applied	Variable aspect of the model that is selected by the organization applying the model	• To identify and maximize leverage of internal knowledge sources and sharing • To enable understanding of current position and the formation of an internal baseline • To enable the model to be reapplied over time to assess progress in a longitudinal study
Coverage	The extent to which BPM practices extend through the organizational entity being assessed	Based on existing practice where organizations can (and do) adopt different approaches to BPM implementation	• To recognize the fact that the standardized and consistent distribution of BPM capabilities deserves recognition
Proficiency	The perceived goodness of BPM practices in the organizational entity being assessed	Concept based on the notions of efficiency and effectiveness in similar models (DeToro and McCabe, 1997)	• To recognize the fact that the quality of BPM capabilities deserves recognition

Table 27.2
Delphi study participants (I, industry; A, academia)

Category	Strategic alignment		Governance		Method		Information technology		People		Culture	
Region:	I	A	I	A	I	A	I	A	I	A	I	A
USA	8	6	10	6	10	5	9	4	9	5	8	5
Australia	2	1	2	1	2	1	2	1	2	1	2	1
Europe	1	–	1	–	1	1	1	1	1	–	1	–
Asia	–	–	–	1	–	1	–	–	–	–	–	–
Category total	*11*	*7*	*13*	*8*	*13*	*8*	*12*	*6*	*12*	*6*	*11*	*6*

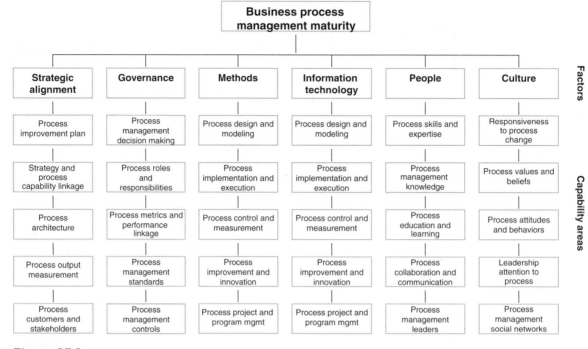

Figure 27.3
The BPM capability areas.

Strategic alignment

Strategic alignment as part of our BPMM model is defined as the tight linkage of organizational priorities and enterprise processes enabling continual and effective action to improve business performance. Through our Delphi study, we identified five principle capability areas to be measured as part of an assessment of strategic alignment capabilities, as they relate to BPM. The sequence in which we present these capability areas reflects the average *perceived importance* weighting assigned by the experts participating in the Delphi study.

1   A strategy-driven *process improvement plan* captures the organization's overall approach towards the BPM initiative. The process improvement plan is derived directly from the organization's strategy, and outlines how process improvement initiatives are going to meet strategically prioritized goals. The process improvement plan provides information related to the targets for the process improvement project, together with planned review and monitoring processes.

2   A core element of strategic alignment, in the context of BPM, is the entire bi-directional *linkage between strategy and business processes*. Do the business processes directly contribute to the strategy, and do organizational strategies explicitly incorporate process capabilities? By way of example, do we know which processes are impacted by a

change of the strategy and which processes could become a bottle-neck in the execution of the strategy, is the strategy designed and continually reviewed in light of process capabilities, how are scarce resources to be allocated to perhaps competing processes, and which processes are we better off outsourcing or off-shoring?

3   *An enterprise process architecture* is the name given to the highest level abstraction of the actual hierarchy of value-driving and enabling business processes. A well-defined enterprise process architecture clearly depicts which major business processes exist, how the industry-/company-specific value chain looks, and what major enabling processes support this value chain – for example finance, HR, IT. A well-designed process architecture derives from a sound understanding of organizational structures from a process viewpoint. In addition, it serves as the main process landscape and provides the starting point for more detailed process analysis.

4   In order to be able to evaluate actual process performance, it is important to have a well-defined understanding of *process outputs* and related KPIs. A hierarchy of cascading, process-oriented and cost-effectively measured KPIs provides a valuable source for translation of strategic objectives to process-specific goals, and facilitates effective process control. Relevant KPIs can be of differing nature, including financial, quantitative, qualitative or time-based, and may be dependent upon the strategic drivers for the specific enterprise process. Often equally important, but more difficult to measure, are KPIs related to characteristics of an entire process, such as flexibility or reliability.

5   Finally, we recognize that strategies are typically closely linked to individuals and influential stakeholder groups. Thus, how well BPM is aligned to the actual priorities of *key customers and other stakeholders such as senior management, shareholders, government bodies and so on* should be evaluated. For example, in practice it can be observed that a change of a CEO will have significant impact on the popularity (or not) of BPM even if the official strategy remains the same. Among others, this also includes investigation of how well processes with touchpoints to external parties are managed, how well external viewpoints have been considered in the process design, and what influence external stakeholders have on the process design.

Governance

Governance in the context of BPM establishes relevant and transparent accountability, decision-making and reward processes to guide actions. In the tradition of corporate or IT governance, a focus is on the decision-making processes of BPM and related roles and responsibilities:

- The clear definition and consistent execution of related BPM *decision-making processes* that guide actions in both anticipated and unanticipated circumstances is seen to be critical. In addition to *who* can make *what* decision, the speed of decision-making and the ability to influence resource allocation and organizational reaction to process change is also important.

- Another core element is the definition of *process roles and responsibilities*. This covers the entire range of BPM-related roles, from business process analysts to business process owners up to chief process officers, and encompasses all related committees and involved decision boards, such as Process Councils and Process Steering Committees. The duties and responsibilities of each role need to be clearly specified, and precise reporting structures must be defined.

- Processes must exist to ensure the direct linkage of process performance with strategic goals. While the actual process output is measured and evaluated as part of the factor strategic alignment, the process for *collecting the required metrics* and linking them to performance criteria is regarded as being a part of BPM governance.

- *Process management standards* must be well defined and documented. This includes the coordination of process management initiatives across the organization, and guidelines for the establishment and management of process management components such as process measures, issue resolution, reward and remuneration structures and so on.

- *Process management controls* as part of BPM governance cover regular review cycles to maintain the quality and currency of process management principles, and compliance management related to process management standards. Such controls will include the degree to which BPM governance standards are complied with in order to encourage desired behaviors.

Methods

Methods, in the context of BPM, have been defined as the approaches and techniques that support and enable consistent process actions. Distinct methods can be applied to major, discrete stages of the process lifecycle. This characteristic, which is unique to the 'methods' and 'information technology' factors, has resulted in capability areas that reflect the process lifecycle stages rather than specific capabilities of potential process methods or information technology. Whilst, arguably, defining capability areas in this way is different from the way adopted for other factors, it is important to note that the capability areas have been derived using the same Delphi process. An advantage of associating the method capability with a specific process lifecycle stage is the resultant ability to assess methods that serve a particular purpose, rather than purely all methods relating to BPM. For example, it is possible to assess the specific methods used for designing processes as distinct from those used for improving processes. This form of analysis is considered to be particularly beneficial, given the common practice of methods (and information technology) being developed, marketed and implemented to meet the needs of a specific process lifecycle stage. The methods maturity assessment therefore focuses on the specific needs of each process lifecycle, and considers elements such as the integration of process lifecycle methods with each other and also with other management methods, the support for methods provided by information technology, and the sophistication, suitability, accessibility and actual usage of methods within each stage.

- *Process design and modeling* is related to the methods used to identify and conceptualize current (as-is) business processes and future (to-be) processes. The core of such methods is process modeling techniques.
- *Process implementation and execution* covers the next stage in the lifecycle. Related methods help to transform process models into executable business process specifications. Methods related to the communication of these models and escalation methods facilitate the process execution.
- The *process control and measurement* stage of the process lifecycle is related to methods which provide guidance for the collection of process-related data. These data can be related to process control (e.g. risks or errors), or could be process performance measures.
- The *process improvement and innovation* stage includes all methods which facilitate the development of improved and more innovative business processes. This includes approaches such as process innovation, Six Sigma and so on.
- The assessment component *process project management and project management* evaluates the approaches that are used for the overall management of the BPM program or projects, including the management of process change.

Information technology

Information technology (IT) refers to the software, hardware and information management systems that enable and support process activities. As indicated, the assessment of IT capability areas is structured in a similar way to that of methods, and refers first to process lifecycle stages. Similarly to the methods maturity assessment, the IT components focus on the specific needs of each process lifecycle stage and are evaluated from viewpoints such as customizability, appropriateness of automation and integration with related IT solutions (e.g. data warehousing, enterprise systems, reporting), in addition to the more generic considerations such as the sophistication, suitability, accessibility and usage of such IT within each stage.

- *IT solutions for process design and modeling* covers IT that enables derivation of process models automatically from log files, and overall tool-support for business process modeling and analysis (e.g. process animation, process simulation).
- *IT-enabled process implementation and execution* focuses on the automated transformation of process models into executable specifications and the subsequent workflow-based process execution. This also includes related solutions such as document management systems or service-oriented architectures. This entire category of software is often labeled 'process-aware information systems'.

- *Process control and measurement* solutions facilitate (semi-)automated process escalation management, exception handling, workflow mining, performance visualization (e.g. dashboards), and controlling based on process log files.
- Tools for *process improvement and innovation* provide automated support for the generation of improved business processes. These could be solutions that provide agile (i.e. self-learning) tools that continuously adjust business processes based on contextual changes.
- *Process project management and project management* tools facilitate the overall program and project management. They are essential, but typically less BPM-specific.

People

While the information technology factor covered IT-related BPM resources, the factor 'people' comprises the human resources. This factor is defined as the individuals and groups who continually enhance and apply their process skills and knowledge to improve business performance. The focus on skills and knowledge of people involved in a BPM initiative could be seen as the 'hard facts' of people. The next capability area ('culture') covers the 'soft side', including behaviors and attitudes leading to the overall appreciation of BPM within the organization.

- *Process skills and expertise* is concentrated on the comprehensiveness and depth of the capabilities of the involved stakeholders in light of the requirements as formulated by the allocated role or position (e.g. business process analyst, process owner).
- *Process management knowledge* consolidates the depths of knowledge about BPM principles and practices. It evaluates the level of understanding of BPM, including the knowledge of process management methods and information technology, and the impact these have on enterprise process outcomes.
- *Process education and learning* measures the commitment of the organization to the ongoing development and maintenance of the relevant process skills and knowledge. The assessment covers the existence, extent, appropriateness and actual success (as measured by the level of learning) of education programs. Further items are devoted to the qualification of the BPM educators and BPM certification programs.
- *Process collaboration and communication* considers the way in which individuals and groups work together in order to achieve desired process outcomes. This includes the related evaluation analysis of the communication patterns between process stakeholders, and the manner in which related process knowledge is discovered, explored and disseminated.
- The final 'people' capability area is dedicated to *process management leaders*. The maturity assessment evaluates people's willingness to lead, take responsibility and be accountable for business processes. Among others, it also captures the degree to which desired process leadership skills and management styles are practiced.

Culture

Culture, the sixth and final factor, is the collective values and beliefs that shape process-related attitudes and behaviors to improve business performance. During the Delphi process, it was surprising to observe that consensus and mutual understanding of capability areas was reached within this factor with a greater degree of ease and considerably less discussion than had occurred in the earlier studies. Arguably, this phenomenon could be the result of 'culture' being one of the last Delphi studies in the series; however, the study for 'people' was run concurrently and similar findings were not present within this study.

- *Responsiveness to process change* is about the overall receptiveness of the organization to process change, the propensity of the organization to accept process change and adaptation, and the ability for process change to cross functional boundaries seamlessly and for people to act in the best interest of the process.
- *Process values and beliefs* investigates the broad process thinking within the organization – that is, do members of the organization see processes as the way things get done? Furthermore, this capability area concentrates on the commonly held beliefs and values on the roles and benefits of BPM. Among them is the longevity of BPM, expressed by the depth and breadth of ongoing commitment.
- The *process attitudes and behaviors* of those who are involved in and those who are affected by BPM are another assessment item in the 'culture' factor. This includes, among others, the willingness to question existing practices in light of potential process improvements and actual process-related behavior.
- *Leadership attention to process management* covers the level of commitment and attention to processes and process management shown by senior executives, the degree of attention paid to process on all levels, and the quality of process leadership.
- Finally, *process management social networks* comprise the existence and influence of BPM communities of practice, the usage of social network techniques, and the recognition and use of informal BPM networks.

Application of the BPMM model

The BPMM model can be applied within an organization in a number of ways, dependent upon the desired *breadth* and *depth* of application.

Breadth refers to the unit of analysis defined for assessment. A unit of analysis can be (in the extreme case) the entire organization, or specific lines of business within the organization. The model can be applied separately to multiple units of analysis, leading to valuable internal benchmarking data.

For each unit of analysis, the model can be applied in two ways: factor level, and capability level. This represents the *depth* of the model application.

A *factor-level* application provides a high-level analysis with results collated on the basis of the six factors contained within the model – that is strategic alignment, governance, methods, information technology, people and culture. Typically, this level of analysis is achieved by BPMM experts undertaking extensive one-on-one interviews with key executives providing complementary views on an organization's BPM initiatives. The BPMM experts then analyze the findings from these interviews, provide a detailed presentation and report back to the organization. This level of analysis is useful for providing a rough understanding of the 'as-is' BPM position from an executive perspective, and provides a good first starting point for organizations in understanding the sophistication of their BPM activities.

A *capability-level* application provides a richer understanding of the 'as-is' BPM position by conducting additional analysis into the five capability areas identified for each of the six factors. In addition to the factor interviews with key executives, this level of analysis involves in-depth workshops with relevant employees with specialist knowledge of BPM activities within each of the capability areas. In addition to a more thorough understanding of the 'as-is' BPM position, this level of analysis enables future BPM strategies to be formulated and targeted to particular aspects of BPM. A further benefit of this level of analysis is that a comparison between BPM perceptions of executives and employees is possible. Moreover, a BPMM assessment on the capability level is complemented by an analysis of BPM-related documents (e.g. process models, job descriptions, definitions of process KPIs).

It is intended that future versions of the model will incorporate a self-assessment component that will enable an organization to achieve a limited maturity assessment without the need to seek external BPMM expertise in addition to being able to have a comprehensive assessment conducted by certified assessors.

Related work

More than 150 maturity models have been developed to measure, among others, the maturity of IT service capability, strategic alignment, innovation management, program management, enterprise architecture, and knowledge management. Many of these models have been designed to assess the maturity (i.e. competency, capability, level of sophistication) of a selected domain based on a more or less comprehensive set of criteria. Unlike CMM, which has reached the level of a compliance standard for software development (Mutafelija and Stromberg, 2003), most of these models simply provide a means for positioning the selected unit of analysis on a predefined scale. Shortcomings of current BPMM models have been the simplifying focus on only one dimension for measuring BPMM and the lack of actual application of these models. Moreover, many existing BPM models do not always clearly differentiate between the evaluation of the maturity of a business process (as measured by its performance) and the maturity of the *management* of business processes. Further shortcomings of many available BPMM models are the missing rigor in the model development process, the limited scope and depth of single facets of BPM, their idiosyncratic nature due to a lack of foundation in related work, the missing consideration of relevant stakeholders, the lack of empirical tests for these models and, especially, the lack of sufficient depth in the assessment levels.

The proposed BPMM model addresses these shortcomings by combining a rigorous theoretical framework with multiple practical applications during the development process to ensure that the resultant model incorporates specific BPM requirements in a practical and useful manner.

Summary

This chapter has provided a brief and selective overview of the structure and components included in a holistic and contemporary model that facilitates the assessment of BPMM. The actual BPMM assessment derived by applying this model can occur on various levels. In its most detailed and recommended form, such assessment takes place one level below the capability areas. The entire assessment kit is based on a maturity assessment questionnaire, semi-structured interviews with key BPM stakeholders, and the evaluation of related documents (e.g. process-related job descriptions, process incentive schema, process models). The triangulation of these three sources of evidence leads to the final assessment score. In analogy to the original CMM, separate evaluations (ranging from one to five) are calculated for each of the six factors. This provides the organization with an overview of its BPM initiatives, and helps to localize the immediate action points necessary for an increased BPMM. A corresponding tool semi-automates the data collection, analysis and presentation activities.

We are currently conducting a number of case studies with European, American and Australian organizations, in order to develop a deeper understanding of the requirements related to a BPMM assessment and to get further feedback on the appropriateness of our proposed model.

Chapter 28

Embedding BPM within the organization

This chapter will focus on how and where BPM should be embedded within the organization. Previous chapters have predominantly focused on the processes from a project or program perspective. Here, the emphasis shifts to one of the ongoing management and sustainability of processes from an organizational perspective.

Why do we need a special BPM organization structure?

Improving processes and obtaining results is not the end but just the beginning of managing business processes. Previous chapters have outlined how to ensure that a culture is in place continuously to improve and monitor processes, but this is not sufficient; the organization should also have an appropriate structure to ensure that the benefits of BPM become clear to the organization and that these benefits are continuous. Process-centric organizations understand they need an appropriate BPM structure. Our experience has shown that although an organization's BPM unit can start from a project, it requires a lasting and structural solution to provide continuous improvement.

As Miers (2005) says,

From an organizational structure perspective, most firms that have embraced process management have adopted a hybrid-style approach. It's not that the functional silos of the past are going to disappear over night. Line of business managers will still run their operations, but for important processes, especially those that cross organizational boundaries, a 'Process Owner' is usually appointed who is responsible for the way in which the process operates in each different business unit.

What are the results of embedding BPM into the organization?

Embedding BPM within an organization requires the following:

- clear organizational positioning of BPM, with clear roles, responsibilities and authorization levels
- a structure that can evolve with the growing importance of BPM within the organization.

We will use the BPM maturity levels from Chapter 27 to indicate the various ways in which BPM can be incorporated into the organization structure, and we highlight the phases shown in Table 28.1.

Table 28.1
Incorporating BPM into the organization structure

Level	Maturity level	Position within the organization
1	Initial state	BPM project
2	Defined	BPM program
3	Repeatable	Center of Business Process Excellence
4	Managed and optimized	Board-level participation and the appointment of a chief process officer

It should be emphasized that the specified BPM project, BPM program, BPM Center of Business Process Excellence and Chief Process Officer (CPO) are fundamentally different, and that each has different objectives, structures, positions within the organization, and challenges.

Table 28.2 shows these four phases and the roles suggested within each level. It also shows the possible number of full-time equivalent (FTE) staff that may be required to staff each phase. These FTE indications will obviously depend upon the size of the organization and the extent to which BPM is being implemented.

Level 1: BPM project objective (Initial state)

To achieve the objectives of the BPM project, this is normally a 'pilot project' scenario and will be defined in the BPM project scope.

Challenges

- The project must generate awareness of BPM in the organization to ensure that there is sufficient support and commitment for it. It is important to balance the message between the general benefits of BPM and the specific results for the project itself.

Table 28.2
BPM organization structure

Role	BPM project (Level 1)	BPM program (Level 2)	Center of BPM Excellence (Level 3)	CPO (Level 4)
CPO				1.0 FTE
Center of Business Process Excellence manager			1.0 FTE	1.0 FTE
BPM program manager		1.0 FTE	As required	As required
BPM project manager	1.0 FTE	As required	As required	As required
Process architect	0.5–1.0 FTE	1.0–2.0 FTE	1.0–2.0 FTE	1.0–2.0 FTE
Process engineer	As required	As required	As required	As required
Process modeler	1.0–2.0 FTE	1.0–3.0 FTE	2.0–4.0 FTE	2.0–4.0 FTE
BPM consultant	0.5–2.0 FTE	1.0–3.0 FTE	2.0–4.0 FTE	2.0–4.0 FTE
Process modeling & management tool administrator	As required	1.0 FTE	1.0 FTE	1.0 FTE
BPM trainer	0.3–0.6 FTE	0.6–1.0 FTE	1.0–2.0 FTE	1.0–2.0 FTE

- The project should not spend too much time on generating BPM awareness, as all project members should remember that their efforts will be predominantly judged by the realization of the project objectives, and not by well-intended awareness of BPM which is outside the scope of the project. The project should provide an excellent showcase of the business benefits of BPM. *The best way to sell BPM is NOT through theories or textbook case studies, but through achieving results within the organization itself!*
- The project should align with other initiatives to establish synergies in process improvement. This will assist in increasing the awareness and the exposure of BPM throughout the organization.
- The project should ensure that sufficient communication is completed at the beginning of the project. Too often, projects start communicating towards the end of the project, when success confidence levels are higher – which is often too little and too late.

Composition

A BPM project should consist of at least the following:

- A BPM project manager, who is the person responsible for achieving the specified project objectives by using BPM. As mentioned in previous chapters, the BPM project manager should be from the business, rather than IT or external.
- A process architect (could be on a part-time basis), whose main responsibilities are to ensure that the project and process architecture align with the overall enterprise architecture, and that relevant people within the organization are informed and involved in the execution of the process architecture.
- A BPM consultant, who assists the business in identifying and realizing benefits that can be achieved through BPM, including new opportunities by changing processes and in coaching the relevant people in achieving them.
- Process modeler(s), whose main responsibilities include the modeling of the Understand and Innovate processes.
- A trainer (on a part-time basis), who provides generic training for BPM.

The following people could also be involved in the project:

- A process engineer, who could be involved where an automated solution is to be used. Where the organization is implementing its first few BPM projects, the process engineer has to ensure that the technical solution fits within the infrastructure of the organization. This can be a major challenge, as it can involve multiple systems, interfaces and platforms, and different versions of software.
- A process modeling and management tool administrator, who has to ensure that the process modeling and management delivers the required functionality.

Most of the project members will be seconded to the project for its duration. It is the role of the BPM project manager to ensure that the team is highly motivated, efficient and effective, making sure that they are ready for bigger challenges after their initial project. Detailed role and responsibilities descriptions for these team members are described in Appendix C.

Place within the organization

The place for this project within the organization should be close to the business unit whose processes are being improved. The project sponsor should have an active participation and commitment to the project and its end result, and should be a senior person within the relevant business unit.

External support

Training and coaching will be the most common form of external support, especially where this is the initial framework-driven BPM project within the organization.

Level 2: BPM program objective (Defined)

At level 2, the organization has had several successes with individual BPM projects and/or has initiated a BPM program consisting of multiple projects. The objective of the BPM program is to be able to achieve results with BPM across multiple projects, organization units, systems, products and services.

Challenges

- The BPM program has to maintain the balance between ensuring that the individual projects are successful and the desire to have them comply with the emerging organizational standards and methods. These standards are crucial to the organization as more and more projects are initiated and people become involved: if standards cannot be enforced during the program, they will certainly not be enforceable throughout the organization.
- The BPM program can gain momentum by leveraging the lessons learned from previous projects and the sharing of best practices. *A BPM program has to prove that the initial success(es) can be repeated and scaled upwards.*
- It is important for the organization to understand that a BPM program is more than a BPM project on a larger scale.

Composition

In addition to underlying BPM projects, a BPM program should include the following staff:

- A BPM program manager, who has the responsibility of ensuring that the various BPM projects under his or her control achieve or exceed their objectives. The BPM program manager is not necessarily the project manager from the previous project or phase, as the skills are different each time.
- A process architect, who is required to ensure that the various projects and initiatives are meeting agreed standards and are not continuously reinventing the wheel. Furthermore, the process architect should liaise with other architects within the organization to establish a *modus operandi.*
- A process modeler or process quality assurer, who should guide the various process modelers in the BPM projects and coach them on the job. This person could also assist in some of the modeling, especially in establishing the initial list of end-to-end process models.

- A BPM consultant, who provides advice on the benefits of levering the various BPM projects and internal account management to the business.
- A process modeling and management tool administrator – with a BPM program it is very likely (and very advisable) to have a process modeling and management tool, otherwise it becomes extremely difficult (or impossible) to maintain the management of the models. The administrator ensures that a minimum set of standards are being maintained, otherwise the tool has the potential to become unmanageable.

The following people could also be involved in the program:

- One or more dedicated BPM project managers, who will be responsible for the more complex BPM projects and coaching and supporting the more junior BPM project managers. These project managers can be called upon to assist when projects get into difficulties.
- Process engineer(s), who will assist in the re-use of various parts of a project within other projects (BPM or otherwise).
- A BPM trainer, who, with an expanding scope and more people involved, can customize training on BPM itself and perhaps provide it internally.

Place within the organization

The BPM program manager should have a close relationship with the major stakeholders of the various projects. With long-term programs there should be significant emphasis on providing communication to the various stakeholders, business and project team members. Consideration should also be given to having a program name, which can be used in internal and external marketing.

External support

Unless an organization is mature in BPM, external support will be crucial at this stage to ensure that the right approach is adopted. In phase 2, BPM is in the take-off phase, and a false start will be extremely energy-, time- and money-consuming. External experts can provide their expertise and experience from multiple other settings.

Level 3: Center of Business Process Excellence (Repeatable)

In this stage, process management gains momentum.

Objective

By now the organization has executed several large-scale project/programs successfully, which means that BPM has gained momentum, and the organization now wants to institutionalize their BPM expertise and experience by establishing a Center of Business Process Excellence (CBPE). A Center of Business Process Excellence brings together people with different skills and experiences to solve complex business problems. It takes the traditional concept of project management far beyond its primary concern of the technical implementation of a project. Indeed, a Center of Business Process Excellence demands a range of competencies to move BPM projects through several lifecycle phases of conception, development, implementation and review.

The CBPE aims to facilitate cooperation between business and IT, giving business greater responsibility for the delivery of automated and non-automated BPM solutions. It will, in effect, pool resources in order to assist a wide range of business units to develop, implement and/or manage self-improvement BPM projects. A CBPE is a group of people who are the organization's experts in BPM. They are not the people who execute all the work associated with a project, as this will not lead to lasting and sustainable results. Rather, the CBPE is a centralized group whose members should provide expertise to facilitate the relevant organizational units to be successful in their BPM efforts. This will enable the organization to have the skills and knowledge to repeat successful BPM projects.

Specific activities that the CBPE should perform include the following:

- Establishment of process standards, which could include methodology, process performance measurement, quality assurance for processes, tools and techniques.
- Providing skilled process resources to the business.
- Ongoing organizational implementation of BPM by the appropriate definition of process owners and process managers.
- Maintaining a leadership position in business process management.

Challenges

- The main challenge for the CBPE is to ensure that it facilitates the business units in achieving their target(s) and assists them in achieving their results. Thus, the CBPE should avoid growing too much or becoming too involved with the BPM project at a detailed level. This is the reason why the CBPE should not be too large and probably not exceed six to eight staff.
- The CBPE should be the guiding light for everyone in the organization who wants to think and work in a more process-oriented way. It should provide coaching and guidance to people who want to start process initiatives. The CBPE should build a process community within the organization, allowing the members from various business units to find each other and exchange experiences and best practices.
- The challenge is to find the right leader for the CBPE. This person should be proactive, and at the same time be able to be patient (e.g. the business has to be encouraged to be enthusiastic about BPM as it must do most BPM work). The CBPE manager has to have a vision for the Center and the organization, and be able to relate this to the day-to-day work. The natural tendency is to appoint

the successful BPM program manager; however, it is important to understand that the roles are quite different.

- The funding of the CBPE is crucial. Ideally, part of the benefits achieved by the business units with BPM should be converted to a monetary contribution to the CBPE, to ensure that the 'missionary' work of the CBPE can be continued. It is crucial that the funding comes from the business units, as this will make the CBPE more demand-driven. Ways to do this are to charge for the services of the CBPE, and for the budget allocation to be provided from the various business units, projects and program. If a budget is provided directly by executive management, it is crucial that the CBPE sets targets in collaboration with the business units, to ensure that the CBPE is still demand-driven.

- The CBPE must maintain the focus on the results that must be achieved by the business units. This is the best advertising for the CBPE. The number of people trained, licenses (of process modelling and management tools) being used and process models created should not be the criteria of success of the Center.

- The CBPE could be centered on a particular process modeling and management tool. However, this is not the ideal situation. A CBPE established in this way should not just train staff in the use of the process modeling and management tool and then let them 'muddle' through projects. The CBPE should also ensure that all the business units understand what the benefits of BPM are, how they are established, and how the tool can contribute. Care should be taken that the approach of such a CBPE is not: 'our tool is the solution, what is your problem?' Remember, the best way of 'selling' the CBPE is to listen to the challenges and requirements of the business units and recommend the most suitable solution, even if it is not the tool of the CBPE.

- Last but not least, communication is crucial in establishing the CBPE and in ensuring that it is able to continue to relate its services to the changing demand and issues within the organization. Communication ensures that everyone understands the benefits the CBPE can bring to the people and organization.

Composition

A Center of Excellence should have (at least) the following staff:

- A Center of Business Process Excellence manager, whose main responsibility is to ensure that the CBPE is capable of assisting the business units of the organization in achieving success. It is crucial that the manager is capable of motivating and guiding staff rather than being the person with the most expertise. It is more important that the manager is capable of communicating and working with the other business managers and executive management.

- Process architect(s), who ensure that the process architecture is formulated, updated and is being used. The process architect(s) will also be closely involved with the formulation and execution of the enterprise architecture.

- A BPM consultant/account manager, who works with the business to identify the opportunities for process improvement and process management within the organization and coordinate how the CBPE can be of assistance. The BPM consultant should be the first person to discuss the BPM opportunities with the business, and the role the CBPE will play. For organizations where the CBPE charges its customers, the BPM consultant is also the account manager for the services of the Center.
- Process quality assurers/senior process modelers, who are required to ensure that the various projects and initiatives are meeting the desired (minimum) standards and are not 'reinventing the wheel' every time. These people should guide the process modelers in the BPM projects and provide coaching *in situ*. They could also assist with some of the modeling – especially establishing the initial process framework.
- A process modeling and management tool administrator – with a CBPE it is required that there is a process modeling and management tool. The administrator ensures that a minimum set of standards are being maintained.
- A BPM trainer, who is responsible for preparing and providing training. With the number of people to be trained increasing, the trainer will also be responsible for customizing the training to the particular requirements of the organization, rather than just providing a standard course.

The CBPE could optionally have a senior BPM project manager, who could assist and coach individual BPM project managers, be involved in BPM project revivals (projects that need assistance) and support the BPM program manager. This person would normally be involved in the start-up phase of a project and then monitor the progress.

The CBPE should ensure that the IT department has dedicated process engineers available in case the organization uses an automated solution. The CBPE should resist the temptation to have its own engineers, as this normally leads to sub-optimization and fragmentation of IT knowledge.

Place within the organization

As mentioned, the CBPE exists to facilitate and support the activities of the various BPM projects and programs. This is why the CBPE should be located centrally within the organization, preferably at the corporate level. It must not report to IT, as BPM is a business-related activity.

Level 4: Chief process officer (Managed and optimized)

Process management is of strategic importance. The ultimate way to ensure that processes receive the maximum commitment and attention from executive management is to appoint a dedicated chief process officer (CPO).

Objective

The CPO is responsible for ensuring that the processes are geared towards contributing efficiently and effectively to the objectives of the organization. This can be achieved by ensuring that the organization's process architecture is well embedded within the overall enterprise architecture, the processes are considered with any major change or initiative within the company, and the Center of Business Process Excellence is accepted and well respected for its contribution to the business.

The CPO will be responsible for coordinating the various organizational strategies and aligning them with the specific process strategies to ensure that they support organizational goals. This involves the following aspects:

- Customer service
- New product development
- Procurement strategy
- Fulfillment strategy
- Human resource and training strategy
- Accounting and finance strategy
- Technology strategy.

The CPO should be made responsible for all end-to-end processes within the organization, which might extend to the processes the organization has with its customers, suppliers and partners. This also involves the IT-related processes. As mentioned previously, IT is aimed at supporting the business processes; a separation between the two domains will lead to sub-optimization.

The CPO will be responsible for:

- end-to-end processes within the organization
- achieving the process goals across the organization, and assuring the smooth flow of data, documents and information between sub-processes
- maintaining a customer focus, constantly working to assure that processes, as a whole, function to satisfy the customer
- ensuring that problems, disconnects or gaps that arise when processes cross departmental lines are resolved to the satisfaction of all stakeholders
- planning, managing and organizing processes as a whole
- ensuring that appropriate process measures are established, monitored and maintained
- establishing and maintaining the BPM project framework or methodology across the organization
- nurturing ongoing and continuous improvement programs for business processes
- smooth running of the Center of Business Process Excellence team
- establishing and maintaining the relationships with the BPM vendors
- ongoing knowledge management for BPM within the organization
- overall quality management.

The main activities for a process owner relate to:

- Process documentation. The process documentation of the relevant processes must be correct, up-to-date and easy to use. Furthermore, the process owner must ensure that the documentation meets all the relevant standards and requirements (e.g. compliance).
- Process improvement. The process owner is the focal point for proposals for process improvement, and will be responsible for the decisions, change management and implementation of these improvements. This includes liaison with relevant stakeholders.
- Interface and boundary management. The process owner has to ensure smooth transition between and across processes, as in many cases the end-to-end process problems arise at the interfaces of the individual processes. The process owner must ensure that the boundaries between various processes are well understood and documented.
- Process automation. The process owner has to be involved in all the relevant automation in relation to the process. It is important to remember that many IT applications span across various processes.
- Process performance management. The process owner must ensure that the performance of the processes and their contribution to the objectives and strategies of the organization are measured, and that the relevant people act on this information. In other words, the process owner must ensure that the processes are managed to ensure that they meet their objectives.
- Process promotion. The process owner must promote the proper use of the process itself, as well as the generic promotion of process thinking.

Challenges

- In order to obtain the buy-in from all process owners and senior management, the CPO should clearly demonstrate his or her added value, as many process owners might consider the CPO to be an extra organization layer.
- The CPO must maintain a strategic orientation and not get too involved in the day-to-day running of the Center of Business Process Excellence, as this is a completely different role that should have a dedicated person with the right capabilities for that job.
- The CPO must be able to provide added value at the Executive Board level, as all other CxOs will have bigger departments, more people and higher budgets. Thus the CPO must have the vision and capabilities to deliver this vision in tangible results, which should ensure that the other CxO's provide the necessary funding, resources and people to make use of BPM initiatives. It will be a challenge in itself to find a person like this, as the person must have a strategic view and also be able to have a detailed understanding of the operational processes, without going too much into detail.

It is important to include a few words of warning. A CPO is especially helpful in a process-centric organization that is mature in its process dealings. If an organization is still evolving to this level of maturity, then the best alternative is to have a BPM program with buy-in from the CEO and senior executives to improve the processes, and then at a later stage appoint a CPO.

Appointing a CPO or establishing a CBPE in an organization that is not mature enough to understand or sustain them will seriously impact the added value they can bring to the organization, and could lead to difficulty in achieving the high expectations of these roles.

Ownership of processes

One of the most challenging parts of business process management is to ensure that the accountability and responsibilities of the processes are clearly and appropriately assigned.

An organization has a number of choices with regard to process ownership; they could

- make the functional managers responsible for their own part of the process only (part of an end-to-end process, that is, a sub-process)
- appoint a functional manager to be responsible for the entire end-to-end process
- appoint a manager who has no functional responsibilities to be responsible for the entire end-to-end process.

Whichever choice is made, there are associated challenges and risks.

1   *Functional sub-process owner.* The risk associated with this approach is that sub-process owners will only see their own part of the process (a silo perspective) and changes to this sub-process may negatively impact other parts of the end-to-end process – which could in turn lead to a sub-optimized end-to-end process.

2   *Functional end-to-end process owner.* The difficulty with this approach is that there is a conflict of interest for the end-to-end process owner. Being responsible for both the end-to-end process and their particular functional silo (a sub-process), process owners may have to make changes that impact their own functional silo profitability and operational efficiency in order to benefit the end-to-end process. Management of processes in this manner has the potential to lead either to the end-to-end situation not being sufficiently considered or to the functional managers using their responsibility for the end-to-end process to pursue their own functional objectives.

3   *Process owner with no functional responsibilities.* While this approach does not suffer from the above issues, it can be extremely challenging to manage because of the need to gain consensus across functional managers. For this to work effectively, the person appointed must be a senior executive or manager with a high level of respect within

the organization. This person must be able to provide the additional persuasion that functional managers sometimes need to look at an end-to-end process perspective. This person can also be called a process 'steward', as he or she does not have the 'normal' operational responsibilities but provide 'stewardship' for the end-to-end process. The challenge is for the end-to-end process owner to be able to counter the sub-optimization efforts of the functional managers and pursue the end-to-end process objectives. In this situation, it is often recommended to have the end-to-end process owner report to the COO or a CPO.

If an organization is extremely BPM mature (some would call it a process-centric organization), then the process responsibility can be arranged along end-to-end process lines. In other words, the organizational structure is totally along end-to-end processes lines, and the organization functional silo structure has been eliminated (or at least minimized). In this case, it is crucial that the various functional employees are still able to share their process expertise and experience.

Part IV

Appendices — tools and techniques

One of the aims of this book is to provide a practical guide to BPM practitioners and managers. To assist in the completion of the guidelines outlined in the framework, we have provided sample templates, checklists, background information and additional information in these appendices. They are aimed at providing hands-on support for the project team to assist them in the execution of BPM projects.

Each phase of the BPM project framework has an appendix, with at least a checklist of the inputs and outputs for that phase; most appendices have additional information. Obviously it is impossible to include all tools and techniques in the book, or it would be hundreds of pages longer, so we have selected tools and techniques that are related to the framework and we believe will add value to the BPM practitioner.

Many of the tools, templates and checklists have been kindly provided with the permission of TouchPoint Business Process Management Consultancy (MPM Group Pty Limited). TouchPoint is continually improving and developing these tools and templates, so if the reader has any suggestions regarding improvement or additional tools and templates that they find useful, please email these suggestions to framework@touchpointbpm.com.au.

7FE Project Management Overview
Framework Summary

Organization strategy	Process architecture	Launch pad	Understand	Innovate	People	Develop	Implement	Realize value	Sustainable performance
Analyze internal & external aspects of organization	Obtain strategy & business information	Initial key stakeholder interviews	Revalidate scope	Management kick-off workshop	Design people strategy	Determine BPM components	Update implementation plan	Benefits management framework	Evaluate project results
Make strategic choices	Obtain process guidelines & models	High level process walk through	Understand workshop	Project set-up	Activity definition	Decide on re-use, buy, make or outsource	Prepare for User Acceptance Testing	Identify Potential Benefits & Plan	Develop/ Fine-tune Sustainability
Determine Impact on Processes	Obtain Relevant IT Principles & Mode	Stakeholder Identification & Engagement	Complete Metrics Analysis	External Stakeholder Focus Groups	Role Design	Update Functional & Technical Specifications	Train Staff	Establish Baseline & Comparative Measurement	Embed Performance Measures in Management
Establish Strategic Measurements	Consolidate & Validate	Executive Workshop #1 & #2	Root Cause Analysis	Initial Innovate Workshops	Performance Management & Measurement	Software Development	Complete Business Tests & Pilots	Refine & Optimize Benefits Mix	Introduce Feedback Loops
Complete the Plan	Apply Architecture	Agree & Plan the handover to the business	Complete People Capability Matrix	Future Process Metrics Projections	People Core Capabilities Gap Analysis	Hardware Deployment	Update Deliverables	Define Benefit Details	Embed Sustainability
Sign-off & Communication	Make it Better	Develop Implementation Plan	Identify Available Information	Simulation	Design Organization's Structure	Testing	Involve Management	Benefits Delivery & Tracking	Reward Sustainability
	Communications	Develop/ Sign-off Business Case	Identify Innovate Priorities	People Change Management Strategy	Update People Change Mngt Strategy	Communications	Develop Rollout, Back out & Contingency Plans	Value Monitoring & Maximization	Institutionalize Process Governance
		Define & Establish Project Team Structure	Identify Quick Wins	Update People Capability Matrix	Update HR Policies		Develop & Run Marketing Programs		Monitor Sustainability
		Complete Initial Project Plan	Understand phase Report	Capacity Planning	Develop Training		Mentor Staff	Communications	Maintaining the Process Models
		Communications	Communications	Workshop Proposed Solutions	Communications		Roll out changes		Communications
				Demonstrate & Validate Feasibility of proposed solution			Monitor & Adjust		
				Process gap analysis			Provide Feed-back to Users & Stakeholders		
				Identify benefits & update business case			Communications		
				Report and Presentations					
				Approvals					
				Business requirements					
				Communications					

Essentials

Project Management: Project Gates; Stakeholder Management; Project Management Risks

Leadership: Sphere of influence: Organization strategy; Leadership style; Communications; Relationships

People Change Management: resistance to change; why change? leadership role; components of change program; getting ready for change; required behavior; how do you get there; communications

© Jeston and Nelis 2006.
Change in colour indicates next step → subsequent similar cell colour indicates parallel activities steps.

Appendix A

Organization strategy phase

This checklist provides a generic overview of possible inputs, deliverables and gates of this phase.

Possible inputs

- Existing information on:
  - mission
  - vision
  - values
- Corporate brochures, websites, annual report and so on to determine the image of the organization
- Induction program to provide input into the key values of the implementation strategy of the organization
- Organization chart to assist in the identification of the main internal stakeholders
- Product portfolio mix to determine the main products
- List of key customer groups/types
- Business model to determine main external partners.

Deliverables

- If not currently available, a documented version of the organization's:
  - vision
  - mission

- goals
- strategic intent
- objectives
- A context or business model, which includes the following:
  - customers (type and volume of customers)
  - services/products
  - suppliers/partners
  - key differentiators
  - resources
- Key differentiators of the organization
- Communication of the results of this phase.

Possible gates

- Understanding magnitude of change
- Organization's capacity to change
- Organization's acceptance of BPM.

Self-assessment strategy

Purpose

The completion of this assessment tool will provide an indication of how the different people within the organization view various aspects of the business strategy. It is crucial to have this insight prior to modeling processes. If there is no consensus on the strategy, it is impossible to obtain consensus on the best way to model the processes.

Completing the questionnaire

1 Distribute the questionnaire to all participants
2 Participants complete the questionnaire, individually, on the basis of the current situation as they see it
3 In principle all the points should be allocated; only allocate lower points if none of the items are applicable
4 Calculate the totals for all five aspects and specify them on the answer sheet
5 Add the totals for all five aspects for all participants in the result overview worksheet
6 Present the individual graph and aspect graph
7 Participants discuss the outcomes and consequences
8 Decide on the changes and actions to be taken.

Questionnaire spreadsheet

The following questionnaire is a Microsoft Excel spreadsheet where participant answers are input. The graphs shown in Figures A.1 and A.2 are automatically generated.

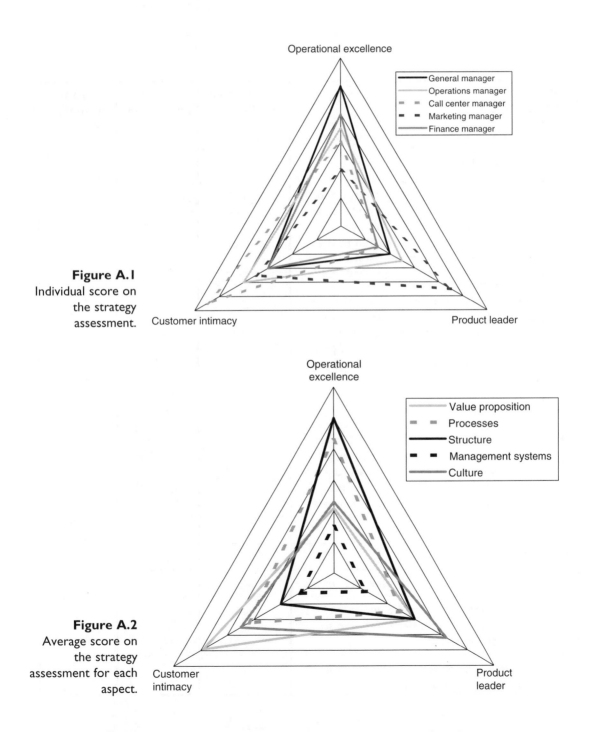

Figure A.1
Individual score on the strategy assessment.

Figure A.2
Average score on the strategy assessment for each aspect.

When distributing the questionnaire to the participants ensure that the column headings at the top of the questionnaire are not shown, as this could prejudice the answers.

This self-assessment strategy questionnaire is attributable to Paul van der Marck, www.managementsite.net, accessed 11 July 2005.

VALUE PROPOSITION			Operational excellence	Product leadership	Customer intimacy
Allocate 20 points <u>across</u> the next three statements					
	a	**Statement 1** We offer our customers a unique combination of price, product range and ease of use. The total costs (combination of money, time and effort) for our customers are minimal compared to the value obtained (product and service)			
	b	**Statement 2** We offer our customers unique value with our products, we are able continuously to increase the value of our proposition and to meet or exceed the expectations (our research, as well as our delivery capability, is 'first class')			
	c	**Statement 3** We offer our customers a unique and valued total solution through our products and services; our service is personal, always friendly and capable; we are able to adjust our solution on the basis of the individual requirements of our customers			
		SUBTOTAL			
PROCESSES					
Allocate 4 points per question to the three statements					
1	a	The throughput time of the end-to-end process for our customer is reduced to the absolute minimum			
	b	Research and Development is our main process to satisfy our customer			

			Operational excellence	Product leadership	Customer intimacy
	c	We focus continuously on the development of a total solution for our individual customers			
2	a	Our end-to-end customer process is managed centrally			
	b	Market research plays an important role in our development			
	c	Our processes are being continuously adjusted to accommodate the needs of our customers			
3	a	Further cost reduction in our processes is not possible anymore			
	b	Rapid development cycles are embedded in our standard processes			
	c	Customer satisfaction is the main measure for our processes			
4	a	Process errors have been reduced to the theoretical minimum			
	b	Parallel development of new concepts is our process model			
	c	Our customer always has a clear picture about what we are doing			
5	a	Process optimization is our main focus			
	b	Our marketing process is aimed at continually exploiting our products and services			
	c	Relationship management is our primary process			
		SUBTOTAL			

			Operational excellence	Product leadership	Customer intimacy
STRUCTURE (ORGANIZATION)					
Allocate 4 points per question to the three statements					
1	a	Our activities are heavily standardized			
	b	Research and Development is a separate division with substantial budget			
	c	Our activities are quite varied and are dependent on the customer			
2	a	Our planning is strongly centralized and 'top-down'			
	b	Product Development is embedded at the top of our organization			
	c	Our planning is developed 'bottom-up' for each client			
3	a	Responsibilities are clearly established; we always work with guidelines and manuals			
	b	There is a extensive freedom within a broad context			
	c	Employees who have operational contact with the customers have a significant level of authority			
4	a	There are many checks and balances within our organization with regard to processes			
	b	We adjust the organization continuously to new products, services, projects and concepts			
	c	Customer relationship management is embedded at the top of our organization			

			Operational excellence	Product leadership	Customer intimacy
5	a	The organization structure is very straightforward (very hierarchical)			
	b	We work more with loose teams around projects: our organization chart looks more like the 'universe' than a hierarchy			
	c	Our organization chart resembles an up-side-down pyramid with the customer at the top			
		SUBTOTAL			
MANAGEMENT SYSTEMS					
Allocate 4 points per question to the three statements					
1	a	All our processes are highly standardized and embedded in our systems			
	b	Our systems adjust to our products on a daily basis			
	c	Our systems are mainly aimed at the ability to select and service customers			
2	a	All our transactions are processed automatically			
	b	Most of the effort in systems development is aimed at the 'development tools'			
	c	All our customer information can be accessed and viewed quickly and easily			
3	a	Our billing system is completely electronic			
	b	Our systems are agile enabling them to continually adjust to the development of products			
	c	Our end customers have direct access to our systems			

			Operational excellence	Product leadership	Customer intimacy
4	a	Our suppliers are directly linked to our systems			
	b	Our systems 'force' us to introduce new products/concepts at a high frequency			
	c	Our systems are focussed on customer retention and repeat business			
5	a	Our customer service is supported with state-of-the-art technology to be able to answer questions promptly and efficiently			
	b	Customer service staff are continuously trained on our newest products, because they change so often			
	c	We track customers who have left us through our systems			
		SUBTOTAL			
CULTURE					
Allocate 4 points per question to the three statements					
1	a	Our people are highly motivated to avoid mistakes			
	b	Our people are highly motivated to continuously develop new ideas			
	c	Our people are highly motivated to satisfy customers			
2	a	Our remuneration systems reward efficiency			
	b	Our remuneration systems reward creativity			
	c	Our remuneration systems reward customer satisfaction			

			Operational excellence	Product leadership	Customer intimacy
3	a	Our recruitment is aimed at selecting efficient working people			
	b	Our recruitment is aimed at selecting innovative and creative people			
	c	Our recruitment is aimed at selecting customer-oriented people			
4	a	Everyone is committed to reducing costs			
	b	Everyone is committed to continuous product improvements			
	c	Everyone is committed to customer satisfaction			
5	a	Our management is a showcase of efficiency			
	b	Our management is a showcase of creativity			
	c	Our management is a showcase of customer orientation			
		SUBTOTAL			
TOTAL SCORE (=100)					

Questionnaire answer sheet

ASPECT		Criteria	Score	
OPERATIONAL EXCELLENCE (first column)				
1	**Value proposition**	Best value for money		
2	**Process**	'End to end' optimized		
3	**Structure (organization)**	Highly controlled and central planning		
4	**Management systems**	Standardized and aimed at fast transactions		
5	**Culture**	Rewards efficiency		
PRODUCT LEADERSHIP (second column)				
1	**Value proposition**	Best product, regardless of the price		
2	**Process**	Focus on R&D and market exploitation		
3	**Structure (organization)**	Ad hoc and reusability of resources		
4	**Management systems**	Measuring of products success with ability to experiment		
5	**Culture**	Rewards vision and innovation		
CUSTOMER INTIMACY (third column)				
1	**Value proposition**	Best total solution, with the best relation		
2	**Process**	Result oriented; customer relationship management		
3	**Structure (organization)**	Authorization closest to customer		
4	**Management systems**	Aims at selected customers, with surrounding the customer with care		
5	**Culture**	Stimulates customization and relationship with customer		

Appendix B

Process architecture phase

Checklist: Process architecture phase

This checklist provides a generic overview of possible inputs, deliverables and gates of this phase.

Possible inputs
From the Organization strategy phase

- A documented version of the organization's:
  - vision
  - mission
  - goals
  - strategic intent
  - objectives
  - implementation strategy
- A context or business model that includes the following:
  - customers (type and volume)
  - services/products
  - suppliers/partners
  - key differentiators
  - resources
- Key differentiators of the organization.

Other inputs

- Enterprise architecture to determine how the process architecture fits in
- Product and service model to be used as part of the models in the process architecture

- HR strategy to include in relevant organization issues to be considered
- Information and technology architecture to determine how this supports the process architecture
- Architecture templates to be followed when completing the process architecture
- Reference models to develop models on the basis of industry standards.

Deliverables

- Documented and agreed process architecture
- Process start architecture
- Organization process view
- List of end-to-end processes
- Benefits management framework (from Realize value phase)
- Communication of results.

Possible gates

- Understanding magnitude of change
- Organization's capacity to change
- Organization acceptance of BPM.

Sample architecture

OVERALL OBJECTIVES

- We want to grow in revenue by 200 percent in the next three years
- We want to increase profits by 150 percent in the next three years.

GENERAL PRINCIPLES

- Our corporate values are as follows:
  - best value for money
  - honesty: we promise what we do, and we do what we promise
  - rewards: results and innovation are rewarded throughout the organization
- We follow an operational excellence strategy with aggressive low pricing and we achieve this through:
  - economies of scale (we only offer services in which we can obtain critical volume)
  - lean and mean organization, processes and application systems
- We openly communicate our objectives and strategic choices
- We implement employee empowerment; employees are encouraged to take responsibility and undertake entrepreneurship within the context of this framework

(Continued)

- We want to be an outstanding national organization; we focus on the entire nation, we have no intention (yet) to go international
- We choose best practices; we will not invent our own methods and tools. If we cannot meet best practice in-house for a particular activity, then we outsource that activity
- We realize we are in a dynamic market and we strive for the organization, and all its elements, to remain agile and flexible.

RELEVANT PRODUCT GUIDELINES

- We have a limited number of products and components
- Customers can obtain the most suitable solution on the basis of our product components
- Discount depends solely on total billable amount and applies for everyone
- We don't invent products ourselves, we adopt promising offerings
- We want to work with other organizations with good value for money within our sector (e.g. phones) or outside (e.g. supermarkets).

RELEVANT ORGANIZATION GUIDELINES

- We have one national organization
- We encourage employee empowerment and we will provide guidance for this
- We challenge people to use their potential and favor internal candidates
- We have a flexible and flat organization structure
- We advocate a learning organization and we define at all levels relevant objectives
- All employees have a bonus depending on their individual performance as well as their business unit as a whole.

PROCESS GUIDELINES

- We consider processes from an end-to-end perspective
- All processes have a business owner
- Only one default process for each business function, exceptions need Board approval
- The process architecture has to include the choice of relevant reference models
- There will be no customized processes for individual customers, if requests reach us, we will evaluate them as required
- We want reduced handovers
- We automate activities where possible, but ensure flexibility
- All processes have performance indicators; they will be open, for everyone to see.

RELEVANT INFORMATION GUIDELINES

- We have for each business function (e.g. customer service, billing, finance) only one system, exceptions need Board approval
- The following applications are standard:
  – A/B/C
- The following applications are available after management approval:
  – Z/Y/X

(Continued)

- All other applications need Board approval
- We outsource all software development
- All data will be entered only once (if similar data exists in multiple places it should be automatically synchronized).

RELEVANT TECHNOLOGY GUIDELINES

- We use x as operating platform
- We use a thin-client server configuration.

In addition to this, models will be part of the process architecture. The process models to be completed in the Process architecture phase include the following:

- organization process view
- list of end-to-end processes.

Other models created in later phases will be added to the process architecture, for example:

- end-to-end process models
- detailed process models (various levels).

Models for the other areas will include all the relevant products and services models, relevant organization charts, relevant information models and the relevant technology models.

Appendix C

Launch pad phase

Checklist: Launch pad phase

This checklist provides a generic overview of possible inputs, deliverables and gates of this phase.

Possible inputs
From the Organization strategy phase

- A documented version of the organization's: vision, mission, goals, strategic intent, objectives and implementation strategy
- A context or business model that includes customers (type and volume), services/products, suppliers/partners, key differentiators and resources
- Key differentiators of the organization.

From the Process architecture phase

- Documented and agreed process architecture (includes organization process view)
- Process start architecture (including relevant end-to-end processes)
- Benefits management framework.

Other inputs

- Business case template
- High-level metrics to assist in the determination of the main processes and bottlenecks
- List of relevant projects to determine synergy and overlap.

Deliverables

- Stakeholders defined in, involved in or associated with the project
- Stakeholder engagement, commitment, and documented and agreed expectations
- Process selection matrix and initial metrics
- A list of agreed process goals
- Process worth matrix
- Prioritized processes for the Understand phase
- Initial implementation strategy
- Project management:
  - project team established
  - project charter document
  - project scope document
  - initial draft of the project plan (in the Understand phase the plan will be completed in detail)
  - determination and documentation of the initial communications strategy
  - initial risk analysis
- Initial business case
- Potential project benefits and realization plan (from Realize value phase)
- Communication of the results.

Possible gates

- Stakeholder analysis
- Understanding magnitude of change
- Organization's capacity to change
- Organization acceptance of BPM
- Technical review
- Availability of participants for workshops.

Project team structure and roles

The project team structure and roles are shown in Figure A.3.

This appendix provides details of a 'strawman' project team structure. This is usually modified to suit the particular organizational requirements. It is, however, a structure that we have found to be particularly effective and workable, so modifying it too much may lead to compromising the effectiveness of the project. Obviously, the size of the BPM project is important in considering the project team structure.

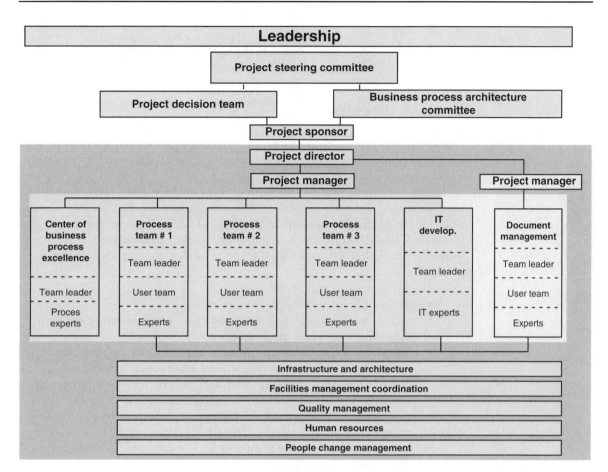

Figure A.3
Sample project team structure for a large-scale BPM project. (Reproduced with the permission of MPM Group Pty Ltd, trading as TouchPoint Process Management Services.)

Project sponsor

The project sponsor has the normal role of a sponsor in a business project. Often the sponsor is a leading business manager. The project sponsor will be the project champion, and will be responsible and accountable for:

- defining and approving the goals, objectives, constraints and success criteria of the project
- signing off the project scope
- signing off the project definition document
- signing off the project plan
- authorizing or obtaining authorization for resources and expenditure for the project
- approving or rejecting any change requests that fall outside the previously agreed project scope

- approval of project budget
- signing off the project as complete, once the defined scope has been achieved.

Project director

The project director is responsible for all activities associated with the project. The project manager(s) and/or process workstream leaders will report directly to the project director.

This role ensures that the implementation of the various project(s) is running smoothly and meeting stakeholder's expectations. The project director must also maintain the relationships with all stakeholders and ensure that the framework described herein is being applied appropriately for the particular organization. Other project-related responsibilities include the following:

- infrastructure and architecture
- facilities management coordination
- quality management and the satisfactory involvement of the staff
- human resources, as outlined elsewhere herein
- people change management and the satisfactory involvement of staff – this area in particular should not be underestimated, as it is possibly the largest component and one of the most important of any BPM project
- supporting project manager(s) and staff, especially in gaining action or agreement from other parts of the organization
- ensuring that adequate resources and facilities, of all kinds, are available to the project team.

While it is the responsibility of the project manager(s) to ensure the day-to-day running and coordination of the above functions, the project director must take a 'big picture' view of the strategic running and alignment of the project.

Project manager(s)

Project managers are responsible for the execution and coordination of the project, which includes the following:

- day-to-day management and execution of their part of the project
- development of the policies and plans to ensure commonality of processes and systems wherever possible
- ensuring that all people change management, human resources and training issues are addressed and implemented
- management of all activities associated with the project to deliver the requirements of stakeholders in the planned timeframe, budget and quality
- preparation and tracking of their part of the budget

- gaining commitment from all stakeholders
- coordinating and gaining agreement for project plans
- establishing and using project control mechanisms to ensure agreed timescale and budgets are managed
- reporting project progress to all stakeholders on the agreed time-frames
- ongoing communication to the organization (business) and IT management
- identifying and establishing communication links with related projects, and managing the risks that any interdependencies may pose
- identifying, managing and elevating, if appropriate, potential or existing issues that may, if left unchecked, impact the project
- monitoring the risks associated with the project and advising the project director and project sponsor.

Process teams

The process teams (often referred to as workstreams) will comprise various groups:

1 The team leader
2 The user leader
3 User team representatives
4 Process experts.

Each of these roles will be briefly described here.

Team leader

This is the normal project team leader role. The team leader will lead his or her team (workstream) and ensure that appropriate workshops are organized, the project plan is developed (in conjunction with the project manager) and the timetable is adhered to, budgets are met and so on. Furthermore, the role includes the following:

- managing assigned tasks by either completing them or delegation to team members
- undertaking periodic team reviews
- completing periodic team status reports for inclusion in the overall project status reports
- participating in periodic project review meetings
- assisting in the resolution of project or business issues
- ensuring that all issues are logged in the issues log and promptly dealt with and/or raised with the project manager and project team
- managing development of the user acceptance testing plan and test cases, and executing the testing successfully
- obtaining sign-off for UAT within their area of responsibility
- completing the implementation plan for their area of responsibility.

User leader

The user leader is a business resource who is appointed by the business management and has the authority to make decisions on behalf of the business. The role includes the following:

- selecting user team members (departmental and across departments)
- technical quality assurance and decisions on process design
- regulation of any conflicts that may arise
- representing the user team on the project decision team
- participating in project meetings of all user leaders
- working with other user leaders to ensure interfaces, hand-offs and so on are correct and that there are no disconnects.

User team representatives

User team representatives are the technical or subject matter experts from the business, and are selected by the user leader. Their responsibilities include the following:

- participating in workshops and interviews
- creating team-specific approaches to project activities
- designing various Innovate phase approaches
- ensuring that quality, compliance and technical assurance issues are addressed
- seeking agreement with other teams on process interfaces and hand-offs, to ensure there are no disconnects
- participating in user acceptance testing planning
- participating in the writing of test plans and cases for user acceptance testing
- participating in the execution of user acceptance testing
- participating in implementation planning and execution.

Process experts

This group will come from the organization's Center of Business Process Excellence (CBPE), and will provide the expertise for:

- process design and redesign
- process design tool(s) used in the project
- activity-based costing
- process simulation
- process interfacing.

Business case template

Outlined below is the purpose of the business case, and a suggested table of content for the BPM project business case.

Purpose of a business case

The business case is an important instrument in managing a BPM project, and has three main functions:

1 At the start of the project, it will provide the information to allow a decision regarding whether to approve and fund the proposed project – in other words, whether the projected benefits warrant the requested investment, considering the risks and alternatives. The benefits to be realized as a result of this project need to be clearly specified.

2 During the project, it will provide guidance to ensure that the project is still on track. This is crucial because the business will evolve during the lifetime of a project, and the project sponsor and project manager must continually check to ensure that the project will still contribute to the organization strategy and yield the desired benefits in relation to the projected costs. In other words, the project sponsor and project manager must continually 'manage the business case'.

3 After the project, it will enable the business and project team to evaluate whether the project has delivered the expected results (benefits) and contributed to the specified objectives, within the agreed budget and timeframe. This evaluation provides crucial lessons, which must be taken into account in the next BPM projects.

Table of content

I	*Executive summary.* The executive summary is aimed at providing the reader with a brief overview of the business case. The text must be sharp and to the point.
1.1	Project description and project owner
1.2	Business requirements
1.3	Strategic contribution
1.4	Financial summary (including benefits and costs)
1.5	Critical success factors
1.6	Risks analysis
1.7	Recommended next steps
2	*Background*
2.1	Problem analysis
3	*Objectives*
3.1	Business objectives
3.2	Project objectives
3.3	Critical success factors

(Continued)

4	*Project scope*
4.1	Outcomes/deliverables
4.2	Inclusions and exclusions
4.3	Dependencies
4.4	Stakeholder analysis
4.5	Assumptions
4.6	Constraints
4.7	Related documents
4.8	Architectural compliance
5	*Project approach*
5.1	Options considered:
5.1.1	Option 1:
5.1.1.1	Expected results
5.1.1.2	Benefits
5.1.1.3	Costs
5.1.1.4	Return of investment etc.
5.2	Preferred approach
6	*Project schedule*
6.1	Project duration
6.2	High-level implementation plan
7	*Resources*
7.1	Internal project stakeholders – interaction with other divisions
7.2	Personnel resource requirements
7.3	Other project resources
8	*Initial risk analysis*

Sample report structure

This is a list of the possible topics that could be included in the report of the project. It includes the Launch pad, Understand and Innovate phases. We suggest that the report be populated as each phase of the project is conducted. Sections 2 and 3 should be completed at the conclusion of the Launch pad phase, Section 4 at the conclusion of the Understand phase, and the remainder of the report at the conclusion of the Innovate phase. There is an overlap between the information in this report and the business case. The report is aimed at the management of the organization, and the business case can be used to populate several of the sections of the report. The business case is aimed at the project sponsor and steering committee as part of the project approval process. It is imperative that these two documents are consistent.

This report is often used at the end of the Innovate phase to justify the continuance of the project into the People, Develop and Implement phases.

A sample report structure is as follows:

I	*Executive summary*
1.1	Background
1.2	Scope
1.3	Approach
1.4	Findings
1.5	Recommendations
2	*Project*
2.1	Background
2.2	Scope
2.3	Success checklist
2.4	Phases and phase components
2.5	Deliverables
2.6	Stakeholders
3	*Launch pad phase*
3.1	Initial process analysis
3.2	Findings
4	*Understand phase*
4.1	Purpose of Understand phase
4.2	Process issues
4.3	Findings
5	*Innovate phase*
5.1	Purpose
5.2	Approach
5.3	Findings
6	*Recommendations*
6.1	Scenario 1 – Quick wins
6.2	Scenario 2 (there could be one or more additional scenarios selected by the business)
6.3	Implementation approach
6.4	Recommended project structure
6.5	Change management
6.6	Risk analysis
6.7	Related projects
7	*Benefits*
8	*Contributors*
9	*Appendix A – Understand phase metrics*
10	*Appendix B – External stakeholder issues*
11	*Appendix C – Legend for process maps*
12	*Appendix D – Current process flows*
12.1	List of end-to-end processes

(Continued)

12.2	Process selection matrix
12.3	Individual process models
13	*Appendix E – Innovated process flows*
13.1	Innovate process matrix
13.2	Scenario 1 – Table of models and file names
13.3	Individual process analysis
13.4	Process 1
13.5	Scenario 2 – Table of models and file names etc.
14	*Appendix G – Estimated Metrics of Innovated Processes*
15	*Appendix H – Risk analysis*
16	*Appendix I – Skills analysis matrix*

Project plan schedule

The project plan schedule will provide an outline of a possible list of tasks and estimated length of time for completion. The project manager will need to modify this to suit the particular BPM project.

Phase 1 – Launch pad phase (~ 2 weeks)

Purpose

The Launch pad phase is the platform from which operational initiative approach BPM projects are selected, scoped, established and launched. While the strategy-driven approach projects will be initiated at the Organization strategy phase, the initial project effort will still need to be estimated. The purpose of this step is to gain an understanding of the effort involved in the completion of these activities.

Step	Duration
Overview of the organization – usually delivered by a senior executive	0.5 day
Initial interviews with stakeholders	2 days
High-level process walkthrough	2–3 days
Executive kick-off workshop(s):	2 days (2 × 0.5-day workshops plus 2 × 0.5 days for documentation)
• identify process goals	
• define project scope	
• design success checklist	
• make list of end-to-end high-level process model(s)	

Step	Duration
• identify business processes • high level – analyze business processes • agree outcomes for understand phase	
Match processes to criteria and prioritize	I day
Produce initial project plan (for Understand phase):	I day
• duration • cost	
Define and establish project team structure – discuss with business and seek agreement of structure and team members. Document team member roles and responsibilities	3 days
Create Understand workshop presentation	0.5 day
Develop/sign off business case	Depends upon project, could be significant time
Complete report and present to management:	2–4 days
• project scope • process goals • list of end-to-end process(es) • list of business processes • next steps	

Phase 2 – Understand phase

Purpose

The purpose of the Understand phase is for the project team members and the business to gain sufficient understanding of the current business processes to enable the Innovate phase to commence. The steps are outlined in Chapter 16.

This phase will lay the foundation for the Innovate phase. The current situation, with its requirements and restrictions, is assessed and analyzed. Quick wins may be identified and implemented.

Steps

The Understand phase will predominantly be conducted in a number of workshops. The duration and number of workshops depends on the scope of the project and the understanding gathered in the Launch pad phase.

A rough estimate suggests planning one week (comprising four half-day workshops) for four to six processes to be documented with metrics and timing.

Step	Duration
Revalidate the scope	0.25 day
Understand workshops:	A function of the number of processes
• gather process flows • gather metrics (time, staff, volumes) • gather costs • document outcomes	
Complete metrics analysis	A function of the number of processes
Root-cause analysis	A function of the number of processes
People capability matrix	1 day
Identify knowledge and information needs	1 day
Identify priorities for Innovate phase	1 day
Identify quick wins (obvious ones, identified in the workshops)	1 day
• discuss with business • select quick wins for implementation • prioritize	
Options for implementation (not part of this project):	2 days
• hand over to business to implement • spawn off separate project(s) (with separate team) • have a time-out for current project team to implement quick wins and then return to the current project	
Complete report and present to management, including: • list of end-to-end process(es) • documentation of current processes with metrics • people capability matrix • knowledge and information needs • quick wins	4–6 days
Develop and deliver phase presentation for management	2 days
Project plan for the Innovate phase, including:	2 days
• duration • cost • project team structure (any changes and estimation of all resources required)	

Phase 3 – Innovate phase (12–20 weeks)

Purpose

The purpose of this phase is to make the process(es) within the scope of the BPM project as efficient and effective as possible to meet stakeholders' current and/or future expectations. This phase also provides a unique opportunity to quantify further, in a more empirical manner, the benefits outlined in the business case.

The Innovate phase is to develop new solutions for the business. The effort and duration will very much depend on the scope and objectives – for example, whether system changes are in scope or not, the timeframe (short-term, mid-term or long-term), and whether revolutionary changes or incremental improvements are desired.

Step	Duration
Executive kick-off workshop	1 day
• process goals • determine overall approach (automation, non-automation, etc.)	
External stakeholder focus group	1 day
Initial Innovate workshop	1 day
Future process metrics projections	5–8 days
Simulation, assumes that:	
• metrics data gathering comes from both the metrics step and additional information gathering during this step	Depends upon the number of processes – as a guide allow 1–3 days per process
• ensure that the process model has been created with simulation in mind	
Update to people capability matrix for new skills required as a result of new processes	1 day
Capacity planning	5–10 days
Workshop proposed solutions	Depends upon the number of processes – refer to comments at the start of this phase
Demonstrate feasibility of proposed solutions	3 days
• with compliance • with audit	
Process gap analysis	3–5 days
Identify and update business case	5–8 days
Complete report and presentation and present to management, could include:	5–10 days
• list of the agreed process goals • documentation of redesigned processes • key findings and an analysis of the process touchpoints • agreed success checklist • business requirements specification, if appropriate • list of recommendations (including more quick wins)	

(Continued)

Step	Duration
• a preliminary risk analysis • cost–benefit overview • suggested next steps • final list of recommendations	
Obtain approval to go ahead	Depends upon the organization
Create business requirements document(s)	Depends upon the number of processes and the level of detail required
Communications plan development	3 days
Communications implementation	Over life of project
Project management activities:	Depends upon the scope and size of the project
• duration • cost • project team structure (all resources required)	

Overall project management

Project management must be planned to ensure that there is enough time and enough resources in the budget. Activities include the following:

- risk management
- project change management
- communication plan
- project status (report for project sponsor)
- project team meetings.

The time needed for these activities depends on the size of the project and the project team.

It is also very important to include enough contingency in the project plan to be able to meet deadlines and budget.

Appendix D

Understand phase

Checklist: Understand phase

This checklist provides a generic overview of possible inputs, deliverables and gates of this phase.

Possible inputs
From the Process architecture phase

- Documented and agreed process architecture (includes organization process view)
- Process start architecture (including relevant end-to-end processes)
- Benefits management framework.

From the Launch pad phase

- Stakeholders defined in, involved in or associated with the project
- Stakeholder engagement, commitment, and documented and agreed expectations
- Process selection matrix and initial metrics
- A list of agreed process goals
- Process worth matrix
- Prioritized processes for the Understand phase
- Project management:
  – project team established
  – project charter document
  – project scope document
  – initial draft of the project plan (the Understand phase plan will be completed in detail)
  – determination and documentation of the initial communications strategy
  – initial risk analysis

- Potential project benefits and realization plan
- Initial business case.

Deliverables

- Process models of current processes
- Metrics baseline
- Prioritized quick wins
- People capability matrix
- Knowledge and information needs
- List of priorities for Innovate phase
- Project plan (in detail) for Innovate phase
- Baseline and comparative measurement (from Realize value phase)
- Report to management
- Presentation to management
- Initial communications plan.

Possible gates

- Unable to obtain satisfactory baseline metrics
- Subject matter experts unavailable.

Overview of process model levels

This describes the five or six levels of process models, with the main benefits of each level.

Level 0 – Organizational relationship map

The organizational relationship map (as first seen in Figure 14.9) shows the organization within its context with its partners: customers, vendors and third parties. This gives the context in which the business can view its processes. Figure A.4 shows an example with some of the processes that occur for a telecommunications service provider, and provides a different perspective to Figure 14.9.

Level 1 – Organization process view

The organization process view represents the highest-level view of the organization from a 'process perspective'. Figure A.5 is an example of an insurance organization. The depiction or grouping of the processes is usually shown in three levels:

1   Strategic processes, which represent the strategic processes that must ensure that the underlying processes are meeting, and continue to meet, the specified objectives

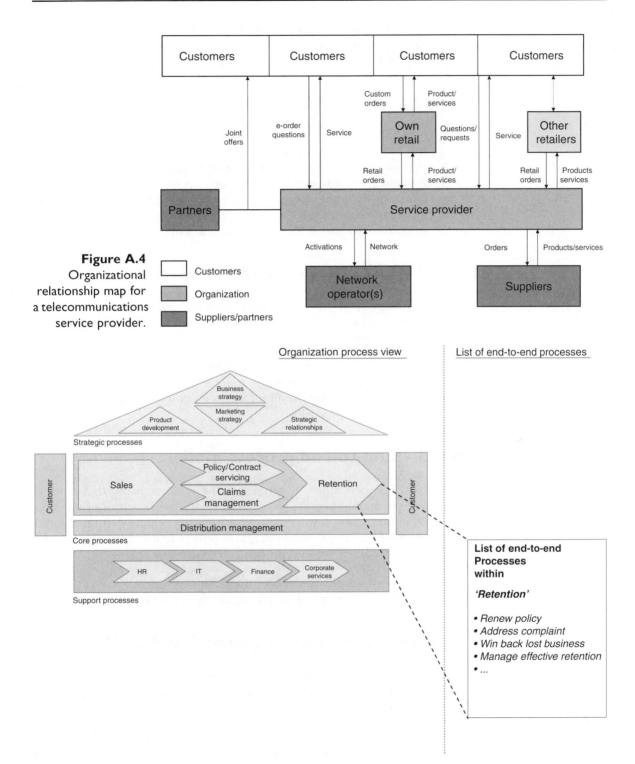

Figure A.4
Organizational
relationship map for
a telecommunications
service provider.

Figure A.5
Organization process view and list of end-to-end processes.

2   Core processes, which represent the core, or main, business activities of the organization

3   Support processes, which are the non-core processes which support the core processes of the organization.

The benefits of an organization process view are as follows:

*   it provides a high-level view of the organization – all other processes will link to this process view
*   it is an excellent way to involve senior management in the process modeling exercise and provides a process view of the organization
*   a process-oriented schematic like this can support process thinking in an organization; if used consistently, it has the potential to replace an organization chart as the only schematic in the organizational context.

Level 2 – List of end-to-end processes

For each of the group of processes identified in the organization process view, a list of end-to-end processes should be created. Refer to Figure A.5.

The benefits of this list of end-to-end processes are that it:

*   provides a link between the organization process view and the individual end-to-end processes
*   ensures that the organization focuses on end-to-end processes rather than on functional silos.

Level 3 – End-to-end process model

An end-to-end process model describes all the main activities that need to be performed in an end-to-end process. It normally crosses various functional areas of the organization. It will include any high-level choices within the end-to-end process – for example, the approval or rejection of a claim (Figure A.6).

The benefits of an end-to-end process model are that it:

*   provides a simple overview of the main activities
*   provides context when preparing the detailed process models.

Process selection matrix (levels 2 and/or 3)

The process selection matrix is a way of showing how the list of the end-to-end processes (or the main activities) within an end-to-end process relate to the specified scenarios. For example, in Figure A.7:

*   main process A is unique for product 1 in market A (process 1)
*   main process B is similar for product 1 and product 2 in market A (process 5)
*   main process C is not applicable for product 1 in market C (no process assigned).

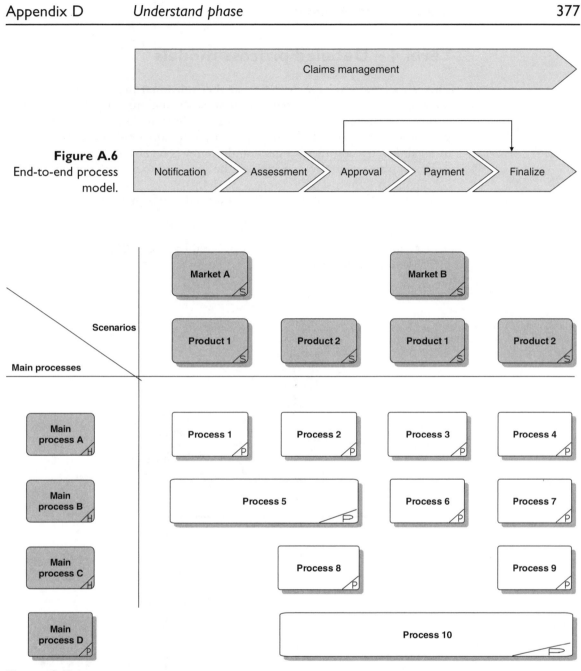

Figure A.6
End-to-end process
model.

Figure A.7
Process selection matrix.

The benefits of the process selection matrix are that it:

- provides an overview of the main end-to-end processes or the main activities and their similarities/variances on one or two pages
- allows selection of which processes need further investigation and determination of the scope of a project.

Level 4 – Detailed process models

This is the first level for modeling at the individual process level. It is also the level where positions/organization units, documents, systems and external entities are specified. At this level it is possible to include more variety (e.g. sales by telephone, email/fax or in person) and more dependencies (e.g. send order only after contract is signed and money is received).

In some cases, certain activities will be specified in a more detailed model. See Figure A.8 for a sample process model.

The main benefits of detailed process models are that they:

- clearly document process flows
- allow easy integration with the main processes in higher levels and other process models.

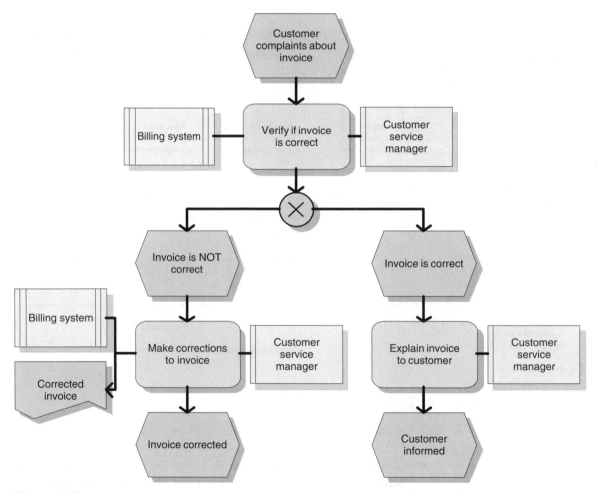

Figure A.8
Sample process model.

Level 5 – Procedures

This level provides a step-by-step description of each individual task. Remember, it is important that process models should only be developed as long as they make sense. Sometimes the procedure level is most effectively executed by the completion of a text document.

The main benefits of procedures are that they:

- provide a clear step-by-step description of the activities
- provide a good guide to train new people on the job.

Swim lanes (levels 3 and/or 4)

Swim lanes could be a useful way of mapping processes and indicating which person or organizational unit is responsible for certain tasks. Here, each person or organizational unit has a column, and all the processes that they execute will be specified in this column (Figure A.9 for a sample swim lane model).

Some process modeling and management tools allow the switching of flow charts to a swim lane model, as it is just another representation of the process flow.

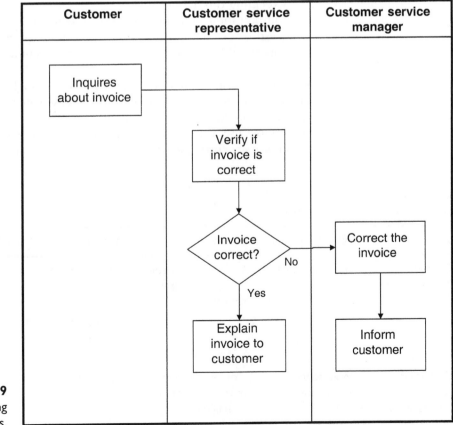

Figure A.9
Process model using
swim lanes.

The main benefits of the swim lane model are that it:

- provides an instant overview of who is doing what activities
- provides a visual representation of the handovers between activities and processes.

Swim lanes can be used from level 3 (list of end-to-end processes) downwards, as these are the levels where the individual processes and their underlying activities can be assigned to people and organization units.

Five-column process model (levels 3 and/or 4)

The five-column process model provides an overview of the source, input, action, output and destination for each activity. It can be specified as text (i.e., a table) or as a flowchart (Table A.1).

The columns are defined as follows:

1   Source: the origin of the input for the action
2   Input: the necessary resource (document or information) for the action
3   Action: the activities and choices (it should also be specified who is executing this action)
4   Output: the result (document or information) of the action
5   Destination: the destination of the output generated by the action; this could be an archive or a subsequent action.

The main benefit of the five-column process model is that it is the best text-based way of describing processes in the case where there is no process modeling and management tool available.

Some people use a three-column structure (input, activity and output) or a four-column structure (activity, person, document and system), but these

Table A.1

Sample five-column process model

Source	Input	Action	Output	Destination
Customer Billing system	Complaint that invoice is not correct	Validate the invoice (customer service representative)	Invoice is not correct: request to correct invoice	Customer service manager
			Invoice is correct: explain invoice to customer	Customer
Customer service representative	Request to correct invoice	Correct invoice (customer service manager)	Corrected invoice	Customer billing system

models do not provide a clear view on how the various actions are related to each other – which is one of the most important issues when preparing models.

Understand workshop – initial workshop presentation

One of the first steps in the Understand phase workshop is to provide a frame for the various workshops that will be conducted. This framing is usually managed by a presentation to the business and certain members of the project team. The following provides a sample of the possible contents of such a presentation.

1 Agenda
   a Introduction:
      i How the Understand workshops will run
      ii Roles and responsibilities of participants
      iii Scope of the project and this phase
      iv What is business process management? (Not all participants will understand it, so a brief explanation or presentation will assist)
   b Agreed list of end-to-end processes
   c Organization process selection matrix
2 Workshop guidelines or rules
3 Workshop participants' expectations (the facilitator needs to understand whether the participants' expectations are different from those planned, and, if so, to reset the expectations)
4 Project scope – reaffirm the scope and ensure that all participants understand it
5 Project objectives – ensure that all participants understand the objective of the project
6 Understand phase outcomes – ensure that all participants understand what is expected at the end of the workshops
7 Perhaps show a few slides on the modeling tool that will be used, describing how models will be created and the types of models that will be used (it is not necessary to provide a demonstration of the tool in detail, as the workshops will commence using it in practice)
8 Individual workshop agenda – each workshop should have an agreed agenda or format, and we suggest the following:
   a Recap and review of the previously completed workshop sessions
      i Discuss and review work completed after workshop end by the project team
      ii Follow-up action items from previous workshop
   b Complete session modeling and discussion of processes
   c Business subject matter experts to present a summary of the sessions
   d Actions to complete outside the workshop, before the next workshop
   e Agree agenda and business processes to be modeled and discussed at the next workshop.

Modeling guidelines

Guidelines to be considered when modeling processes are as follows.

- *Purpose and audience of the model:* before modeling, it is important to specify the purpose and audience for that process model. We often see that process models are being used by more people and for more purposes than initially envisaged.
- *Approval and governance:* prior to modeling, it is important to specify who will approve and maintain the process models. Too often we have heard people saying at the end of the project: 'If I had known that I would be the person formally approving these process models, I would have been more intensively involved.'
- *The BIG picture:* the first step in process modeling is to specify how the process fits into the overall processes of the organization, and then to drill down to the more detailed processes; this provides the participants with the required BIG picture.
- *Process model steps:* it is crucial that a clear set of steps for this is outlined specifying how the process model is to be developed, reviewed, approved and maintained, and what the roles and responsibilities of the various people will be.
- *Standards and reference models:* ascertain the standards and reference models that are applicable.

The following modeling principles are listed (Davis, 2001):

- *Principle of correctness.* A model must have the correct semantics and syntax. The method must be complete and consistent, and the model must comply with the method. Only then can the model be validated against the real world, using the modeling tools, and shared with other modelers and business users. *Stick to the modeling method (well, mostly).*
- *Principle of relevance.* Items should only be modeled if they are relevant to the model's purpose. Modeling in too much detail wastes time and money, and confuses people. In general, if your model is larger than two A4 pages, you are modeling at too detailed a level. *Don't model the universe.*
- *Principle of cost versus benefit.* The amount of effort to gather the data and produce the model must balance with the expected benefit. In general, 80 percent of the benefit comes from 20 percent of the effort. Getting the last 20 percent will cost you another 80 percent in effort. *Know when you've done enough.*
- *Principle of clarity.* The model should be understandable and usable. Business process models are complex, so break the models down into understandable chunks that fit into an overall structure. *Keep it simple – clever models often confuse.*

- *Principle of comparability.* A modeling tool can be very powerful. It can be used in lots of different ways to achieve the same end. The real benefit comes from communication and sharing. To do this, you must take a common approach to modeling within the modeling tool. *Define standards and stick to them.*
- *Principle of systematic structure.* Models produced in different views should be capable of integration. Again, stick to the method, stick to the common naming conventions, and produce and reuse libraries of common objects. *Don't re-invent the wheel, re-use whenever you can.*

Issues and opportunities register

An extremely important part of the Understand phase is the capture of ideas, opportunities and issues, and registering them in the Issues and opportunities register. This register should be maintained throughout the Understand phase (and other phases), and contain the following information:

- Issue number
- Process name
- Description of the issue
- Consequence (is it broad or narrow?)
- Priority
- Does it affect the strategy, business, organization, architecture (including compliance) or IT?
- What is the solution?
- Is it a short- or long-term issue?
- Responsibility (whose?)
- Likely benefits:
  - description
  - amount ($)
  - how derived
  - constraints
  - assumptions
  - qualitative/quantitative impact
- Associated costs?

Appendix E

Innovate phase

This checklist provides a generic overview of possible inputs, deliverables and gates of this phase.

Possible inputs
From the Organization strategy phase

- A documented version of the organization's: vision, mission, goals, strategic intent, objectives and implementation strategy
- Key differentiators of the organization.

From the Process architecture phase

- Documented and agreed process architecture
- Process start architecture
- Benefits management framework.

From the Launch pad phase

- Stakeholders defined in, involved in or associated with the project
- Stakeholder engagement, commitment, and documented and agreed expectations
- Process selection matrix and initial metrics
- A list of agreed process goals
- Process worth matrix
- Project management
- Potential project benefits and realization plan
- Initial business case.

From the Understand phase

- Process models of current processes
- Metrics baseline
- People capability matrix
- List of priorities for Innovate phase
- Project plan (in detail) for Innovate phase
- Baseline and comparative measurement.

Other input

- List of relevant projects to determine synergy and overlap.

Deliverables

- A list of agreed process goals
- New process models and documentation
- Simulation models
- Activity-based costing information
- Capacity planning information
- Stakeholder engagement, commitment, and documented and agreed expectations
- Process gap analysis
- Updated process selection matrix
- Metrics for the various innovate scenarios
- Benefits side of a cost–benefit analysis for the business case
- Project plan (in detail) for People and Develop phases
- Report to management
- Presentation to management
- Updated communications plan
- People capability matrix for new processes
- Initial business requirements
- Refined and optimized benefits mix (from Realize value phase)
- Communication of the results.

Possible gates

- Stakeholder analysis
- Understanding magnitude of change
- Organization's capacity to change
- Organization acceptance of BPM
- Technical review
- Compliance issues
- Risk management issues
- Expectations not achieved.

Innovate executive kick-off workshop

Sample agenda

Attendees

Objectives

1. To provide an update on the project status
2. To provide a context for the Innovate phase of the project:
   - ensuring that the outcomes are consistent with the strategic objectives of the organization
   - providing written guides for the process goals for the various processes
   - providing guidelines for constraints, issues and timeframes.

Outcomes

We will have an agreed written list of:

- process goals
- guidelines for the Innovate phase, in terms of the constraints from the business, business issues and desired timeframes to implement the redesigned processes.

Format

Item	Topic	Who
1	Project status report:	
	• Project plan – to date and future	
	• Findings to date	
2	Project scope review	
3	Business process innovation versus redesign	
	• Existing application system opportunities and constraints	
4	Guidelines for the Innovate phase ('rules of the game'):	
	• Opportunities	
	• Constraints	
	– people	
	– applications	
	– cultural	
		(Continued)

Item	Topic	Who
	• Issues • Timeframes (3, 6, 12 or 24 months?)	
5	Establish future process goals – where do you want to take the business from a process perspective?	
6	How do the goals for the redesigned processes relate to organization strategic objectives?	
7	Review process worth matrix	
8	Success checklist agreed at the initial executive workshop; ensure items are still consistent with the decisions of this workshop	
9	Project deliverables for this Innovate phase	
10	Other business	

Steps of an Innovate workshop

Structure of Innovate workshops

This section provides a suggested structure and organization for the Innovate phase workshops.

Workshop organization

Workshop organization will vary depending upon many factors – the size of the organization, the number of workshops and workshop participants, and the complexity of the processes being reviewed, to name but a few of the variables. The best configuration of roles, assuming a reasonably large organization and complex processes, is as follows:

- 'Facilitator' – this is the person who controls the workshop, ensuring that the direction and guidelines are strictly adhered to and that the timeframe and outcomes are kept in mind at all times.
- 'Process modeler' – this assumes that the process modeling will be conducted on-line, using a process modeling and management tool during the workshop and projected onto a screen for all participants to view. We have found this to be the best approach as it allows the participants to become intimately involved. The process modeler not only 'creates' the models for all to see during the workshop, but also participates in the workshop discussion.
- 'Scribe' – this person takes notes of the discussion; collects metrics, issues, opportunities, thoughts and ideas; and notes any 'parked' ideas for future consideration. Individual team members (especially

those from the business) should be tasked, after a workshop has been completed, to investigate ideas back in the business and present back to the workshop – for example, an improvement opportunity may require further investigation to ensure that there are no impacts on other business areas, IT systems, suppliers or customers. The scribe needs to keep track of these tasks, as well as taking detailed notes from the workshop. Our experience is that the scribe provides added value; however, the necessity for the role will depend upon the size and complexity of the workshop, and a scribe is not always needed.

The behavior of the facilitator and other project team members should reflect the difference between the Understand and Innovate phase workshops. An experienced BPM workshop facilitator will understand these differences and be aware of the following:

- Business participants may feel threatened by suggested changes to the processes and their possible future roles; the facilitator and group need to be sensitive to this.
- Whether an issue or suggestion fits within the timeframe is being considered.
- The facilitator (and the non-business participants) must remain neutral for as long as possible during the discussions. Business participants must be given the opportunity of making the processes better. This also ensures that the business owns, and is committed to, 'its' ideas for process improvement.
- The facilitator must create an environment where there can be lots of questions asked – this is achieved by the facilitator asking lots of questions, and keeping criticism and negative comments to a minimum and under control.
- There must be lots of 'why?' questions asked.
- There must be no significant disagreement from non-business/ project team members within the workshop.
- There may be a high level of passionate disagreement between the business participants as to how a process should be modified or totally changed. While this is good because it promotes better outcomes, it does need to be sensitively handled by the facilitator.
- The facilitator must work on the creative members of the group and perhaps guide them to make suggestions first, ensuring that all workshop participants contribute and have an opportunity to have their say.
- Very detailed information should be avoided. For example, if there is a need for a new business 'form', then agree on this, but do not go into the detail of 'form' design.
- Always ensure that all business participants are recognized and praised for their contributions.
- At the conclusion, it must be the business that owns the new process options, not the project team members or facilitator.

Short-term horizon

Below is a sample workshop agenda for three- and twelve-month timeframe scenarios.

Introduction
Request a senior executive to open the session and describe the following:

- the objectives to be achieved
- the goals and vision for the workshop(s) – this will have been agreed in the executive workshop
- the constraints to be taken into consideration during the workshops – for example, the timeframes are three and twelve months; are changes to IT applications, to distribution channels or to product configurations allowed?

Sequence
1   Review the list of end-to-end processes developed for the area under consideration during the Understand workshops. If necessary, this should then be redesigned.
2   Present the top two items selected during the strengths and weaknesses (strengths represents opportunities) discussion in the Understand phase workshops. Ensure that these are placed in a prominent position (e.g. on a whiteboard or wall), are referred to on a regular basis and are taken into account during the Innovate phase discussions.
3   Review the process goals and organization objectives to ensure that the new processes take account of them.
4   There are then two ways to commence the innovate process discussion:
   - discuss the shortcomings of the current process and improve it
   - completely redesign the process.
5   Commence the creative innovate work. If it is warranted, during the modeling of the innovate process ensure that model components are colour coded, highlight the differences from the old process (if appropriate) and represent the timeframes involved in the introduction of the suggested improvements. Differing timeframes may also be shown by separate process models.
6   Capture ideas and tasks that need to be checked regarding feasibility. Team members should then be tasked with the responsibility of going back into the business and validating the feasibility of the suggestions. They should then return to the group and present their findings.
7   At various stages during the workshops, it is essential that a business participant 'presents' the suggestions back to the group and invites managers to ensure or consolidate the business ownership of the new processes. The facilitator should ensure that the business participants are credited with the ideas.

8 Several new process scenarios should be developed; do not stop at one and think you have done a good job. The first one or two redesigned processes only start the creative flow, and it is the later innovated processes that are the most creative and efficient.

After workshop activities
- Immediately after the workshop, the Innovate workshop project team must complete a review of the model(s) against the notes taken by the scribe to ensure that the notes and the model(s) record all aspects discussed and are consistent
- Expand details to shortlist alternatives
- Further investigate the technical feasibility of the alternatives
- Reapply the evaluation criteria in more detail to ensure consistency
- Select no more than three options for management consideration
- Build a plan (next steps).

Long-term horizon

The details and agenda for this workshop are mainly the same as those for the short-term horizon, with the following exceptions:

1 Rather than starting with the process created during the Understand workshops and slightly or significantly modifying it, you start with a 'clean sheet of paper'.
2 Clearly, there is an opportunity 'totally' to rethink how the business is to operate. Radical ideas and process innovation should be considered. A useful approach is to brainstorm 'outside the box' ideas.
  - the facilitator should ask the participants for radical ideas and there should be no criticism or comment from the group at this stage; ideas should be written on Post-It notes and placed on a whiteboard
  - the next step is to have participants place the ideas into groups
  - discussion should then take place to eliminate the ideas that are outside the criteria set by the executive workshop for this Innovate phase
  - ideas can then be debated on their merit.
3 These ideas and suggestions can be used in the design of the new process.

Workshop preparation

It is essential that the team members involved in conducting the Innovate workshops prepare in advance. Preparation should include the following:

- reviewing the Understand models being addressed during the workshop to ensure a common understanding

- if necessary, confirming aspects of the Understand process in the initial workshop
- thinking through possible innovation process solutions so that the workshop may be 'directed', if appropriate, by the facilitator.

Workshop execution

How to start the workshops? Clearly, the obvious way to commence an Innovate workshop would be to ask the business participants to think of a new, more efficient process that will meet the timeframe and other constraints agreed at the start. Sometimes this approach meets with blank faces and no response.

Other methods to enable this process to commence in a more structured and clear manner could include the following:

1   *Control points.* If the process to be modeled is a financial or control process, then you could brainstorm the various control points that are required within the process. For example, in a receipting and bank reconciliation process, the control points might be the following:
    - ensure all data have been entered by operators into the application system
    - a single person collects audit trails of the information entered into the application system
    - balance these audit trails to the application system
    - combine all these audit trails into one report
    - balance audit trails to bank statements to ensure physical banking has been completed and ensure that the bank statements are correct
    - review bank statements for items that have been deposited directly into the bank and must be entered into the application system
    - send reports (audit trails or consolidated reports) to the finance department for completion of the bank reconciliation
    - ensure all reports reach the finance department.

    Once these control points have been agreed, the development of the process can be relatively quick and easy because you have agreed the essential steps that must be met by the process.

2   *Critical activities.* For a non-financial process, a list of critical activities could be brainstormed and written on a whiteboard or Post-It notes. Again, the process could be relatively quickly and easily developed. Always question the critical activities to ensure they are really necessary. Process innovation may allow the circumvention of some of the current critical activities.

3   *Business participants' resistance and push back.* If you are experiencing this within the session – for example, the business participants believe their Understand (current) process is 'perfect' and cannot be improved, or do not wish it to be improved – then do not start by trying to redesign the current process. Ask for suggestions for improvement activity by activity in the current process, and brainstorm the issues and areas that could be improved. The new process

could then be developed from these brainstormed suggestions and shown to the business participants.

Questions for an Innovate workshop

This section contains the most important questions to be considered before redesigning a process. It is best if these questions are discussed at the start of the workshop.

This document is based on the belief that a business process and the related process models are not goals in themselves, but a means to achieving a business objective within a given context. Therefore, before commencing the Innovate workshop process and indulging in process modeling, it is important to have the correct focus and context on which the modeling should be based. Furthermore, these considerations should be discussed and made explicit.

It is important to understand that everyone has implicit assumptions about the possibilities and limitations of process innovation. The potential for the Innovate workshops will be hampered by these implicit assumptions unless they are addressed, shared, understood and agreed upon. The questionnaire below only relates to process-oriented redesign, and not to system- or organizational-oriented redesign.

How to use this document

Prior to the commencement of the Innovate phase, the questions listed in the table below should be discussed. It is crucial that the scope of the Innovate phase is specified before conducting the workshop. Then the modeling can start.

Questionnaire

SCOPING

1   What is the scope and extent of the process(es) to be redesigned?
     What is out of scope?

BUSINESS

2   To which overall business objective do these processes contribute? (WHAT?)
3   Which strategy should be used as a basis for the processes? (HOW?)
     Customer intimacy
     Product leadership
     Operational excellence.
4   What are the main driver(s) of process change? (WHY change?)

(Continued)

PROCESSES

5   What is good in the current process(es)?

6   What are the bottlenecks/issues to be overcome in the current process(es)?

7   Which best practices can be included? This can be done on the basis of reference models, ideal models, industry practices and benchmarking.

8   What are the most significant improvements that can be made to the process(es)?

9   What are the performance indicators/SLAs (quality and quantity)?

10 What are other relevant metrics associated with the process(es) – including relevant decompositions?

11 How are the process(es) monitored and by whom, and which variables can be used to adjust the process(es)?

12 What rules and regulations must this process comply with (internal and external)?

13 What significant interfaces does this process have with other process(es)?

ORGANIZATION

14 What organizational units are involved, and what criteria do they impose on the process?

15 What positions and people are involved in the process, and do we need to take this into consideration in the innovate workshops?

INFORMATION SYSTEMS

16 What information systems are involved, and what restrictions and opportunities does this provide?

DOCUMENTS

17 What outputs and/or documents must be generated, and must they comply with any particular requirements (e.g. legal)?

Innovate case study

This Innovate case study takes all the steps and suggestions from Chapter 17 and provides an example of how they may be applied in a large financial institution with several thousand employees and multiple offices spread throughout a country. The leadership of the financial institution understood that moving to a process-centric organization was essential for its future and embarked upon a program to move the organization towards this process-centric view. The organization leadership was willing to back the program with sufficient funding, and had a goal of making significant progress towards goals within the next two or three years.

(Note: the steps are not in exactly the same sequence as explained in Chapter 17, which shows that the framework steps must be flexible to accommodate different organizational needs and situations.)

It was agreed that the business drivers were the following:

- the need to compete in the marketplace
- the need to decrease the expense ratio (revenue to expense), currently above industry average, to significantly below the industry average in order to gain a competitive advantage
- the need to increase the time spent by branch staff with customers rather than on administrative activities (providing the opportunity for increased revenue)
- the desire to build long, deep relationships with customers
- better use of staff by increasing employee satisfaction and providing customers with stable service, even during peak periods
- the need to enter new markets.

A strategy was devised to approach the program (see Figure A.10).

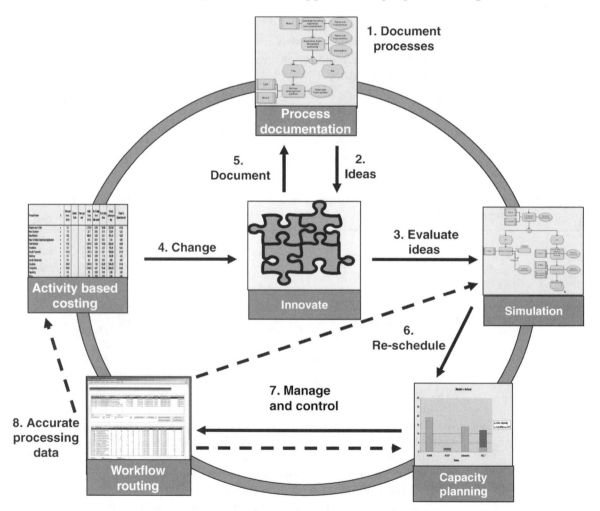

Figure A.10
Strategy for increased efficiency (reproduced with permission of the case study organization).

We will now take you through a summarized version of the steps and order in which this organization approached this program of improvement projects.

1   First, the organization embarked upon a number of activities to establish the foundations for the program, establishing a set of guidelines and standards (process architecture) that included the following:

    • selecting a modeling and management tool with a central repository capability
    • agreement that all modeling would be completed on an end-to-end basis
    • agreement upon a standard of how processes would be modeled and to what depth
    • appointment process owners for every process
    • standardization of processes across the organization
    • agreement, across the organization, that 'perfect is the enemy of good' (by this it meant they were not seeking perfection; perfection costs too much money and does not return the level of benefits that justify the expenditure).

    Workshops and workplace investigations were then completed to document the existing processes, and standardized across the organization. Ideas were collected for process improvement and innovation. These ideas were fed into the central project team for consideration and evaluation.

2   Simulation was completed, on an end-to-end basis, for several reasons and outcomes:

    • the existing processes were simulated to gain a thorough understanding of the processing timings and compared with current staff levels and utilization
    • this analysis also established baseline measurements to evaluate and measure future process innovate suggestions
    • bottleneck and simulation analysis provided further understanding for process simplification and improvement
    • suggested process improvement alternatives were analyzed and compared to the existing processes and each other, assisting in determining the optimal process environment
    • staff capacity planning was simulated for various process scenarios (variable transaction volume analysis assisted in providing stable service levels by providing input into the capacity planning activities)
    • simulated matching and optimization of staff skills to the sequence of the process flow was carried out
    • simulation provided a method for testing and evaluating new processes before they were implemented.

3   Before any new processes were implemented, they were evaluated via activity-based costing. This determined the true cost of a process on an end-to-end basis, which provided the following:

    • the ability to attribute costs to the processes that generate the products
    • the opportunity and information for more accurate and effective cost management

- the ability to provide management with an understanding of the cost of processes
- input into more accurate product and service pricing, as processes could be costed more accurately (in case of cost-based pricing)
- the capability for 'what if?' analysis, where it was deemed necessary.

4 This information was fed back into the analysis of process innovate suggestions and then on to simulation.

5 The above information was then fed back into the process repository to document any changes to ensure the information was continuously available to all staff. The information (process models) was then made available to staff via publication on the organization's intranet site.

6 Capacity planning was then carried out. This was about having the right number of suitably skilled people available at the right time to meet customer and organization needs. It resulted in the simultaneous satisfaction of staff, customer and organization needs. It was about understanding and analyzing the following:

- transaction volumes and the timing of receipt within the organization to understand the busy times of the day and the busy days of the week
- types of transactions received, when received, and the skills required to process them
- the skill levels of individual staff and any training requirements.

A skills inventory (matrix) was then completed, comprising the following:

- a ranking of an individual's skill level against each process, from 1 to 5, where a person with a skill level of 1 was a novice and with 5 was an expert. The determination of skills was conducted by interviews, tests and reviews of staff function profile and competence, and skills matrix.
- training requirements to increase skill levels, coupled with the transaction types and volumes (it is no good training people and thus increasing skill levels for transactions that occur infrequently).
- handling times for each transaction for each level of skill – for example, a person with a skill level of 5 ('expert') would be faster at processing a transaction than would a person with a skill level of 1 ('novice'). A decision was made about speed (use of experts) versus flexibility (use of multi-skilled staff).

An understanding of capacity planning and its associated aspects enabled the organization to optimize staff satisfaction and staffing levels, and reduce costs. This capacity planning and work forecasting was completed by a centralized group for the entire organization, and in small enough intervals (say thirty minutes) to ensure that the right staff were available when required. While this sounds like a great deal of work (and it was, to establish), it actually made this complex planning issue less complex over time, especially when integrated with a workflow work-routing solution.

The capacity planning information also provided feedback to the simulation models, which may require further analysis and adjustment.

7   Work-routing (process engine) was where the implementation of all the planning and effort took place. Work was received by the organization and captured in a BPM-automated solution. The work-flow work-routing component selected the appropriate process, and accessed information on the current processing queues and back-logs and on the skills matrix. This information enabled an individual transaction to be routed to the next available and highest skilled (or appropriate) person. This routing was to either an individual or a work group.

This aspect is the means by which the organization managed and controlled the operation of its business.

This routing and status checking, coupled with business activity monitoring, allowed precise calculation of process cycle times, which were then used to refine the processes, as discussed in the next step. This also identified any process errors.

8   The last step was the one that provided sustainability. It was where the 'actual' transaction processing was monitored and data were collected regarding the actual processing times, costs, volumes and issues (bottlenecks, excess capacity). This information was continually monitored and analyzed, and fed back to the simulation, activity-based costing, and flowthrough into capacity planning to adjust staffing levels.

This information was also used to provide performance measurement data for process owners, management, processing groups and staff.

Results

The financial result for this organization was a significant drop in expense to sales ratio, from about 70 percent to under 40 percent in three years. Obviously there were other benefits, such as increased customer and staff satisfaction and the highest branch office staff–customer facing time in the industry.

Sample process gap analysis

The process gap analysis documents the differences between the Understand phase findings and the Innovate phase, and should contain the following information:

1   An overall analysis of the impact of the changes in processes on the organization
2   Implementation options and comments

3   Per individual process:
    - a brief description of the Understand process
    - a brief description of the selected new Innovate process
    - a summary of the key changes between the two
    - any process issues
    - the impact of appropriate metrics
    - general impact discussion and comments
4   An identified general impact assessment
5   Identified project timelines
6   Identified training impacts and requirements
7   Identified change management issues
8   Identified organization structure impact and requirements
9   Process and implementation risks.

Appendix F

People phase

Checklist: People phase

This checklist provides a generic overview of possible inputs, deliverables and gates of this phase.

Possible inputs

From the Understand phase

- Process models of current processes
- People capability matrix
- Knowledge and information needs.

From the Innovate phase

- A list of agreed process goals
- New process models and documentation
- Capacity planning information
- Stakeholder engagement, commitment, and documented and agreed expectations
- Process gap analysis
- Project plan (in detail) for Develop phase
- Updated communications plan
- People capability matrix for new processes
- Refined and optimized benefits mix.

From the Develop phase

- High-level overview of the solution
- Detailed business requirements.

Other inputs

- HR policies and guidelines
- Existing job descriptions and roles.

Deliverables

- People strategy documentation
- New roles descriptions
- Role measurement (goals) creation
- Performance measures
- People core capabilities gap analysis
- Redesigned organization structure
- Updated HR policies
- Training documentation
- Defined benefits details (from Realize value phase)
- Communication of the results.

Possible gates

- HR policy inflexibility
- Employee council or trade union inflexibility
- Stakeholder analysis
- Understanding magnitude of change
- Organization's capacity to change
- Organization's acceptance of BPM.

Appendix G

Develop phase

Checklist: Develop phase

This checklist provides a generic overview of possible inputs, deliverables and gates of this phase.

Possible inputs
From the Understand phase

- Process models of current processes.

From the Innovate phase

- A list of agreed process goals
- New process models and documentation
- Simulation models
- Process gap analysis
- Metrics for the selected solution
- Project plan (in detail) for People and Develop phases
- Refined and optimized benefits mix
- Initial business requirements.

From the People phase

- Role measurement (goals) creation
- Performance measures
- Training documentation.

Other inputs

- List of relevant projects to determine synergy and overlap
- Enterprise or IT architecture.

Deliverables

- High-level overview of the solution
- Detailed business requirements
- Software selection documentation
- Software specification and design
- Software development and configuration
- Software test scripts and results
- Hardware specifications and availability
- Hardware test scripts and results
- Integration test scripts and results
- Defined benefits details (from Realize value phase)
- Communication of the results.

Possible gates

- Development and testing hardware and software configuration not the same as it will be in the live environment
- Stakeholder analysis
- Understanding magnitude of change
- Organization's capacity to change
- Organization's acceptance of BPM
- Technical difficulties
- Testing difficulties.

Components of an automated solution

What are the components of an automated BPM solution?

We believe that there are nine automated components to a fully automated BPM solution (see Figure A.11).

Case study: We already have all the components

We have seen very large organizations who have all the nine automated components and still do not know how to bring them together into a BPM solution. Sometimes they do not know why they should.

Message: Without an understanding of BPM within the organization's leadership, without a framework and the BPM expertise and experience, the automated components will either not be used or be used in a sub-optimized way.

Does this mean that every BPM solution must be automated? Absolutely not. The degree of automation can range from zero to almost fully automated. The level of automation will depend upon the needs of the organization.

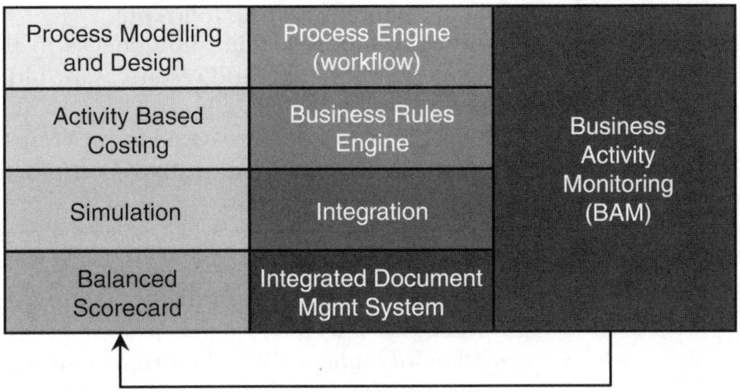

Figure A.11
BPM automated
components.

The automated components are described in more detail below.

1 *Process modeling and design.* This is where an organization models its processes and sub-processes. This does not require a BPM technology tool, as it could be completed in several of the Microsoft products (or pencil and paper) if you wish, it will just take longer and be far less flexible. A technology-based modeling tool will be significantly more efficient. The tools available range from unsophisticated tools that record a process in a simple format, with no links to other processes, to tools that are extremely sophisticated, linking processes, sub-processes, an overview of an organization, high-level value chains and the re-use of sub-processes, all on server-based central repository technology.

The main benefits are the following:
- the ability for multiple modelers to use and modify models at any one time in any location, resulting in more consistency, less delays and lower costs
- the ability to manage the process model, for example validate its correctness, up-to-date status and effectiveness, resulting in better quality and more results
- the ability to publish process models so that people can refer to them and the related information (e.g. current templates for letters, webpages, application forms), resulting in more people using the process models, better quality and lower costs.

2 *Simulation.* This is where an organization wishes to simulate the viability of its processes to identify process weak points and resource bottlenecks. This is where you determine whether your process can be executed in the way you expect. Based on the simulated process KPIs specified (assumptions made), you can evaluate different alternatives and perform realistic benchmarking prior to making any cost-intensive process changes within the organization. With this in mind, the following fundamental question should always be asked regarding the functioning of your redesigned business processes: Who does what and in what order? It is not enough just to describe business processes. In order to be able to judge the dynamic interplay between different processes, simulation provides numerous analysis options.

The main benefits are the following:

- the ability to determine bottlenecks in the process and dependencies of processes and resources, resulting in better results and lower costs
- the ability to compare various processes on the basis of their efficiency and speed, and share best practices, resulting in lower costs and better results
- the ability to validate an improved process and test it against various scenarios
- the ability to reduce implementation costs and more efficient processes.

3   *Activity-based costing* (ABC). This represents an important add-on tool for existing cost accounting systems. ABC makes the success of BPM projects measurable, and creates transparency in the understanding and, therefore, potential control of process costs. It is the tool to help secure strategic organizational decisions on the cost side and to achieve long-term cost reduction. The ability to generate and utilize competitive advantages requires knowledge of the 'right' costs.

The main benefits are the following:

- the ability to understand cost components of processes, resulting in prices and costs being more aligned
- the ability to compare various processes and identify areas for improvement, resulting in lower costs.

4   *Balanced score card* (BSC). This provides the ability to establish various measures within the organization – measures such as KPIs or other critical measures for the measurement of processes. It can be used not only for the establishment of the quantitative measures, but also for the determination of what parts of the business processes to measure and subsequently report. These can then be linked to the strategic objectives of the organization. BSC will provide the platform for the business activity monitoring (BAM) component described below. For example, measures can be established for the expected processing costs and timeframes for the execution of processes. These targets can then be compared to the actual costs and timeframes achieved within the BAM component.

The main benefits are the following:

- the ability to link processes and their outcome to objectives of the organization, resulting in better results and lower costs
- the ability to monitor the progress of processes and their contribution to the organization objectives, resulting in better results and lower costs
- the ability to modify objectives and determine their impact on the processes, resulting in more agility of the processes and the organization as a whole.

5   *Process engine (workflow)*. The common term used for a process engine is a workflow system, which describes the automation of internal business operations, tasks and transactions that simplify and streamline current business processes. The process engine is the software

component that executes transactions or events. In order to execute processes via a process engine, the organization must first model its processes either in the process modeling tool provided by the process engine software provider or in a specialized process mapping tool.

The main benefits are the following:
- the ability to automate work that can be standardized, resulting in decreasing cost and throughput time and increased quality
- the ability to route work on the basis of dependencies and skills, resulting in reduced throughput time and better quality
- the ability for staff to focus on more interesting and important work, resulting in more employee satisfaction and better quality.

6   *Business rules engine* (BRE). This provides the kind of agility that the organizations of today need, because it allows an organization to 'extract' its business rules from code-based legacy application systems into a business rules engines (BRE). It is part of the drive to give 'power' back to the business, rather than relying on the ever present technology bottleneck. BREs of today provide the ability for a technically competent business analyst, working within the business (not IT), to change business rules very quickly. Rather than the business specifying business rule changes, by giving this to the IT department to review, write technical specifications, quote, schedule, develop and test, a business-based business analyst can complete and test the change, thus providing the business with much increased business agility. This ability to provide instant changes must be kept within the bounds of production promotion policies and management audit needs of the organization, although these policies may require significant review as a result of the new technology ability.

The main benefits are the following:
- the ability to automate more work, resulting in improved quality and reducing costs and throughput time
- the ability to test and manage the business rules prior to releasing any changes, resulting in better quality and reduced costs
- the ability for the business to define, monitor and manage the business rules as it doesn't have to rely on IT, resulting in more effective, manageable and agile processes.

7   *Integration.* This provides the interface layer between the process models within the process engine and the legacy applications of the organization. Integration is a significant component and, unless addressed early within a project, it has the potential to cause a project to fail. We addressed this aspect in Chapter 24, when we discussed the potential gates a project must go through.

The main benefits are the following:
- the ability to implement BPM automation while keeping the existing system, resulting in substantially more benefits with limited costs
- the ability to reduce redundancy and inconsistencies of data, resulting in reduced costs and improved quality

- the ability to make changes more quickly than can be done via the traditional legacy systems approach, resulting in more agility and substantial lower costs.

8 *Integrated document management system.* Most processes, certainly in the financial services sector, are accompanied by some form of paper. Hence, if an automated BPM solution is implemented without an accompanying integrated document management system, the organization risks making its processes extremely fast, and then having to wait for the physical paperwork to catch up. Clearly it is much better, from a process perspective, to have scanned images of the paperwork available on an 'as required' basis by a process. There are organizations that made a conscious management decision to implement a BPM solution without the imaging component of document management, and this placed the entire implementation at considerable risk and did not provide the expected benefits to the business.

The main benefits are the following:
- lower costs and better quality in processing documents
- documents are electronically available, so work can be completed from an electronic version, reducing throughput significantly (no waiting for the paper to arrive)
- retrieval and tracking of documents can be completed more easily, resulting in lower costs and faster throughput times.

9 *Business activity monitoring.* The collection and examination of performance-related process information is an essential prerequisite for successfully implementing and evaluating measures for the continuous optimization of business processes. BAM provides the actual performance measures that can be compared to the targets established within the BSC component. It automatically identifies performance data from organization processes, especially those that span systems, and thus makes it possible to analyze them. This information can be gathered from the various software application systems within the organization, not just the process engine component. BAM provides information that helps to uncover weaknesses in process handling and to optimize processing throughput times. It acts as an early warning system by providing not only historical information but also predictive information for the monitoring of business processes. Reporting can be via printed reports or, more likely, management dashboards.

The main benefits are the following:
- the ability to monitor processes in real time (or near real time) and drill down into problem areas, resulting in less problems and lower costs
- the ability to forecast delays and service level agreements (SLAs) that cannot be met, thus allowing for proactive action resulting in better quality
- the ability to benchmark the processes against competitors and industry standards, resulting in better results.

These nine automated components are our suggestions of what automation tools are desirable within an automated BPM solution in a BPM-mature organization. This does not, however, mean that all nine components must be present for a project to be successful. An organization may choose to not use the first four components, or document management may not be required in certain implementations. Clearly, the more components used, the more likely it is that an implementation will achieve more benefits. However, 'a tool is only a tool'! Unless the tool is used effectively, it will not solve a business problem. It is like purchasing a saxophone – unless the person knows how to play the instrument and then how to play with 'heart and soul', the outcome will not be pleasant for anyone!

The example in Figure A.12 shows how the technology components may work together in an address-change transaction within a large complex organization with multiple legacy application systems. This example does not describe the integrated document management system component.

Imagine that before the change of address 'transaction' is commenced, the organization has process modeled the process (probably redesigned it to be more efficient), perhaps completed simulation and activity-based costing steps, and then devised process targets for cost and time. These will be used as targets against which actual performance will be compared in the future.

In this example, the customer contacts the organization via one of the staff/customer interfaces (touchpoints) on the left-hand side of Figure A.12

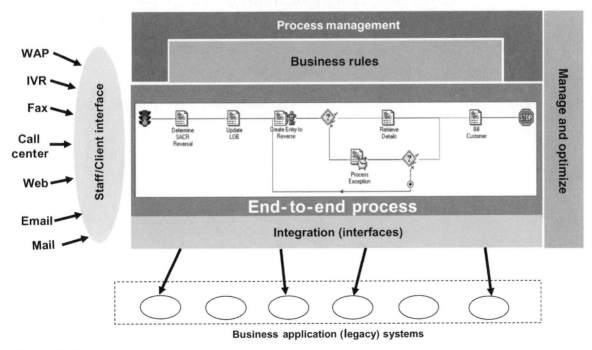

Figure A.12
BPM automation example.

(WAP, IVR, fax, call center and so on). This initiates the change of address process.

This process type initiates the process engine (workflow component) to schedule, prioritize and manage the processing. The process engine 'calls' the business rules engine to apply any applicable business rules to the transaction, and then 'calls' the integration component to access the various legacy application systems that require updating. In this example, there are four legacy application systems that require the address to be updated. The process engine monitors this updating activity to ensure that it is completed successfully. If one of the legacy application systems is not currently available, the process engine continues to try to update it once it is available. If the legacy application does not become available for a defined period of time, the process engine reports this fact (exception) to a designated supervisor or manager.

While all this is being performed, the BAM component is recording the information into a process data warehouse. It is this information that will then be reported against in the BSC component – that is, a comparison is reported as to the targeted time and cost against the actual time and cost. Process managers may then plan, investigate and optimize future processing accordingly.

While this example appears to be a trivial matter, changing addresses within large complex organizations can be an extremely complex and error-prone event. This is often due to the many and the varied nature of the organization's legacy application systems. We have seen large organizations that have in excess of thirty legacy application systems, with customers having products in several of these systems. From a customer's perspective, the customer notifies the organization and expects all his or her dealings (products) to be amended. This 'simple' change of address event can therefore cause significant process time, complexity and errors, much to the dissatisfaction of the customers.

Appendix H

Implement phase

Checklist: Implement phase

This checklist provides a generic overview of possible inputs, deliverables and gates of this phase.

Possible inputs
From the Launch pad phase

- Initial implementation strategy.

From the Understand phase

- Knowledge and information needs.

From the Innovate phase

- A list of agreed process goals
- New process models and documentation
- Capacity planning information
- Process gap analysis
- People capability matrix for new processes
- Refined and optimized benefits mix.

From the People phase

- People strategy documentation
- New roles descriptions
- Role measurement (goals) creation
- Performance measures
- People core capabilities gap analysis
- Redesigned organization structure

- Updated HR policies
- Training documentation
- Defined benefit details.

From the Develop phase

- High-level overview of the solution
- Detailed business requirements
- Software test scripts and results
- Integrated test scripts and results
- Defined benefit details.

Other input

- HR policies – to assist with the training.

Deliverables

- Trained and motivated staff
- Roll-out, back-out and contingency plans
- Marketing programs
- Implementation strategy
- Business UAT tests
- Completed UAT tests and results improved processes or new processes that work satisfactorily, according to the identified stakeholders requirements and needs
- Implemented solution
- Final defined benefits details (from Realize value phase)
- Communication to the relevant stakeholders.

Possible gates

- UAT testing fails
- Roll-out, back-out plans do not work
- Training does not work or is given too early
- Stakeholder analysis
- Understanding magnitude of change
- Organization's capacity to change
- Organization's acceptance of BPM
- Technical review.

Training guidelines

This appendix gives an overview of BPM-specific aspects of training. Because there are many books about training, and because training depends very much on the objectives, audience and context, we will not provide a full listing of establishing training; we will limit ourselves here to the specific BPM aspects of training.

General guidelines for training

- Specify explicit learning objectives and outcomes. We have experienced occasions where a two-day training session for a modeling tool was used as the means for briefing project managers about the possibilities of that tool (which could be done in half a day). Needless to say, the project managers were highly disinterested and frustrated when they realized this.
- Determine the audience: does it makes sense to split the groups on the basis of varying backgrounds, experience with BPM/BPM tools, skills, seniority and so on?
- Communicate the objectives and expected outcomes to the audience well ahead of time. Provide them with an opportunity to ask questions and give feedback. *We have seen occasions where people were told in the morning to attend training in the afternoon, without even clearly knowing the reasons why.*
- Start each training session by eliciting the expectations of the participants and writing them on a flip-chart for all to see throughout the sessions. This is a good way to ensure that the training is suitable for the participants. Start each new session by checking progress.
- All processes should be related as much as possible to the situation of the participants; this provides them with a clear understanding of how their work environment will be impacted.

Example: How too much is not good

Whenever we need to ensure that people understand the importance of objectives and uniformity in processes, we use the following exercise. We ask people in groups of two or three to model the process of going to the shop to buy groceries. We notice that each group will do one of the following three things:

1   Produce a long checklist of things to consider and to do
2   Model a long flowchart with a lot of 'if–then–else' flows
3   Disagree on how to proceed.

After ten minutes, we ask people to present their effort. Some groups are proud to show how long, complete or complex their checklists or models are, while others do not have much to say.

When we ask *what is the audience and objective of this model?*, the groups realize that they were so involved in modeling that they had forgotten to ask the most obvious questions. We underline this message by asking the following question: *would you use this description when you have to do the shopping? If not, why not?* This is the moment when people realize the importance of thinking before modeling. We ask people to consider what would have happened if they had had three weeks to model their business processes: this could result in an overkill on the process models, without much added value to the business.

Then we can look at the various descriptions and wide variety of models, symbols, methods and wording that are being used in modeling the trip to the shop to buy groceries. This is where we can emphasize the importance of modeling conventions, so that all models are modeled according to uniform guidelines so that they can be related to each other.

Appendix I

Realize value phase

Checklist: Realize value phase

This checklist provides a generic overview of possible inputs, deliverables and gates of this phase.

Possible inputs
From the Process architecture phase

- Benefits management framework

From the Launch pad phase

- Potential project benefits and realization plan

From the Understand phase

- Baseline and comparative measurements

From the Innovate phase

- Refined and optimized benefits mix

From the People, Develop and Implement phases

- Defined benefits details

From the Sustainable performance phase

- Value monitoring and maximization

Table A.2
Benefits tracking matrix

Benefit	Measure	Target	Deadline	Actual achievement	Date realized	Responsible project member	Business sponsor	Process Owner	Status	Comment

Deliverables

- Benefits delivery and tracking
- Communication of the results.

Possible gates

- Development strategy does not deliver benefits
- Implementation strategy does not deliver benefits
- Stakeholder analysis
- Understanding magnitude of change
- Organization's capacity to change
- Organization's acceptance of BPM
- Technical review.

Benefits tracking matrix

This provides a template for a benefit tracking matrix (see Table A.2).

- *Benefit* is the objective that the project aims to achieve (e.g. reduce processing time)
- *Measure* is the way the organization can measure whether the benefit has been achieved (from order to delivery)
- *Target* is the actual target set for the measure to achieve (e.g. two days)
- *Deadline* is the date by which the benefit will be achieved.

It is crucial that the responsible project member and business sponsor are specified. It is possible that a single benefit has various measures and targets.

Appendix J

Sustainable performance phase

Checklist: Sustainable performance phase

This checklist provides a generic overview of possible inputs and deliverables of this phase.

Possible inputs
From the Launch pad phase

- Initial implementation plan (future process owners).

From the Innovate phase

- New process models and documentation.

From the People phase

- People strategy documentation
- New roles descriptions
- Role measurement (goals) creation
- Performance measures
- People core capabilities gap analysis
- Redesigned organization structure
- Updated HR policies
- Training documentation
- Defined benefits details (from Realize value phase).

From the Develop phase

- High-level overview of the solution
- Defined benefits details (from Realize value phase).

From the Implement phase

- Implemented solution
- Defined benefits details (from Realize value phase).

From the Realize value phase

- Benefits delivery and tracking.

Deliverables

- Mechanisms to manage business processes, and identify and realize opportunities for process improvements
- Managed and improved processes
- Value monitoring and maximization (from the Realize value phase).

Appendix K

People change management essential

Drivers for cultural change

The forces of cultural change provide a useful framework to specify the roles of leadership, employees and management in the cultural change program and to assign specific project initiatives.

Figure A.13, in conjunction with Chapter 25, shows the areas that will need to be addressed and should be ready.

Forces of cultural change			Project initiatives
Purpose (leadership)	**Necessity**	Leads to movement	• •
	Vision	Gives direction	• •
	Success	Creates belief	• •
	Spirit	Gives power	• •
Action (management)	**Structures**	Invites	• •
	Capacities	Guarantee	• •
	Systems	Reinforce	• •

Figure A.13
Forces for cultural change. Published with permission of Berenschot.

Clarification of the terms used

- *NECESSITY* leads to movement – it increases the willingness to change. The ability to make the promise of a successful future tangible and realistic and stimulates the need to take action. It should not create fear (as fear paralyzes people), but it should create a sense of urgency.

- *VISION* gives direction – it provides a goal and objective for the change. The leadership believes in this vision and 'walks the talk' on the basis of the proposed new culture.
- *SUCCESS* creates belief – it will increase the confidence that the new culture is able to be achieved. Success must be propagated quickly and broadly. Success increases the motivation to participate.
- *SPIRIT* gives power – it is the source of energy for change. It is about the dynamics of the change process itself. It is about providing people with the additional strength to break the existing barriers, to think outside the box and to make things happen.
- *STRUCTURE* invites change – people's behavior will be influenced by changes in various aspects of the organization. Physical changes in the work environment could also trigger changes. It is important to mobilize all the available and potential willingness, within both the organization and the people, for change.
- *CAPACITIES* guarantees the change – providing the capacity for change will increase the confidence of employees. The required capacities will be achieved through training, education, information and promotional campaigns, and personal successes of employees in the change project.
- *SYSTEMS* reinforce changes – feedback on results will provide further willingness to change. Performance review systems, remuneration systems and information systems play an important role. They must ensure that the new culture is reinforced.

Appendix L

Embedding BPM in the organization

BPM interest group

Chapter 28 described the positioning of BPM within the organization structure. Many organizations have several people interested in, or even passionate about, BPM; however, they can often find it difficult to convince management to take any structural steps to embed BPM.

One way to ensure that the interest of BPM is captured and can expand within the organization is to establish a BPM interest group. This group can bring people from all over the organization (or even from partners and customers) together to discuss how BPM could provide opportunities for the organization.

The interest group should generate awareness within the organization regarding what BPM is (and what it is not), what the benefits will be for the organization and how each employee could contribute. The group should have clear, specific objectives and targets. The group could present examples on how the organization might benefit from BPM, and have people from various parts of the organization share experiences and ideas. It is recommended that the group distinguishes various focus points, as BPM is so broad and varied – for example, the technical, regulatory and business aspects.

A BPM interest group is a great way to generate initial interest. Some organizations need some initial interest and results prior to taking the first steps to embed BPM within the organization.

If this group is initiated from a BPM project, it is crucial that the emphasis of the project remains on the achievement of the project objectives. It is recommended that the BPM interest group be coordinated by an enthusiastic sponsor from the business, to ensure that the project staff remains focused on the project and to obtain sufficient buy-in from the business.

The best way to balance multiple initiatives and at the same time have an overview of all these initiatives is to ensure that all initiatives are coordinated by a member of the BPM Center of Excellence, as can be seen in Figure A.14.

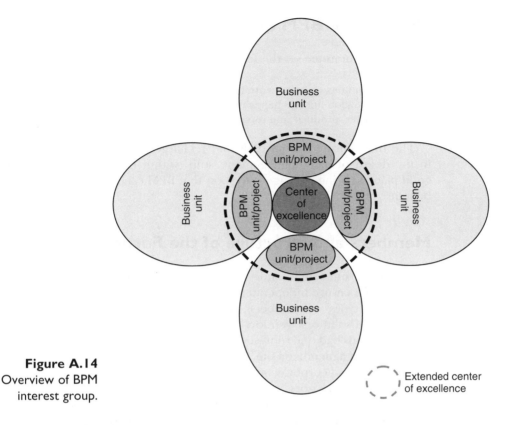

Figure A.14
Overview of BPM
interest group.

BPM Forum

Many people have tried to capitalize on the hype surrounding BPM. We have seen various initiatives and organizations fail miserably, as they have tried to make money in the name of sharing BPM expertise.

This section provides an overview of how a small-scale initiative to share BPM experiences and ideas across many organizations became a nationwide success in The Netherlands and has now started in Belgium, Poland and Australia (see www.bpm-forum.org.). This is a non-profit organization for the members, through the members and with the members with no (hidden) commercial interests.

What was the trigger for the BPM Forum?

BPM was a major hype in 2003, and was presented as the 'silver bullet' for all an organization's problems. Some organizations were saying *BPM is the solution. . . . . What is your problem?'* Some vendors realized the business opportunity and started re-branding all their existing products as BPM. Potential and actual users of BPM solutions became very confused; they needed to understand what BPM really is and how to implement it.

What is the BPM Forum?

The initial committee set the following objective for the Forum:

> The Forum aims to be a neutral, independent and quality embedding Forum for the initiation and exchange of BPM knowledge and experiences, methods, best practices, products and services and proven solutions.

> The BPM Forum was an oasis and recharge point for the BPM prophets in the desert of daily management 'stuff' within their organizations, and a good place to bring colleagues to show that BPM can actually realize business benefits.

Members and structure of the Forum

The BPM Forum was intended to have activities for, with and through its members. To ensure independence, it was important to balance the power of the various 'types' of members. They distinguished three types of members: users of BPM solutions, vendors (services and software) and academics. Each of these groups had one representative in the committee. Most of the activities were hosted at a member's site. Contributions to fund the Forum are obtained via individual and corporate membership fees. Figure A.15 shows the structure of the Board of Advisors.

The types of activities included bi-monthly meetings, site visits, conferences, a website, book reviews, the establishment of an agreed BPM vocabulary, and informal activities (e.g. 'BBQ with BPM').

The critical success factors for the group were agreed as follows:

- neutrality and independence (clear founding principles)
- balancing users, suppliers and academics
- thinking BIG starting small: '*under-commit and over-deliver*'

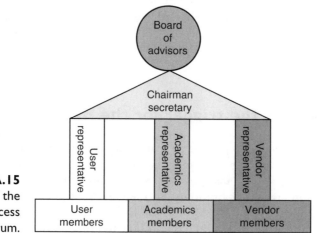

Figure A.15
Structure of the Business Process Forum.

- communicate, communicate, communicate
- balancing critical mass versus quality
- run it like a business: objectives, strategy, SWOT, customers, services, projects and processes.

Outline for process modeling convention

This section provides an outline of suggested process modeling conventions. These include the following:

- *Uniformity.* Only a uniform presentation of information in the tool creates a communication basis for employees in different business units and departments. This communication basis is important if employees are to inform each other about the interfaces of various work areas, as part of process orientation, or if employees from different departments organizations are to work together on projects. Uniformity in this sense applies to designing graphics, naming conventions and the envisaged degree of detail.
- *Reduce complexity and increase readability of process models.* Definition and documentation conventions will ensure that all employees involved in process modeling, as modelers or readers, will only be confronted with the information of importance for them and the organization. This is particularly important with the selection of models, objects, symbols and attributes, how the process structure will link, and formal settings of the master database. The benefits of reduced complexity and increased readability are especially noticeable during the familiarization of new employees and when carrying out new projects with the process modeling and management tool.
- *Integrity and reusability.* Integrity and reusability of information in the process management and modeling tool are prerequisites for a consistent overview of an organization and its structure and processes. This overview in turn is a prerequisite for being able to interpret the information already stored.
- *Consistency and analyzability.* The objective must be to enable the unambiguous, complete and accurate analysis of process database information across departments and project teams.

To achieve this, the modeling conventions should be

- practical – the modeling conventions document itself must be useful for the modelers, while they model processes, and must provide practical information (not theoretical) on modeling with the selected tools and methods within the organization
- accessible – the reader should be able to access the required information easily and intuitively; the best way to achieve this is to have a clear and logical table of contents and use a list of diagrams, a glossary and an index.

Conventions should be 'fit for use' for the modelers, and should not duplicate the training manuals or user guides; rather they should provide practical tips and guidelines for modeling with the selected process modeling and management tool within the organization.

Elements of modeling conventions

1   Version control
2   Table of contents
3   PART I – INTRODUCTION
   a   Introduction to the Conventions document:
      i   Purpose of the conventions
      ii   Target audience
      iii How to use this document (specified for each target audience)
      iv   Overview of the document (describe each chapter)
      v   Other documentation related to the Conventions (e.g. training material)
      vi   Who has compiled the document?
      vii What is the process to amend the Conventions?
   b   Introduction to business process management:
      i   What is the vision of the organization for BPM?
      ii   What is the current state of BPM in the organization (e.g. relate to BPM maturity model) and what state does the organization aspire to achieve?
      iii What is the approach of management to business processes (BPM)?
      iv   Which methods/techniques/frameworks/tools are being used?
      v   Who is responsible for BPM in the organization?
      vi   What are the roles in relation to BPM? (Provide a list of tasks, responsibilities and mandates)
      vii Overview of process architecture of the organization.
   c   Introduction to process modeling and management tools and methodology:
      i   Which tool(s) have been selected?
      ii   What are the main features?
      iii What were the main drivers for this choice?
      iv   High-level overview of the tool/methodology.
4   PART II – MODELING CONVENTIONS
   a   Modeling approach:
      i   Top-down versus bottom-up modeling
      ii   Process from modeling to approving to publishing and maintaining the models.
   b   Modeling guidelines:
      i   Modeling principles
      ii   Lessons learned from previous modeling within the organization.

    c Overview of model types and model objects:
       i   Provide real-life samples
       ii Benefits of model types and model objects
       iii List when you should which models and objects.
    d Naming conventions:
       i   Naming conventions for models
       ii Naming conventions for objects
       iii Use real-life samples.
    e Graphical display:
       i   Model information to be included
       ii Model lay-out
       iii Positioning and size of objects.
    f Model and object entities:
       i   List model and objects entities and indicate which fields are mandatory (if the list is long, then this should be included in an appendix).
    g Commonly made mistakes:
       i   List most commonly made mistakes, include real-life samples, and provide a step-by-step approach of how to avoid or correct errors.
    h Producing reports.
5 PART III – PRACTICAL USER ASPECTS
    a Installation
    b Configuration and settings
    c Folder structure
    d Change password.
6 Glossary
7 List of diagrams
8 Index.

Checklist for process modeling and management tool

Pitfalls during the selection of a process modeling and management tool

An appropriate tool for an organization should not be determined solely by its functionality or price, but by the suitability of the tool for the purpose for which the organization chooses to use it. There are two commonly made mistakes in selecting a process modeling and management tool (Figure A.16):

1 *Waste* (over-priced): the organization's requirements for a tool are quite basic and a state-of-the-art, high-functionality tool is purchased. This results in higher than necessary costs (purchase and maintenance) and dissatisfied users (as the tool requires substantial training), and only limited use is made of the wide variety of functionality that the tool offers.

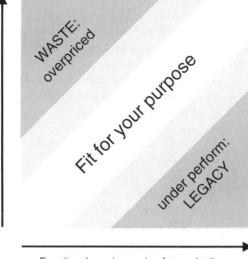

Figure A.16
Mapping of
functional
requirements
required and
provided.
(Reproduced with
the permission of
MPM Group Pty
Ltd, trading as
TouchPoint Process
Management
Services.)

2 *Legacy* (under-perform): the organization wants to start with a basic set of requirements and purchases a basic tool. The requirements evolve over time and the organization finds that the incumbent tool is unable to keep up with the new functionality required. This results in increased effort in process modeling, frustrated staff, and additional costs and rework when eventually migrating to another tool.

If the organization's initial requirements are basic and it wishes to start with a simple tool, there are basically two strategies that could be employed:

1 The modular approach: select a tool that can either be extended at a later stage with additional modules or be initially configured in a limited manner and easily reconfigured later for wider use. These additional modules could either be part of the same suite or be modules from other vendors. Care should be taken that the tool is also scalable and usable with an increased number of users.
2 The tactical approach: select a tool that serves the initial purpose and make a conscious decision to replace the tool if and when your requirements increase. It is important to realize that the more effort put into the models in the tool, the harder and more expensive it becomes to migrate the tool to a new one – for example, all process models will need to be recreated.

Using this checklist

This checklist provides a high-level overview of aspects that should be considered when selecting a process modeling and management tool. The information should be used as a high-level indication only; each selection project has its own unique characteristics which should be catered for, to ensure an optimal solution. This checklist only applies to a process modeling and management tool and does not cover the selection of an automated BPM solution, which will involve many more components (e.g. process engine (workflow), business activity monitoring).

The selection process

Aspects to consider during the selection of a process modeling and management tool include the following:

1 Specify the most important objectives for which the tool will be used in the next twenty-four months, such as:
   * the purpose it will be used for
   * the type of models to be created
   * the type of documentation required
   * who will use the tool
   * how many people will be modeling and using the models.

   Remember that most tools are used for longer and for more purposes than initially thought. Converting all the developed process models to another tool is a large task, which can involve significant effort and resources. Thus, it is important to specify whether the organization requires a short-term easy design tool or a more robust, architecturally based modeling and management tool.

2 Use the checklist provided below as a starting point to develop a customized organizational checklist from which to select the process modeling tool. Specify the high-level requirements of the tool (functionality, technical and usability). This should also include the methodology to be supported. Use a Request for Information and product demonstrations to orientate the organizational requirements to the functionality available in the marketplace. Some vendors will promote features that will not be relevant to the organization; therefore, validating the functionality offered by products against whether this provides any tangible benefits to the organization is essential. Ask vendors about the main strengths and weaknesses of their products, and determine what benefits and restrictions this will provide for the organization.

3 Review the responses from the Request for Information, specify detailed requirements for the tool and issue a Request for Proposal.

4 Check references and complete existing-user site visits: check the functionality and support, the impact on the organization, and whether the vendor keeps its promises. A useful question is to ask the referee 'with the benefit of hindsight, would you purchase this tool or deal with the vendor again?'

5 Complete a pilot before actually purchasing the tool to ensure that all assumptions and promises are valid. Involve the relevant stakeholders

(such as management, business, finance, IT, users, BPM staff, partners, architects).

6   When negotiating with the preferred vendor, always keep one or two fall-back options (it is difficult to negotiate on price when only one vendor is left).

High-level checklist

This checklist has the following five components:

- Functionality (each functionality module has its own set of questions)
- Technical aspects
- Usability
- Price
- Vendor.

I   FUNCTIONALITY
Functional modules

1   Process modeling
2   Reporting and analysis
3   Management of processes
4   Publishing
5   Optimization
6   Enterprise architecture
7   Activity-based costing
8   Automated BPM solution

- Can modules be added at a later stage?
- Is there scalability in terms of functionality and model depth?

1   Process modeling:

- What types of models can be produced (e.g flowcharts, organization charts, value chains)?
- Which modeling methods are supported (e.g. IDEF0, event-driven process chains)?
- Is there the ability to hyperlink to documents, HTML pages and so on?
- How is multi-level modeling achieved?
- Which objects can be modeled?
- What type of semantic checks can be made?
- Which templates/reference models are available?
- Is a library with objects available?
- Does the tool provide reusability of objects (e.g. with a change in an object in one model, the changes are visible wherever the object is used)?

2   Reporting and analysis:

- What standard reports are provided?
- How easy is it to develop customized reports?

(Continued)

- What standard analysis is available?
- How easy is it to perform customized analysis?

3   Management of processes:

- Is there an integrated overall process management approach that forms the basis of the models?
- Does the system support strategic, tactical and operational views of the processes?
- Is balanced score card supported?
- Can KPIs be specified and monitored?
- Does the tool provide business activity monitoring or an interface to a business activity monitoring tool?
- Does the tool support compliance and risk management (e.g. Sarbanes Oxley)?

4   Publishing:

- Can models be presented on the Internet/intranet?
- How easy is it to navigate in the published version? (e.g. do links/drill-downs work on the Internet/intranet like they do in the tool?)
- How easily can users understand the models?
- What search functionality is available?
- Is it easy to customize the lay-out?

5   Optimization:

Simulations can provide benefits, but can require substantial effort to develop. Distinguish between the following three levels of simulation.

- *What if?* analysis – simple what if? analysis based on a predefined data set
- *Dynamic simulation* – events generated and processed by configured parameters
- *Full-fledged simulation* – includes resourcing and dependencies with other processes
- What analyses does the tool provide (e.g. identification of bottlenecks)?
- What reporting on the simulation is provided?

6   Process and/or enterprise architecture:

- Which architectural models are available (e.g. systems and interfaces, data models, products and services, etc.)?
- Can cross-references be made between the various models and objects?
- What architectural method is used?
- What type of reporting is available?
- What type of analysis is available?

7   Activity-based costing:

- Does the tool support activity-based costing?
- Does the tool interface with financial systems? If so, which ones?
- What type of calculations can be performed?
- What type of reporting is available?
- What type of analysis is available?

8   Automated BPM solution:

This section only contains a couple of basic questions, as selecting an automated BPM solution requires a different, more thorough, approach.

(Continued)

- Does the tool provide process engine (workflow) management and business rules engine?
- Does the tool interface with a process engine (workflow) management system and business rules engine (an ability to upload process models)? If so, which ones?
- Does the tool interface with an integrated document management system? If so, which ones?

II   USABILITY
Usability:

- How user-friendly is the tool?
- What is the minimum required training?
- Does the tool support multiple concurrent users?
- Does the tool support drill-down and cross-reference functionality?
- What is the search functionality?
- How does the tool provide user management (access, passwords, security, etc.)?
- Does the tool use a repository (central database)?
- What is the search functionality?
- How does the tool provide user management (access, passwords, security, etc.)?
- Does the tool use a repository (central database)?

Support:

- What on-line help is available?
- Is support available via a helpdesk? If so, what are the costs?
- What local support is included and available?

Model management:

- Does the tool provide an audit trail that reports on what changes have been made, and by whom?
- Does the tool contain a change management module to identify, track and authorize changes to the models?
- Does the tool allow authorizations to be set at an individual and a function level?

III   TECHNICAL ASPECTS
Hardware and software:

- What operating platform is required?
- What are the software requirements (check version numbers)?
- What database options does the tool support?
- What are the hardware requirements for workstations and server?
- What are the infrastructure requirements?
- How scalable is the solution to deal with more data, more models and more users?
- What impact will growth in the data and the number of users have on the performance (time-based) of the tool?

Interfaces:

- What interface standards does the tool support (e.g. XML)?
- What interfaces to other applications does the tool provide (e.g. process engines (workflow) management system, ERP, etc.)?
- What are the supported BPM standards (e.g. BPML, BPEL)?
- What are the import facilities for data, models and images?
- What are the export facilities?

(Continued)

IV   COSTS

Purchase prices:

- What is the purchase price for a modeling license?
- What is the purchase price for an administrator license?
- What is the purchase price for viewing on the Internet and intranet?
- What is the purchase price for additional modules (e.g. simulation, activity-based costing)?
- What discount is applicable in the case of multiple licenses?

Support fees:

- What are the maintenance or support fees? What is included?
- What are the training fees?
- What are the consultancy fees?

V   VENDOR

- How is local support provided?
- What is the track record of the vendor? Are there references to support this?
- How does the tool rate in comparative test results (e.g. Gartner or Forrester)?

Business process outsourcing (BPO)

Organizations are facing ever-increasing pressure to perform better, cheaper, faster and more responsively. This applies not only to the core processes and products of the organization, but also to all processes, even the supporting processes. Most organizations find it challenging enough to be competitive in their core processes, let alone their supporting processes. This is where the outsourcing of the supporting business processes to a third party is an option for an organization. With the current state of technology (Internet security, broadband connection, web services and increased worldwide computer literacy), it is now more than ever an option to consider the outsourcing of at least the supporting processes of the organization.

Reasons for outsourcing

Many organizations are seriously considering outsourcing their business processes for the following reasons:

- Lack of best practice process expertise. This especially applies when the processes to be outsourced are supporting processes that are not performing well. This normally occurs for processes that have not been analyzed and improved.
- Lack of technical expertise and required investment. This applies to organizations that have legacy IT systems which require substantial

upgrading or replacement. Given the current constraints on IT investment, especially for supporting processes, outsourcing is a serious option.

- Focus on core processes and the outsourcing non-core processes. This allows the managers to spend their attention, effort and available investment capital on core processes.
- Lower cost. However, if lower cost is the only motivation, then this should not be the sole reason for outsourcing.

Criteria to look for in a business process outsource vendor

When considering the outsourcing of business processes, the following criteria should be considered:

- specific process expertise
- ability to scale volume and time
- ability to add additional services
- total cost involved (including the initial set-up costs) and flexibility in pricing
- service levels and related penalties for not meeting the agreed service levels
- flexibility to change contract and conditions
- IT application (flexibility and functionality)
- track record of the vendor in business process outsourcing of their existing client base.

Conduct site visits of the existing vendor clients to ensure the vendors' ability to validate their service level claims. Remember that business process outsourcing is more than just data entry.

Conditions that should be met prior to outsourcing

The following conditions should ideally be met within the organization prior to the outsourcing of business processes:

- Process metrics should be in place, understood and realistic.
- Processes should have already been streamlined. Remember that outsourcing an inefficient process will in all probability result in the continuation of the inefficient process by the vendor.
- Have a plan for employees who are currently performing the processes (they could either be employed elsewhere within the organization or be moved to the outsource vendor).
- Review the business model and identify any business opportunities that may occur as a result of outsourcing.

- Develop a business case and project planning. This should cover not just the processes being outsourced but also the impact upon the other business processes within the organization. The outsourced processes should contribute to the new strategies and objectives of the organization.

Type of business process outsource vendors

The types of business outsourcing vendors include the following:

- IT companies
- process specialist companies (e.g. specialists in loans processing)
- industry specialist companies (e.g. a teleco billing vendor)
- offshore companies (which are one of the above-mentioned type of companies or a combination of them).

An alternative to outsourcing is insourcing

A recent reaction to the large-scale outsourcing of the last five to ten years is that companies have brought previously outsourced processes back in house. In most cases this occurs as the organization realizes that these processes are core processes – for example, the call center provides valuable information on customer feedback.

Some companies, whose processes are extremely effective and efficient, go one step further and offer servicing to other organizations.

Important BPM methodologies

In this section we will describe the main BPM models and methodologies.

BPM has evolved over a long period. The current view of BPM is the merger of three main streams that have independently evolved over many years. The three main streams we are referring to are the following:

1 Business process thinking: from the first 'wave' of scientific management, in which business processes where seen as assembly line activities, to the second 'wave' business process reengineering.
2 Automation: from the initial automation of calculations to the attempts to automate workflow. With the expansion of the Internet and related software (e.g. web services), it became possible to cross the boundaries of organizations.
3 Quality thinking: from inspecting to including quality as an integral part of business as usual (e.g. Total Quality Management and *kaizen*) and the measurement of this (e.g. Six Sigma).

Smith and Fingar (2002) describe how the third 'wave' is where automation and business process and quality management come together.

The third wave of BPM is a synthesis of process representation and collaboration technologies that removes the obstacles blocking the execution of management intentions. BPM is therefore the convergence of management theory, total quality management, Six Sigma, business engineering and general systems thinking – with modern technologies.

First wave: Scientific management

The most significant approach towards processes in the first wave is symbolized by scientific management. In the early twentieth century, Adam Smith and Frederick Taylor introduced a scientific approach to the processing of business processes, especially in the manufacturing sector. Adam Smith, in his book *The Division of Labor* (the first volume of *Wealth of Nations*, by Smith, 1909–1914), described how productivity could increase significantly if each worker had a specific and specialized task. Frederick Taylor (1911) introduced scientific management, in which he relied upon time and motion studies to find the 'one best method' of performing a task.

In both approaches there was a clear division of labor between the manager and the worker. The manager had to 'think' and the worker had to 'work'. This also resulted in clear divisions between design, production and quality control. Furthermore, they considered workers more as machines than as individuals and unique people. These approaches included a drive towards:

- standardization
- specialization
- optimization
- centralization.

The first assembly line of Henry Ford was very much based on these concepts. The problems with this approach were the monotony of work, and the initial unemployment of people whose skills were not required anymore. Furthermore, employees had no interest in the overall result and were not encouraged to do so.

Many administrative and service processes were initially established along these same lines, as in the manufacturing assembly line. As time passed, people began to realize that most, if not all, administrative and service processes are fundamentally different from assembly-line work and should be treated differently, which has led us to where we fundamentally are today.

Second wave: BPR overview

What does it mean?

BPR stands for Business Process Reengineering. In their book *Reengineering the Corporation*, Hammer and Champy (1993) defined BPR as 'the fundamental reconsideration and radical redesign of organizational processes, in order to achieve drastic improvement of current performance in costs, service and speed.'

In the early 1990s, BPR gained enormous momentum, and was based on the vision that administrative processes cannot be compared to the Taylor approach found in manufacturing, where each person has a small designated task and the design and management are performed by specialists and not by the workers themselves.

What is the main approach?

Davenport and Short (1990) distinguished the following five steps in a BPR approach:

1   Develop the business vision and process objectives
2   Identify the business processes to be redesigned
3   Understand and measure the existing processes
4   Identify IT levers
5   Design and build a prototype of the new processes.

A sixth step that is often mentioned is to adapt the organization structure and the governance model towards the newly designed primary processes.

Hammer and Champy (1993) distinguish the following characteristics that are common to a BPR project:

1   *Several jobs are combined into one.* Too often the process was previously performed by too many people (e.g. each employee tightened one screw in an assembly line), which resulted in long lead times.
2   *Workers make decisions.* The division between doing and deciding is thus eliminated, as this resulted in delays and lower employee satisfaction.
3   *Steps in the process are performed in a natural order.* Too often the processes were described as a sequential chain of activities that had to be performed one after the other. By having a natural order of process steps and allowing processes to be performed in parallel, the throughput time can decrease significantly.
4   *Processes have multiple versions.* Flexibility can be created by ensuring that processes are executed depending on the specific circumstances, rather than a single mass-production approach.
5   *Work is performed where it makes most sense.* To reduce time and money, unnecessary hand-offs can be reduced.
6   *Checks and controls are reduced.* This is done by empowering workers and making them more accountable for their actions.
7   *Reconciliation is minimized.* Reconciliation does not provide added value and can be minimized by reducing the number of hand-offs and activities.
8   *A case manager provides a single point of contact.* For complex activities, appointing a case manager ensures that there is a single point of contact between the complex processes and the customer.
9   *Hybrid centralized/decentralized operations are prevalent.* IT allows organizations to gain the economies of scale of centralization while decentralizing decision-making to its operational units.

Third wave: Smith and Fingar

Smith and Fingar (2002) wrote out of necessity, as there was much confusion about how organizations were to compete in the twenty-first century. They restated that:

> [the] re-engineering mantra – 'don't automate, obliterate' – has given way to a deep respect for, and an effective means of, leveraging existing business and technology assets. This opportunity arises now because it is only recently that methods and technology have become available to fully enable process management in the sense defined here.

They described a new method of working, as organizations can make use of the advanced technology and the new ways of thinking, working and competing. They state that processes are no longer just a group of activities; they are characterized by being end-to-end and dynamic; responding to demands from customers and changing market conditions; being widely distributed and customized across boundaries within and between businesses; and often spanning multiple application of disparate technology platforms. They are also long running (such as order to cash) and at least partly automated. Furthermore, they are difficult to make visible. In many organizations, business processes have been neither conscious nor explicit. They are undocumented, embedded, ingrained and implicit within the communal history of the organization, or, if they *are* documented, the documentation or definition is maintained independently of the systems that support them.

Smith and Fingar describe the impact of new technology and how:

> BPM is a synthesis of process representation and collaboration technologies that removes the obstacles blocking the execution of management intentions... For the first time in business history, this synthesis makes it possible for companies to do what they have wanted to do all along – manage their business processes with great agility... The radical breakthrough lies in using process calculus to define the digital representation of business processes, the basis for new corporate information assets. 'Process data' based on an open standard for process description allows managers to leverage both old and new technologies for process management.

One of the main benefits of their book is that they describe how, with their new thinking, old rules (read barriers) are no longer applicable and fundamental new ways of working and managing become possible. For example:

Old rule	A choice must be made between incremental process improvement and radical reengineering
Disruption	Lifetime process lifecycle management
New rule	There are no discontinuities

We strongly advise any person who uses BPM to read and apply these new rules ('opportunities').

The framework described in this book provides guidance on how to identify and implement the new way of working, which involves processes as well as the management of these processes.

Quality management ISO 9001:2000

(This material is reproduced with the permission of the ISO Central Secretariat from the website of ISO (International Organization for Standardization – www.iso.org)

What does quality management mean?

ISO stands for the International Organization for Standardization, which is a non-governmental organization. Its members are the national standards institutes of each country.

What is the main approach?

ISO has developed more than 15 000 standards in a wide variety of sectors. One of the main standards that relates to business processes is referred to as ISO 9001:2000, which is a generic requirement (e.g. it applies to any organization). This standard deals primarily with quality management in dealings between an organization and its customers, primarily business-to-business. It relates to:

- the fulfillment of the customer quality requirements
- the fulfillment of applicable regulatory requirements
- the enhancement of customer satisfaction
- the achievement of continual improvement of performance in pursuit of these objectives.

It is important to note that ISO 9000 relates to the process and not to product standards.

ISO 9001:2000 specifies requirements for a quality management system for any organization that needs to demonstrate its ability consistently to provide a product that meets customer and applicable regulatory requirements and aims to enhance customer satisfaction.

Principles

The ISO 9001:2000 series of standards includes a list of quality management principles that improve an organization's performance. These are the following:

- customer focus
- leadership
- involvement of people
- a process approach
- a systems approach to management
- continual improvement
- a factual approach to decision-making
- mutually beneficial supplier relationships.

Steps

ISO has identified the following steps to implement ISO 9001:2000 – the quality management system:

1 Identify the goals you want to achieve
2 Identify what others expect from you
3 Obtain information about the ISO 9000 family
4 Apply the ISO 9000 family of standards in your management system
5 Obtain guidance on specific topics within the quality management system
6 Establish your current status, and determine the gaps between your quality management system and the requirements of ISO 9001:2000
7 Determine the processes that are needed to supply products to your customers
8 Develop a plan to close the gaps in Step (6) and to develop the processes in Step (7)
9 Carry out the plan
10 Undergo periodic internal assessment
11 Decide whether you need to demonstrate conformance – if yes, go to Step (12); if no, go to Step (13)
12 Undergo independent audit
13 Continue to improve your business.

ISO does not issue certificates for organizations who meet the requirements of ISO 9001:2000. Certification is carried out independently of ISO, although ISO does develop standards and guidelines to encourage good practice in certification activities.

Quality management: *Kaizen*

What does it mean?

Kaizen is an excellent approach to include in an organization's process thinking. This thinking should be included in everyone's job profile. *Kaizen* is a Japanese concept indicating continuous step-by-step improvement on the following three levels: management, teams of employees, and the individual employee. '*Kai*' means 'to change' or 'to modify', while '*Zen*' means 'good' or 'right'.

Kaizen, compared to BPR, is more focused on gradual and incremental improvements coming from the employees themselves, and has a lower threshold for implementation.

What are its principles?

Kaizen has the following principles:

1 Teamwork
2 Personal discipline

3   Improved morale
4   Quality circles
5   Suggestions for improvement.

What is the approach?

Quality circles play an important role in *Kaizen*. A quality circle is a small group of workers. This group of workers focuses on improvement in their own workplace, with special attention to cost, productivity and safety. In most cases the quality circles are voluntary and are usually not chaired by a department manager, but by one of the workers.

Masaaki Imai (1986) distinguished the following steps of quality circles:

1   Select a theme or problem
2   Understand the situation
3   Set the target for improvement
4   Analyze factors and measures
5   Report results
6   Prevent backsliding
7   Develop insights and future directions.

Quality management: Six Sigma

What does it mean?

Sigma is the Greek letter that is used in statistics to measure how far a given process deviates from perfection. Six Sigma means a failure rate of 3.4 parts per million, or 99.9997 percent perfection. The objective of Six Sigma is to improve profits through defect reduction and improved customer satisfaction. It involves a systematic and analytical process of identifying, anticipating and solving problems, and has become more and more a way of working.

Motorola developed the Six Sigma methodology in the mid-1980s, and it was initially used in the manufacturing industry; however, nowadays it is being used more and more in service organizations (e.g. financial institutes).

Steps of Six Sigma

Six Sigma contains the following steps:

1   **Define** – determine the intended improvement, provide a high-level model of the process and identify what is important to the customer
2   **Measure** – provide baseline data on the current process performance, identified problems areas and a focused problem statement
3   **Analyze** – perform root-cause analysis of the identified problems, validate these with the data and provide tested solutions

4 **I**mprove – pilot and implement the suggested solutions that should eliminate or reduce the identified root cause

5 **C**ontrol – evaluate the implemented solution and the original plan, and ensure the sustainability of the solution by embedding the solution in the standards.

Six Sigma concepts

The following concepts are key to the Six Sigma approach (see www.ge.com, accessed 15 August 2005):

Critical to quality	Attributes most important to the customer
Defect	Failing to deliver what the customer wants
Process capability	What your process can deliver
Variation	What the customer sees and feels
Stable operations	Ensuring consistent, predictable processes to improve what the customer sees and feels
Design for Six Sigma	Designing to meet customers' needs and process quality

Who does Six Sigma?

Six Sigma identifies different skill levels:

- Green Belt – someone who has completed the basic training
- Black Belt – someone who has responsibility for leading a team
- Master Black Belt – someone who supervises the Black Belts.

Lean Six Sigma

Lean processing is a philosophy which started at Toyota in the 1940s. It aims to achieve continuous improvement and customer satisfaction. It aims to achieve perfection, and targets the reduction in waste, lead time and costs, while being able to deliver on-time quality goods. Together with the just-in-time (JIT) approach, it generated enormous interest within the manufacturing sector. In the last few years, lean processing has also gained momentum within the administrative and service industries, especially coupled with Six Sigma, and has thus become known as Lean Six Sigma.

What are the main principles?

Lean processing aims to address the following problems:

- incorrect determination of market and customer requirements
- product design that is not based on customer requirements but on manufacturability

- overproduction (especially due to inflexible processes)
- inventory
- defects
- waiting
- activities without any added value
- unnecessary transport or moving
- inefficiencies.

When to use Six Sigma?

Six Sigma should be used,

- when problems are commonplace and not well defined
- when there are unknown causes of errors
- in complex situations with many variables.

Six Sigma fits well within our framework as outlined in this book, and is considered to be a sub-set of the framework.

When NOT to use Six Sigma

Six Sigma requires commitment from the top of the organization, so unless this is available, do not use Six Sigma.

Six Sigma requires a significant investment in training and the subsequent program; if such funds are not available, it is no use trying to do 'half' a Six Sigma implementation.

Six Sigma and our framework

As outlined above, Six Sigma is a useful and rigorous approach to improving quality. However, Six Sigma is only a portion of the overall aspects required in a BPM project or a process-centric organization. The main issues missing are the following:

- the alignment with organization strategy
- the process architecture, including the alignment with the business and IT as well as process guidelines which are the foundations for the subsequent process models
- fundamentally changing (or reengineering) the business process, especially in the case of a change in strategy or merger/acquisition
- the use of automated BPM tools and the process model and management tool
- the *essentials* of a BPM project, namely people change management, project management and leadership; these are especially crucial when innovating rather than just improving the processes
- end-to-end focus of processes, across functional silos and even across organizational boundaries, as a traditional Six Sigma approach might get too much data to handle in these situations.

Some people argue that these aspects are or could be included in a Six Sigma project. It is our strong opinion that any method or framework should be complete and not leave crucial elements to the insight of the project managers.

Thus, Six Sigma and our framework are complementary, whereby the added value of Six Sigma comprises the following:

- a strong quality focus and awareness
- stringent measurement of quality and data
- a mechanism to identify process errors and solutions.

We will now outline how a project will flow if Six Sigma is included in our framework, in the case of an operational-initiative project.

- The Launch pad phase will be the starting point. It is about identifying the scope and purpose of the project: the *Define activities* of Six Sigma will assist in this regard in identifying the areas with the highest number of errors and biggest opportunities for improvement. Preliminary data and error analysis will be helpful in quantifying and qualifying leads, rather than relying on intuition or anecdotal evidence.
- The Organization strategy and Process architecture phases of the Framework will not be completed in their entirety, but only referenced for relevant information. It remains crucial to ensure alignment with the organizational strategy, as this provides the objectives and context for the processes. Six Sigma will not be used in these phases.
- In the Understand and Innovate phases, once the project has been 'launched' the project can go through the *Measure, Analyze* and *Improve*. In general, some of the steps of the Understand and Innovate phases can be covered by the Six Sigma approach, including the root-cause analysis. Special attention must to be given to the steps related to communication, involvement of the stakeholders and the innovate decisions. The innovate steps of our framework will help the people involved in thinking outside the box and developing new processes or use of BPM automation.
- During the People, Development, Implement, Realize value and Sustainable performance phases, it is recommended that the steps of the framework be used to ensure that the people, processes and IT are aligned. The *Control* step of Six Sigma can be used to monitor the benefits and ensure sustainability control and management of the improved processes.
- The essentials – project management, people change management and leadership – are critical for the success of any BPM project, as they are for a Six Sigma/BPM project. Remember, the success of a BPM project depends heavily on how well the BPM project and its impact upon the business are managed, and not on having the best solution or the best methodology.

In summary, as a generalization we would say that BPM is about the management of process improvement sustainability within the organization. It is about the establishment of a business process architecture, process governance, organizational change management capability, sustainable process performance and increasing BPM maturity, among others. Six Sigma, on the other hand, can be a useful intervention strategy for a business process improvement problem. Therefore, we see Six Sigma as a useful sub-set of the framework.

Appendix M

Framework summary

The purpose of this table is to provide a complete checklist and review mechanism of each phase and step. We have provided examples of the tools and techniques that could be used for each step, together with who is most likely to be responsible for the completion of the activity and the deliverables from the step. Where appropriate, we have shown any likely project gates that may be encountered.

Phase	Step	Tools/Techniques	Roles Involved	Deliverables	Gates	Comment
Organization Strategy	Performing this phase is not part of a project, it is an Organizational activity		Executive Management	Documented • vision • mission • objectives • strategy • how to implement the strategy)		e.g. annual
Process Architecture	Performing this phase is not part of a project, it is an Organizational activity	Enterprise Architecture Process Architecture	Enterprise Architecture Group Executive management	• Documented and agreed process guidelines • Document and agreed Benefits Management Framework • Organization Corporate Process View Including – ARIS Modeling Hierarchy – Process Matrices		e.g. annual
Launch Pad	Communications	Communication Planning Change Management	Project Manager • assign change manager	Initial Communications Strategy	Stop immediately unless: • the project is funded sufficiently Resolve or determine impact of: • an ill-defined or not clear project scope • project scope is not finally agreed	
	Initial key stakeholder interviews	Understand key business drivers and "what is keeping them awake at night"	Project Manager or senior project member	Information that will be important in prioritization and project direction		
	High-Level Process Walk Through	Observation/Interviews asking questions until you gain an understanding of how the processes work in practice	Process Analyst	Documented high-level process overview		Can be omitted, if the High Level process is well known to the Process Analyst
	Stakeholder Identification & Engagement	Stakeholder Identification Meetings	Project Manager Process Analyst	List of Stakeholders		

Phase	Step	Tools/Techniques	Roles Involved	Deliverables	Gates	Comment
Launch Pad (continued)	Management Workshop	End-to-End Process Thinking Redesign width Project Width Process Selection Matrix Process Worth Matrix Process Metrics Red Wine Test Facilitation	Project Manager Process Analyst Executive Management	Agreed Process Goals Process selection matrix with initial metrics Prioritized Processes		
	Agree & plan the handover to the business	Handover document	Project Manager Business Owner	Handover Plan		
	Develop Implementation Plan	Implementation Planning	Project Manager Project Sponsor Business Owner	Initial Implementation Plan		
	Develop & Sign-off Business Case	Cost/Benefit Analysis Business Case Template	Project Manager Project Sponsor	Initial Business Case		
	Define & Establish Project Team Structure	Project Management	Project Manager	Established Project Team		
	Complete Initial Project Plan	Project Planning	Project Manager	Initial Project Plan		
	General Project Management	Project Management	Project Manager	Project Charter document Project Scope document Initial risk analysis		
Understand	Revalidate Scope	Review with management and Stakeholders	Project Manager Project Sponsor Key Stakeholders	Reconfirmed and documented Scope		
	Communications	Change Management	Project Manager Change Manager	Informed people		
	Understand Workshops	Process Modeling Facilitation skills Workshop Preparation Workshop Facilitation	Process Analyst Business Subject Matter Experts	Process models of current process (in process modelling tool)	Stop immediately unless: • Processes are reviewed on a genuine end-to-end basis • have the correct business people in the workshops	Only as much as needed

Phase	Step	Tools/Techniques	Roles Involved	Deliverables	Gates	Comment
Understand (continued)	Complete Metrics Analysis	Data Analysis	Process Analyst	Metrics for baseline & prioritization	• sufficient metrics are gathered – else baseline is difficult or impossible to determine – future improvement benefits comparison impacted	
	Root Cause Analysis	Fishbone 5 Whys?	Process Analyst	Understanding of the processes & Root Causes		
	Complete People Capability Matrix	People Capability Matrix	Process Analyst	Current people capability matrix		
	Identify Available Information	Knowledge & Information Needs Map	Process Analyst	Knowledge & Information Needs Map		Identification of available documentation for training & knowledge perpetuation
	Identify Innovate Priorities	Prioritization	Process Analyst Project Manager	Priorities for Innovate Phase		
	Identify Quick Win Opportunities	Prioritization	Process Analyst Project Manager	List of Quick Wins Issues and opportunities register		
	Understand Phase Report	Report Writing	Responsibility: Project Manager Executing: e.g. Process Analyst	Report for Understand phase		Only if necessary Brief report to document findings
Innovate	Communications	Change Management Communications Plan	Change Manager All members of the project team	Informed people Documentation supporting the redesigned process models	Stop immediately unless: • the organization has a vision for the Innovate phase and is able to establish process goals, nor determine the scenarios for the phase	
	Management Kick-Off workshop	Facilitation	Project Manager Project Sponsor	Opportunities & constraints defined by management		
	External Stakeholder Focus Group	Interviewing Facilitation	Process Analyst Project Manager	Documented stakeholder requirements		If business thinks this is useful
	Innovate Workshops	Facilitation Creative Thinking Process Design Principles	Process Analyst Facilitator (this could range from the Project Manager, Team Leader or Process Analyst).	Documentation supporting the redesigned process models		
	Future Process Metrics Projections	Data Analysis Excel Spreadsheet	Process Analyst	Estimated future metrics		

Phase	Step	Tools/Techniques	Roles Involved	Deliverables	Gates	Comment
Innovate (continued)	Simulation	Process modelling & simulation tool	Process Analyst	Simulated process models via selected scenarios		Only complete if necessary & has a specific purpose
	Create Initial People Change Management Strategy	Initial People Change Management Strategy report	Human Resources Project Manager Change Manager	Strategy document		Could significantly influence people capability matrix
	Update People Capability Matrix	People Capability Matrix	Process Analyst	Documented gap in capabilities & skills		
	Capacity Planning	Capacity planning tools	Process Analyst	Capacity Planning document		Will assist in providing input into performance measures & skills mix
	Workshop Proposed solutions	Baseline Comparison	Process Analyst Project Manager	Sign-Off from Audit, Risk & Compliance, IT		
	Demonstrate & validate feasibility of proposed solution processes	Knowledge of IT systems; risk management; compliance requirements	Project Manager IT staff	Demonstrate feasibility of solution		
	Process gap analysis	Gap Analysis	Process Analyst	Documented gap		
	Update Business Case with Benefits & Obtain Sign-off	Cost/Benefit Analysis Business Case Template	Project Manager	Refined Business Case	The organization does not have a vision for the Innovate Phase and is unable to establish process goals.	
	Report & presentations	Report template	Project Manager Project Sponsor	Report		
	Business Requirements	Business Analysis Documentation writing skills	Business Analyst Process Analyst	Business Requirements		
People	Communications	Change Management Communication Plan	Change Manager All members of the project team	Informed people	Stop immediately unless: • staff performance targets are realistic (business unit not understaffed) • people being consulted or	
	Design people strategy	Knowledge of working environment, e.g. employee union issues	Project Manager	Strategy document		This relates to organization structure change options & approach

Phase	Step	Tools/Techniques	Roles Involved	Deliverables	Gates	Comment
People (continued)	Activity definition	Activity, job & structure analysis RASCI for Role Design	Project Manager Process Analyst	Suggested role definitions	engaged in the performance measurement establishment Resolve or determine impact of: • HR not engaged early enough or at all • judging the performance of people within the organization before the process and structural issues have been addressed	
	Role Redesign	RASCI for Role Design	Project Manager Process Analyst Human Resources Management	New role definitions		
	Performance Management & Measurement	Performance Management	Process Analyst Management Human Resources Management	Integrated & aligned performance management		
	People Core Capability Gap Analysis	People Capability Matrix	Process Analyst Human Resources Management	Capability gaps & action plan		
	Design organization's structure	New roles descriptions Organization structure matrices	Project Manager Process Analyst Human Resources Management	New organization structure		
	Update People Change Management Strategy	Previous strategy document	Project Manager Change Manager	Updated strategy document		
	Update HR Policies	RASCI for Role Design	Process Analyst with HR Consultant	Updated HR policies		If appropriate
	Develop Training	Training needs analysis Training development	Training Consultant Process Analyst	Training plan & Training material		
Develop	Communication	Change Management Communication Management	Change Manager all project staff	Informed people	Stop immediately unless: • Business fully understand what will be delivered. This does not mean that	
	Update functional & technical specifications	Previous specifications	Process Analyst IT staff	Revised functional & technical specifications		

Phase	Step	Tools/Techniques	Roles Involved	Deliverables	Gates	Comment
Develop (continued)	Software Development	e.g. SDLC, RAD	Business Analysts, Developers, Test Analysts, ...	• high-level overview of the solution • detailed business requirements • finalize software selection documentation • software specification/design • software development/configuration • software test scripts and results • hardware specification • hardware availability • hardware test scripts and results • integration test scripts and results	the business has ONLY signed off on specifications Resolve or determine impact of: • UAT has not been developed by business & fully communicated to developers	According to organizations approach
	Testing	System testing strategy, plan and scripts	Process analyst IT staff Test analysts and test team	Bug free developed software		
Implement	Communication	Change Management Communication Management	Change Manager all project team members	informed & motivated people within the organization	Stop immediately unless: • Business Testing and/or Training as a show-stoppers has been resolved	
	Update Implementation Plan	Implementation Planning Scenarios	Project Manager Business Owner	finalized implementation plan		
	Testing	Testing	Test Analyst Process Analyst to focus on facilitating the business users to carry out the testing itself Business Users	test cases & results tested & updated systems	• the business has sufficient expertise or resources to complete User Acceptance Testing Resolve or determine impact of:	
	Train Staff	Training	Training Consultant	trained staff, enabled to work on the new process	• the core project team is unable to deal with all	

Phase	Step	Tools/Techniques	Roles Involved	Deliverables	Gates	Comment
Implement (continued)	Mentor Staff	Mentoring & Coaching	Change Manager Project Team Super Users	Better skilled and motivated staff	the enquiries and problems at the start of the implementation and during the early stages	
	Roll out changes; monitor & adjust	Roll-out performance indicators	Project Manager	rolled out solution (updated after testing) which contributes towards addressing the project objectives		
Realize Value	Communications	change management	Change Manager Project Manager		Stop immediately unless: • development strategy does not deliver benefits • implementation strategy does not deliver benefits	
	Benefits Management Framework (Proc. Arch)	Benefit Management Framework	Process Governance Committee	Benefits Management Framework		
	Identify Potential Benefits & Plan (Launch Pad)	Benefit Summary Plan	Project Manager Change Manager	Benefit Realization Register Benefit summary plan	• stakeholder analysis • understanding magnitude of change	
	Establish Baseline & Comparative Measurement (Understand)	Data Analysis	Project Manager Change Manager	Baseline Measures	• organization's capacity to change • organization's acceptance of BPM	
	Refine & Optimize Benefits Mix (Innovate)	Benefit Milestone Matrix	Project Manager Change Manager	More realistic and correct benefits	• Technical Review	
	Define Benefit Details (People, Develop & Implement)	Benefit Delivery Matrix	Project Manager Change Manager	Benefits Delivery Matrix		
	Benefits Delivery & Tracking (Realize Benefit)	Benefit Delivery Matrix	Project Manager Change Manager	Benefits Delivery Matrix		

Phase	Step	Tools/Techniques	Roles Involved	Deliverables	Gates	Comment
Realize Value (continued)	Value Monitoring & Maximization (Sustainable Performance)	Benefit Realization	Benefit Owner Project Sponsor	Delivery of Results		
Sustainable Performance	Communications	Communication management	Change Manager Benefit Owner	Better informed & committed managers & employees		
	Evaluate Project Results	Baseline Comparison	Project Manager Benefit Owner	Impact of project assessed		
	Develop Fine-Tune Sustainability	Process Governance	Project Manager Benefit Owner	Better & more sustainable results		
	Embed performance measures in management	Information from previous phase & steps Management KPIs	Project Sponsor Project Manager Executive management Business managers	Process improvement & management is embedded within the organization		
	Introduce feedback loops	Feedback loops Feedforward loops	Project Sponsor Project Manager Business managers	Systems to support the loops		
	Embed Sustainability	Publication of processes	Project Manager Benefit Owner	Process improvement & management is embedded within the organization		
	Monitor Sustainability	Process performance measurement	Benefit Owner	Monitor mechanism & indicators in place		
	Continuous Improvement	Process Governance: • Process Stewards (Owners)	Benefit Owner (Process Analyst)	Documented & agreed roles & responsibilities for processes & their management		

Appendix N

7FE Project Framework Quality Assurance Checklist

This checklist should be used by a project director or project manager as a quality assurance document. It will provide the reviewer or manager with the ability of ensure the integrity, risks and likely success of the project.

This is a document that should be completed over the life of the project, probably updated each month on an incremental basis, depending upon where the project is on its life cycle. It is a growing live document rather than a one off project status report.

<Project Name>
Business Process Management Framework

Prepared by: <project team member>

Date: <date>

1. Purpose of this Document

This BPM framework project checklist aims to enable project directors, managers, process analysts or other project members to follow the Business Process Management Framework outlined in this book.

The BPM framework is a 'toolkit' from which the appropriate steps and deliverables are chosen, it is not compulsory to follow it to the letter. However, it is highly recommended to <u>consider</u> every step and deliverable of this framework. Decisions to skip parts of the framework (phases or steps) should be made consciously and should be documented, as to why, in this checklist.

2. Project Detail

Project:			
Scope			
Business Benefit			
Project Approach (strategy-driven, business issue-driven, or process-driven)			
Approved End Date		**Forecast End Date**	
Approved Budget		**Forecast Budget**	
Project Sponsor		**Project Manager**	

3. Project Summary

Phase #	NAME	COMMENTS
Phase 1	Organization Strategy	
Phase 2	Process Architecture	
Phase 3	Launch Pad	
Phase 4	Understand	
Phase 5	Innovate	
Phase 6	Develop	
Phase 7	People	
Phase 8	Implement	
Phase 9	Realize Value	
Phase 10	Sustainable Performance	

4. Detailed Deliverable Checklist:

Phase	Step	Deliverables	Used?	Why not used?	Planned Finish Date
Organization Strategy	Performing this phase is not part of a project, it is an organizational activity	documented • vision • mission • objectives • strategy • how to implement the strategy		*note if available for your project*	
Process Architecture	Performing this phase is not part of a project, it is an organizational activity	• Documented and agreed process guidelines • Benefits Management Framework • Corporate Process View, including – Modeling Hierarchy – Process Matrices		*note if available for your project*	
Launch Pad	Communications	Initial Communication Strategy			
	Initial Key Stakeholder interviews	Information that will be important in prioritization and project direction			
	High-Level Process Walk Through	Documented high-level process overview			
	Stakeholder Identification & Engagement	List of Stakeholders			
	Executive Workshops	Agreed Process Goals Process selection matrix with initial metrics Prioritized Processes			
	Agree & plan the handover to the business	Handover Plan			
	Develop Implementation Plan	Initial Implementation Plan			

Phase	Step	Deliverables	Used?	Why not used?	Planned Finish Date
	Develop & Sign-off Business Case	Initial Business Case			
	Define & Establish Project Team Structure	Established Project Team			
	Complete Initial Project Plan	Initial Project Plan			
	General Project Management	Project Charter document Project Scope document Initial risk analysis			
Understand	Communications	Informed people			
	Revalidate project scope	Agreed project scope as a result of what has been learned from the project to date			
	Understand Workshops	Process models of current process Documentation of what works well and what could work better			
	Complete Metrics Analysis	Metrics for baseline & prioritization			
	Root Cause Analysis	Understanding of the processes & Root Causes			
	Complete People Capabilities	Current people capability matrix			
	Identify Innovate Priorities	Priorities for Innovate Phase			
	Identify Quick Win Opportunities	List of Quick Wins			
	Understand Phase Report	Report for Understand phase			

Phase	Step	Deliverables	Used?	Why not used?	Planned Finish Date
Innovate	Communications	Informed people			
	Management Kick-Off workshop	Opportunities & constraints defined by management			
	External Stakeholder Focus Group	Documented stakeholder requirements			
	Innovate Workshops	Redesigned Process Models Documentation supporting the redesigned processes			
	Future Process Metrics Projections	Estimated future metrics			
	Simulation of processes	Process simulation and assumptions			
	People change management strategy	Documented and agreed initial strategy			
	Update People Capability Matrix	Documented gap in capabilities & skills			
	Capacity planning	Capacity planning document and agreement			
	Select future processes	Sign-Off from Audit, Risk & Compliance, IT			
	Process gap analysis	Documented gap			
	Update Business Case with Benefits & Obtain Sign-off	Refined Business Case			
	Approval to proceed from management	Sign-off agreement			
	Business Requirements	Business Requirements			

Phase	Step	Deliverables	Used?	Why not used?	Planned Finish Date
People	Communications	Informed people			
	Design people strategy	Strategy Document			
	Activity definition	Suggested role definitions			
	Role design	New role definition			
	Performance Management & Measurement	Integrated & aligned performance management			
	People Core Capability Gap Analysis	Capability gaps & action plan			
	Design organization's structure	New organization structure			
	Updated people change management strategy	Updated document outlining strategy			
	Update HR policies	Updated HR policies			
	Develop Training	Training plan & Training material			
Develop	Communications	Informed people			
	Determine BPM components				
	Decide on reuse buy, make or outsource				
	Update functional & technical specifications	Revised functional & technical specifications			
	Software Development	High-level overview of the solution Detailed business requirements Finalize software selection documentation Software specification/design Software development/configuration Software test scripts and results Hardware specification Hardware availability Hardware test scripts and results Integration test scripts and results			
	Testing	Bug free developed software			

Phase	Step	Deliverables	Used?	Why not used?	Planned Finish Date
Implement	Communications	Informed & motivated people within the organization			
	Update Implementation Plan	Finalized implementation plan			
	Testing	Test cases & results Tested & updated systems			
	Train Staff	Trained staff, enabled to work on the new process			
	Mentor Staff				
	Roll out changes; monitor & adjust	Rolled out solution (updated after testing) which contributes towards addressing the project objectives			
Realize Value	Communications				
	Benefits Management Framework (Process Architecture)	Benefits Management Framework			
	Identify Potential Benefits & Plan (Launch Pad)	Benefit Realization Register Benefit Summary Plan			
	Establish Baseline & Comparative Measurement (Understand)	Baseline Measures			

Phase	Step	Deliverables	Used?	Why not used?	Planned Finish Date
	Refine & Optimise Benefits Mix (Innovate)	More realistic and correct benefits			
	Define Benefit Details (People, Develop & Implement)	Benefits Delivery Matrix			
	Benefits Delivery & Tracking (Realize Benefit)	Benefits Delivery Matrix			
	Value Monitoring & Maximization (Sustainable Performance)	Delivery of Results			
Sustainable Perfor-mance	Communications	Informed people who accept the changes and using the new processes			
	Evaluate Project Results	Post implementation review report			
	Develop Fine-Tune Sustainability				
	Embed Sustainability	Agreed and used process and people targets			
	Monitor Sustainability	Appropriate reporting			
	Continuous Improvement				

References and bibliography

Ahern, D. M., Clouse, A. and Turner, R. (2004). *CMMI Distilled: A Practical Introduction to Integrated Process Improvement*, 2nd edn. Addison-Wesley.

Blatter, P. (2005). Learning from manufacturers and industrialization. Presented at the *IQPC BPM Conference*, Sydney, April 2005.

Bloem, J. and van Doorn, M. (2004). *Realisten aan het roer, naar een prestatiegerichte Governance van IT*. Sogeti Nederland.

Blount, F. (1999). Changing places: Blount and Joss. *Human Resources Monthly*, December.

Burlton, R. T. (2001). *Business Process Management*. Sams Publishing.

Cavanagh, J. (1999). Australia's most admired. *Business Review Weekly*, 15 October.

Chibber, M. L. (undated). *Leadership*. Sri Sathya Sai Books and Publications Trust.

Collins, J. (2001). *Good to Great*. Random House.

Cope, M. (2003). *The Seven Cs of Consulting, The Definitive Guide to the Consulting Process*. FT Prentice Hall.

Covey, S. (1989). *The Seven Habits of Highly Effective People*. Simon & Schuster.

Curtis, B., Alden, J. and Weber, C. V. (2004). *The Use of Process Maturity Models in Business Process Management*. White Paper. Borland Software Corporation.

Davenport, Th. H. (2005). The coming commoditization of processes. *Harvard Business Review*, June, 83(6), 100–108.

Davenport, Th. H. and Short, J. E. (1990). The industrial engineering information technology and business process redesign. *Sloan Management Review*, Summer.

Davis, R. (2001). *Business Process Modelling with ARIS, A Practical Guide*. Springer.

DeToro, I. and McCabe, T. (1997). How to stay flexible and elude fads. *Quality Progress*, 30(3), 55–60.

Drucker, P. (1991). The new productivity challenge. *Harvard Business Review*, November–December.

Fisher, D. M. (2004). *The Business Process Maturity Model. A Practical Approach for Identifying Opportunities for Optimization*. Available online at http://www.bptrends.com/resources_publications.cfm (accessed 17 March 2005).

Gartner (2005). *Delivering IT's Contribution: The 2005 CIO Agenda*. EXPPremier Report, January.

Gerstner, L. V. Jr (2002). *Who Says Elephants Can't Dance?* Harper Business.

Goldsmith, J. (1995). *Fortune*, 12 April.

Gray, B. (1989). *Collaborating: Finding Common Ground for Multiparty Problems.* Jossey-Bass Publishers.

Hakes, C. (1996). *The Corporate Self-Assessment Handbook*, 3rd edn. Chapman and Hall.

Hamel, G. and Prahalad, C. K. (1994). *Competing for the Future.* Harvard Business School Press.

Hammer, M. (1993). *Fortune*, 4 October.

Hammer, M. (1994). *Fortune*, 22 August.

Hammer, M. (1995). *Fortune*, 12 April.

Hammer, M. and Champy, J. (1990). Reengineering work: don't automate, obliterate. *Harvard Business Review*, July.

Hammer, M. and Champy, J. (1993). *Reegineering the Corporation, a Manifesto for Business Revolution.* Harper Collins Publishers.

Harmon, P. (2003). *Business Process Change.* Morgan Kaufmann.

Harmon, P. (2004). *Evaluating an Organisation's Business Process Maturity.* Available online at http://www.bptrends.com/resources_publications.cfm (accessed 17 March 2005).

Harmon, P. (2005a). Service orientated architectures and BPM. *Business Process Trends*, 22 February.

Harmon, P. (2005b). BPM governance. *Business Process Trends*, 8 February.

Harper, P. (2002). *Preventing Strategic Gridlock: Leading Over, Under and Around Organizational Jams to Achieve High Performance Results.* CAMEO Publications.

Hawley, J. (1993). *Reawakening The Spirit in Work.* Berrett-Koehler Publishers.

Hriegel, R. and Brandt, D. (1996). *Sacred Cows Make the Best Burgers.* Harper Business.

Jeston, J. and Nelis, J. (2006–2007). Various articles in BP Trends (www.bptrends.com).

Jeston, J. and Nelis, J. (2006–2007). Various articles (www.managementbyprocess.com).

Kaplan, R. and Norton, D.(1996). *The Balanced Score Card, Translating Strategy into Action.* Harvard Business School Press.

Kaplan, R. and Norton, D. (2004). *Strategy Maps: Converting Intangible Assets into Tangible Outcomes.* Harvard Business School Press.

Keen, P. (1997). *The Process Edge.* Harvard Business School Press.

Koop, R., Rooimans, R. and de Theye, M. (2003). *Regatta, ICT implementaties als uitdaging voor een vier-met-stuurman.* ten Hagen Stam.

Lewin, K. (undated). Frontiers in group dynamics. *Human Relations Journal*, 1.

Lewis, L. (1993). Tandy Users Group Speech 1993 Convention, Orlando, Florida.

Luftman, J. N. (2003). Assessing strategic alignment maturity. In: *Competing in the Information Age: Align in the Sand* (J. N. Luftman, ed.), 2nd edn. Oxford University Press.

Masaaki Imai (1986). *Kaizen: The Key to Japan's Competitive Success.* McGraw-Hill/Irwin.

Masaaki Imai (1998). *Kaizen.* McGraw-Hill Professional Book Group.

Maull, R. S., Tranfield, D. R. and Maull, W. (2003). Factors characterising the maturity of BPR programmes. *International Journal of Operations & Production Management*, 23(6), 596–624.

McCormack, K. P. (1999). The Development of a Measure of Business Process Orientation. Presented at the *European Institute for Advance Studies in Mangement: Workshop on Organizational Design*. Brussels, Belgium, March 1999.

Miers, D. (2005). BPM: driving business performance. *BP Trends*, 5(1).

Mutafelija, B. and Stromberg, H. (2003). *Systematic Process Improvement using ISO 9001:2000 and CMMI*. Artech House.

Neely, A., Adams, C. and Kennerly, M. (2002). *Performance Prism: The Score Card for Measuring and Managing Business Services*. FT Prentice Hall.

Nelis, J. and Jeston, J. (2006–2007). Various articles (www.management byprocess.com).

Nelis, J. and Oosterhout, M. (2003). Rendement uit processen. *Informatie*, May (available online at www.informatie.nl).

Nelson, M. (2003). *Enterprise Architecture Modernization Using the Adaptive Enterprise Framework*. The Mercator Group.

Newsletter for Organizational Psychologists, 1995.

Nohria, N., Joyce, W. and Roberson, B. (2003). What really works. *Harvard Business Review*, July.

Oxford University Press. (2004). Oxford English Dictionary : The definitive record of the English language. Retrieved 5 January 2006, from http://dictionary.oed.com

Paulk, M. C., Curtis, B., Chrissis, M. B. and Weber, C. V. (1993). *The Capability Maturity Model for Software, Version 1.1* (No. CMU/SEI-93-TR-24). Software Engineering Institute.

Pol, M., Teunissen, R. and van Veenendaal, E. (2002). *Software Testing, A Guide to the TMap®*. Pearson Education.

Porter, M. (1980). *Competitive Strategy: Techniques for Analyzing Industries and Competitors*. Free Press.

Porter, M. (1985). *Value Chain, Competitive Analysis: Creating and Sustaining Superior Performance*. Free Press.

Pritchard, J.-P. and Armistead, C. (1999). Business process management – lessons from European business. *Business Process Management Journal*, 5(1), 10–32.

Rosemann, M. (2005; unpublished). *22 Potential Pitfalls of Process Management*.

Rosemann, M. and de Bruin, T. (2004). Application of a holistic model for determining BPM maturity. In: *Proceedings of the AIM Pre-ICIS Workshop on Process Management and Information Systems (Actes du 3e colloque Pre-ICIS de l'AIM), Washington, DC, 12. December 2004* (J. Akoka, I. Comyn-Wattiau and M. Favier, eds). AIM.

Rosemann, M. and de Bruin, T. (2005). Towards a business process management maturity model. *Proceedings of the 13th European Conference on Information Systems (ECIS 2005), Regensburg, 26–28 May 2005*. ECIS.

Rummler, G. A. (2004). *Serious Performance Consulting*. International Society for Performance Improvement and ASTD.

Rummler, G. A. and Brache, A. P. (1995). *Improving Performance*. Jossey-Bass Publishers.

Scheer, A.-G., Abolhassan, F., Jost, W. and Kirchmer, M. (2003). *Business Process Change Management*. Springer.

Smith, A. (1909–1914). *Wealth of Nations*. The Harvard Classics.

Smith, H. and Fingar, P. (2002). *Business Process Management – The Third Wave*. Meghan-Kiffer Press.

Smith, H. and Fingar, P. (2004). *Process Management Maturity Models.* Available online at http://www.bptrends.com/resources_publications.cfm (accessed 23 July 2005).

Spanyi, A. (2004). *Business Process Management is a Team Sport: Play it to Win!* Meghan Kiffer.

Stace, D. and Dunphy, D. (1996). *Beyond the Boundaries.* McGraw-Hill.

Taylor, F. W. (1998). *The Principles of Scientific Management.* Dover Publications (reprint of 1911 original).

Treacy, M. and Wiersma, F. (1997). *The Discipline of Market Leaders.* Perseus Books.

Van de Berg, H. and Franken, H. (2003). *Handbook Business Process Engineering.* BizzDesign B.V.

van den Berg, M. and van Steenbergen, M. (2002). *DYA©: Speed and Alignment of Business and ICT Architecture.* Sogeti Nederland.

Van der Marck, P. (2005). Scoren met uw Waardecreatie (Scoring with your value proposition), at www.managementsite.nl/content/articles/298/298.asp.

Vo Oech, R. (1990). *A Whack in the Side of the Head,* Thorsons.

Wagter, R., van den Berg, M., Luijpers, J. and van Steenbergen, M. (2002). *DYA©: Dynamic Enterprise Architecture: How to Make it Work.* Sogeti Nederland.

Walton, M. (1986). *The Deming Management Methods.* The Berkley Publishing Group.

Ward, J. and Peppard, J. (2002). *Strategic Planning for Information Systems.* John Wiley & Sons.

Wertheim, E., Love, A., Peck, C. and Littlefield, L. (1998). *Skills for Resolving Conflict.* Eruditions Publishing.

Wheatley, M. J. (1994). *Leadership and the New Science.* Berrett-Koehler.

Zachman, J. A. (1987). A framework for information system architecture. *IBM Systems Journal,* 26(3).

Index